LAUGHTER AFTER

LAUGHTER AFTER

Humor and the Holocaust

Edited by
DAVID SLUCKI, GABRIEL N. FINDER,
and AVINOAM PATT

WAYNE STATE UNIVERSITY PRESS
DETROIT

Copyright © 2020 by Wayne State University Press, Detroit, Michigan 48201. All rights reserved. No part of this book may be reproduced without formal permission.

ISBN 978-0-8143-4478-1 (paperback); ISBN 978-0-8143-4738-6 (hardback); ISBN 978-0-8143-4479-8 (ebook)

Library of Congress Control Number: 2020931376

Wayne State University Press
Leonard N. Simons Building
4809 Woodward Avenue
Detroit, Michigan 48201-1309

Visit us online at wsupress.wayne.edu

Contents

Acknowledgments — vii

INTRODUCTION: TO TELL JOKES AFTER AUSCHWITZ IS BARBARIC, ISN'T IT? — 1
David Slucki, Gabriel N. Finder, and Avinoam Patt

AFTERMATH

HITLER HANGING ON THE TREE: HUMOR AND VIOLENCE IN SOVIET YIDDISH FOLKLORE OF WORLD WAR II — 15
Anna Shternshis

TOO SOON? YIDDISH HUMOR AND THE HOLOCAUST IN POSTWAR POLAND — 39
Marc Caplan

IS IT STILL FUNNY? LIN JALDATI AND YIDDISH SATIRE BEFORE AND AFTER THE HOLOCAUST — 59
David Shneer

I. B. SINGER'S ART OF GHOST WRITING IN *ENEMIES, A LOVE STORY* — 85
Jan Schwarz

"A RING OF FIRE": HUMOR AND THE HOLOCAUST — 105
Stephen J. Whitfield

BREAKING TABOOS

NEBBISHES, NEW JEWS, AND HUMOR: THE CHANGING IMAGE OF AMERICAN JEWISH MASCULINITY POST-HOLOCAUST   133
Jennifer Caplan

"WE'RE SAFE HERE, BUT POLAND IS A STATE OF MIND": THE EXPLOITATION OF HOLOCAUST CONSCIOUSNESS IN JEWISH FICTION AND MEMOIRS   155
Jarrod Tanny

"THIS WAY TO THE OVENS, SEÑORAS Y SEÑORES": HOLOCAUST CARTOONS IN LATIN AMERICA   181
Ilan Stavans

THE IMAGE OF ANNE FRANK: FROM UNIVERSAL HERO TO COMIC FIGURE   195
Liat Steir-Livny

"I'M ALLOWED, I'M A JEW": OLIVER POLAK AND JEWISH HUMOR IN CONTEMPORARY GERMANY AFTER THE HOLOCAUST   219
Gabriel N. Finder

"THE HOLOCAUST WAS THE WORST": REMEMBERING THE HOLOCAUST THROUGH THIRD-GENERATION JOKES   241
Jordana Silverstein

"YAD VASHEM, YOU SO FINE!" THE PLACE OF THE SHOAH IN CONTEMPORARY ISRAELI AND AMERICAN COMEDY   261
Avinoam Patt

"DID YOU EVER SEE OUR SHOW?" HOLOCAUST COMEDY IN AMERICAN SITCOMS   285
David Slucki

THE LAST LAUGH?   313
Ferne Pearlstein and Robert Edwards

Contributors   335

Index   341

Acknowledgments

We started talking about working together on a book on humor and the Holocaust at a 2016 conference at Brandeis University on the legacy of Lenny Bruce. What began as a conversation during a coffee break became a traveling road show and ultimately this book. We are grateful to all the colleagues who spoke to us, challenged us, and argued with us about the significance and value of Holocaust-themed humor at conferences, workshops, and lectures. Special thanks go to all the authors in the volume, whose cutting-edge scholarship has contributed to the production of what we think is a groundbreaking volume. Their diligence and brilliance have made working on this volume a real pleasure.

We owe a deep debt of gratitude to Kathy Wildfong and Annie Martin, our editors at Wayne State University Press, for championing this project, despite its controversial nature. We further wish to thank Kristin Harpster, Emily Nowak, Kristina Stonehill, and Jamie Jones, members of the press staff, for helping bring this book to fruition. We are, moreover, grateful to Mimi Braverman for her careful and professional editing of the manuscript.

We would be remiss if we did not thank one another. This book is the fruit of a cooperative effort from start to finish. We were close friends before we embarked on this book project. We're even closer friends now upon its completion.

We would each like to thank our families for putting up with all our bad jokes.

We dedicate this book to our funny children, Arthur Slucki, Chloe and Hillel Finder, and Maya, Alex, and Micah Patt. Their peals of laughter instill hope in a better world.

David Slucki
Gabriel N. Finder
Avinoam Patt

Introduction

To Tell Jokes After Auschwitz Is Barbaric, Isn't It?

David Slucki, Gabriel N. Finder, and Avinoam Patt

> Do you know why the German Wehrmacht girls are in the Netherlands? As mattresses for the soldiers.
>
> Anne Frank, 28 September 1942

Act I: Jokes and the Holocaust

IN MAY 2018, RESEARCHERS at the Anne Frank House in Amsterdam uncovered hidden pages of the iconic diary that Frank kept during her years in hiding. The newly uncovered pages show a different side of Frank. They reveal her thoughts about sexuality, sex education, and sex work and even include dirty jokes. The revelation raises questions about how our perception of Anne Frank is changed and how these new findings should be incorporated into the dissemination of the diary. Is it right to publish materials that the diarist clearly wanted to remain out of view? How does this change her legacy and image, so ingrained in Western popular culture? To what extent do these two pages of taboo material undermine the idea of innocence that Frank has embodied for so long? One commentator in England thinks that it was a betrayal of Frank to publish the jokes and that publication merely created a spectacle that dehumanized the young author.[1]

What is most interesting here is not so much the fact of the jokes themselves. It has been well-enough established that those living under totalitarian regimes tell jokes for a variety of reasons: as a coping mechanism, as a form of resistance, or as a way to maintain a sense of humanity through laughter, even in the face of dire circumstances.[2] More pertinent is how the new revelations change our perceptions of Anne Frank, the emblem of innocence, a young girl who maintained hope and her belief in the goodness of humankind despite her worsening circumstances. It helps to raise questions about what role humor played in the Holocaust experience, but even more pertinent, what role it plays in our remembering of the past. The new discovery may make Frank look more human, more cynical, more naïve, certainly not the messenger of purity that many have imagined her to be. Or perhaps it reveals taboos that may not sit easily with people—that humor does not fit neatly into discussions of the Holocaust.

Act II: Jokes About the Holocaust

Seinfeld creator Larry David appeared in late 2017 as guest host on the weekly sketch comedy juggernaut *Saturday Night Live*. It was the *Curb Your Enthusiasm* star's second appearance as host, having cemented his relationship with the show in 2016, when he appeared regularly as Democratic presidential hopeful Bernie Sanders. David had just recently launched the latest season of his hit HBO comedy after a six-year hiatus and was by then a household name.

The monologue opened with David imagining what it would have been like had he been homeless in New York City. It then veered into uncomfortable territory as he turned to the recent spate of sexual assault allegations against powerful public figures, observing that many of those making the biggest headlines, such as film producer Harvey Weinstein, were Jewish. If this was not already making the audience squirm in their seats, David then took a left turn, speculating on whether or not he would have tried to woo women in concentration camps had he lived during the Holocaust era. Imagining what his pick-up line might be, he mused, "How's it going? They treating you OK? You know, if we ever get out of here, I'd love to take you out for some latkes. You like latkes? What, what'd I say? Is it me or is it the whole thing? It's 'cause I'm bald, isn't it?"[3]

The audience reaction was muted, the uncomfortable laughter clear in the background. The critical reaction was more mixed. Some found the monologue to be a desecration of the memory of the victims who perished in the camps.[4] For another commentator the central problem was that the jokes diminished the severity of the serial sexual assaults of which Weinstein and others stand accused.[5] Jewish literature scholar Jeremy Dauber sought to locate the monologue within its historical and cultural context, explaining that the success of such controversial humor depends on its ethical framework.⁶ For regular viewers of David's oeuvre, the *SNL* monologue was not so surprising or shocking. *Curb Your Enthusiasm* dealt with the Holocaust on a regular basis, as David mocked revered icons of Holocaust memory. It was David's brazenness in bringing that taboo so starkly to network television that shocked audiences so much and sparked a mini-wave of opinion pieces on the possibilities or acceptability of humor that invokes the Holocaust, and where the boundaries fall on this question.

Only eighteen months later, the Netflix series *Historical Roasts*, hosted by "roast master" and comedian Jeff Ross, included an episode in which Anne Frank (played by Rachel Feinstein) is roasted by Franklin Delano Roosevelt (played by Jon Lovitz), Don Rickles (played by his daughter, Mindy Rickles), and, most controversially, Adolf Hitler (played by Gilbert Gottfried). The humor is risqué and even cringe-worthy, with jokes making fun of Frank's hiding place, satirizing the popularity of her diary, and lampooning FDR (with allusions to current atrocities: "Just do what FDR did and look the other way") and the Greatest Generation. The main butt of the jokes, though, is Hitler. The lion's share of Lovitz's Roosevelt routine is devoted to jokes about Hitler having only one testicle. Feinstein's Anne Frank, however, has the last laugh, taking Mel Brooks's cue in roasting Hitler, a kind of posthumous Jewish victory. "Guess what, Hitler?" she taunts. "You're being played by a Jew right now, and it's the loudest and most annoying Jew we could possibly find," as though to emphasize the fact that one-third of Europe's Jews survived the Holocaust and could laugh at his expense.

The writers seem to have been keenly aware of the potential criticism and to have written a script that anticipated any outrage. A few factors point to that. First, Ross gives context by summarizing Frank's story in a manner that makes it clear that it is a serious story and that Frank is a figure that he reveres. (That said, he can't help himself and makes a joke here: "Please enjoy the roast of Anne Frank . . . and the end of my career. After this, I may have to go into hiding for a while.") Second, each of the actors is Jewish, a fact that Ross highlights to give them license to insert Anne Frank into the series. "Us Jews," he says, "always get through the pain with laughter, and if we don't laugh, we cry." The episode is also topical; contemporary references to climate change and refugees in the United States are used as justification for the episode. That is, it is the urgency of contemporary political issues that requires comedians to highlight historical figures such as Anne

Frank. Another way in which Ross anticipates criticism is to point out that, typically, roast subjects are popular figures, not villains. Ross says that they are roasting Frank rather than Hitler because "I only roast the ones I love."

The audience reaction was, as with David and his *SNL* monologue, often marked by uncomfortable laughter, and the critics reacted with outrage.[7] Yet, like David's monologue, the roast asks the audience—perhaps more explicitly than does David—to consider the boundaries and function of humor and to question who the butt of the joke really is. It suggests that humor can indeed be part of a Holocaust memorial landscape as well as perform an educational function, as Ross seems legitimately to believe that he can use the forum to teach his audience about Anne Frank, the current plight of refugees, and the dangers of indifference.

In this volume the contributors argue that humor *is* possible after the Holocaust. They examine what is at stake in deploying humor in representing the Holocaust. What are the boundaries? What is still considered taboo and why? What are the functions of humor in the context of the Holocaust? Clearly, there has been comedy and laughter in the decades since. However, the extent to which humor can be ethically deployed in representing and discussing the Holocaust is not as clear. The issue is becoming more pressing. In the last two decades, humor that invokes symbols of the Holocaust has become more prevalent in American, Israeli, Canadian, Latin American, Australian, and European popular culture. Whereas a film like Mel Brooks's *The Producers* (1968) was controversial in its day for its use of Nazi symbols and imagery, today it has been adapted as a Broadway musical, and it would be considered relatively tame alongside other examples of humor that touch on the Shoah. The boundaries have shifted when it comes to the relationship between laughter and the Holocaust.

Still, there is little agreement on where those boundaries lie, and episodes such as the discovery of jokes in Anne Frank's diary or Larry David's *SNL* monologue highlight a certain kind of discomfort that persists around this topic. Many questions still remain unanswered: Is humor totally off-limits when the subject matter is so serious, so devastating? Is the only possible approach to Holocaust remembrance one that is earnest and reverential and conveys historical events in a sober, factual manner? Who is allowed to make such jokes? Survivors, Jews, anyone? Did the Shoah itself create a rupture in the modern Jewish tradition of "laughter through tears," exemplified by Yiddish writer Sholem Aleichem?[8] If Theodore Adorno's oft-misinterpreted maxim that "to write poetry after the Holocaust is barbaric" contains an ounce of truth, how much more so does that apply when discussing humor after the Holocaust?[9]

Scholars have been grappling with this question since the late 1980s, after the critical and popular success of Art Spiegelman's graphic memoir, *Maus*. The literary scholar Terrence Des Pres argues that works such as *Maus*, which used humorous forms and could elicit laughter from readers, offer an alternative to the "tradition of high seriousness" that is typical of representations of the Holocaust. This approach is the result of a certain kind of Holocaust etiquette that developed over decades, a set of fictions that function as "regulatory agencies to influence how we conceive of, and write about, matters of the Holocaust." These fictions, which took decades to crystallize, are that "the Holocaust is unique, its data cannot be trifled with, and we respect those conditions by staying within the bounds of high seriousness."[10]

Des Pres claims that a certain weariness had set in with this earnest approach, a weariness that could be debilitating. For him, laughter is another way to begin to think through the challenges of remembering the Holocaust, something that can add to how we understand it: "I want to consider the energies of laughter as a further resource. We know, to begin with, that a comic response to calamity is often more resilient, more effectively equal to terror and the sources of terror than a response that is solemn or tragic." Or, in short, "laughter revolts." Comic approaches "refuse to take the Holocaust on its own crushing terms." It is the comic, and the act of displacement that laughter offers, that allows us to move forward in the world, even with the devastating knowledge of the Holocaust.[11]

The late 1990s saw the release of three Holocaust films that would reignite this discussion: Roberto Benigni's Academy Award–winning *Life is Beautiful* (1997), Radu Mihăileanu's *Train of Life* (1998), and Peter Kassovitz's remake of *Jakob the Liar* (1999), starring Robin Williams. Only a few years after *Schindler's List* (1993) had taken the world by storm with its hyperrealistic depiction of the rescue of more than 1,000 Jews by the German industrialist Oskar Schindler, filmmakers were pushing back against the

Holocaust etiquette identified by Des Pres. If *Schindler's List* marked the apex of high seriousness in representing the Holocaust, these later films showed the possibility of laughter in a world after Auschwitz.

Slovenian psychoanalyst Slavoj Žižek suggests that these films emerged as a direct response to *Schindler's List*, and what he argues is the failure of Holocaust tragedies: "All three films are centered on a lie that allows the threatened Jews to survive their ordeal." He claims that they emerged because realist films such as *Schindler's List* are based on a fiction that the Holocaust can be faithfully represented.[12] "Why not turn to comedy," he writes, "which at least accepts in advance its failure to render the horror of the holocaust?"[13] For Žižek, the emergence of Holocaust comedies on film is directly related to the "elevation of the holocaust itself into the metaphysical, diabolical Evil—the ultimate traumatic point at which the objectifying of historical knowledge breaks down and even witnesses concede words fail them. The holocaust cannot be explained, visualized, represented or transmitted, since it marks the black hole, the implosion of the (narrative) universe. Any attempt to locate it in its context, to politicize it, equals an anti-Semitic negation of its uniqueness."[14]

Literary scholar Sidra DeKoven Ezrahi goes a step further than Žižek, picking up on Des Pres in arguing that the comic is a necessary part of what allows us to move forward in a world beyond the Holocaust: "So let me state what might seem obvious: yes, life is beautiful. No, the Shoah cannot be funny. What is at stake in the reinstatement of laughter '*nach Auschwitz*,' *after* Auschwitz, is not the fidelity of a comic representation *of* the Shoah but the reinstatement of the comic as building block of a post-Shoah universe."[15] Clearly, the Holocaust is not funny, does not elicit laughter. But finding those moments of irony and lightness, those times when humor served to give victims a sense of dignity, helps us to see the possibilities for another way to remember that offers a way back into a world that can indeed be beautiful.[16]

Twenty years after *Life Is Beautiful*, it is now time to take stock of how the genre has developed and how it has shaped or been shaped by how we remember the Holocaust. *Life Is Beautiful* marked a turning point, if not in humorous representations of the Holocaust, then at least in discussions about the ethics and functions of such humor. This volume is possible because of the distance from the popular emergence of the Holocaust comedy genre in the late 1990s. The decades since have also seen the explosion of Holocaust humor on television, in stand-up comedy, and in literature in the Americas, Israel, Europe, and Australia.

This volume comes at an important moment in the trajectory of Holocaust memory. As the generation of survivors continues to dwindle, scholars and community leaders are greatly concerned about how memories and lessons of the Holocaust will be passed to future generations. Without survivors to tell their stories, to serve as constant reminders of what they experienced, how will future generations understand and relate to the Shoah?

Moreover, recent years have seen a spike in antisemitism in the United States, Europe, and Latin America. Against the backdrop of events such as the massacre of Jews in a Pittsburgh synagogue in 2018, the white supremacist march in Charlottesville, Virginia, in 2017, or the ongoing targeting of Orthodox Jewish institutions in France and the United States, the urgency of remembering the Holocaust and taking it seriously has increased. Does laughing at aspects of the Holocaust and its aftermath, particularly when neo-Nazis march in the streets of the United States and Europe, minimize its gravity? Does humor that invokes the Holocaust then trivialize the severity and horrors of the Holocaust? Does it undermine the moral authority of survivors and their descendants? Does it make the victims' suffering seem less extreme, easier to dismiss? Moreover, who is permitted to make jokes invoking the Holocaust? Are we all survivors of the Shoah? Or do descendants of survivors reserve the right to determine what is funny?

Another corollary is that the very groups reviving antisemitism often deploy their own twisted humor to harass Jews and stoke the flames of hatred, regularly invoking the gas chambers and Hitler's planned extermination of Europe's Jews in their online forums. Drawing on historic Nazi techniques, they use humor as a form of humiliation and propaganda to attract supporters. Humor and satire can also serve to normalize new manifestations of fascism; laughing at those in power can soften them and lead people to let their guard down against the threat of antisemitism and racism.[17] These issues challenge the conception of humor as therapeutic or as a weapon of the disenfranchised, when it is those who enjoy positions of privilege who can benefit most from the use of humor.

The contributors to this volume examine case studies from World War II to the present day in considering and reconsidering what role humor can play in the rehabilitation of survivors, of Jews, and of the world more broadly. Does comedy have a place in the landscape of remembering tragedy? Several contributors deal with the question of what boundaries exist for humorists and comedians, if any boundaries exist at all. If boundaries do exist, who is responsible for enforcing them? What type of humor can exist in the depravity of the Einsatzgruppen, the cold efficiency of Treblinka, and the quiet, calculated mass murder of people with disabilities by the Nazis? In what ways, if any, does Jewish humor change because of the Holocaust? Who is permitted to invoke the Holocaust for humorous purposes and to what ends?

Humor has been a factor in how we think about the Jews' experiences under Nazism since World War II. Whether revelations about humor during the war (including jokes, satirical songs and plays, and films) or satirical plays in Displaced Persons camps that mocked the Jews' vanquished enemies, humorous treatment of issues surrounding the Holocaust date back to the war itself.[18] More recently, humor has been used to investigate the role that Holocaust memory plays in contemporary societies, such as Israel, Germany, and the United States. Humor after the Holocaust can serve different functions. It can serve as a weapon against Nazism or against the rise of new forms of fascism, as in *The Producers*. It can be a coping strategy for survivors and their descendants; the Yiddish film *Undzere kinder*, produced in immediate postwar Poland, shows how humor could be therapeutic for survivors. Humor can help illuminate the plethora of ways that victims and survivors experienced the war and can show the complexity that underpins those experiences. This is most famously the case in *Life Is Beautiful*, which, although fictional, suggests that humor could operate even under the most dire circumstances. Finally, humor can challenge memorial conventions around the Holocaust and help shape the way we think about the past.

The question is not whether or not Holocaust-related humor is appropriate or how it should be policed. To reinforce Ezrahi, the Shoah is obviously not funny in itself, and with the exception of Holocaust-inflected "humor" deployed for antisemitic purposes, that is not the starting point for the artists under consideration. The Holocaust, for these writers and comedians, is not the butt of the joke but the background to explore contemporary political, social, and cultural issues. In a world in which Holocaust memory is ubiquitous, even if the Holocaust itself is barely understood, it is perhaps not surprising that humor that invokes the Holocaust has become part of the memorial landscape. The contributors to this volume seek to uncover how and why such humor is deployed and what the factors are that shape its production and reception. They are concerned with the ethical underpinnings and implications of such humor, a task that has become more urgent as we enter a memorial landscape in which the contact with that past continues to recede.

Notes

1. Tanya Gold, "Publishing Anne Frank's 'Dirty' Jokes Demeans the Human Who Wrote Them," *The Guardian*, 17 May 2018, https://www.theguardian.com/commentisfree/2018/may/17/publishing-anne-frank-dirty-jokes-demeans-human [accessed 18 May 2018].
2. The best collection of such humor from the Holocaust era is Steve Lipman, *Laughter in Hell: The Use of Humor During the Holocaust* (Northvale, NJ: Aronson, 1991).
3. Larry David stand-up monologue, *Saturday Night Live*, 4 November 2017, https://www.youtube.com/watch?v=G0eeNijdv3I [accessed 22 May 2018].
4. Jeffrey K. Salkin, "Pretty, Pretty, Pretty Tasteless," *Forward*, 6 November 2017, https://forward.com/scribe/386961/larry-david-pretty-pretty-pretty-tasteless/ [accessed 1 July 2018]; Dvir Abramovich, "Standing Shoulder to Shoulder with Survivors," *Australian Jewish News*, 16 November 2017, https://www.jewishnews.net.au/standing-shoulder-shoulder-survivors/71133 [accessed 1 July 2018].
5. Lila MacLellan, "What Will It Take to Make Men Stop Making the Wrong Jokes About Rape?" *Quartz*, 5 November 2017, https://qz.com/1120692/larry-david-snl-monologue-when-will-men-stop-joking-about-sexual-assault/ [accessed 1 July 2018].
6. Jeremy Dauber, "Why Larry David's Holocaust Joke Was So Uncomfortable," *The Atlantic*, 7 November 2017, https://www.theatlantic.com/entertainment/archive/2017/11/why-larry-davids-holocaust-joke-was-so-uncomfortable/545105/ [accessed 1 July 2018].
7. See, for example, Julia Métraux, "Netflix's Roast of Anne Frank Is as Bad as It Sounds," *Hey Alma*, 5 June 2019, https://www.heyalma.com/netflixs-roast-of-anne-frank-is-as-bad-as-it-sounds/ [accessed 17 June 2019]; Marcy Oster,

"Episode of New Netflix Series Mocks Anne Frank," *Jewish Telegraphic Agency*, 29 May 2019, https://www.jta.org/quick-reads/episode-of-new-netflix-series-mocks-anne-frank [accessed 17 June 2019]; and Sue Surkes, "Uproar over Netflix Show in Which Hitler 'Roasts' Anne Frank," *The Times of Israel*, 30 May 2019, https://www.timesofisrael.com/uproar-over-netflix-show-in-which-hitler-roasts-anne-frank/ [accessed 17 June 2019].

8. A spate of scholarship examining the tradition of Jewish humor has appeared recently. Among the most important works are Ruth Wisse, *No Joke: Making Jewish Humor* (Princeton, NJ: Princeton University Press, 2015); Jeremy Dauber, *Jewish Comedy: A Serious History* (New York: Norton, 2017); Eli Lederhendler and Gabriel N. Finder, eds., *A Club of Their Own: Jewish Humorists and the Contemporary World* (New York: Oxford University Press, 2016); Lawrence J. Epstein, *The Haunted Smile: The Story of Jewish Comedians* (Oxford: Public Affairs, 2001); and Sarah Blacher Cohen, ed., *Jewish Wry: Essays on Jewish Humor* (Detroit: Wayne State University Press, 1990).

9. Adorno is not, as many have assumed, proscribing poetry and art. Instead, he suggests that the Holocaust necessitates a shift in how we think about culture and its role in society. After the brutality of the Nazis, Western assumptions about the freeing potential of art needed to be rethought, as totalitarian regimes showed how easily culture could be usurped and brought into the service of oppression and violence. See Marianne Tettlebaum, "'Nothing Is Meant Quite Literally': Adorno and the Barbarism of Poetry After Auschwitz," in Dorian Stuber, ed., *Holocaust Literature* (Ipswich, MA: Salem Press, 2016), 200–213.

10. Terrence Des Pres, "Holocaust *Laughter*?" in Berel Lang, ed., *Writing and the Holocaust* (New York: Holmes and Meier, 1988), 217.

11. Des Pres, "Holocaust *Laughter*," 220–21.

12. At least in film. As Slucki and Patt show in their chapters in this volume, television series such as *Seinfeld* and *HaHamishia HaKamerit* (The Chamber Quintet) highlight the absurdity of the representation being conflated with the event itself.

13. Slavoj Žižek, "Camp Comedy," *Sight and Sound* 10, no. 4 (2000): 26. The lowercase *h* is in the original text.

14. Žižek, "Camp Comedy," 26.

15. Sidra DeKoven Ezrahi, "After Such Knowledge, What Laughter?" *Yale Journal of Criticism*, 14, no. 1 (2001): 287.

16. Other studies of the genre of Holocaust humor, which tend to focus particularly on films, include Sander Gilman, "Is Life Beautiful? Can the Shoah Be

Funny? Some Thoughts on Recent and Older Films," *Critical Inquiry* 26, no. 2 (2000): 279–308; Yosefa Loshitsky, "The Politics and Ethics of the Holocaust Film Comedy," in Ronit Lentin, ed., *Re-Presenting the Shoah for the Twenty-First Century* (New York: Berghahn, 2004), 127–37; Aaron Kerner, *Film and the Holocaust: New Perspectives on Dramas, Documentaries, and Experimental Films* (New York: Continuum, 2011), 79–100; Eyal Zandberg, "'Ketchup Is the Auschwitz of Tomatoes': Humor and the Collective Memory of Traumatic Events," *Communication, Culture, and Critique* 8 (2015): 108–23; and David Slucki, "Making Out in Anne Frank's Attic: Humor and the Holocaust in Australia," in Eli Lederhendler and Gabriel N. Finder, eds., *A Club of Their Own: Jewish Humorists and the Contemporary World* (New York: Oxford University Press, 2016), 204–29.

17. For a discussion on this side of satire, see Malcolm Gladwell, "The Satire Paradox," *Revisionist History*, podcast, 17 August 2016, http://revisionisthistory.com/episodes/10-the-satire-paradox [accessed 20 March 2018]; and Heather L. LaMarre, Kristen D. Landreville, and Michael A. Beam, "The Irony of Satire: Political Ideology and the Motivation to See What You Want to See in *The Colbert Report*," *International Journal of Press/Politics* 14, no. 2 (2009): 212–31.

18. See, for example, Avinoam Patt, "Laughter Through Tears: Jewish Humor in the Aftermath of the Holocaust," in Eli Lederhendler and Gabriel N. Finder, eds., *A Club of Their Own: Jewish Humorists and the Contemporary World* (New York: Oxford University Press, 2016), 204–29.

AFTERMATH

Hitler Hanging on the Tree

Humor and Violence in Soviet Yiddish Folklore of World War II

Anna Shternshis

Adolf Hitler is a brown Haman,
A thick robe awaits you.
We are building, in your honor
A coffin, a beautiful one.

To the grave will bring you
Our Stalin, our joy.
On the right side will hang
Hitler, Goebbels, Himmler, Frick.
From the left side will swing around
Rosenberg and Ribbentrop.
Flying right with their
Heads down into the ground.

And we will bury you
So deeply into the ground.
From your corpse, the ugly one
There will be no stink![1]

THIS SOMEWHAT PROPHETIC[2] YET not entirely sophisticated ditty promoting violence and savoring dark details of Hitler's death was first collected in 1943 from Shifra Perlina, a young Jewish woman from Lithuania who lived in Alma-Ata, Kazakhstan.[3] She sang it to Hirsh Blosteyn (1895–1978), a Yiddish poet and journalist who was on a mission to write about Soviet Yiddish anti-fascist humor for the Soviet Yiddish weekly *Eynikayt* (Unity); the magazine was published in Moscow by the Soviet Jewish Anti-Fascist Committee between 1942 and 1947.[4] *Eynikayt*'s agenda included mobilizing Jews from around the world to support the Soviet war effort. Bloshteyn was probably assigned to write a piece featuring jokes and humorous songs that promoted Soviet Jewish resistance and expressed support for the Soviet war effort. These sentiments were indeed popular among the 1.6 million Jews in the Soviet Union, including the 250,000 Polish and Romanian Jewish refugees surviving the war in Kazakhstan and other parts of the Soviet rear.[5] But it is one thing to agree that Hitler and Nazi Germany are enemies of the Soviet Union and a completely different thing to create entirely politically correct jokes to this effect. Moreover, as we have learned from memoirs and diaries written during the war by Polish Jewish refugees, their fears of the Soviet state often equaled their fears of Nazi Germany, especially since many of them ended up in the Soviet Union precisely because Stalin's government arrested them shortly after the annexation of Poland and deported them to Soviet jails.[6]

None of this ambivalence is recorded in songs, jokes, stories, and anecdotes collected between 1941 and 1947 by Soviet Yiddish journalists, historians, folklorists, and ethnomusicologists. Some of these materials appeared in *Eynikayt* between 1942 and 1947; others, although intended for publication, never made it to print but were instead preserved in the archives of the Kiev Cabinet for Jewish Culture, a Jewish studies research bureau of the Ukrainian Academy of Science.[7] I argue that the fact that a joke was publishable did not necessarily mean that it was not popular. It also did not mean that people who read it would not find it funny.

I write this chapter to explore how we can best use the newly found corpus of these patriotic Yiddish jokes and other humorous pieces. Do these jokes indeed give us a sense of what people found funny during the war? Or do they tell us more about what the state ideologues believed people should laugh about? Above all, I argue that these officially approved jokes give us a chance to see what was relevant to Yiddish speakers living in the Soviet Union, many of whom read *Eynikayt*. Although there is no way of knowing how they reacted to these jokes (laughed, ignored, rolled their eyes), we do know that they understood them. We also know that people who printed these jokes believed that someone should laugh at them or at least approve of them. Discussing Soviet Yiddish jokes also gives us a chance to obtain insight into cultural products that merged the state ideological message with the folkloric forms that were either circulated or designed to be circulated among the people targeted by these ideological messages.

Uncensored Soviet Yiddish songs, stories, anecdotes, and jokes probably existed, and these would arguably be the most interesting ones because of their spontaneous and uncensored nature. But to date, I have not been able to find them. Therefore, as a point of contrast, I rely on humorous pieces collected outside the Soviet Union but during the war. One collection is by Rabbi Shimon Huberband (1909–1942) in the Warsaw Ghetto, as part of Emanuel Ringelblum's *Oyneg Shabes* initiative;[8] another one is from the corpus cited by Steve Lipman in his anthology *Laughter in Hell*.[9] A comparative analysis of censored Soviet Yiddish jokes, circulating in relative safety, and uncensored Polish Yiddish jokes can help us to determine what people found funny and what the Soviet government thought they should laugh at.

Some scholars who analyze Holocaust humor suggest that jokes can serve as a window on the zeitgeist of the milieu in which they had been popular. Others argue that ghetto humor is best understood through the prism of spiritual resistance.[10] I believe that studying Yiddish humor published in the Soviet Union during the war does not provide this insight into how Soviet Jews resisted fascism. Instead, it helps us to understand how Soviet ideologues intended to use Yiddish jokes and humorous songs as motivational pieces to fight the enemy. The best approach for contextualizing these pieces, I believe, is thinking about them as an attempt by the state to use Yiddish humor as a weapon against fascism.

Motivating the population to fight in a war partly by creating a satirical image of the enemy in popular culture is an aspiration of all governments at war.[11] But, as sociologist Christie Davies demonstrates, although authorities often succeed in mobilizing artists for the production of patriotic cartoons, jokes, and songs, they actually expend more effort on censoring spontaneous yet subversive humor.[12] This was probably also the case with Soviet Yiddish patriotic humor, although no hard evidence, in the form of letters, directives, or instructions, exists to this effect. The only evidence we can rely on comes from the analytical pieces written by Soviet Jewish ideologues themselves.

For example, based on the analysis of dozens of songs and jokes that he collected among Jewish refugees and evacuees in Kazakhstan[13] between

1942 and 1943, Bloshteyn argued that 1943 would be remembered as the year when Soviet Jewish humor blossomed.[14] Today, this assertion seems outrageous. It is indeed strange to think of 1943 in Europe as the year of Jewish laughter; by the beginning of the year the majority of Jews of Poland and Ukraine had been killed, the last surviving French Jews were about to be deported, and others began to learn of the loss of their families and communities. The worst was yet to come for Hungarian Jews. If anything, we tend to think of 1943, as David Roskies has suggested we should, as ground zero of Jewish culture[15]—the time when the centuries-old Yiddish civilization was almost completely destroyed in Poland and the Soviet Union.

From Bloshteyn's perspective, however, and maybe from the perspective of some Jews who lived then in Soviet Central Asia and had limited information on the scope of the destruction of the Jewish communities in Europe, 1943 could indeed seem more cheerful compared to 1941, when most of these people were on trains traveling to unknown destinations and fates. With the Soviet victory at Stalingrad and encouraging news from the Western Front, 1943 probably marked the moment when the enemy became a lot less scary, a lot less invincible, and easier to mock. This is the time, possibly, when official humor, first designed to motivate soldiers not to be scared of a much better equipped and organized German army, began to resonate. In this sense, the Soviet Jewish humor of 1943 was indeed "postwar" humor, although the war was still going on.

Hitler the Haman, Stalin the Hero: Purim Imagery in Soviet Wartime Humor

Perlina's song makes fun of German political leaders and ridicules their unsuccessful attempts to invade the Soviet Union. In the context of Soviet satire of the 1940s, her choice of villains is unremarkable, as Hitler, Göring, Rosenberg, Ribbentrop, and Frick became iconic villains of the Soviet struggle against fascism. Caricatures of these politicians filled the Soviet press, some drawn by professional artists such as Boris Efimov, who wrote in his memoirs that he used his art to nurture antipathy for the enemies.[16]

The comparison between Hitler and Haman, the villain from the Purim story, is less expected in the Soviet context and more specific to Jewish humor, but it is quite common in the framework of Jewish rhetoric of World War II, when Hitler and Haman were used interchangeably in popular speech, on gravestones,[17] in Yiddish-language speeches by officials,[18] in Polish ghettos, in postwar displaced persons camps in Germany,[19] and even by Hitler himself.[20] The story of Purim and its characters made a triumphant comeback during World War II everywhere in Europe, including the Soviet Union, where it is likely that Polish Jewish refugees, who were usually more familiar with the Jewish holiday than Soviet Jews of the 1940s, contributed to resurrecting the popular tradition.

Purim is a Jewish holiday commonly associated with comedy, often performed for the public on stage. The story of Purim is often reinterpreted in the context of contemporary events that Jews experience.[21] Therefore it is not entirely surprising that Haman's character became interwoven with Hitler. Soviet Yiddish folklore relied on both the humor of the celebration and the hopeful nature of the story to create songs and jokes that related to the war. Consider, for example, another song from the time, also recorded in Kazakhstan, but a little later, in 1945, from an anonymous singer who insisted that the song should be called "Purim Gifts for Hitler."

> You're not my first enemy,
> Before you I've had many others!
> I only need to add your name
> To this little note, the one that begins with "Haman."
> Haman, Antiochus, Torquemada, Krushevan,
> Were provoking the world long before you [arrived].
> A longer note—Haman's—already exists,
> There wouldn't be enough paper [for yours] . . .
> You all set a goal
> To erase me from the world,
> Except . . . [my fate] does not depend on you—
> Stalin has already tied your hands!
> You've burned my joyful home
> And disgraced my daughters.
> You've trampled my infants
> And sworn to get rid of me too.

> Your angry dreams are wild and silly!
> We're alive! And [we] will survive no matter what.
> Your bleary end will be on Haman's tree
> While the Jewish people live on and on![22]

The song compares Hitler not just with Haman but also with other failed enemies of the Jewish people, such as Antiochus IV Epiphanes (215–164 BCE), known for his persecution of Jews in antiquity, a tale that is recounted during the Jewish holiday of Chanukah; Tomas of Torquemada (1420–1498), the head of the Spanish Inquisition; and Pavel Krushevan (1860–1909), the alleged author of the *Protocols of the Elders of Zion*. Importantly, the song also vows cruel revenge on Hitler and his supporters; it promises Hitler a fate worse than that of other failed enemies of the Jews. The praise of Joseph Stalin as the powerful crusher of fascism seems genuine here. Unlike many Soviet Yiddish patriotic songs of the 1930s, where mentions of Stalin seemed like later additions and felt artificial, the wartime songs praise him front and center, without reservations.[23]

What seems less genuine in this song and in Perlina's song, however, is their actual humor, which feels fully officially sanctioned and lacks crucial characteristics of a good joke: spontaneity, subversiveness, or a dose of cynicism.[24] Certainly, there are elements of morbidity, such as savoring the beauty of the coffin, the thickness of a rope, the stink of a corpse, and profanities, but somehow the song lacks the emotional power that leads to spontaneous laughter. If anything, the songs seem funnier today in the twenty-first century because the contemporary American audience perceives Yiddish culture as kitchen-based, full of cynical humor, and vulgar, and it does not expect Yiddish-language songs to savor violence, comment on politics, and call for revenge. The shock of hearing these words today provokes laughter, which it most likely failed to produce in 1944 and 1945, when the songs were written and when they could be seen as boring and dry for the same reasons that today's audience finds them funny—the full absence of kitchen humor, personal vulgarity, and self-deprecation.

At the same time, a listener in the mid-1940s probably did not need to look up who Frick and Rosenberg were, just as we do not need to look up who Hillary Clinton and Donald Trump are. The joke might not have been funny in 1943, but it was completely clear to its audience; it commented on contemporary events and, in some cases, clarified them. In this sense, Soviet Yiddish jokes and humorous songs, collected and published (or ready to be published) through state-sponsored institutions, give us a sense of what was relevant to Yiddish speakers living in the Soviet Union during this time and what intellectuals believed could be publishable to represent Jewish humor.

Crimea, Donbass, Oil, and Coal: Yiddish Jokes and Songs Reflect on Current News

Every joke, anecdote, song, or ditty cited in this chapter was published or recorded as the war was still being waged, giving us a chance to discuss the attitudes and sensitivities of the time rather than perceptions of them decades later. Yiddish jokes, songs, and stories created in the Soviet Union during the war are probably the only Yiddish literary pieces created and disseminated with the goal of helping official government ideology, as opposed to works created by people in response to discrimination, harassment, or unjust treatment. As a result, most of these pieces have little in common with the songs and jokes created in the Vilna, Warsaw, or Łódź ghettos, mostly because the Soviet songs and jokes (unlike the ghetto ones) never criticize the Red Army or indulge in self-deprecation. Instead, they praise Stalin, the Russian people, and the Soviet military and laugh at easy targets: German soldiers, fascist ideology, and Nazi leaders. Many of these pieces do not mention Jews at all. Consider, for example, a humorous song, "Afn Hoykhn Barg" (On the High Mountain), collected by poet Sholem Kupershmidt (1881–1968) in the summer of 1944 in Krasnogvardeiskoe, Uzbekistan, from Veli Shargorodskii (born in Odessa, 42 years old at the time).

> On the high mountains, and on the green fields
> The Germans are shuffling around with their faces fallen.
> "How have you been greeted, dearest Germans, so
>   esteemed?"
> "Ach, [the Soviets] showed us the way out from Crimea."
> "Stop with your sulking, don't be so upset,
> What happened in Caucasus, and what's with Donbas?"

> "*Nu*, Hitler had plans for businesses there:
> Dig out the coal, pump out the oil,
> *Nu*, but the Russians—they blocked our route,
> And so we were forced to run away."
> "Tell us about Ukraine, what sent you away [from there]?"
> "We didn't get a lick of honey [in Ukraine] either."
> On the high mountains, and on the green fields
> The Germans are shuffling around with their faces fallen.
> "Look at what bumbling soldiers you are now!"
> "Ah, misery and woe are upon us from all sides!
> We're out of options—it's not looking good
> Germany is in trouble, Hitler is kaput!"[25]

The song comments on the events of 1943–1944 and satirizes Hitler's unsuccessful attempts to seize the natural resources of Ukraine, such as coal and oil, as well as his failure to capture Crimea. The lyrics point to the old Yiddish counting riddle that sarcastically refers to impious Jews as *taychalakh* (Germans). But in Veli Shargorodskii's version, the *taych* is a real German and the song fights against German fascism. This folk song was previously incorporated into Alexander Krein's (1883–1951) version of "Afn Hoykhn Barg."

Shargorodskii's song provokes laughter today because it has an unusual contemporary feel. We still hear the words *oil, coal, resources, Caucasus, Ukraine,* and *Crimea,* because they are in the news today. These sites and issues are scenes of violence and ethnic conflicts. In the second decade of the twenty-first century we do not expect Yiddish songs of the past to care about issues that seem contemporary to us, such as oil resources (which in the song rhymes with business [*neft/gesheft*]) and coal. We (wrongly, of course) expect them to be concerned with old-fashioned "eternal" values, such as love, family, and community, because this is how we imagine Yiddish culture—functioning in the realm of "the good old days." This song destroys these expectations, and the shock of this discrepancy creates cognitive dissonance, which in turns provokes laughter. But if anyone laughed at the song in 1944, it would have been for different reasons; it would have been because the song ridicules the German attempts to occupy Ukraine, and the comical figures of German soldiers running away with their pants down (physical humor) are at the epicenter of the satire. In addition, listeners could not help but chuckle because they would have recognized the popular melody but with completely different lyrics—again, an effect lost in the twenty-first century, when the original tune is no longer in the realm of popular everyday music.[26]

Reading the texts of officially sanctioned jokes and humorous songs does help us understand the strategies of creating an ideologically acceptable image of a laughable and therefore vulnerable enemy that was not frightening. In "Afn Hoykhn Barg," Germans are depicted running away with their pants down, complaining and whining (like women), and looking forlorn. It is hard to say whether the audience of the song or its creator got a chuckle from visualizing these images, but we know that the Soviet scholars, who most likely self-censored, thought it would be ideologically acceptable to preserve these pieces and present them as a form of a patriotic folklore.

Laughing at Hitler

The lack of sophistication of ideologically correct humor can seem stunning or even patronizing, similar to early Soviet communist propaganda songs of the 1920s.[27] But one can also make an argument that the nature of this humor is juvenile, filled with physical comedy and intentionally crude comparisons, because it was directed at a young audience, one that could be more receptive and appreciative of such content. In fact, pieces recorded from children seem to promote exactly that kind of humor. Consider, for example, the song "Di Naye Khasene" (The New Wedding), first collected from Klara Rosenberg, a pupil from School Number 18 in Mogilev-Podolsk in the Vinnitsa Region of Ukraine in December 1944.

> The street is boiling hot with excitement,
> The Germans are running away!
> They run and lose their health,
> They run around crazily.
> Hitler screams: "oy, oy, oy,
> Dear in-laws,
> Do not drive away my people so fast
> They fall face down [in such a rush!]"

"Oy, oy, oy, the Reds are coming, the Reds, the Reds!
Oy, oy, the Reds are coming, the Reds are here!"
One can see that on the mountain
Red flags.
Jews are eager
To see the new bride.
She is coming from the mountain,
Great like Noah's Ark.
Jews rejoice and joke:
"Who is the maiden?"

This is a Katyusha, Katyusha, Katyusha,
Katyushas, Katyushas are here!
Hitler sits in Berlin,
He mourns his troubles.
Whereto should his [Third] Reich's Army run, whereto?
It is now good for nothing [*toygt shoyn af kapore*].
It seems to be that he almost
Wipes away his tears . . .
Göring stands by his side
And asks him:
"Hitler, oy, why are you crying, why are you crying?
Hitler, why are you crying and complaining?"
"Woe to me and woe to us
Where are my roses?"
Just look at this Reich's Army
It is shitting in its pants!
My young years are spoiled
By them forever,
It was a sweet dream,
Tugs from my soul!

Because it was sweet, my dream, it was
Because it was sweet, my dream, so sweet!
Maybe God can still perform a miracle
Like it says in the Book . . .

Hitler, oh, forget, forget
Look at these Red banners!
Look at Stalin,
Today he is unmatched,
The power of his rage can break walls,
Angry, like thousands of [evil] spirits!

To bury the Reich's Army, to bury, to bury!
To bury the Reich's Army once and for all [*for ale shvartse yor*].
Our dear Jews are happy
And get even happier.
They play violins
Each one is like an angel!

Praised be he [Stalin], for his heroism
The one, who should live forever.
It was miserably hard,
But we survived!

Mazel tov, to all of us, all of us, all of us
Mazel tov to all of us—we are coming home![28]

"Di Naye Khasene" is a wartime remake of the Yiddish *badkhen* (wedding joker) song "Di Khasene." The remake makes fun of Hitler and his army, whereas the original prewar version makes fun of a clumsy groom, his mother-in-law, and other elements of the wedding that went slightly wrong.[29] The profanity *raykhs armey bagrobn tsu ale shvartse yor* (to bury the Reich's Army in hell) adds to the comical effect.

The image of Hitler as fearful, stupid, and effeminate was common in Yiddish jokes of the time, probably representing a variation of compensatory humor.[30] In fact, Soviet caricatures of the 1940s often depict both Hitler and German soldiers dressed as women, partly commenting on German soldiers' use of scarves as hats and therefore dressing in seemingly women's garments, partly signaling their weakness and unpreparedness for war. In "Di Naye Khasene" Hitler behaves "like a woman"—he complains, moans, and cries. He "marries" a rocket with a female name, but it is clear who would wear the pants in that family.

Unlike most other officially published and collected humorous songs and jokes, this one seems genuinely funny because it adds a layer to the story of the wedding-gone-wrong situation by replacing a groom accidentally almost marrying his mother-in-law with Hitler as the groom actually marrying a rocket named Katyusha, which we presume, kills him during the ceremony.

Praise of weapons was popular in Soviet songs, which proclaim love of machine guns, pistols, rifles, and rockets. Mendel Man (1916–1975), a Polish Yiddish poet, collected a song titled "My Machine Gun" in 1944, which praised a weapon for its ability to kill as many Germans as possible so that "the Jewish people should live."[31] In the Vilna ghetto in 1943, Hirsh Glick wrote a song "Never Say" ("Zog Nit Keynmol") that later became known as the anthem of Jewish resistance during the Holocaust, in which he called for "singing, holding revolvers in one's hands."[32] In another song, Glick glorified a young girl who successfully learned how to use a gun.[33] There is not much humor in these songs, only admiration for people who know how to use guns to kill the enemy. Not laughing at guns is actually a new thing in Yiddish army songs, which are usually self-deprecating in their ridicule of newly drafted Jewish soldiers who do not know how to use weapons (e.g., Itzik Manger's famous song "Yosl Ber") and thereby reflect ambivalence about serving in the army.[34] All of this is gone from the Yiddish wartime music created both with and without Soviet censorship. Yiddish humor turns the tables and tends to attack German soldiers as unable to use weapons. "Di Naye Khasene" manages to combine Soviet patriotism and spontaneity by putting a German enemy in a situation so laughable that not even the traces of Nazi ideology can suppress a chuckle from a listener. Ultimately, these Soviet Yiddish songs reject the stereotypes of Jewish men lacking masculinity and insist that Jewish men fight enthusiastically, fiercely, and violently. Old jokes that hinted otherwise did not fit into either Soviet official or unofficial humor. In the context of official humor, such jokes could be perceived as implying that Jews were not behind the Soviet effort. In the unofficial context, such sentiment would have fed into a popular (and wrong) belief that Jews sat out the war in Tashkent while people of other ethnicities fought. Such an accusation was not even subversively, even remotely, even unofficially a laughing matter. The jokes about incapable Jewish soldiers seemed to have disappeared the moment Hitler's army invaded the Soviet Union.

Bloshteyn collected a number of Yiddish jokes about Hitler pretending to be a Jew, asking for help from Jews, or being outsmarted by Jews. Many of these jokes seem similar in spirit to those popular in the ghettos—humor that scholars often describe as a sign of the lack of moral defeat.[35] Bloshteyn claims that the following joke was among the most popular ones in Kazakhstan:[36]

> When Hitler realized that his *gesheft* was over, he put on a fake beard, dressed up as a *frum* Jew, and asked Goebbels about the whereabouts of the last Jews in his Third Reich. He then headed there and found a Jew.
>
> "Hide me, brother!" he said. "Hitler's people are running after me!"
>
> The whole thing seemed suspicious to the Jew. He had not heard, until now, that a Jew could call Hitlerite garbage "people" (*mentshn*). They could be called animals, dogs, scum (*paskudnyakes*), but not "people"! So he says to his interlocutor: "You see, uncle, I myself am hiding, in deep disguise. I fully dropped my Jewish face. So, first, we need to fully cut off your beard and leave a small moustache on, just like that. And before Hitler managed to answer, the Jew quickly stretched his hand toward Hitler's beard. Hitler began trembling, which fully betrayed who he really was."
>
> The Jew said: "I have seen goats with beards, which is quite natural. I have even seen Beck[37] with beards in his hands, but a Jewish beard on a dog's muzzle—this is something new!"
>
> The Jew said to Hitler, "Beard or no beard, the beard is not an issue. Your true place is six feet under."[38]

The focus on the Polish politician Beck and the evocation of a pious Jew suggest that this joke originated among Polish Jewish refugees. Importantly, we do not see any references to the government, the Red Army, or any other attributes of the Soviet state. In fact, had we not known that the joke was collected in Kazakhstan, we could have attributed it to any place in Europe where Jews were interned and persecuted during this time and where their humor was not censored. In fact, intentionally or unintentionally, most seemingly spontaneous (rather than specifically ideologically produced) jokes in Bloshteyn's collection actually do not contain any references to the Soviet state. Those that do seem to lack any specific references to Jews. Here is one example:

> Hitler calls Goering and issues him an order: "Marshall! Prepare the fastest plane for me, and it should take me straight to Paulus.[39] I want to hear from him personally about Stalingrad!" Goering answers: "Sorry, Herr Führer, I cannot execute your order, Paulus is very busy right now: he is giving a personal account to General Rokossovsky!"[40]

The absence of Jewish characters does not necessarily mean that this joke seemed irrelevant to Jews, because they, of course, followed the news closely and made jokes and stories based on what they learned about the progress of the war. But one does observe a disinclination to connect the Soviet success with victory for Jews, especially in jokes and stories recorded in the field rather than created by professional writers and artists.

Censored and Uncensored Humor

One can make an argument that the Soviet Union gained popularity even in anti-Communist circles during World War II, especially after the Soviet victory at Stalingrad; thus patriotic jokes reflected genuinely popular sentiments. For example, the magazine *Crocodile*, a Soviet-sponsored humorous weekly, was one of the most sought-after publications. It contained exclusively state-approved humor. Caricature sections of Soviet newspapers, again filled with the ideologically appropriate humor, were read first. Beyond the Soviet borders, *Time Magazine* named Joseph Stalin man of the year in 1942. Soviet military success could not escape the world's attention. Moreover, laughing at Hitler and his miscues became a staple of comedy in many places, including the United States, where, to name but one example among many, Ernst Lubitsch produced the classic anti-Hitler comedy *To Be or Not to Be* in 1942. Why, then, should we not expect that Soviet humor that laughed at Hitler and praised the Red Army originated from grassroots sources rather than from officially sponsored ones? In particular, why would the Soviet government need to censor any Yiddish-language art, including humor, when by 1944 it became clear that Stalin's government actually saved some European Jews? I think the answer to that question comes from comparing the Soviet materials discussed here with the Yiddish jokes that were collected in the ghettos.

Humor in the ghettos developed more in accordance with the observations of Christie Davis, who points out that uncensored wartime humor focuses on black market injustice and features puns on propaganda that always exaggerate one's own victory and diminish one's losses, expose the corruption of leaders, and, above all, thrive on self-deprecation.[41] The jokes created in the ghettos did not shy away from the topics of the Red Army, the Eastern Front, and Stalin. Yet the tone and the content of these jokes, at least the ones that ended up being preserved, are strikingly different from those preserved in the Soviet Union. For example, here is a joke from the Warsaw ghetto:

> British Radio announces: "Today we destroyed two hundred enemy aircraft." German Radio announces: "Today, we caused the enemy to lose two hundred aircraft." Soviet Radio announces: "Today the enemy lost four hundred aircraft."[42]

Another joke, also from the Warsaw ghetto, comments on the Red Army's lack of resources.

> A strange-looking airplane was noticed in the sky. Onlookers found it difficult to determine what country it belonged to. Suddenly one of the spectators said, "I know whose airplane it is. It's Russian." "How do you know?" everyone asked him. "Simple," he answered. "I saw the pilot's bare feet."[43]

Both of these jokes could potentially be told in the Soviet Union, as people routinely joked there about the lies of propaganda and the lack of resources, even in the 1930s, when it was really dangerous. Yet we do not have a record of such jokes in Yiddish during wartime. Most likely, it was because such pieces were not only too dangerous to record but also even too dangerous for Yiddish oral tradition to preserve.

Another topic that was popular in the ghettos was the corruption of Jewish leaders. Eighteen-year-old David Sierkowiak spent a considerable number of pages in his diary complaining about corruption and unfairness in the Jewish-led food distribution system in the Łódź ghetto and cited a number of jokes to this effect.[44] In Theresienstadt the musical *Prince Bettliegend* satirized favoritism and corruption among Jewish leaders.[45] In the Warsaw ghetto Jewish councils were not spared from ridicule either.

> The Führer inquires of General Franco: "Comrade, how did you solve the Jewish problem?"
> Franco answers: "I instituted the yellow badge."
> "That's nothing," says Hitler. "I imposed tributes, instituted ghettos, lessened their food rations, imposed forced labor." . . . Finally, Franco says: "I gave Jews autonomy and Jewish councils."
> "Ah," says Hitler, "that's the solution."[46]

Corruption, the black market, speculation, and the lack of information were all discussed in Russian-language Soviet wartime jokes, which were usually preserved only through oral tradition.[47] They were surprisingly similar to the ones circulated in the ghettos among Jews, especially jokes about the Siege of Leningrad, which commented on how thin people can get from starvation before they die, or the military ones, which mocked the generals and newspaper propaganda. Unofficial Soviet jokes sometimes contained antisemitic statements about Jews' surviving the war in Tashkent, their getting rich while speculating on the black market, and even their mass killings. According to one such joke:

> The Red Army liberates a village in Western Ukraine and discovers the ditch where Jews were killed. A soldier tells his friend:
> "Mikola, look what Germans did with our kikes!"

"Never mind, when we get to Berlin, we will do even worse to their kikes!"

There are definitely no positive images of Jews in Soviet Russian-language wartime jokes. Yiddish counterparts addressed Soviet state-run and popular antisemitism after the war, in the 1960s and 1970s, but there are no such jokes, not ones that I could find anyway, dating from the war. I also was not able to find jokes about the Holocaust in Yiddish (or in Russian) in the Soviet Union from the 1960s and 1970s. Jokes about pogroms and rapes exist, but not jokes about the Holocaust. The silences, omissions, and absences in officially preserved Soviet Yiddish jokes speak louder than the words they hide. If anything, they demonstrate that Soviet patriotic Yiddish jokes did not address all aspects of the Soviet Jewish experience and therefore cannot be studied as insights into folk culture, as the scholars who collected and recorded them recommended that we should. Instead, these jokes, all published in Yiddish in Soviet official publications or prepared to be published in a book, tell the story of how Soviet propagandists chose pieces of Yiddish folk culture and tried to use them for ideologically appropriate purposes during the war. Unfortunately, neither archives nor public memory has preserved unofficial Yiddish jokes, the ones that were never meant for publication or the ones that undermined Soviet official messages in Yiddish. It is hard to imagine that such jokes did not exist, but it is even harder to imagine what they were laughing at and how.

Epilogue

The most optimistic, most humorous, boldest, and funniest official Yiddish songs and jokes celebrating Soviet victory in World War II appeared before the victory actually occurred and definitely while Jews were still being victimized by fascism. Their function was probably to give hope rather than celebrate the actual victory.

Later Yiddish songs, those written in 1946, 1947, and 1948, rarely celebrate victory with such enthusiasm. Instead, they almost always mention the deceased: dead children, dead spouses (more often dead wives than dead husbands; the chances of survival for Jewish women who remained under the German occupation were much lower than the chances of survival of

Jewish men drafted into the Red Army),[48] dead cities, and dead souls. Jokes condemning Hitler no longer seemed acutely relevant.

The projects of collecting Yiddish folklore in the Soviet Union came to an end in the late 1940s. In 1949 the Kiev Cabinet for Jewish Culture was shut down. In 1950 the head of its ethnomusicology section, Moisei Beregovsky (1892–1961), was arrested, only to be released in 1956. With the exception of a few centers where Yiddish public culture continued to function in the Soviet Union, such as Chernovtsy and Vilna, Yiddish moved to the home sphere, where jokes and stories probably flourished but were not collected and recorded, even in their censored versions. In effect, this means that the wartime humor analyzed in this chapter was the subject of the last Soviet-sponsored academic research on Yiddish folklore. No matter how limited and ideologically censored these results were, research of this topic was still crucial, given that the new research in the field became possible only in the 1990s when the Soviet Union collapsed.

In a strange twist of fate, many Jewish jokes produced in the ghettos, the ones that seemed genuinely funny in the 1940s, are a lot less funny today, because unlike the creators and the audience of these pieces, we know that the objects of these jokes, such as corrupt or demagogic Jewish leaders, were murdered just like the people who enjoyed telling jokes about them. As a result, we cannot laugh at these jokes. Instead, we study them as valuable historical documents.

Quite the opposite is true, it seems, about Soviet Yiddish official humor, the humor that failed to produce a genuine comical effect in the 1940s, largely because it kept silent on some of the most controversial issues facing Yiddish-speaking Jews, such as bigotry, corruption, and the lack of unity in their own community. But the official anti-fascist humor, the humor that seemed stale and unsophisticated in the 1940s, produces laughter today, in the twenty-first century, even (or especially) if reproduced in translation. The jokes about world leaders fighting, often greedily, for natural resources, starting wars for their own personal interests, lying in the name of propaganda, are relevant and subversively funny, partly because we do not expect them to have been first produced in Stalin's Soviet Union in Yiddish and partly because the issues of wars and politics are still acute.

Bloshteyn, Beregovsky, Kupershmidt, Meyerson, and other professional and amateur collectors of Soviet patriotic folklore in Yiddish during the war preserved these jokes to prove that Jews, like all other ethnic groups living in the Soviet Union, did their fair share in the war effort and in the promotion of Soviet ideology. They were restricted by funds, ideological constraints, their own hunger, and the uncertainty of wartime. Yet they managed to write down the material that would never survive in public memory and allowed us to gain insights into what was relevant to Soviet Yiddish speakers during World War II. I do want to think that they did not want this material to remain relevant many decades later, as the dangers of fascism are still too real in so many parts of the world. Maybe it is indeed the time to study how one can use humor as a more effective weapon.

Notes

1. H. Bloshteyn, *Funem Yidishn Sovetishn folklor*, Russian State Archive (GARF), 8114, p. 2, located at the United States Holocaust Memorial Museum, Washington, DC; translation by Anna Shternshis.
2. Joseph Goebbels was German propaganda minister; Heinrich Himmler was head of the SS; Wilhelm Frick was minister of the interior; Alfred Rosenberg was a Nazi ideologue; Joachim Ribbentrop was minister of foreign affairs. All these people and Hitler, of course, died an unnatural death: Hitler and Goebbels committed suicide in Hitler's bunker as Soviet forces closed in on Berlin; Himmler took his own life while in British custody; Frick, Rosenberg, and Ribbentrop were convicted at the Nuremberg trial and hanged.
3. Bloshteyn, *Funem Yidishn Sovetishn folklor*, 2.
4. Bloshteyn was born in Keydan, Lithuania, and moved to Ukraine after the outbreak of World War I. In 1925 he immigrated to Argentina but finally returned to the Soviet Union in 1931 and settled in Kharkov, Ukraine.
5. Yitzhak Arad, *The Holocaust in the Soviet Union* (Lincoln: University of Nebraska Press, 2009).
6. Mendel Mann and Alexander Bogen, *Mentshn fun Tengushay: roman* (Tel Aviv: Farlag Y. L. Perets, 1970); Dov Levin, *The Lesser of Two Evils: Eastern European Jewry Under Soviet Rule, 1939–1941* (Philadelphia: Jewish Publication Society, 1995); Ben-Cion Pinchuk, *Shtetl Jews Under Soviet Rule: Eastern Poland on the Eve of the Holocaust* (Oxford, UK: Blackwell, 1990); Shimon Redlich, *Life in Transit: Jews in Postwar Lodz, 1945–1950* (Brighton, MA: Academic Studies, 2010).

7. For more on the history of the Cabinet, see Alfred Abraham Greenbaum, *Jewish Scholarship and Scholarly Institutions in Soviet Russia, 1918–1953* (Jerusalem: Hebrew University of Jerusalem, Center for Research and Documentation of East European Jewry, 1978).
8. David G. Roskies, *The Literature of Destruction: Jewish Responses to Catastrophe* (Philadelphia: Jewish Publication Society, 1989), 399–408.
9. Steve Lipman, *Laughter in Hell: The Use of Humor During the Holocaust* (Northvale, NJ: Aronson, 1991).
10. David G. Roskies and Naomi Diamant, *Holocaust Literature: A History and Guide* (Waltham, MA: Brandeis University Press, 2012).
11. Alexander Watson and Patrick Porter, "Bereaved and Aggrieved: Combat Motivation and the Ideology of Sacrifice in the First World War," *Historical Research* 83, no. 219 (2010): 146–64; Edward Madigan, "'Sticking to a Hateful Task': Resilience, Humour, and British Understandings of Combatant Courage, 1914–1918," *War in History* 20, no. 1 (2013): 76–98.
12. Christie Davies, "Humour Is Not a Strategy in War," *Journal of European Studies* 31, no. 123 (2001): 396.
13. Thousands of Jews (the exact number is not known) survived World War II in Kazakhstan along with 400,000 Soviet citizens and Poles.
14. Bloshteyn, *Funem Yidishn Sovetishn folklor*, 1.
15. David Roskies, "1943: The Jewish World at Ground Zero," lecture presented at Washington University, St. Louis, https://source.wustl.edu/2007/03/the-jewish-world-at-ground-zero/ [accessed 9 July 2018]. See also David G. Roskies, *Against the Apocalypse: Responses to Catastrophe in Modern Jewish Culture* (Cambridge, MA: Harvard University Press, 1984).
16. Stephen Norris, "The Sharp Weapon of Soviet Laughter: Boris Efimov and Visual Humour," *Russian Literature* 1, no. 2 (2013): 40.
17. Arkady Zeltser, *Unwelcome Memory: Holocaust Monuments in the Soviet Union* (Jerusalem: Yad Vashem, 2018).
18. Shimon Redlich, K. M. Anderson, and I. Al'tman, *War, Holocaust, and Stalinism: A Documented Study of the Jewish Anti-Fascist Committee in the USSR* (Luxembourg: Harwood Academic, 1995), 28.
19. Avinoam Patt, "'Laughter Through Tears': Jewish Humor in the Aftermath of the Holocaust," in Eli Lederhendler and Gabriel N. Finder, eds., *A Club of Their Own: Jewish Humorists and the Contemporary World* (New York: Oxford University Press, 2016), 113–17.

20. Jo Carruthers, *Esther and Hitler: A Second Triumphant Purim*, ed. Michael Lieb, Emma Mason, Jonathan Roberts, and Christopher Rowland, Oxford Handbooks Online, 2011, http://www.oxfordhandbooks.com/view/10.1093/oxfordhb/9780199204540.001.0001/oxfordhb-9780199204540-e-36.
21. Jeremy Dauber, *Jewish Comedy: A Serious History* (New York: Norton, 2017).
22. Vernadsky National Library of Ukraine, Manuscript Department, fond 190, delo 151, p. 74; English translation of Yiddish song by Tova Benjamin. See also the liner notes for Yiddish Glory, *The Lost Songs of World War II* (Six Degrees Records, 2018).
23. On Stalin in Soviet Yiddish music, see Anna Shternshis, *Soviet and Kosher: Jewish Popular Culture in the Soviet Union, 1923–1939* (Bloomington: Indiana University Press, 2006), ch. 4.
24. Delia Chiaro, *The Language of Jokes: Analyzing Verbal Play* (London: Routledge, 2006); Vikram Ahuja, Taradheesh Bali, and Navjyoti Singh, "What Makes Us Laugh? Investigations into Automatic Humor Classification," *Proceedings of the Second Workshop on Computational Modeling of People's Opinions, Personality, and Emotions in Social Media* (Stroudsburg PA: Association for Computational Linguistics, 2018); Peter McGraw and Joel Warner, *The Humor Code: A Global Search for What Makes Things Funny* (New York: Simon & Schuster, 2014).
25. Yiddish Glory, *Lost Songs of World War II*; Vernadsky National Library of Ukraine, Manuscript Department, fond 190, delo 150, pp. 105–6; translation by Tova Benjamin.
26. Linda Hutcheon, *A Theory of Parody: The Teachings of Twentieth-Century Art Forms* (Urbana: University of Illinois Press, 2000); Linda Hutcheon, "The Politics of Postmodernism: Parody and History," *Cultural Critique* 5 (1986): 179–207; J. Peter Burkholder, "The Uses of Existing Music: Musical Borrowing as a Field," *Notes* 50, no. 3 (1994): 851–70.
27. Shternshis, *Soviet and Kosher*, 106–42.
28. Vernadsky National Library of Ukraine, Manuscript Department, fond 190, delo 147, p. 87.
29. "Di Khasene," by Meir Khartiner (1880–1972), performed by Leibu Levin (1914–1983), https://www.youtube.com/watch?v=KY53tM1nIjA [accessed 7 July 2018]. See also Evgeniya Kazdan, "Velikaya otechestvennaya voyna v evreyskom folklore (po materialam iz sobraniya M. Ya. Beregovskogo)," *Vremennik Zubovskogo Instituta*, St. Petersburg, issue 6, nos. 96–105 (2011): 99.
30. Michael Billig, *Laughter and Ridicule: Towards a Social Critique of Laughter* (London: Sage, 2005).

31. Yiddish Glory, *Lost Songs of World War II*; Vernadsky National Library of Ukraine, Manuscript Department, fond 190, delo 322, p. 44.
32. Hirsh Glik, "Never Say," 1943. For the full text and the history and bibliography of the song, see Gila Flam, *Singing for Survival: Songs of the Lodz Ghetto, 1940–45* (Urbana: University of Illinois Press, 1992).
33. For the full text and the history of the song, see http://holocaustmusic.ort.org/places/ghettos/vilna/shtil-di-nakht-iz-oy/ [accessed 9 July 2018].
34. For more on Yiddish songs about wars and soldiers, see Ruth Rubin's archive: https://exhibitions.yivo.org/categories/browse/Item+Type+Metadata/Genre/Soldiers+and+War?site=site-r [accessed 9 July 2018].
35. Lipman, *Laughter in Hell*.
36. Bloshteyn, *Funem Yidishn Sovetishn folklor*, 2–3.
37. Józef Beck (1894–1944) was a Polish statesman who served the Second Republic of Poland as a diplomat and military officer; he was a close associate of Józef Piłsudski.
38. Bloshteyn, *Funem Yidishn Sovetishn folklor*, 2–3.
39. Friedrich Wilhelm Ernst Paulus (1890–1957) was a German general during World War II who commanded the Sixth Army. He attained the rank of field marshal two hours before the surrender of German forces in the Battle of Stalingrad.
40. Konstantin Rokossovsky (1896–1968) was a Soviet officer of Polish origin who became marshal of the Soviet Union, marshal of Poland, and Polish defense minister from 1949 to 1956. He is considered responsible for the eventual success of the Red Army in World War II. Bloshteyn, *Funem Yidishn Sovetishn folklor*, 4.
41. Davies, "Humour," 397.
42. Shimon Huberband, "Jokes and Puns," in David G. Roskies, *The Literature of Destruction: Jewish Responses to Catastrophe* (Philadelphia: Jewish Publication Society, 1989), 399.
43. Huberband, "Jokes and Puns," 400.
44. Dawid Sierakowiak, Alan Adelson, and Kamil Turowski, *The Diary of Dawid Sierakowiak: Five Notebooks from the Łódź Ghetto* (New York: Oxford University Press, 1996), 148–78.
45. Lisa Peschel, "'Prince Bettliegend' in Australia and Cape Town," http://ptja.leeds.ac.uk/2018/07/06/prince-bettliegend-in-australia-and-cape-town/ [accessed 8 July 2018]. The full reconstructed play can be viewed at https://vimeo.com/246407843 [accessed 8 July 2018].

46. Huberband, "Jokes and Puns," 400.
47. Mikhail Melnichenko, "Fenomen frontovogo anekdota," *Rossiyskaya Istoriya* 6 (2009): 28–40.
48. The survival rate of Jews under the German occupation was less than 5%. Women and children were overrepresented among 2.5 million Jews killed during the war. Meanwhile, of 440,000 Jews who served in the Red Army, two-thirds returned home.

Too Soon? Yiddish Humor and the Holocaust in Postwar Poland

Marc Caplan

Two factors figure in the significance of Yiddish to humor addressing the Holocaust. First, Yiddish was the language of the overwhelming majority of Holocaust victims, and as such Yiddish authors and their readers around the world were already contemplating the cataclysmic effects of European antisemitism even before the genocide itself began. By March 1941, about three months before the Nazi invasion of the Soviet Union and the accompanying mass slaughter of Jews that signaled the genocidal phase of the Holocaust, Yiddish journals in America were using the term *Khurbn*[1] to describe the catastrophe befalling European Jewry.[2] The focus of the Yiddish press on these developments was pervasive, and by 1943 Yiddish literary journals in New York such as *Svive* and *Di Tsukunft* were dedicating whole issues to the destruction of Polish Jewry and its implications for the future of Yiddish culture. Even before the outbreak of World War II, two of the most popular works in Yiddish in the late 1930s decried the menacing climate of antisemitism and violence then weighing on Jewish culture: "S'brent" (It Burns), a song by the Krakow folk poet Mordkhe Gebirtig (1877–1942); and "A Gute Nakht, Velt" (Good Night, World), by the American poet Jacob Glatstein (1896–1971). Both works were written in 1938. They would be incorporated into a canon of Holocaust literature *avant la lettre*, and they established a primary tendency for this literature in Yiddish toward an impassioned, collectivist tone, at once defiant and despairing of the world's apparent indifference to Jewish suffering.

The other factor in the development of Yiddish humor runs directly contrary to the first trend: the role that Yiddish belles lettres had created for itself more than a century before World War II as a primarily satirical, comic, socially engaged literature. Although writing in Yiddish stretches back to the Middle Ages, the primary language for expressing theological, legalistic, philosophical, and poetic ideas among Ashkenazic Jews had historically been Hebrew; the essentially medieval linguistic model through which this culture developed until well into the nineteenth century distinguished between writing in Hebrew and speaking in Yiddish. What was left for Yiddish, therefore, were ideas considered too plainspoken, too impious, or too dangerous to be expressed in either a language legible to non-Jews or the sanctified writing of rabbinic Hebrew. Accordingly, when modern Yiddish literature began to take shape at the beginning of the nineteenth century, it was perfectly attuned to satire, ridicule, and mirthmaking. The first ideologues to use Yiddish for consistently humoristic purposes—although in the early days of these efforts they were often not terribly funny people—developed what Dan Miron has termed a "language of Caliban." They conceived of Yiddish not only as a demotic language but as an intrinsically deformed and ugly one, fit only for the expression of grotesque and distorted caricatures of their culture and therefore best suited to the ridicule of superstition and corruption that the writers sought to change in traditional society.[3]

The first efforts to create a humorous response to the Holocaust in Yiddish were therefore caught between the conflicting imperatives of Yiddish humor and Holocaust commemoration. Remarkably, however, such cultural productions began to emerge in the immediate aftermath of the war.[4] Two documents that bear witness to the dialectical relationship between humor and commemoration, as well as the dilemma between the everyday nature of joke telling and the monumental solemnity of the subject matter, are *Gelekhter durkh trern* (Laughter Through Tears, 1947), a volume of humorous sketches and feuilletons by Moyshe Nudelman (1905–1967), and the film *Undzere kinder* (Our Children), produced in 1947 but suppressed in Poland until after the Cold War. *Undzere kinder* was directed by Natan Gross (1919–2005) from a script by leading Yiddish writers such as Rachel Auerbach (1903–1976) and Binem Heller (1908–1998), and it starred the comedy team Shimen Dzigan (1905–1980) and Yisroel Shumacher (1908–1961).[5]

Gelekhter durkh trern and *Undzere kinder* share both social and thematic commonalities, starting with the overlapping experiences of their creators.

Nudelman was, from the 1920s, one of the most prolific and popular humor writers for the Yiddish press in Poland; he took refuge during the war in the Soviet Union, where he participated in the reorganized Polish army that reclaimed Polish territory and contributed to the final defeat of the Nazis. After the war he worked briefly for the Yiddish press in Łódź, where much of the material for *Gelekhter durkh trern* originally appeared, before emigrating to Paris and eventually the United States, where he continued his career as a leading humor contributor to the New York daily *Der Tog-Morgn Zhurnal*. Although Gross, the director of *Undzere kinder*, began directing films only after the war—he was 20 when the war began—the stars of the film, Dzigan and Shumacher, were well-established comedians in interwar Poland. Nudelman had contributed comedy skits to the Ararat theater troupe in Łódź, where Dzigan and Shumacher were stars both in cabaret performances and on film. Like Nudelman, the director and stars of *Undzere kinder* fled to the Soviet Union during the war, and they were in Poland during the immediate postwar era before the Communist consolidation of power at the end of the 1940s, when they relocated to the State of Israel. There, Dzigan and Shumacher defied the official censure of Yiddish in the public sphere to become leading comic performers until the end of their respective lives.[6]

Nudelman begins his collection with a feuilleton from May 1945, in which he describes the significance of writing humorously after the war:

> I've decided to title this feuilleton without words, and instead simply with a big question mark. But at the last minute I realized that I was heading down a slippery slope. How can a Yiddish newspaper in Poland today permit itself the luxury of being able to print a big question mark? . . . If one has to wait for London to send so many linotype materials, one would have to wait, accordingly, for America to send its shipment of question marks, for Australia to send its shipment of exclamation marks, and for South Africa to send a transport of periods.

Soon, the author concludes that titling his feuilleton with a big question mark is a poor allocation of resources because there are so many questions that require regular-size punctuation, such as "How long will it be for the other nations to 'acquaint themselves' with the condition of Polish Jewry, before they will provide a real plan for reconstruction (question mark)."[7] The fate of Yiddish punctuation signifies the fate of the Yiddish language and of the people still speaking it; it bespeaks the strategy of Nudelman's collection as a whole that he elides the "big" question mark in favor of a series of ordinary questions devoted to everyday life among survivors rather than the philosophical question of how such a life is possible. Yet the homelessness of Yiddish typeface stands in for the stateless condition of displaced Jews, whether in Poland or in the diasporic centers to which survivors such as Nudelman would soon emigrate. In keeping with the conventions of the feuilleton genre, Nudelman presents himself in writing as a voice speaking to his readers, and the only form of embodiment he can depict is the typeface through which his words become text.

By contrast, in *Undzere kinder* the actors themselves embody a comparable sense of displacement. Filmed in the same year as Nudelman's book was published, 1948—it proved to be the final Yiddish-language film to be produced in Poland—*Undzere kinder* strives to maintain an ideological equanimity that would pass muster for the emerging Communist hegemony in Poland by avoiding references to Polish collaboration with the Nazis and depicting Jews, unlike Nudelman's sketches, as eager to remain in Poland and rebuild their life there. The film nonetheless was never shown in Eastern Europe and was only rediscovered in 1979.[8] It is thus a kind of time capsule; just as Nudelman begins his collection with a feuilleton titled "After Six Years," describing the absurdity yet necessity of commencing life again after the Holocaust, *Undzere kinder* depicts a kind of double suspension: of life resuming after the Holocaust yet finding resuscitation only during the waning decade of the Cold War, long after more than 90% of surviving Jews had left Poland.

Although the documentary appeal of Nudelman's collection consists in its record of postwar burlesques of the wartime experience, relatively little of the book is devoted to these subjects, for the understandable reason that the recollection was still too raw, the situation in Poland too precarious, and the feelings of Nudelman's audience too sensitive to allow for a full exposition of the subject. He nevertheless offers a handful of sketches on the theme, including a reminiscence of ghetto humor, even though he had left Poland before the ghettos were established. The most significant of these set pieces, both for its documentary value and the laughs it provides, is "Yidn Hobn in Geto Oykh Gelakht" (In the Ghettos Jews Also Laughed). Although Nudelman acknowledges the difficulty of hearing such jokes in the immediate aftermath of the war, when the full extent of the devastation was becoming common knowledge, he stresses that for Jews in the ghettos and concentration camps, humor was not only a means of resistance but also the only such means available. "There was a special category of 'revenge' jokes," he writes. "Jews were unable to take revenge with weapons in their hands—so they defended themselves with the weapon of jokes [*vits-gever*] instead of grenades."[9] The primary example Nudelman offers of this genre is a song sung in the Warsaw ghetto.

Vos darfn mir vaynen,	Why should we weep,
Vos darfn mir klogn,	Why should we mourn,
Mir veln nokh Frank'n a kadish nokh zogn.	We'll say Kaddish for [Hans] Frank.
Lomir zayn fraylekh un zogn zikh vitsn,	Let's be happy and tell jokes,
Mir veln Hitler'n shiva nokh zitsn.	We'll be sitting shiva for Hitler yet.
Lomir zikh traystn, di tsores fargesn,	Let's comfort one another, and forget our sorrows,
Es veln di verem nokh Hitler'n fresn.	The worms will be eating Hitler.
Di sonim, vos firn indz dort kayn Treblinka,	The enemies who bring us to Treblinka
Zey veln dokh vern in dr'erd ayngezinkn.	They'll sink in the earth yet.
Mir veln tsuzamen nokh orem ba orem,	We'll go together arm in arm,
Miretshem tantsn af daytshe kvorim.	And God willing dance on German graves.[10]

Yiddish Humor and the Holocaust in Postwar Poland • 43

The use of humor to exert revenge on more powerful non-Jewish adversaries was one of the uses to which Yiddish speech had been put since time immemorial, but this is a remarkably explicit example in print. Its expression of contempt is closer to Glatstein's "A Gute Nakht, Velt" than to the satires of Sholem Aleichem or Y. L. Peretz.

In the same account, Nudelman describes a fixture of the ghetto named Rubinstein, who tells jokes in exchange for donations: "Why are you giving me just two [zlotys]?" he would ask. "Two [*a tsvayer*] zlotys can go to hell. Three zlotys [*a drayer*] can go to hell. Even those four zlotys [*firer*—a play on words with the German term *Führer*] can go to hell!"[11] A similar wordplay lies at the heart of a joke about the world's seeming indifference to the fate of Jews in the ghetto: "In this world [*di velt*] nobody cares about us, and in the world to come [*yene velt*] nobody cares about us, that much I can understand, only what's keeping Roosevelt [*Roz-velt*] from doing something?"[12] Also on the geopolitical level, Nudelman records a joke in which Hitler prepares for an invasion of the British Isles by consulting with a religious Jew: "Listen here, *Jude*, your Moses is said to have a magic stick, which he just had to raise and it would change water to dry land, and with that he led the Jews over across the sea. Tell me, does such a stick still exist, and if so, where can I find it?" The Jew replies, "Yes, the stick still exists. It's locked in the British Museum, and Churchill has the key!"[13] This joke, it may be noted, does double duty, simultaneously mocking Hitler's thankfully frustrated plan to invade Great Britain while satirizing the legacy of British imperialism for looting the treasures of Egypt and other colonial possessions.

In addition to recording these jokes from the ghettos, Nudelman offers his own account of Germany's fate in the immediate aftermath of the war as a running commentary on the Nuremberg trial. In one such sketch he bemoans the slow pace of the deliberations: "All of Nuremberg has been transformed into a tortoise."[14] Göring in Nudelman's account complains, "Never in my life could I have imagined that a trial having to do with *me* could be so boring!"[15] Julius Streicher meanwhile suffers a nightmare while dozing off during his trial; his comrades in the dock must comfort him when he wakes up by saying, "Don't worry, Jules [Yulek]. First of all, you can see it's not so bad.... Even if your case comes to trial, you'll already be so old, or even better—by then, you'll have lived out your life in pleasure and comfort and you'll already be long dead."[16] Concluding the sketch, Nudelman appeals to the court, "Perhaps it's not possible to hang the accused—then shoot them, as long as they're shot. Only be quick about it. And if you're uncertain about how it's done—just ask the accused. They can give you some great pointers. You're not dealing with dilettantes; they're past masters."[17] The sarcasm offers its reader an increasingly rare sense of immediacy and urgency to the events of 1946, underscoring that, however quickly it seems in hindsight that (some of) the principal perpetrators were brought to justice after the war, such justice could never come fast enough for the survivors of their crimes.

These skits burlesque the Nazis at Nuremberg. However, it is remarkable that none of Nudelman's satires of postwar life in Poland refer to non-Jews. The same holds true for the essentially all-Jewish setting of *Undzere kinder*, where even the farmer who offers Dzigan and Shumacher a ride in his wagon to the orphanage is a Yiddish-speaking Jew, and, of course, a professional actor in his own right. In keeping with the conventions of prewar Yiddish comedy, derived from nineteenth-century Yiddish satire, the Poland of both Nudelman's book and the film is still completely Jewish, even though 90% of the Jews in Poland had been murdered just a few years before. At the same time, the film's eager depiction of Jews—living in harmony with nature, working the land, and building for a future that is invested in the courage, independence, and strength of child survivors—reflects the Zionist motivations of the filmmakers, including the cast of child actors, almost all of whom would relocate to the State of Israel soon after the film's completion. Considered in hindsight, the film's combination of genres—mixing satire, idyll, Holocaust testimony, and expressions of defiant hope—reflects the contradictory ideological imperatives of the film: the adult Yiddish-speaking survivors who were its primary audience, children preparing to relocate to Israel and learn the Hebrew language, and a Polish-speaking Communist hegemony overseeing and eventually suppressing the entire production.

Nudelman was free of these contradictions, because of both his artistic autonomy as an author and his ideological autonomy as a refugee leaving for the West rather than attempting to make peace with the political establishment in Poland. His writing is nonetheless as schematic as *Undzere kinder*, and he divides his work between recording the experiences of survival and recovery and the imperative to distract from this history to entertain his readers, for whom its most harrowing aspects would already have been familiar. The most interesting dimension of Nudelman's work offers documentation about humor during the Holocaust disguised as entertainment. By contrast, *Undzere kinder* constructs a dramatic narrative using the trappings of documentary. Natan Gross himself was primarily a documentarian, but the film's screenplay is meticulously scripted, and aside from the context out of which it emerges, much of what it depicts is fictional.[18] Following a portentous prologue by Binem Heller, the main narrative commences with a group of orphans from the Helenówek colony traveling to Łódź to see a performance by Dzigan and Shumacher.[19] The children enter the modern industrial city of Łódź in a horse and buggy, just as Dzigan and Shumacher later in the film travel to Helenówek in a horse-drawn wagon led by a Yiddish-speaking Jewish farmer. For the children, who serve as a collective and scarcely individuated presence in the film, this contrast suggests the emerging harmony between country and city extolled in Communist and Zionist iconography, whereas Dzigan and Shumacher, though only about 40 years old at the time, appear as members of an older generation and thus outsiders in the emerging order by virtue of their awkwardness in the rustic setting.

On stage, Dzigan and Shumacher perform a song praising traditional Jewish cuisine with a mix of sentimentality and self-conscious irony—that is, kitsch—staged in the "ghetto" as a beggar's lament to cadge donations of food. The viewer senses what the children soon protest by interrupting the performance with shouts and whistling: that the professionals' shtick is performed with neither accuracy nor sensitivity toward the actual experience that these children, performing the role of survivors, would have known firsthand. The film offers a comic affirmation of play, humor, and even ridicule as necessary values for a new life, associated with the vitality and optimism of the children themselves, but the "old" Yiddish humor that Dzigan and Shumacher perform and embody seems to be out of place in the new dispensation. Or so it would seem; after the performance, which has been staged to depict its own failure, to provide an opening for Dzigan and Shumacher to interact with their orphaned hecklers, the two comedians are left alone for a spare minute of dialogue in their dressing room. Here already a dramatic dynamic re-emerges, based on their comic personae but shorn of its humor. Dzigan is at once cynical and instinctual, complaining that their performance has failed as performance because Jews do not want to remember the war and because children should not be allowed in the theater. Shumacher presents a more reflective and empathic response, as he will throughout the film; he understands that the children are orphans and recognizes that they should teach the adults rather than the other way around.

Nudelman similarly grapples with the question of how his memories and his humor negotiate between past and present. In this respect the greater part of Nudelman's collection deals neither with the experience of the war nor with thoughts of revenge but with the absurdities and indignities of everyday life in the precariously liberated Polish state. Although frequent targets of his ridicule include the sometimes outlandish efforts of individual survivors to game the system for additional foreign aid, as well as the endless labyrinth of committees and bureaucracies to distribute that aid, the ultimate object of Nudelman's satire is the slow pace of aid itself and the apparent indifference of foreigners, including Jewish emigrants settled in the West before the war, to the fate of the Jews still living in Poland. In this a significant pattern emerges: Although governments and agencies from Western Europe as well as North and South America are taken frequently to task, the Soviet Union and the inexorably hegemonic Polish Communist Party receive at best a single muted, quasi-anthropological joke, taking them in tandem with another otherwise unmentioned presence on the political spectrum, Zionism. "Party politics among Jews in Poland is a multi-colored phenomenon; blue and white or red—but leaving the country is undertaken in black," that is, surreptitiously.[20]

By the time his collection appeared in book form, Nudelman himself was already living in Paris. The final section of the book, "Menakhem-Mendl the Emigrant," is devoted explicitly to this theme. Here, Nudelman casts himself in the guise of the first popular hero in the work of Sholem Aleichem, the greatest comic writer in Yiddish—or, indeed, Jewish—literature. Two features, however, distinguish Nudelman's Menakhem-Mendl from the original. First, Sholem Aleichem's Menakhem-Mendl, conceived nearly a half-century earlier, wrote letters from cities such as Odessa or Kiev (Yehupetz in Sholem Aleichem's fictional world, because most Jews at the time were officially barred from living in Kiev) to his wife, Sheyne-Sheyndl, in the shtetl, with Sheyne-Sheyndl replying to him sarcastically at the beginning of the series. Nudelman's Menakhem-Mendl writes monologues; Nudelman's Menakhem-Mendl, to the extent that any continuity exists between him and his prototype, is a widower. Second, Sholem Aleichem's motivation for the series was to register the shock and exploitation of the modern world, in particular, the world of speculative capitalism, from the standpoint of a perennially naïve, perpetually luckless young man from the provinces, desperate for a big score in a series of incompetently conceived get-rich-quick schemes. Modernity, for Sholem Aleichem's Menakhem-Mendl, is both a foreign country and an enchanted forest. By contrast, Nudelman's Menakhem-Mendl is a survivor of World War II, and thus he arrives in the metropolis, Paris, already disenchanted. The big city and its Western modernity are no less absurd for Nudelman's Menakhem-Mendl than for Sholem Aleichem's, only in Nudelman's version the protagonist is already in on the joke.

Undzere kinder also evokes Sholem Aleichem—the definitive comic author in Yiddish of modern discontent—when Dzigan and Shumacher "stage" a performance of Sholem Aleichem's *Kasrilevker sreyfes* (A Conflagration in Kasrilevke) at the orphanage.[21] The performance is a skillful cinematic montage, in contrast to the previous awkward and maudlin performance on stage, and it is performed to connect with the audience at the orphanage because it makes no pretense to speak for their experience. The staging begins with the two stars intoning the Gebirtig song "S'brent," signifying its canonical status less than a decade after its composition, yet incorporating it into a comic performance that dispels the song's pathos.[22] Their choice of texts for adaptation is astute; whereas the letters of Sholem Aleichem's Menakhem-Mendl depict the seductions of the metropolis through the eyes of a luckless shtetl dweller desperate to escape his limited horizons, the Kasrilevke stories, as a distinct genre within Sholem Aleichem's fiction, present a more complex portrait of modernity's discontents superimposed on the traditional community. *Kasrilevker sreyfes* accordingly presents the efforts of the shtetl Kasrilevke to establish a fire department, which when put to its first test realizes that it has everything necessary to put out a fire, except water. Dzigan and Shumacher's comic performance leads associatively and organically to a discussion among the children of fires they had witnessed in the ghettos, along with other reminiscences of depravation and depravity during the war. Although the film is not primarily comic and is only in telltale moments funny, it is through comedy as a performance style and specifically Yiddish theatrical convention that the serious work of reconstruction is addressed and engaged.

At the same time, the Sholem Aleichem sketch creates a stylistic and narrative rupture in the film; it is an exposition of Dzigan and Shumacher's artistry that is deliberately severed from the naturalistic and documentary aesthetics that frame it. Although it is undeniably a more enjoyable performance than what had been on display at the theater in Łódź, its pleasures are more cinematic than thematic. It is therefore unclear why this performance would resonate with its on-screen audience where the previous one had failed—except for the demands of the main narrative to illustrate a progression from estrangement to empathy, from past to future, and from incomprehension to hope. That is, this interpolation is no less ideological or overdetermined than the other scenes in the film, even though it literally cuts the narrative in two. It harkens back to the superseded time that had ostensibly been repudiated in the failure of the comedians' stage performance in the Łódź theater, yet in this instance the children accept the performance and the performers and appropriate their work for the "play" of their morning games the next day. In this respect, Sholem Aleichem fails to function as a representation of the Jewish experience during or after the war, yet he can still be adapted to the therapeutic work of reconstituting the relationship of child survivors to the past—that is, as long as the children actually speak Yiddish and understand the author's references to the shtetl and Jewish practices that had been institutionalized there.[23]

Such connections would prove fleeting in the upheavals then affecting survivors en route from Poland, so that the assurances the film offers are directed to the audience watching the film instead of the children who make up its subject. Nudelman's goals are less ambitious, but one must wonder, counterfactually, what either of these productions might have been had circumstances allowed for more ideological freedom. Might Nudelman have been angrier and for that reason funnier? One can suggest a contrast with another work from the same moment, *This Way for the Gas, Ladies and Gentlemen* (*Proszę państwa do gazu*) by Tadeusz Borowski (1922–1951).[24] The stories in this collection portray the Holocaust from a self-annihilating perspective that replicates the experiences that Borowski had been party to as a non-Jewish political prisoner at Auschwitz and Dachau. Borowski's freedom was neither granted by the state nor affirmed on behalf of a collective but was exerted out of a nihilistic dissociation from the concept of community that Nudelman, who was not a survivor in the same sense as Borowski, could not affect and that his readers in the Yiddish press could not accept. The film, in equal measure, is riven by aesthetic contradictions between entertainment and documentation but also by its ideological affirmations of progress and triumph. It highlights a vision of harmony between Poles and Jews, and adults and children, as well as Jewish resistance to Nazi terror, while at the same time foregrounding the devastating grief still afflicting the survivor community. The most compelling moments in the film—for example, when the head of the orphanage reenacts her pain at having lost children during the war—occur when the pretense of entertainment and hope is dropped to give expression to collective yet private grief.

It is likely, however, that such a complex emotional balancing act was what led *Undzere kinder* to be repressed in the postwar political order; for all the excesses and contradictions of late Stalinism, it was rigorously consistent in its rejection of emotional or philosophical subtleties. Instead, one can search for this combination of memorialization and critique—or laughter through tears—in an ongoing project that involved Dzigan and Shumacher as well as Nudelman, collectively, for the remainder of their career: the task of writing and performing comedy in Yiddish for a reconstituted audience in Israel and around the world.[25] When Dzigan recorded later Nudelman sketches such as "Der Soyne Fun Vakatsyes" (The Enemy of Vacations) or "Tsvey Yidn Khapn Fish" (Two Jews Fishing), he relocated the sarcasm and verbal aggression that had characterized Yiddish comedy of the interwar era to postwar Israel—although Nudelman himself settled in the United States—thereby rendering Israel as a national home into a reconfiguration of the Polish nation-state where their humor had first found its voice.[26]

One such sketch, a monologue recorded by Dzigan titled "Yankl der Katsev" (Yankl the Butcher), illustrates some of the same paradoxes that Nudelman's work had underscored in the immediate postwar era.[27] The butcher who relates his life story in the recording has opened his shop on

Dizengoff Street, the main street in Tel Aviv, using reparations money from Germany; he applies for the funds at his wife's insistence, because, as she reasons, "If people who had suffered under the Germans but don't want to accept their reparations, that's their business, but you have nothing to be ashamed of since you were in Russia the entire time!" This reiterates the most frequent jokes in Nudelman's post-Holocaust collection, of Jews trying to work the system for personal gain and of everyday life shaped not by the traumas of the war years but by the absurdity and banality of postwar bureaucracy. As Yankl explains, every aspect of his life is guided by his wife's vision: She took him out of the meat locker to open the business. She led him to the wedding canopy and had even given birth to two children "all by herself—I had nothing to do with it!" So too was it her idea to take a trip to Europe, but rather than seeking out places of memory for Yiddish-speaking Jews, sites closed off by the Cold War, they travel to England, France, and Switzerland.

The Europe they encounter is therefore a de-Judaized space, even if Yankl can only understand it from a perspective shaped by his experiences as a Yiddish speaker and an Israeli. Paris, accordingly, is "a city, just like any other. A dirty city, with dirty streets. Everyone there has dirty hands. In Israel that would be impossible, because in Israel one hand washes the other." When his wife brings him to the Louvre, Yankl remembers that he has heard of it, but he can't remember if it's a kosher butcher shop or if it was the synagogue where Rothschild heard Kol Nidre. Despite seeing Paris through Jewish eyes, Yankl's vocabulary is so limited that at every meal he is only able to order a single dish, filet mignon—a conspicuously nonkosher cut of meat. This suggests that something is similarly less than kosher about the butcher himself, and the suspicion is confirmed when Yankl returns to Israel from Switzerland. While going through customs, he insists that his wife not be searched or questioned because she is in a state of advanced pregnancy. The customs officer takes her away, however, and returns to offer Yankl congratulations: His wife has just given birth to septuplets—seven yards of silk fabric. Unfortunately, the officer adds, it was a difficult birth and she had to be delivered by C-section. The entire journey thus serves as a vehicle for further satirizing daily life in Israel, particularly the pervasiveness of its bureaucracy and taxes. Yankl is a "typical" Israeli, but only by virtue of his status as a disempowered outsider;

linguistically and culturally he is still a refugee and immigrant, regardless of how many years he has lived in Israel.

Paradoxically, however, the status that Dzigan and Shumacher perform as outsiders and new *olim* and their exclusive use of Yiddish on stage account for their stardom in the new State of Israel. As John Efron makes clear in a study of Dzigan and Shumacher, "Their arrival in Israel in 1950 occasioned a lengthy and glowing article in *Davar* [the leading Labor Zionist organ of the era], which while not fully appreciating the difficulties they faced, nonetheless fully understood what megastars the duo were and what their presence in Israel meant for the Yiddish speaking public and Israeli theater in general."[28] The duo, and particularly Dzigan, used this status to offer an ongoing critique of David Ben-Gurion (1886–1973), both for the prime minister's contempt of Yiddish and what Dzigan perceived as his contempt for recent arrivals in the new state. His celebrity status nonetheless led him to socialize with other politicians with whom he felt greater affinity, such as Levi Eshkol (1895–1969), Golda Meir (1898–1978), and even Ben-Gurion's protégé Shimon Peres (1923–2016). As Efron states, when Dzigan met with these politicians, the language spoken was always Yiddish.[29]

Dzigan's acclaim in Israel depended on the ability to present himself as an outsider to the new national consciousness for which Yiddish remained as marginal and powerless as it had been previously in interwar Poland. Such celebrity status, however, could only have developed in a Jewish state during an era when virtually every citizen had been born elsewhere, and the vast majority of those places of origin had been Yiddish-speaking spaces destroyed during the Holocaust. The ability to mock the new society in the murdered language constituted both an act of commemoration for the past and a statement of defiance toward the present. What Dzigan and Shumacher demonstrate in this gesture, with frequent help from Nudelman's writings, is the force that unites their comic energy with subsequent generations of Jewish humor referencing the Holocaust: that humor can function as a weapon of resistance, what Nudelman had described as *vits-gever*, and it is in the hands of the marginalized that this weapon cuts sharpest and deepest.

Notes

1. Although the terms *Holocaust* (from the Greek *holókaustus*, "wholly burnt"), *Shoah* (from Hebrew, "catastrophe"), and *Khurbn* (also Hebrew, "destruction") are essentially synonymous, the adoption of *Khurbn* in Yiddish—a word signifying ruination throughout Jewish history, harking back to the destructions of the Temple in Jerusalem (in 586 BCE and 70 CE)—signifies not merely the physical annihilation of European Jewry but the sense of cosmological rupture separating pre-genocide Jewry from what followed. If each of these terms effectively, or even ineffectively, conveys the immensity of human devastation that the Jews of Europe suffered, only *Khurbn*, because of its association with the earlier loss of homeland and spiritual rootedness centered on the ancient Temple, resonates with the sense of a lost civilization, a lost world, a lost metaphysical connection with what preceded the invasion of Poland in 1939.
2. On this point, see Anita Norich, *Discovering Exile: Yiddish and Jewish American Culture During the Holocaust* (Stanford, CA: Stanford University Press, 2007), 24.
3. See Dan Miron, "A Language as Caliban," in Dan Miron, *A Traveler Disguised: The Rise of Modern Yiddish Fiction in the Nineteenth Century* (Syracuse, NY: Syracuse University Press, 1996), 34–66. To be clear, what Miron describes is the process whereby the author Sh. Y. Abramovitsh (Mendele Moykher-Sforim, c. 1835–1917) overcame the early antipathy toward Yiddish that he had inherited from a previous generation of Eastern European modernizers; by the time he achieved artistic maturity, in the 1870s, Abramovitsh had laid the groundwork not only for modern Hebrew literature but also for the "classic" phase of Yiddish literature characterized by the comic masterworks of Sholem Aleichem (1859–1916) and Y. L. Peretz (1852–1915), in addition to his own great satires.
4. For an illuminating survey of Yiddish humor in the immediate aftermath of the Holocaust that focuses primarily on writing and performances in the displaced person camps, see Avinoam Patt, "'Laughter Through Tears': Jewish Humor in the Aftermath of the Holocaust," in Edi Lederhendler and Gabriel N. Finder, eds., *A Club of Their Own: Jewish Humorists and the Contemporary World* (New York: Oxford University Press, 2016), 113–31.
5. My understanding and appreciation of this film has been enriched considerably thanks to Professor Ian Biddle. See Ian Biddle, "Music, Sound, and Affect in Yiddish-Language Holocaust Cinema: The Posttraumatic Community in Natan Gross's *Undzere kinder* (1948)," *Music and the Moving Image* 11, no. 3

(2018): 40–59. My thanks to Professor Biddle for giving me permission to read his essay in draft form.

6. Virtually the only source of information on Nudelman is to be found in the entry on him written by Benyomin Ellis in the *Leksikon fun der nayer yidisher literatur* [Lexicon for the New Yiddish Literature], trans. Joshua Fogel (New York: Alveltlekhn yidishn kultur-kongres, n.d.), v. 6, columns 176–78, http://yleksikon.blogspot.com/2018/01/moyshe-nudelman.html [accessed 10 May 2019]. Virtually no information in English is available on Natan Gross, other than an excellent article by Haggai Hitron that focuses on *Undzere kinder* in the 20 September 2006 issue of *Haaretz*, https://www.haaretz.com/israel-news/culture/1.4866764/1.4866764 [accessed 10 May 2019]. In Hebrew, see the obituary by Shimon Redlich, "Natan Gross, 1919–2005," *Gal-Ed: On the History and Culture of Polish Jewry* 21 (2007): 157–60. For basic information on Dzigan and Shumacher, see http://www.yivoencyclopedia.org/article.aspx/Dzigan_and_Shumacher [accessed 10 May 2019]. More extensively, a recent study by Diego Rotman is a worthy candidate for translation to amplify the appreciation of these two figures in the study of Yiddish internationally; see Diego Rotman, *Habamah k'vayit ara'i: Ha-teatron shel Dzigan ve-Shumacher (1927–1980)* [The Stage as a Temporary Home: The Theater of Dzigan and Shumacher (1927–1980)] (Jerusalem: Magnes Press, 2017).

7. M. Nudelman, *Gelekhter durkh trern: Zamlung fun humoristish-satirish shafungen funem nokhmilkhomedikn lebn fun poylishe yidn* [Laughter Through Tears: A Collection of Humoristic-Satirical Creations on the Postwar Life of Polish Jewry] (Buenos Aires: Tsentral-Farband fun Poylishe Yidn in Argentina, 1947), 15–16; all translations from this source are my own.

8. For more on the rediscovery of the film at the dawning of the Solidarity movement in Poland, and just a few months before Dzigan's death in Israel, see Ira Konigsberg, "Our Children and the Limits of Cinema: Early Jewish Responses to the Holocaust," *Film Quarterly* 52, no. 1 (1988): 19n19.

9. Nudelman, *Gelekhter durkh trern*, 113.
10. Nudelman, *Gelekhter durkh trern*, 113–14.
11. Nudelman, *Gelekhter durkh trern*, 114.
12. Nudelman, *Gelekhter durkh trern*, 115.
13. Nudelman, *Gelekhter durkh trern*, 117.
14. Nudelman, *Gelekhter durkh trern*, 94.
15. Nudelman, *Gelekhter durkh trern*, 95; emphasis in original.
16. Nudelman, *Gelekhter durkh trern*, 95.

17. Nudelman, *Gelekhter durkh trern*, 96.
18. One example of this practice is noted in Hitron's article in *Haaretz*. When the film describes the burning of the Warsaw ghetto, the actress who introduces the subject is Lydia Shumacher, the (then) 8-year-old daughter of Yisroel Shumacher; not only had she not witnessed the burning of the Warsaw ghetto—she had spent the war with her parents in the Soviet Union—but she had to learn Yiddish specifically for her role on camera.
19. One reason that both Dzigan and Shumacher as well as Nudelman found themselves in postwar Łódź is because Łódź had been a significant center for Yiddish culture before the war. As Chone Shmeruk (1921–1997) explains, Łódź was considered one of the most "Jewish" cities in interwar Poland; in 1921 it had a Jewish population of 156,155, more than 34% of the city's total—a higher proportion than either Warsaw or Vilna. Furthermore, as home to a large Jewish working class, popular culture for Jews in Łódź was more often conducted in Yiddish rather than in Polish. See Shmeruk's introduction to Yisroel Rabon, *Di gas* [The Street] (Jerusalem: Magnes Press, 1986), xxxvi–xxxvii. Moreover, Łódź became the center of Jewish life in immediate postwar Poland, absorbing a large number of Jewish survivors. See Shimon Redlich, *Life in Transit: Jews in Postwar Łódź, 1945–1950* (Boston: Academic Studies Press, 2010). Gabriel Finder also notes that Łódź was the center of Polish film production in the immediate aftermath of World War II; see Gabriel N. Finder, "Child Survivors in Polish Jewish Collective Memory After the Holocaust: The Case of *Undzere kinder*," in Nick Baron, ed., *Displaced Children in Russia and Eastern Europe, 1915–1953* (Leiden: Brill, 2017), 225.
20. Nudelman, *Gelekhter durkh trern*, 20.
21. The skit is an adaptation of *Kasrilevker sreyfes*, the sixth section of *Dos naye Kasrilevke* (The New Kasrilevke, 1901), and should not be confused with *Kasrilevke nsrofim* (The Refugees of the Kasrilevke Conflagration, 1903; 1910). Both narratives are collected in Sholem Aleichem, *Ale verk fun Sholem Aleichem*, vol. 4, *Alt-nay Kasrilevke* (New York: Morgn-frayhayt oysgabe, 1937).
22. For an additional perspective on the incorporation of Gebirtig's anthem into the film, see Konigsberg, "Our Children," 17.
23. Gabriel Finder, however, argues persuasively that the language of everyday life in the Helenówek home was already Polish, not Yiddish, and this confirms the testimony of child actors in the film, including Shumacher's own daughter, that their Yiddish dialogue had to be coached because they were unaccustomed to speaking Yiddish in unprompted situations. See Finder, "Child Survivors," 241.

Finder's essay is particularly commendable not only for his review of prior criticism of the film but also for his research into verifying the sources for the film's composite documentary testimony; see in this respect Finder, "Child Survivors," 242.

24. See Tadeusz Borowski, *This Way for the Gas, Ladies and Gentlemen*, trans. Michael Kandel (New York: Penguin, 1976 [1967]).

25. In a later collection, *Lakht a yid in erets-yisroel* (A Jew Laughs in the Land of Israel), Nudelman describes Dzigan and Shumacher's career in the new state; although the collection is similar in tone and structure to *Gelekhter durkh trern*, the author writes in a straightforwardly journalistic, though sympathetic and admiring, tone about the difficulty of performing Yiddish theater in Israel and the popular and artistic success that Dzigan and Shumacher achieved there despite this adversity. Interestingly, Nudelman takes little note of his collaboration with the two stars before and during the war or his continued role as one of their contributing writers after the war. See M. Nudelman, "Dzigan-Shumacher teater" [The Dzigan and Shumacher Theater], in M. Nudelman, *Lakht a yid in erets-yisroel* (New York: Shulsinger, 1956), 165–71.

26. My source for the audio recordings of these and other Dzigan performances—many recorded after Shumacher's death with other actors and some transcribed from live and television productions in Israel during the 1960s and 1970s—is the multivolume CD series *Yiddish Humor*, produced for Israel Music by Dr. Motel Friedman; the two Nudelman sketches referenced here are included in volume 2 (1996). For a full bibliography of Nudelman's postwar writing for Dzigan, see http://digital.library.upenn.edu/webbin/freedman/lookupartist?hr=&what=6828 [accessed 10 May 2019].

27. The recording, which also appears on the *Yiddish Humor* CD, is Dzigan's longest audio monologue. I have been unable to find a reference to the author of the skit, and although the style is similar to Nudelman's writing for Dzigan, he is not credited in the digital bibliography cited from the University of Pennsylvania library. Also missing is the original date of the recording, although I infer that it is from the early 1960s because it is a solo monologue, meaning that it was recorded after Dzigan had stopped working with Shumacher in the year preceding Shumacher's early death, and because it makes reference to Ben-Gurion as prime minister, which means it was probably recorded before Ben-Gurion stepped down in 1963.

28. See John M. Efron, "From Łódź to Tel Aviv: The Yiddish Political Satire of Shimen Dzigan and Yisroel Shumacher," *Jewish Quarterly Review* 102, no. 1 (2012):

78. Efron's article is an excellent analysis and celebration of Dzigan and Shumacher's art and its significance to both prewar Polish Jewish culture and postwar Israeli culture. If I may offer a single critique, however, Efron makes no distinction between the comedians as performers and the many writers who collaborated with them and provided their best jokes, Moyshe Nudelman included.

29. Efron, "From Łódź to Tel Aviv," 78.

Is It Still Funny?

Lin Jaldati and Yiddish Satire Before and After the Holocaust

David Shneer

> Thanks to Rob Adler-Peckerar, Jewlia Eisenberg, and Jalda Rebling, who were key interlocutors in the production of this essay, in addition to the editors and the anonymous reviewers. Thanks also to the Hadassah Brandeis Institute and the Louis P. Singer Fund for financial support to carry out the research.

ON APRIL 4, 1936, SHORTLY before joining the Communist Party of the Netherlands, 23-year-old Lin Jaldati performed in an "Evening of Cabaret" (*Cabaret-Avond*). Kunstwereld, an arts production company in Amsterdam headed by S. Frank, put on the cabaret to a packed hall in the city's Adyar Club at Tolstraat 160.[1] An emcee (in cabaret parlance, a *conférencière*) hosted a series of performances divided into two acts. The concert program lists the names of the performers and a generic description of what they performed. Jaldati, the stage name of Dutch Jewish dancer, mime artist, and singer Rebekka (Lientje) Brilleslijper, was the only performer appearing in both acts. In the first act she performed "Hasidic dances" (*chassidische dansen*), and in the second, Yiddish songs (*jiddische liedjes*). She learned the Hasidic dances from the Amsterdam-based Ansky Society's Yiddish theater troupe, with whose members she developed and choreographed several popular Jewish dance characters. In the second act, she sang Yiddish (and in some cases Hebrew) songs that had been part of her repertoire since her teenage years at a Jewish summer camp, including one that would appear regularly throughout her long career. That song, the subject of this essay, was "How Does the Tsar Live?" ("Vi Azoi Lebt der Kayzer?"), but on most programs, it was abbreviated to "Gentlemen!" ("Raboysay!"), the opening salutation in the song.[2]

Twenty years later—after the German occupation of Holland, Jaldati's deportation to Auschwitz and Bergen-Belsen, her return to Amsterdam, and then her marriage to a German communist and their subsequent relocation to his hometown of (East) Berlin, capital of the German Democratic Republic (GDR)—Jaldati began building her career as the leading Yiddish performer in the self-defined anti-fascist country.[3] In this essay I explore how and why this Auschwitz survivor kept alive Yiddish satiric songs in her repertoire for fifty years. I describe how the performance of songs and their social, cultural, and political contexts changed over time.

At the birth of anti-fascism as an oppositional cultural and political movement before World War II, Jaldati's Yiddish performances represented forms of indigenous Eastern European Jewish culture that often satirized both "ossified" patriarchal Judaism and state authoritarianism. They were meant to make an audience, Yiddish-speaking or not, laugh at both rabbis in traditional prayer houses and the powerful states that were becoming an increasing threat in the daily lives of audience members. After the war, Jaldati's performances of Yiddish satire became post-genocide songs presented as memorial rituals, remnants of a destroyed culture, and cultural reflections of a downtrodden people. How could they be otherwise, for the war destroyed the entire European Yiddish cultural apparatus along with most of the people who produced that culture? And yet, I suggest that if we examine the *affect*—the mood, gestures, and rapport Jaldati created with her audiences—of Jaldati's postwar performances rather than just the ephemera left behind, the potential for satire and laughter in her prewar Yiddish songs persists into the postwar period alongside the role of Yiddish culture in memorializing the Holocaust.

"How Does the Tsar Live?" Adyar Club, April 4, 1936

Jaldati started singing at home and then at Jewish summer camps. Eventually, she trained in dance with some of the Netherlands' leading lights of modern dance and became a member of the chorus line for the National Revue. She also performed with the theater troupe of the local Jewish immigrant society, the Ansky Society, named after the famed Eastern European

Jewish ethnographer and political activist S. Ansky, whose plays such as *The Dybbuk* and *Day and Night* would become well-known cultural creations across Europe.[4] Jaldati developed her early dance and song repertoire under its members' tutelage, including songs that would remain with her for her entire fifty-year career. Because of her relationship with these Amsterdam Yiddish-speaking immigrants and her then Polish-born Yiddish-speaking boyfriend, the photographer Borukh (Boris) Kowadlo, Jaldati became drawn not only to Eastern European Jewish culture but also to its indigenous leftist politics. She joined the Communist Party of the Netherlands sometime in 1936 as a result of the Spanish Civil War and because of her relationship with Kowadlo.

Jaldati had her first breakout performance dancing and singing solo in an explicitly non-Jewish context in 1936 at the Kunstwereld Cabaret at the Adyar. This Amsterdam club served as a hub for the Dutch Theosophical Society and hosted events for the movement. Eventually it broadened its mandate to function as a home for Amsterdam's liberal synagogue and as a leftist performance space.[5] In that iteration the Adyar hosted events, cabarets, and fundraisers for "victims of Spanish fascism" as well as organ concerts of Jewish liturgical music.

The emcee for the cabaret was Amsy Moina, stage name of the Indonesian actress Amsy Jacqueline Ettij. Moina was born in 1908 in Surabaya, an important trading post in the Dutch East Indies, and made her way to the Netherlands, where she became an actress of Dutch cinema, playing ethnic roles that, casting directors assumed, fit her racially marked Indonesian appearance. Moina's cabaret sated the Dutch leftist audience's orientalist fascination with the "exotic"; act after act presented a new vision of "the East," in particular of the Dutch "East" of Indonesia, but also of authentic "eastern" Jewish culture.

The first half of the show featured ethnic dances, including Jaldati's Hasidic dances. Stylized Hasidic dances and their culture more generally were popular in the interwar period on both sides of the Atlantic. Although in the late nineteenth century acculturated Jews of Western and Central Europe feared losing their hard-earned social and cultural capital because of the so-called *Ostjude*'s presence on the streets of major European cities, in the early twentieth century a new trend among acculturated Western Jews, especially intellectuals, to find a reservoir of Jewish authenticity in the culture of the *Ostjude* took hold. This trend continued and expanded after World War I, as Hasidic culture moved off the pages of books and journals and onto the stages of theaters and cabarets.[6] Jaldati created both male and female Hasidic characters through the use of fantastic costumes, dramatic gestures, and Yiddish music drawn primarily from contemporary Yiddish theater and film.[7] She trained and performed with the Ansky Society's theater troupe, where she learned these Eastern European dances and songs. She also had help from members of the famed Vilna Troupe, with whom she performed just two months before she appeared at the Adyar.

In late March 1936 Kunstwereld also organized a performance by the Ansky theater troupe at the Bavohuis, a former church that had been turned into a performance space, of Ansky's *Tog un nakht* (Day and Night), in which Jaldati performed several dances.[8] Her dances included "Rebecca at the Well," "The Yeshiva Boy," "The Sukkot Dance," and other well-known Jewish dances for a female solo that appeared on stages in Europe and the United States in the 1930s.[9] The dances were meant to edify and entertain the audience, both Jewish and non-Jewish; in her comments to the audience directly from the stage, Jaldati said that she would perform dances rooted in an "authentic" Jewish experience.[10]

One week after the Yiddish theater performance, at the Kunstwereld cabaret, after Jaldati danced, Masha Polak performed music on violin, and then Moina introduced Indra Kamadjaja (in some other places his name is spelled Kamadjojo), who was born in Indonesia in 1906 as Jan Broekveldt. Kamadjaja was known in the Netherlands for his classic Indonesian dance, although in the cabaret program he was presented simply as an "exotic dancer."[11] Joining those two performers were a grand dame of the Dutch opera, Faniella (the stage name of Fanny Ella Poons), and actress and comedienne Eline Pisuisee, who performed an operetta. In the second act of the cabaret, Jaldati performed Yiddish songs. Although her songs are not listed, one of them was likely "Raboysay," which she performed in nearly every concert in the 1930s.

"How Does the Tsar Live?" has become a classic Yiddish satire, and in the Freedman Jewish Song Archive at the University of Pennsylvania, there are no fewer than twelve versions of it.[12] The song is a mock conversation that echoes a dialogue that might take place in a yeshiva, a traditional Jewish study house. Yeshivas were reserved for young Jewish men, whom Jaldati impersonated in the first act on stage when she danced "The Yeshiva Boy." The student poses a series of questions (*shayles*) to rabbis in the study house, whose "wisdom is limitless [*on a breg*]." The "wise" elders are surprised at the audacity of the student, asking such mundane questions of these esteemed men: How does the tsar drink tea, eat potatoes, and sleep at night? This leads the rabbis to produce a vision of luxury and excess, the truth of which is left to the listener to determine.

The point of the song is to provoke laughter at the scenario in the study house—as though these questions rose to the level of Talmudic debate—and at the ridiculous daily routine of the tsar, emperor, or any autocratic ruler. The rabbis paint an image of the autocrat ordering unnamed people, his minions, to create a pile of sugar with a hole in it and then to pour hot water in it, presumably to sweeten the sugar (where the actual tea is, one never knows). The next stanza is similarly satiric, with the autocrat "eating" his potatoes as soldiers shoot them through a "wall of butter." The final stanza portrays the "sleeping" tsar in a room stuffed full of feathers, while a regiment of soldiers surrounding the room screams at the top of their lungs, "Quiet! Quiet! Quiet! The tsar is sleeping."

The song's lyrics are already satiric, but their satiric potential can be heightened through their performance. Perhaps the most important aspect of Jaldati's performance of Hasidic songs was her costuming. Jaldati performed in the clothes of a young Jewish male when she danced "The Yeshiva Boy." Therefore we should assume that she performed dressed as a male subject for her second act when she sang this song about a yeshiva boy asking his rabbis questions. A photo of Jaldati in costume shows that her attire echoes that of a yeshiva boy, albeit an androgynous one. Her hair is tucked into the cap with strands of it peeking out like traditional Jewish male sidelocks (*peyes*), and her fitted jacket shows off her female figure. At the same time, her costume also suggests a jester or clown, thus satirizing the presumed studiousness of the yeshiva boy. Her face and impish smirk only add to the mischief that the yeshiva boy-jester intends. Her cocked arms also imply someone who will question anyone with authority. In writing about cross-dressing and Jewish performance, dance scholar Rebecca Rossen says, "In these drag performances, stagings of Jewishness became entangled with choreographies of gender and nation, resulting in ethnically ambiguous and androgynous figures who simultaneously bolstered and evaded the frameworks that defined them."[13] In other words, cross-dressing Jewish female dancers both subverted the anthrocentrism of Judaism and simultaneously reinforced it by making Jewish men (in the form of a cross-dressed Jewish woman) something to laugh at.

Cross-dressing was common in European and American cabarets. As Beth Holmgren writes about Polish cabaret, "Talented cabaret performers tried on the city's many identities, including real-life politicians, high society hostesses, jazz-age bon vivants, lower-middle-class shopkeepers, poor shop girls, cabbies, gigolos, and dancers for hire. Men played women and women played men. One celebrity mimicked another. Sometimes Gentiles impersonated Jews, though these Jewish characters differed markedly in language and sophistication from the actual Jewish performers. Much more often, Jews impersonated almost every type of Gentile."[14] The best Jewish cabaret performers managed to pass as non-Jews during the war because they had already had much practice with impersonation. This held true for Jaldati as well, whose background in theater allowed her to pass as an Indonesian-Dutch mixed-heritage citizen during the first two years of German occupation.[15]

Jaldati performed each of the three stanzas of "How Does the Tsar Live?" using her hands, face, and gestures to paint a picture of how the tsar (or the emperor, depending on one's geography) conducted his daily routine—from lapping up sweet water from a mound of tea (cue the tongue), to eating a potato that had just been shot through a wall of butter (cock the gun), to sleeping at night with soldiers shouting "Quiet." Who knows how loud she would have screamed "*Sha!*" (quiet) on the stage that evening? What we do know is that at the cabaret and her subsequent shows of Jewish song and dance, she represented "exotic" and authentic Eastern European Jews to a Dutch crowd. And Eastern European Jews, as she introduced them to the crowd that evening, had an indigenous tradition of satire that poked fun at everyone in power, from rabbis and cantors to generals and emperors.

Members of the Amsterdam audience may have previously seen a Jewish cabaret performer playing the cross-dressed role of a yeshiva boy if they had attended a performance by Chaja Goldstein, who performed in the Adyar the previous Saturday, March 28, 1936.[16] Goldstein was a Polish Yiddish performer who had been based in Berlin. She performed with the Berlin-based Tip Top Cabaret but fled the city in 1933 for Amsterdam.

"Lin Jaldati as the Yeshiva Boy," 1935, photo by Boris Kowadlo. Courtesy of the Nederlands Fotomuseum, Rotterdam, and the Akademie der Künste, Berlin.

She performed with the Tip Top Cabaret until it closed down in 1934, but Goldstein maintained a successful solo career throughout the 1930s, including her performances at the Adyar. Immediately upon settling in Amsterdam, she performed "Eastern Jewish songs and dances that the crowd, both Jewish and not," was unfamiliar with, as a reporter for *Het Volk* wrote in a review of Goldstein's show.[17] She also served as Jaldati's foil, as reviewers of Jaldati's evenings of Jewish dance and songs often compared her to Goldstein. In her memoir, Jaldati writes about attending one of Goldstein's classes and how disappointed she was with their interactions.[18]

Jaldati performed Jewish songs and dances at most of her 1930s solo performances of Jewish song and dance after she quit the National Revue, at the prompting of her future husband, the Berlin-born-but-living-in-the-Netherlands non-Jewish leftist pianist and musicologist Eberhard Rebling.

One has to imagine that as Germany expanded its borders, especially after Kristallnacht in November 1938, which drove waves of Jews across the border, the satire of Jaldati's Yiddish songs took on an increasing sense of political urgency.

Jaldati and Her Yiddish Satire During and After the War

World War II and the German occupation of the Netherlands on May 10, 1940, put an end to Jaldati's solo Jewish evenings of song and dance, at least in public. She earned a living by teaching privately after she opened her own dance studio. But she was constantly afraid of being arrested by the police, especially given her short stature, dark hair, and dark complexion. To continue being out in public, she obtained fake documents saying that she was half-Dutch, half-Indonesian, thus explaining her "exotic" appearance.[19] When she and her family received deportation orders in 1942, they ignored them and went into hiding with the Communist underground, which smuggled weapons and hid people.

In the underground Jaldati and Rebling continued performing. They gave illegal house concerts under the auspices of De Vrije Kunstenaar (The Free Artist), the illegal Dutch artists' union, until July 10, 1944, when their safe house about 30 miles from Amsterdam was betrayed and nearly everyone arrested.[20] During his transport from the safe house to Amsterdam, Rebling escaped out the back of the police wagon. Jaldati was interrogated as a political subversive for several days and sent to Westerbork, the Dutch transit camp.[21] During her short time there, she gained a reputation for her music—entertaining the depressed inmates with material from her Yiddish repertoire—before she and her entire family, save Rebling and their 3-year-old daughter, Kathinka, were put on the last train bound for Auschwitz, the only death camp still operating in Poland, on September 3.[22] This was the same train that carried the family of Anne Frank.

Losing all but her sister Janny, Jaldati survived Auschwitz, a death march to Bergen-Belsen, and imprisonment there, a place she describes as hell. She fought hunger and a bout with typhus before the British liberated Bergen-Belsen on April 15, 1945. She and Janny nursed the dying Anne and Margot Frank before they succumbed to the disease shortly before liberation.[23] Jaldati and Janny, two broken camp survivors, made their way back to the decimated Netherlands, itself only liberated on May 5 and still reeling from the Germans' 1944–1945 occupation policies that led to mass starvation, known as the Hunger Winter.[24] In late May Jaldati reunited with Rebling. In August she was back on stage singing Jewish songs, but her wrecked body would not allow her to dance the choreography she had performed in her 1930s shows.

During the war and her incarceration in Westerbork, Auschwitz, and Bergen-Belsen, Jaldati had learned other songs, primarily by memorizing them by ear, and expanded her repertoire to include these so-called "camp and ghetto songs." These were songs of resistance, such as "The Partisan Hymn" ("Never Say," or "Zog Nit Keynmol"), or sober melodies of Jewish pathos, such as Mordechai Gebirtig's "It's Burning" ("S'brent"). In the postwar years she went back on the road with Rebling, touring Jewish displaced persons camps in Scandinavia, Switzerland, and Berlin, singing and storytelling as the yeshiva boy for Yiddish-speaking displaced persons.[25] In the program for her 1946 concert in Copenhagen, during a Scandinavian tour, Jaldati and Rebling, her husband who served not only as her accompanist but also as her agent, reproduced the same 1930s Kowadlo photograph I described earlier. So Jaldati continued playing the role of the yeshiva boy, at least in printed material for her postwar concerts. (I do not have evidence that she actually performed in those costumes, because none of the reviews I consulted mention it.)

The image on the advertisement for her 1946 Stockholm concert, slightly different from the one in the Copenhagen program, again shows Jaldati dressed as a yeshiva boy. Even in the face of tragedy, Jaldati projected an image of playfulness. And yet times had changed. In this photograph, her eyes are narrowed and her lips pursed, suggesting frustration, sadness, or even depression. And she has only one hand visible, raised in a gesture of resignation with the other one hidden behind her back—a far cry from the first image of her two arms wildly cocked with incredulity. The reviews of the Stockholm show do not mention her costumes and therefore do not mention her being dressed as a yeshiva boy, but they do note with enthusiasm her brilliant hand gestures, facial expressions, and body movements that communicated as much if not more than the words she sang.

In 1947 Rebling joined the Communist Party of the Netherlands and became a leading functionary in the party. In 1949, as part of the wave of

Advertisement for "An Evening of Song and Dance by the Famous Yiddish Artist from Holland, Lin Jaldati," Stockholm, November 25, 1946. Courtesy of the Akademie der Künste, Berlin.

German leftists returning to the Soviet occupation zone to rebuild a new democratic Germany, Rebling was offered a job as editor-in-chief of the East German state music journal. Struggling to find work and to support their family in the Netherlands and with their communist politics and a job offer in hand, Rebling and Jaldati moved to the GDR in 1952. What Jaldati's fate would be was unknown. Anna Seghers, the well-known German writer who moved back to postwar East Germany from her exile in Mexico, suggested that if Jaldati moved with her husband to East Germany, she could participate in the repair of German society through her performances of Yiddish music. Seghers implored her to move, so that she and her Yiddish music could "clean out the rubble [*Trümmer*] in people's heads" after twelve years of Nazism.[26] Jaldati would be no ordinary German *Trümmerfrau*, the "rubble woman" who loomed large as a symbol of wartime German suffering.[27] She would be a rubble woman of the German soul.

Six years after her arrival in the GDR and twenty-two years after the Kunstwereld cabaret, the Auschwitz and Bergen-Belsen survivor Jaldati had established herself as one of the leading interpreters of Yiddish music in the self-proclaimed anti-fascist state, whose leadership had also been in fascist concentration camps, as Jaldati had been, or at least that was the prevailing rhetoric. (Jaldati also reintroduced non-Jewish Germans to their own German-language folk culture, which had been co-opted and racialized by Nazism, by teaching German folk dancing and performing German folk songs.) Jaldati established this reputation through her regular live performances on the GDR's anti-fascist holiday calendar, including GDR Memorial Day, the second Sunday of September, and Kristallnacht, November 9, which was also considered a major holiday. She also gave solo concerts of partisan and battle songs, both in Yiddish and in other languages, as her repertoire grew to incorporate German progressive music and progressive songs from other linguistic and cultural traditions. She appeared on radio with relative frequency in the 1950s and 1960s and even had roles in several GDR films.

From her first concerts in the GDR, Jaldati embedded her Yiddish music in the anti-fascist cultural framework of her new home. This meant that Yiddish music needed to treat the wartime experience of fascist violence as a somber tragedy and as a source of moral edification. The titles of her concerts changed too. From "An Evening of Jewish Song and Dance" in the interwar Netherlands, her concerts in the GDR had such titles as "Battle and Partisan Songs," "Joy and Suffering, Work and Struggle in the Song of the Peoples," and "Suffering and Hope."[28] In other words, if, in the interwar Netherlands, Jaldati performed Yiddish music as an exotic and authentic expression of Yiddish satire, in the GDR Yiddish music would be absorbed into an international world folk music culture of downtrodden peoples.

A packed audience came to Berlin's House of Culture of the Soviet Union to hear the first solo concert in the GDR by Jaldati, who had overnight become the city's newest musical sensation. The *Berliner Zeitung* featured her show as one of the "concerts of the week," with Yiddish songs that were "a testament to a rich folk culture and sound a protest, which rises to the point of becoming an indictment against racial hatred." The only song the reviewer mentions by name is "Raboysay": "She attends to the satiric song 'Rabjassaj' with such grace, with such taste and in just a few striking gestures!" But then the review shifts tone, clearly in reference to her other song, and once again comments on her gestures, facial expressions, and body movements: "Her eyes flare, her whole face blazes with the song of the Jewish fighter, condemned to death yet facing the future."[29] From her earliest shows in the GDR, critics understood Jaldati's Yiddish performances through an anti-fascist cultural framework. They understood her work as an expression of an oppressed people but one that resists that oppression.

None of Jaldati's concert programs in the GDR, even those in Berlin—the epicenter of cross-dressing cabaret until the rise of Nazism—ever showed her cross-dressed. A combination of factors likely led her to stop presenting herself that way: the culturally conservative environment that reigned globally in the 1950s and the GDR's approach to culture that emphasized vigilance against recurrent fascism and a moral seriousness, as opposed to playfulness. Perhaps most important was Jaldati's own camp survivor body and her maturity as she passed 40 years of age. The moment for her yeshiva boy act had passed. Instead, as a *diseuse*, a singer-storyteller, she animated the lyrics of the songs through facial expressions, gestures, and bodily movements rather than dance.

A 1954 solo concert program for the show *Song of the Peoples* (*Das Lied der Völker*) opens with a Marxist interpretation of Jewish history—a story of a downtrodden people, in which culture, and music in particular, is merely the reflection of that downtrodden status: "There is no people on earth, who in countless songs has not expressed its centuries-long suffering by oppression, and yet its indefatigable joie de vivre, its fight for a better life and hopes for a final liberation." The program goes on to describe how music both reflects and generates a spirit fighting for liberation going back to the French Revolution. It then turns specifically to Jewish anti-fascist music from the war: "We remember how the heroic Jewish partisans in the war against Hitlerite fascism went to their deaths with their partisan song on their lips." Jaldati performed this concert throughout the GDR in the mid-1950s as well as on tour to Denmark, Finland, the Federal Republic of German (FRG), and other countries in the Communist eastern bloc.

Das Lied der Völker included six acts. In the first, Jaldati opened with classic German folk songs such as "Es waren zwei Königskinder" (There Were Two Children of the King), a medieval German folk song about generational conflict, and "Phyllis und die Mutter" (Phyllis and Her Mother). According to her daughter Jalda, Jaldati taught herself these German folk songs and then taught them to her audiences.[30] She then moved to Yiddish folk songs, which included "Raboysay." The remaining four segments included two piano solos by Rebling and an international folk song medley; the show closed with more German folk songs, ending with the classic "Heinrich und Liese," better known as "There's a Hole in the Bucket, Dear Liese, Dear Liese."[31]

It is hard to imagine Jaldati, an Auschwitz survivor and Yiddish *diseuse*, singing these German folk songs, but sing them she did. Perhaps she took seriously the role cast for her by Seghers back in 1949 of being a "rubble woman of the soul." Not only did she bring to German audiences music in Yiddish, the native language of the people murdered in Nazi atrocities against European Jewry, but she also taught herself German folk music and performed it for German audiences. Although she might not have intended it, non-Jewish Germans listening to her concerts may have felt that, by listening to an Auschwitz-tattooed Jewish Holocaust survivor singing Yiddish and German folk songs, they were given permission to join in the singing and might feel absolved of their wartime guilt. For Jews in the audience, Jaldati's shows were spaces of secular Jewish community in a country lacking in forms of public cultural, as opposed to religious, Jewish expression. (Perhaps ironically, Jewish religious institutions were state-sponsored, not just in communist East Germany but throughout the postwar communist world.)³²

Overall, we see that reviewers of Jaldati's concerts emphasized the Marxist class critique present in the work rather than viewed her Yiddish songs as representative of authentic Jewish culture (or German culture for her German songs). They wrote about her "freedom and resistance songs of diverse peoples," which happened to include Jews. For her concerts of Jewish music from the 1950s, the program's interpretive material usually emphasized the "centuries-long oppression of Jews," including pogroms and the "millions exterminated by fascism" in gas chambers. Unlike interwar Amsterdam, where indigenous Eastern European Yiddish satire was the point of her performance, in the GDR, Jaldati's Yiddish songs were interpreted through a global socialist framework of downtrodden peoples.³³

A 1958 feature article about Jaldati described her learning Yiddish in an Amsterdam Yiddish-speaking club, presumably the Ansky Society (it did not mention that her grandmother spoke Yiddish, so she had also heard it in the home) and that she always included Yiddish songs in her concerts. The writer described Yiddish music as "having a particular 'laughing through tears' musicality. There are joyous songs, but those are outweighed by the sad ones."³⁴ "Suffering" and "hope" were frequently used in the titles of her concert reviews, attempting to neuter the biting and funny satire that the songs conveyed. Instead, Jaldati's Yiddish music was intended to become a statement about the moral seriousness of what fascism had done to Jews and that, through it all, Jews persisted.

"How Does the Tsar Live?" Leipzig, March 7, 1958

Every spring and fall since the Middle Ages, Leipzig has hosted a fair (*Messe*). The city and its fairs have always been an economic and cultural crossroads where Eastern and Western Europe meet to trade goods, books, and ideas. This did not change in the GDR. On the contrary, the Leipziger *Messe* was a time for the GDR to showcase itself to the world.³⁵

The state invited cultural performers, especially well-known classical music and dance groups, from across Europe to entertain and edify the many visitors who came to town. For the spring 1958 *Messe*, the state invited a Parisian ballet as well as the "famous Soviet violinist David

Oystraikh," at least according to L. Arvin, a journalist covering the fair for the Polish Yiddish newspaper *Folksshtime*. But among these classical cultural offerings that the Communist world had cultivated in its Cold War battle against the "decadent," "rock music-obsessed" capitalist West, Arvin encountered something unusual: "a poster that read as follows, 'The German Concert and Guest Artist Directorate is hosting an evening of Jewish Folk Art at which Lin Jaldati will sing, and she will be accompanied by Eberhard Rebling... at the Leipzig Fair."[36] He decided to attend the concert, interview the performer, and then write about it for the *Folksshtime*.

On March 7, Jaldati performed an evening of Jewish folk art (*jüdische Volkskunst*) at the Weisser Saal. The program that Arvin procured from one of the ushers included an essay about the show: "Especially among peoples who have been oppressed by the ruling classes of other peoples and expelled to foreign lands, music has the power to unite groups of this particular people, who have been scattered as national minorities, as well as to strengthen each individual and to foster unity."[37] There was no mention of Jews per se, but given the context, a reader would have assumed that Jews were the oppressed group in question. The next sentence talked about African Americans and their downtrodden status, and then, halfway through the first paragraph, the program introduces the specific Jewish experience, which includes a history of pogroms. The narrative continues: "Eastern [European] Jews' joy is sad, their sadness often exaggerated in grim self-mockery."[38] The final paragraph describes the Jewish experience of gas chambers and fascism's failed attempt at genocide of European Jewry.

Despite this melancholic description of Yiddish music as exaggerated self-mockery and the overwhelming lament with descriptions of millions murdered in gas chambers, Jaldati's performances attempted to offer a counterpoint to this lugubrious approach to Jewish music. Each song had a description next to it, listed on the advertisement for the concert that appeared around Leipzig: a "song for accordion," a "hasidic song," or a "*Spottlied*" (a satiric song that in some programs is included as part of the title, not as a description of its genre). "Raboysay" was labeled as a *Spottlied*.

Spottlieder have a long history in German revolutionary politics, going back to the 1848 revolutions. Given how Nazism had tainted German folk music, postwar Germany, both East and West, struggled to find an appropriate way to reclaim a German folk music tradition. One place postwar musicians turned to was the *Spottlied*. As David Robb writes in his book about protest songs in West and East Germany, "Singers identified with the basic gesture of rebellion in the satirical Spottlieder, the parodies of authority and servility and the anti-army songs. Above all, the interest in the 1848 songs lay in the discovery of something new: distinct from the tradition of folk song that had been co-opted by the Nazis and was now viewed as Nazi-tainted, the 1848 songs represented a 'low' tradition of oppositional art."[39] German musicians, such as the popular GDR balladeer and eventual exile Wolf Biermann, used the *Spottlied* especially in the 1960s.

Biermann went into exile, as did other culture makers who used their art to criticize the East German state. But satire existed throughout the state's history in the satiric magazine *Die Eulenspiegel* and the series of short films called *Das Stacheltier* (The Porcupine), which were shown before the newsreels, which themselves preceded the feature film in cinema houses. In 1978, with a state license, cabaret clubs opened throughout the country; one of the most important was located in Potsdam. According to Sylvia Klötzer, these regulated spaces for satire neutered their potential political bite against the East German regime. They were, according to Klötzer, pressure valves for social discontent, not unlike Mikhail Bakhtin's late medieval carnivals, similar ritualized reversals of power that maintained the existing power structure. After 1954, before which a short window for satire of domestic politics was allowed, rarely if ever was the socialist state the direct object of satire. That said, especially by the 1970s and 1980s, audiences and presenters frequently used code to communicate a particular critique of the GDR, and by the 1980s satire about the regime itself was becoming more explicit.[40]

Little of this holds true for Jaldati's Yiddish-language *Spottlieder*, which were not positioned as political challenges to the GDR. On the contrary, by labeling the song a *Spottlied*, Rebling and Jaldati incorporated it into a German folk music tradition that poked fun at *external* authority, whether that was West Germany's leadership with Chancellor Konrad Adenauer hiring unreconstructed members of the Nazi Party into his cabinet or the "capitalist" United States and its Cold War with the "peace loving" Communist world. In contrast to her GDR-era Yiddish satiric performances, there was no mention in the interwar Dutch programs or in reviews of her concerts about "Raboysay" as a "satire [*spotlied* in Dutch]." Rather, the performances were presented as indigenous forms of specifically Jewish satire in the fight against regnant fascism, not to mention traditional Judaism.

At this point, I want to spend some time with Arvin's review of Jaldati's Leipzig concert so that we can learn how a journalist for a Polish Yiddish newspaper reacted to her GDR show. First, Arvin notes that although the hall was filled "with a diverse audience, the majority of the audience was made up of Leipzig residents." Despite the propaganda potential for the GDR to demonstrate state support for Jewish culture to its foreign guests at the *Messe*, especially in light of the 1952–1953 purge of the GDR Jewish leadership, Leipzig locals made up the majority of the audience. Arvin also comments on the "interesting" introduction in the program and its description of the particular Jewish experience during the war. In commenting on the recognition of centuries-long Jewish suffering, especially Jewish suffering during the war and fascist atrocities, Arvin notes that even though millions were murdered in the gas chambers, "the survivors fought against the overpowering enemy in the Krakow, Vilna, and Warsaw ghettos and Jewish partisans [fought them] in concentration camps."

Arvin's biggest surprise, however, is "the sympathetic singer, Lin Jaldati," who "gave short explanations in German but produced Jewish folk songs . . . in a rich, juicy Yiddish [*geshmakn, zaftikn yidish*]." He also describes how Jaldati stood on stage discussing her relationship with another famous Dutch Jewish victim of the Nazi regime, Anne Frank, "with tears in her eyes." As a witness to the last months of Anne's life, Jaldati was a much sought-after speaker in the wake of the surprising success of the 1955 theatrical version of the *Diary of Anne Frank*. She discussed her own wartime experience through the lived experience of the most famous victim of the Nazis from stages throughout the GDR and all of Europe.

Arvin describes Jaldati as an "artist of high caliber . . . each nuance, every word and the selection of songs was done very intelligently." In particular, he points to her performances of "Tsip Tsapkl" and "Az der Rebbe Elimelekh," songs that Jaldati had performed since before the war, as sung "with much charm [*mit vifl khen*]." Arvin lauds the tenderness with which Jaldati rendered her songs and the powerful way she recited Moyshe Shulshteyn's "A Mountain of Shoes" ("A Barg Shikh"), leaving the audience "trembling in its seats." "Next to me," Arvin closes, "sat a German girl, who cried as Jaldati explained the words of her last two songs," one of which was "Raboysay."[41]

Let's think about this for a moment. Jaldati is on stage singing Yiddish satiric songs such as "Raboysay," "Tsip Tsapkl," and "Az der Rebbe Elimelech," and the frame of the evening is her experience surviving the extermination camps. As a *diseuse*, she used song, in the form of "S'brent" and "Zog Nit Keynmol," and narration of Shulshtein's "A Barg Shikh" to convey her wartime experience. She even made a German girl weep during the show. Therefore, Jaldati's show functioned as a collective memorial, at least, but not only, for Jews in the audience. But she punctuated those experiences of Jewish suffering with levity. On one level, her Yiddish *Spottlieder* functioned as satire (or as Arvin wrote, they were "light and playful"), in the tradition of the *Spottlied* going back to the nineteenth century. What was being satirized was left unsaid, but likely it meant something different for each person in the audience. On another level, after the Holocaust all of Jaldati's Yiddish music, including a Yiddish *Spottlied*, was heard as a reminder of the murder of most of its speakers.

Conclusion: Is Yiddish Satire Possible After the Holocaust?

The earliest audio recording I have of Jaldati singing "Raboysay" is from 1960, when she performed it on Berliner Rundfunk, the GDR's leading radio station. In that recording, Rebling opens on the piano with a few short bars and then Jaldati comes in with the words "A sholem aleichem, reb yid," a basic greeting, something like "Hello, good sir." Unlike the original version, which is set in a yeshiva and opens with the collective greeting "Raboysay," Jaldati's later version of the song with the storytelling aspect, after she had relocated to the GDR, evokes a scene in which one Jew encounters another on the street.

Many well-known performers—from Molly Picon and Paul Robeson to Adrienne Cooper and Leah Koenig—sing "Raboysay," but in all other versions of the song I have heard, the opening word is just "Raboysay" (Gentlemen), pointing to the assembled group of men. In one translation of the song, the word *raboysay* was in fact translated as "rabbis." Moreover, in the original song, the word for "question," *shayle*, is not the word one would use for a mundane question, such as inquiries about the eating habits of the emperor. That word would have been *frage*. *Shayle* is an elevated form of legal question to which rabbis generally provide the answer. In none of the recordings of Jaldati does she ever open the song with *raboysay*. In fact, *all* of Jaldati's recordings of "Raboysay" have the frame story, which opens with a greeting in the singular, "A sholem aleichem, reb yid."

As we have seen, the song initially appeared in Jaldati's repertoire in the 1930s, and although I do not have any recordings from the prewar period, Jaldati likely sang the original version set in the traditional Jewish yeshiva as she might have heard it from Amsterdam's Yiddish-speaking immigrants. After all, that was the goal of her performances in the 1930s—to conjure up a world of indigenous Eastern European Jewish religious culture for the assembled audiences and then poke fun at it. The addition of the opening address in the singular shifts the song's setting away from a Jewish study house and highlights the interaction between two simple Jews, presumably both poor. In this case the responses are meant to showcase the class divide between their own poverty and the tsar's ostentatious wealth.

Jaldati always opened the song with an explanation to her assembled audiences. I have only one live recording of her explaining the song, this one to a Dutch audience in 1985, but in my conversation with her daughter Jalda, this was how Jaldati always introduced the song. In her explanation, Jaldati sets the song in the Hapsburg Empire and describes how one "shtetl Jew" from Galicia approached another shtetl Jew, who had in theory just come from Vienna and met the emperor (*der kayzer*). She then translates the three questions and performs the song, in this case with her daughter Jalda playing the shtetl Jew who poses the questions to the second one, played by Jaldati. Given the laughter one hears in the recording, one has to assume that the two performers used their bodies, gestures, and facial expressions to generate the clearly humorous satire. It is also clear that the Jew who returned from Vienna did not actually meet the emperor. He is creating a fantasy for the two impoverished shtetl Jews to bond over. As Jalda suggests, it would be like asking someone from the provinces who visited the nation's capital, "Did you meet the president?"

As one listens to the beginning of the song, Rebling begins on the piano as though it were the setup to a play, and then Jalda enters with her opening line over the piano, "A sholem aleichem, reb yid." This emphasizes the happenstance nature of the encounter, which elicits Jaldati's response, "Aleichem sholem [and greetings to you]." Then the piano goes silent, as the stage morphs into a play with Jalda the daughter and Jaldati the mother creating the scene. Jalda then replies, "Du bist geven in Vin un az dortn gezen undzer kayzer, a-yo?" ("You were in Vienna, weren't you, and there you saw our emperor, right?"), to which Jaldati replies, "Ver? Frantsl Yosl?" ("Who? Little Franz Joseph?").

According to Jalda, in the 1980s, the family used the name "Frantsl Yosl" not only to invoke, and mock, the past emperor of the Hapsburg Empire, who reveled in luxurious excess, but also to poke fun at a prominent contemporary right-wing politician in West Germany by the same name (Franz Joseph Strauss, in this case). Strauss would have been known throughout the German- and Dutch-speaking worlds and certainly among European Jews, who were aware of his conservative politics in successive West German governments and his wartime past fighting for the Wehrmacht.[42] Jalda then closes the frame narrative with a general question, "Ot azoi a guter kayzer, zog zhe mir?" ("And so, was he a good emperor, tell me?"), to which Jaldati replies in a lilting, singsong way, "a giter, a giter, a giter, a mamzer" ("a good one, a good one, a good one, a bastard"). The audience erupts in laughter.

Jalda showed me in a video call how her mother did this. She said the repeated word *giter* more or less straight and then she accompanied the word *mamzer* with a dismissive gesture with her hand, and she turned her head away. Although *mamzer* is a Yiddish word, the audience burst out in laughter, both because of her gestures and because *mamzer* means something similar in the Amsterdam dialect of Dutch, which has incorporated many words from the western Yiddish that was once spoken there. Only then does the traditional song begin with "raboysay."

The simple Jew asks the Jew who had been in Vienna the series of three questions as the second Jew responds with ever more elaborate gestures but singing the original lyrics (drinking tea, eating potatoes, and sleeping at night). The audience, made up of speakers of Amsterdam's Yiddish-inflected Dutch dialect, understood some if not most of the Yiddish, given the linguistic similarities. It is clear from the audio recording that the audience laughs at times when Jalda and Jaldati used their bodies to conjure up images of excess (about sugar, butter, and feathers) about which the simple Jew could only fantasize. I had an image in mind of Sholem Aleichem's "If I Were Rothschild," in which the poor Jew imagines what it must be like to live like Rothschild. To the first question about sugar, as Jaldati says the word *licking* three times, the audience moves from a mild to uproarious laughter.

In other studio recordings Jaldati sings both parts, but she is always clearly playing two different characters. She emphasizes this because after each verse the simple Jew remarks with wonder, "Really?" ("Emes?") or "So that's how he does it" ("Ot azoi"), to which the second Jew declares, "Really" ("Emes"). The song closes with the simple Jew parting ways with the other Jew and wishing him a long life ("blayb gezunt biz hundert un tsvontsik").

In the 1930s, when Jaldati sang Yiddish satiric songs such as "Raboysay" to Dutch audiences, she used humor and satire to conjure up and then poke fun at a world of patriarchal Judaism, in which rabbis field naïve questions from a student and make up answers imagining the opulent wealth of the autocrat living far away. After the Holocaust, Jaldati's Yiddish satire had to become something different, because the Eastern European Jewish world that she had conjured up in the prewar period no longer existed. First, she added the frame story, setting it as a dialogue between two shtetl Jews fantasizing about how the emperor lived in Vienna. This secularized the song's story and emphasized a class dimension about poor Jews imagining the distant emperor with no rabbis present. Second, with the GDR's anti-fascist ideology needing to be constantly invoked and legitimated, Yiddish music, even satiric music, was a constant reminder of the remnants of a Jewish world destroyed by fascism. Therefore anything in Yiddish, the language of the always downtrodden Jews, could not help but be a form of both memory about genocide in the past and an admonition about fascism in the present.

But by the 1980s, when the live recording was made and we hear Dutch audiences rolling with laughter, Yiddish satiric music regained some of its ability to make audiences laugh. Unfortunately, although I have studio recordings, I do not have live recordings of Jaldati's concerts in 1980s GDR to know whether an audience there would have been laughing as hard as a Dutch audience. Therefore I am loath to speculate about an answer to the question I asked myself going into this project: whether by the 1980s the GDR regime's legitimacy would have been so undermined that the satiric potential of Jaldati's songs might have been unwittingly evoking the GDR party secretary Erich Honecker's government. Jalda and others with whom I spoke think this was the case, and perhaps with the emergence of political cabaret in 1980s GDR, this might be true.

The question remains: What was the Dutch audience laughing at? Was it at the empathetic fears of people living under autocracy in the past? Probably not. Potential fear of contemporary right-wing politicians taking power in the 1980s? Remember, this is the era of Margaret Thatcher, Ronald Reagan, Helmut Kohl, and in the Netherlands Ruud Lubbers, who championed similar privatization policies as the others. Possibly.

But the more likely answer is that the audience may have been poking fun at Jews by laughing at Jaldati's rendition of the Yiddish language itself, which evoked romanticized lost worlds and quaint "extinct" cultures. No matter the answer, in 1980s Amsterdam, Jaldati and her audience may have "resurrected" the original satire in "Raboysay," which as she and her daughter rendered it, added a new layer of meaning to the song. Even though it remained a memorial to the murdered Jews of Europe, "Raboysay" had a new overlay of broad political satire. And if Jaldati were to sing the song today, how would it resonate with audiences, who would laugh at images of the emperor (read: Donald Trump, Vladimir Putin, Recep Erdoğan, or Abdel Fattah el-Sisi) and his ostentatiousness as he licks and licks and licks at the mound of sugar?

Notes

1. "Cabaret in 'Adyar,'" *Algemeen Handelsblad*, 28 March 1936, p. 5.
2. The Yiddish word *kayzer* refers to any authoritarian figure, be it an emperor, tsar, or kaiser. See, for example, the words to "Ein Lid Vegn Nikolai der Tsveitn (Kaiser Fun Rusland)," which were sent to Jaldati by Jacob Scheinin, a Moscow-based Yiddish musicologist who was helping Jaldati excavate music from the 1905 revolution. Lin Jaldati Archiv 184, Akademie der Künste, Berlin. Note that the transliteration of *raboysay* varies, depending on the language into which it is being transliterated (Yiddish, for her postwar Swedish concert program; German; Dutch; or English).
3. David Shneer, "Yiddish Music and East German Antifascism: Lin Jaldati, Post-Holocaust Jewish Culture, and the Cold War," *Leo Baeck Institute Yearbook* (2015): 1–25.
4. David Shneer, "How Eastern European Jewish Immigrants, Modernist Yiddish Culture, and Anti-Fascist Politics Dragged the Netherlands into the Twentieth-Century," *East European Jewish Affairs* 46, no. 2 (2016): 139–59. On Ansky's

plays and their European-wide popularity, see Debra Caplan, *Yiddish Empire: The Vilna Troupe, Jewish Theater, and the Art of Itineracy* (Ann Arbor: University of Michigan Press, 2018).

5. Matthias Havinga, *Orgel in de Diaspora: Een Onderzoek naar Joodse Orgelcultuur in Nederland* (Amsterdam: Conservatorium van Amsterdam, 2008), 22.

6. On Hasidic dance, see Jill Gellerman, "With Body and Soul: An Introduction to the Ecstatic Dance of the Hasidim," MA thesis, Ohio State University, 1972. On the transformation of the image of the *Ostjude*, see David Brenner, "Promoting East European Jewry: *Ost und West*, Ethnic Identity, and the German-Jewish Audience," *Prooftexts* 15, no. 1 (1995): 63–88. As an example, Martin Buber's fascination with Hasidic culture resulted in several collections of Hasidic tales.

7. Although groups of men tend to be involved when Hasidim dance, Jewish women performed most Hasidic dances on stages in the interwar period. Some American female dancers who performed solo Jewish dances, such as Dvora Lapson or Pauline Koner, actually conducted performance ethnography among Hasidic communities in New York, Poland, and Palestine in the 1930s to inform their work. According to Lapson, "Hasidic dancing begins slowly, with a touch of sadness, and gradually assumes faster rhythms until it climaxes in a state of ecstasy. The movements are basically characteristic Ghetto gestures and motions. At first there is swaying, then the forearm is used in quick choppy gestures from the elbow out. As the dance progresses, the feet begin to be raised in jerky movements, the arms, from finger to shoulder, begin to function freely with the clapping of hands and the snapping of fingers." See Dvora Lapson, "Hasidism and the Dance," manuscript version of her article on Jewish dance for the *Jewish Encyclopedia*, Wolfe Papers, New York Public Library, box 16, folder 11. See also Pauline Koner, *Solitary Song* (Durham, NC: Duke University Press, 1989).

8. "Sch. Ans-ki," *Nieuw Israelitsch Weekblad*, 20 March 1936, p. 12. For a broader context about the Ansky Society, Amsterdam's Yiddish cultural organization, see Shneer, "Eastern European Jewish Immigrants." See also "Lien Jaldati en haar kunst: Joodse ritus en Joodse volkskunst leverden de fundamenten," *Vooruit* (The Hague), 27 March 1939.

9. Rebecca Rossen, *Dancing Jewish: Jewish Identity in American Modern and Postmodern Dance* (New York: Oxford University Press, 2014).

10. Some programs from the 1930s include several sentences describing not only the dances but also what their meaning was in traditional Eastern European Jewish culture. But from the reviews in Dutch newspapers, we know that Jaldati

explained from the stage how her dances should be understood as reflecting "authentic" Jewish traditions.

11. Matthew Isaac Cohen, "Indonesian Performing Arts in the Netherlands, 1913–1944," in Bart Barendregt and Els Bogaerts, eds., *Recollecting Resonances: Indonesian-Dutch Musical Encounters* (Leiden: Brill, 2014), 214–58.

12. http://digital.library.upenn.edu/webbin/freedman/lookupwork?hr=&what=Vi%20Azoy%20Lebt%20Der%20Keyser%20%3F [accessed 18 April 2019].

13. Rebecca Rossen, "Hasidic Drag: Jewishness and Transvestism in the Modern Dances of Pauline Koner and Hadassah," *Feminist Studies* 37, no. 2 (2011): 335.

14. Beth Holmgren, "Cabaret Identity: How Best to Play a Jew or Pass as a Gentile in Wartime Poland," *Journal of Jewish Identities* 7, no. 2 (2014): 27.

15. Lin Jaldati and Eberhard Rebling, *Sag nie, du gehst den letzten Weg* (Berlin: Buchverlag Morgen, 1986), 341.

16. "Chaja Goldstein," *Algemeen Handelsblad*, 28 March 1936, p. 13.

17. P. F. S., "Dans- en chansonavond: Chaja Goldstein," *Het Volk*, 6 April 1933, p. 13.

18. U., "Lien Jaldati: Dans en zang in het Muziek-Lyceum," *Algemeen Handelsblad*, 28 September 1939, evening edition. Lin Jaldati and Eberhard Rebling, *Sag nie, du gehst den letzten Weg* (Marburg: BdWi Verlag, 1995), 188.

19. David Shneer, *Lin Jaldati: Trümmerfrau der Seele* (Berlin: Hentrich & Hentrich, 2013).

20. On the harrowing and horrifying story of how their safe house was betrayed, see Ad van Liempt, *Hitler's Bounty Hunters: The Betrayal of the Jews* (New York: Berg, 2005), 129–34. See also Eberhard Rebling to Irma and Mordecai Bauman, Mordechai Bauman Collection, Box 3, Folder 7 (Letters to/from Lin Jaldati and Eberhard Rebling, 1970s–1990s), TAM222. For the definitive account of their safe house, see Roxanne van Iperen, *'t Hooge Nest* (Amsterdam: Lebowski, 2018).

21. Westerbork had a cabaret, officially named Gruppe Bühne Westerbork, that operated between July 1943 and June 1944 and at which Max Ehrlich, Chaja Goldstein, and others who had been well-known figures in theater and cabaret before the war performed. See Brigitte Sion, *Max Ehrlich: Le Théâtre contre la Barbarie* (Geneva: Metropolis, 2004); and Aviva Atlani, "The Ha-Ha Holocaust: Exploring Levity Among the Ruins and Beyond in Testimony, Literature, and Film," PhD diss., University of Western Ontario, 2014.

22. For more on cabaret, see Peter Jelavich, *Berlin Cabaret* (Cambridge, MA: Harvard University Press, 1993). Jelavich discusses how German Jews interned at Westerbork organized the Westerbork cabaret.

23. On the liberation of Bergen-Belsen and the experience of survivors, see Suzanne Bardgett, David Cesarani, Jessica Reinisch, and Johannes-Dieter Steinert, eds., *Survivors of Nazi Persecution in Europe After the Second World War*, vol. 1 (London: Vallentine Mitchell, 2010).
24. Henri A. zan der Zee, *The Hunger Winter: Occupied Holland, 1944–1945* (Lincoln: University of Nebraska Press, 1998).
25. In her Scandinavian concerts, most members of the audience were Jewish survivors (*ibergeblibene*), according to a review of her Stockholm show from December 1946. See Rakhmiel Briks, "A yidisher kunst ovent in Stokholm," *Shtime*, 11 December 1946, in Lin Jaldati Papers, Akademie der Künste, Berlin, file 70.
26. References to the story appear frequently in 1980s interviews with Jaldati. See, for example, Maja Ulbrich, "Lin Jaldati," *Weltbühne*, 13 September 1988; or Rainer Bratfisch, "Lin Jaldati: Au Service de la Culture Yiddish," *RDA, Realités*, 1985.
27. Elizabeth Heineman, "The Hour of the Woman: Memories of Germany's 'Crisis Years' and West German National Identity," *American Historical Review* 101, no. 2 (1996): 354–95.
28. See, for example, Horst Rabetge, "Leid und Hoffnung in der jüdischer Volkskunst," *Leipziger Volkszeitung*, 11 March 1958; and "Freude und Leid, Arbeit und Kampf im Lied der Völker," concert program, 14 May 1954, Lin Jaldati Archiv, Akademie der Künste, Berlin, file 71.
29. "Konzerte der Woche," *Berliner Zeitung*, 8, no. 296 (19 December 1952): 3.
30. Conversation with Jalda Rebling, 22 January 2018.
31. *Das Lied der Völker* concert program, Betriebsgruppe der Gesellschaft für Deutsch-Sowjetische Freundschaft des VEB-Zentrale Grafische Lehrwerkstatt Gross-Berlin, 29 November 1954.
32. For more on Jewish religious life in the GDR and throughout the communist world during the Cold War, see David Shneer, "An Alternative World: Jews in the German Democratic Republic, Their Transnational Networks, and a Global Jewish Communist Community," in Kateřina Čapková, Stephan Stach, and Kamil Kijek, eds., *Jewish Lives Under Communism* (under review with Rutgers University Press). On seeing Yiddish cultural performances as opportunities for the development of secular Jewish identity, see Susan Stern, ed., *Speaking Out: Jewish Voices from United Germany* (Chicago: Edition Q, 1995).
33. *Möwe* concert program, 18 April 1957, Lin Jaldati Archiv, Akademie der Künste, Berlin, file 71.

34. "Wir stellen Lin Jaldati vor," *Melodie und Rhythmus* 2 (November 1958): 28.
35. Katherine Pence, "'A World in Miniature': Leipzig Trade Fairs in the 1950s and East German Consumer Citizenship," in David Crews, ed., *Consuming Germany* (London: Bloomsbury, 2003), 21–50.
36. L. Arvin, "Af a yidishn kontsert in Leipzig," *Folksshtime* 43, no. 1733 (7 March 1958).
37. *Jüdische Volkskunst* concert program, Weisser Saal, Leipzig, Lin Jaldati Archiv, Akademie der Künste, Berlin, file 71.
38. The German in the concert program reads "Die Freude der Ostjuden ist traurig, ihre Betrübtheit oft in grimmigem Selbstspott überhöht."
39. David Robb, ed., *Protest Song in East and West Germany Since the 1960s* (Rochester, NY: Camden House, 2007), 12.
40. For more on satire in the GDR, see Sylvia Klötzer, "'Volldampf woraus?' Satire in der DDR: 'Eulenspiegel' und 'Kabarett am Obelisk' in den siebziger und achtziger Jahren," in Thomas Lindenberger, ed., *Herrschaft und Eigen-Sinn in der Diktatur: Studien zur Gesellschaftsgeschichte der DDR* (Böhlau: Köln, 1999), 12: 267–313; also available at Dokserver des Zentrums für Zeithistorische Forschung Potsdam, http://dx.doi.org/10.14765/zzf.dok.1.837 [accessed 1 April 2018]. See also Sylvia Klötzer, *Satire und Macht: Film, Zeitung, Kabarett in der DDR* (Böhlau: Köln, 2006).
41. L. Arvin, "Af a yidishn kontsert in Layptsik."
42. Conversation with Jalda Rebling, 22 January 2018.

I. B. Singer's Art of Ghost Writing in *Enemies, A Love Story*

Jan Schwarz

> I like to write ghost stories and nothing fits a ghost better than a dying language. The more dead the language, the more alive are the ghosts. Ghosts love Yiddish, and as far as I know they all speak it . . . I am sure that millions of Yiddish-speaking ghosts will rise from their graves one day and their first question will be, "Is there any new book in Yiddish to read?"
>
> Isaac Bashevis Singer, *Conversations*, 166.

YITSKHOK BASHEVIS'S EARLY WRITINGS, published in Warsaw journals between 1925 and 1936, were written in the stark naturalist style typical of Yiddish trends in the interwar period.[1] Following Singer's emigration to the United States in 1935, his first American Yiddish book, *Satan in goray un andere dertseylungen* (Farlag Matones, 1943) included a series of demon monologues, collectively called "The Diary of the Evil One" (*Der togbukh fun yeytser-hore*). These monologues were the first time Singer used the "I" narrative, followed two years later by the seminal "Gimpel tam" (Gimpel the Fool). Singer's artistic turn to the classical Yiddish monologue opened a rich artistic resource, one that he would continue to tap throughout his long career. In a retrospective article from 1943, Singer characterized Yiddish writers as "split personalities": "Modern Yiddish literature did not represent either a new beginning or true continuity; it was rather the aftergrowth of a great and rich culture. Its creators were split personalities, and everything they said had to have the dual meaning of mockery (or stylization), even when their intentions were completely serious."[2]

Like the classical Yiddish writers' folksy narrators, such as Mendele the Bookseller and Tevye the Dairyman, Singer's return to the monologue allowed him to use the "dual meaning of mockery (or stylization)." He first used this technique in the monologue of the dybbuk at the end of *Satan in goray* (1935). A dybbuk who has possessed Rechele, the novel's protagonist speaks from her mouth in a long monologue of stylized and subversive old Yiddish speech. By returning to the classical monologue of Yiddish literature, Singer also discovered the artistic possibilities of Yiddish humor that had been absent from his earlier writings. In his first monologues, Singer used the rich resources of Eastern European Jewish folklore, humor, and archetypical figures, such as the fool, the trickster, and the schlemiel. He also increasingly employed I-narratives in novellas, short fiction, and life writing in postwar America.

In this essay I examine how Singer's novel *Enemies, A Love Story* (1972) uses farce and a tragicomedy rooted in classical Yiddish literature. The novel addresses the ghostlike lives of Jewish Holocaust survivors in New York while depicting the actual ghostwriting of its protagonist, Herman Broder. Ghostwriting is the novel's central theme, which Singer tailors to the very different reader expectations in the Yiddish and the American (Jewish) contexts. *Enemies* enabled Singer to address his conflicting loyalties to both his Yiddish and American Jewish readerships by satirizing his own split personality as a bilingual writer.

I also examine what was lost in translation, in the transformation from the Yiddish newspaper series (1966) to the English novel (1972) and how the novel was adapted by Paul Mazursky as a feature film (1989). *Enemies* is Singer's third novel to address the plight of Holocaust survivors in New York, and it is the only one about this topic to appear in English during his lifetime. The two other novels about Holocaust survivors in a postwar New York setting, *Meshugah* (1994) and *Shadows on the Hudson* (1998), were published posthumously. Their original composition and serialization in Yiddish occurred in the mid- to late 1950s, before *Enemies*.[3]

In his author's note to *Enemies*, Singer states, "Although I did not have the privilege of going through the Hitler holocaust, I have lived for years in New York with refugees from this ordeal." Here, Singer rejects the postwar Yiddish literature of eyewitness accounts and commemoration that dominated the pages of the postwar Yiddish press, exemplified in the Buenos

Aires book series *Dos poylishe yidntum*.⁴ The novel's two main characters, Herman Broder, the sexually hyperactive survivor, and the phony American rabbi Lampert, subvert the generic and narrative conventions of Yiddish literature in the post-Holocaust period.⁵ Together, they embody the split personality of their creators, the Yiddish Yitskhok Bashevis and the American I. B. Singer.

While serializing *Sonim, a geshikhte fun libe* (Enemies, A Love Story) in the *Forverts* in 1966, Singer published the short story "Der toyter klezmer" (The Dead Fiddler) in nine segments in September 1966 in the *Forverts*.⁶ This story depicts a shtetl woman, Liebe Yentl, who is possessed by two dybbuks, a klezmer and a whore. The dybbuks entertain the shtetl inhabitants, who come to the woman's house at night to enjoy the spectacle of their argumentative, operatic, and vulgar voices. The dybbuks decide to get married in a mock wedding, conducted in their own voices but impersonating a *badkhn*, klezmorim, and a rabbi reciting religious blessings. Only when Liebe Yentl's father, Reb Sheftel, swears that he will say Kaddish, burn memorial candles, and erect a headstone for the two dead souls, do they depart her body. "The Dead Fiddler" is framed as a story from a nonspecific mythical past located in the town of Shidlovtse, "which lies between Radom and Kielce, not far from the Mountain of the Holy Cross."⁷ At the end, the story becomes part of the mythical past of the town's Jewish inhabitants.

> In autumn, when leaves fell and winds blew from the Mountains of the Holy Cross, a low melody was often heard in the chimneys, thin as a hair and mournful as the world. Even children would hear it, and they would ask, "Mama, who is playing?" And the mother would answer, "Sleep, child. It's the dead fiddler."⁸

Part of the story's narrative spell is its stylistic play with the two dybbuks' blasphemy and vulgar language, which challenge the hegemonic unity of the shtetl's religious universe. Both "The Dead Fiddler" and the children's stories that Singer published in 1966 use the style and narration of the traditional storyteller. The humorous aspects of dybbuk possession in "The Dead Fiddler" are similar to those in *The Slave*. There, the dybbuk possession is depicted as a comedy of disguise and exposure, highlighting the shtetl Jews' superstitious beliefs. The novel's protagonist, Sarah, who pretends to be deaf, reveals her true identity as a Polish woman while being possessed by a dybbuk and giving birth.

"The Dead Fiddler" is an operatic shtetl vaudeville of two dead souls from the lowest social rung who in the voices of dybbuks create an imaginary world of make-believe and entertainment. In contrast, the theatrical comedy of *Enemies* is based on the sudden appearance of Holocaust survivors in New York who were thought to be dead. The character Pesheles points out the commonality of this phenomenon in the late 1940s.

> Well, it's a small world. Extraordinary times. Once I read a story in the paper about a refugee who was eating supper with his new wife. Suddenly the door opened and in walked his former wife, who he thought had died in the ghetto. That's the kind of mess Hitler and Stalin and the rest of their gangs cooked up.[9]

Singer creates high comedy when Tamara shows up unannounced at the door and scares Yadwiga to death. Exposing a Polish peasant woman to the "ghost" of her former mistress who supposedly had perished in the war allows Singer to elaborate on the ghost motif as comedy and farce. Singer highlights Yadwiga's Polish speech and Catholicism in her response to Tamara: "'Oh, Holy Mother! My heart!' Yadwiga crossed herself. At once she realized that a Jewish woman doesn't make the sign of a cross and clasped her hands together. Her eyes bulged from their sockets, her mouth became twisted with cries she couldn't utter."[10]

The survivor's return from the dead is presented as a farce rather than as a redemptive act with the potential for exploring the emotional, existential, and religious ramifications of Tamara's reunification with Yadwiga and Herman. Tamara reflects on her self-perception as simultaneously alive and dead: "I'm alive but I am as good as dead. They say dead people sometimes come back to pay a visit and in a way, I'm that kind of visitor. I came to see how things are, but don't worry, I won't come again."[11]

Like the two dybbuks in "The Dead Fiddler," Tamara has returned from the dead to reconstitute an obliterated reality. Like a dybbuk, she ventures into antinomian, subversive speech. Suddenly Herman, Tamara, and Yadwiga are thrown back to their prewar roles as a middle-class Jewish couple with a Polish servant. The shtetl universe in "The Dead Fiddler" and the contemporary New York setting of *Enemies* indicate Singer's artistic range, unified by the theme of ghost writing.

From Singer's earliest days as a Yiddish writer in interwar Warsaw, Sholem Asch served as an artistic foil that he negated, subverted, and parodied—a clear indication of the strong influence Asch continued to exert.[12] After the Holocaust, Asch's humanism and neo-Romanticism seemed out of sync with the Jewish American readership, whereas Singer's nihilistic, subversive storytelling grew increasingly popular in English translation. In the obituary of Asch that Singer wrote for the *Forverts*, Singer compared Asch to Sholem Aleichem.

> Sholem Aleichem wrote like an insider from the inside. From the beginning, Sholem Asch viewed the Polish Jews like a guest from a faraway country. Like a rich uncle who arrived from abroad to visit the poor family. Sholem Aleichem had empathy, but he laughed like one of his people. Sholem Asch was only empathy. How can one ridicule the poor Jews who struggle for a piece of bread? Over Sholem Asch's black eyes always hang a tear. And this tear also hangs over his work.[13]

Instead of Asch's sentimental weeping, Sholem Aleichem used Jewish humor in the style of "laughter through tears." Asch represented the assimilated Jews' universalism and humanism, as Jewish authors writing in German, such as Stefan Zweig and Franz Werfel, did. Singer, on the other hand, identified with the *yidishe yidn* (salt-of-the-earth Jews), similar to the characters in Sholem Aleichem's work. He viewed himself as an insider among the Polish Jewish people. Singer also stressed that Asch and he belonged to a generation of alienated Jews who had rejected their grandfather's *emune* and *bitokhn* (religious faith and belief). Singer's obituary reveals an ambivalent appreciation of Asch. In the art of translating and marketing his work in English, Asch served as a role model: "Asch had the talent of a writer, but the energy of a banker, or an industrialist. That is the secret of his popularity. Asch was the first among the Yiddish writers to discover the importance of being translated into European languages."[14]

Asch's death in 1957 gave Singer the opportunity to pay tribute to him in his romantic pastiche *The Slave*, serialized in the *Forverts* and published in both English (1962) and Yiddish (1967).[15] *The Slave* is the most Asch-like novel Singer would ever publish. Set during the Chmielnicki pogroms in the mid-seventeenth century, *The Slave* deepened Singer's artistic vision, which was rooted in a distinctly Polish Jewish universe that was suffused with religious sensibility and moral edification. At the end of *The Slave* the righteous Jacob is put to rest with his departed wife, the Jewish convert Sarah, like a religious hagiography, an anachronism that subverts the modern novel's complexity of character and plot.

In *Enemies* Singer departs from both Sholem Asch's Romanticism and the Russian family chronicle of his older brother, I. J. Singer (1893–1944). Instead, he creates a farce inspired by Sholem Aleichem.[16] The novel was serialized in the *Forverts* in 1966, the same year that Singer published his first children's book, *Zlateh the Goat and Other Stories*, and began to publish Chelm stories in the *Forverts*, which were collected in *The Fools of Chelm and Their History* (1973). The Jewish humor of the children's stories, the archetypical fools of Chelm, and Sholem Aleichem's laughter through tears inform the use of farce and tragicomedy in *Enemies*. Moreover, Singer portrays Rabbi Lampert, one of the novel's main characters, as a parody of an Asch-like figure.

Enemies trims Herman's self-reflective and philosophical ruminations in the Yiddish version to create a simpler, unified English narrative of rootless Jewish survivors in postwar New York. The satirical jab at Jewish American materialism and vulgarity in the original Yiddish version of *Shadows on the Hudson* (1957–1958) is replaced by *Enemies'* comedy of manners in which the survivor characters are portrayed as *luftmentshn* (without social, existential, and religious foundations).[17] *Enemies* is indebted to Singer's post-Holocaust monologues of fools and schlemiels and is steeped in the melodrama of the Yiddish popular press to which Singer contributed under various pseudonyms. The novel's plot would have fit right into the human interest section of the *Forverts* as a "true story" about "The Incredible Herman and His Three Wives."[18]

In a letter to Singer dated February 23, 1966, only a few weeks after commencing the serialization of *Sonim* in the *Forverts*, Aliza Shevrin reports the progress in translating the first installments of the novel into English.¹⁹ From the start, Singer intended to make the novel available in English, but it took six years until the English book was published by Farrar, Straus & Giroux.²⁰ By then, Shevrin's relationship with Singer had soured and Elizabeth Shub had taken over the translation of the work. Shub, the daughter of the Yiddish literary critic Shmuel Niger, persuaded Singer to write children's stories and worked with Singer in translating and editing them through the 1970s.²¹

Like Rabbi Lampert's Judaica publications, *Enemies* is the result of a collaborative effort of editing and translating the Yiddish newspaper version for an American readership. Singer's author's note states that "it was translated by Aliza Shevrin and Elizabeth Shub and edited by the latter, Rachel MacKenzie, and Robert Giroux." Similarly, Herman Broder's articles for the rabbi are described as first drafts in Yiddish or Hebrew that are translated and edited by a team. The following quote, translated from the Yiddish, is from the serialized version in the *Forverts*.

> Herman Broder did for the rabbi, as it were, what the latter called "research"; truthfully, he authored his books, his essays for the Judaic journals, even his speeches. Herman wrote everything in Hebrew or in Yiddish, but someone translated the scribbles into English. A third edited, a fourth made "publicity" for the rabbi. The rabbi made a lot of money.²²

In *Enemies* the same text is rendered as follows:

> The rabbi referred to what Herman did for him as "research." Actually, Herman ghosted the rabbi's books, his articles, his speeches. He wrote them in Hebrew or in Yiddish, someone translated them into English, and a third person edited them.²³

The Yiddish version maintains Herman's point of view while using the English word *research* to describe his work. The same quote in *Enemies* is from the rabbi's point of view instead. The Yiddish *shraybekhtser* (scribbles) and the English "publicity" have been removed in *Enemies*, as is the fact that the rabbi made a lot of money. *Enemies* recreates the bare bones of the Yiddish without its subtle linguistic games and delineation of Herman's internal point of view. A humorous element of the Yiddish version derives from the play with a foreign language, English, which highlights the farcical character of Herman's work as a ghostwriter for a rabbi. The use of English words creates a contrast between two worlds. In *Enemies*, "ghosted" as a verb is used to designate a common practice in the American literary world, ghostwriting, a word with no equivalence in Yiddish. The serialized version simply states that Herman "authored his books." In English, he is reduced simply to a ghostwriter.

In another section Herman's profession is described in more detail.

> His livelihood is so bizarre and crooked like everything happening to him. He became a "ghostwriter" [*gayst-shrayber*] for the rabbi. Among all the professions built on air [*luftparnoses*] which Jews employ, it was his, Herman's, destiny to fall into the most insubstantial [*di same luftikste*]. . . . He wrote about things he didn't believe in. . . . He promised a better world and hopeful future [*a besere velt un a likhtike tsukunft*]—in paradise.[24]

In the translated book, the same text is reduced to the following.

> His livelihood was as bizarre as everything else that had happened to him. He had become a ghost writer for a rabbi. He, too, promised a "better world" in the Garden of Eden.[25]

The word *gayst-shrayber* (ghostwriter) is translated in *Enemies* as "ghostwriter" without the quotation marks in the original. This Yiddish neologism refers to Singer's monologues of dybbuks, demons, and the evil inclination (*yeytser-hore*), his artistic trademark. The centrality of Herman's self-perception as a *luftmentsh*, akin to a Sholem Aleichem character, is elaborated on in an extra paragraph that was cut out of the English book. It describes Herman's prewar life as a university student in Krakow and Warsaw, where he worshipped humanism and culture.[26] The Yiddish phrase "besere velt un a likhtike tsukunft" ("better world and promising future"), referring to the promise of humanism and socialism, is applied only to the religious concept of "paradise" in *Enemies*. The Yiddish version has a much broader range in its criticism of the secular ideologies.

In the following paragraph, the Yiddish delineates a set of associations quite different from those in *Enemies*.

> He read the manuscript and grimaced. He, Herman, traded with God as Terah did with the idols. Herman had only one justification: those who listened to the rabbi's sermons or who read his essays were also not honest. All of modern Jewishness is one big system of mutual deception [*gegenzaytike opnareray*].²⁷

In *Enemies* the paragraph is translated as:

> As Herman read, he grimaced. The rabbi was selling God as Terah sold idols. Herman could find only one justification for himself: most of the people who listened to the rabbi's sermons or read his essays were not completely honest either. Modern Judaism had one aim: to ape the Gentile.²⁸

A major change in the transition from Yiddish to English is the deliberate mistranslation of *moderne yidishkeyt* (modern Jewishness), as equated in Yiddish with "one big system of mutual deception" (*opnareray*). In English, it becomes, "Modern Judaism had one aim: to ape the Gentile." Again, the Yiddish refers to Singer's artistic universe, particularly the story "Gimpel the Fool," with its play on the various meanings of the words *nar* and *opnarn* (deceiving and tricking) as opposed to *tam* (the simpleminded, holy fool derived from the Bible). The English has a narrower semantic range; the assimilated (German) Jews are merely accused of "aping the Gentile." The humor in the Yiddish is specifically related to the deception of textual manipulation and authorial identity theft that characterizes ghostwriting. In *Enemies* these subtleties are replaced with a cruder satire against a phony American Reform rabbi who tries to pass as a *goy*. In both versions the Germanic-sounding name Herman Broder is emblematic of the assimilated German Jewish universe of "aping the Gentiles."

Herman's writings exist in a ghostly universe of "scribbles." They are similar to the short-lived existence of *Sonim*, published as short segments in the daily Yiddish newspaper. The English translation of Herman's Yiddish and Hebrew writings published with Rabbi Lampert's authorial signature transforms them into English prose. This is similar to the way in which *Enemies*' author, I. B. Singer, provides the English book with a textual authority that supersedes the Yiddish writing of *Sonim*'s author, Yitskhok Bashevis.

Yasha Kotik is a minor character who appears only once in *Enemies*. He introduces himself as a comedian and a veteran of the Yiddish theater when he meets Herman, his former lover Masha, and the real estate mogul Nathan Pesheles at Rabbi Lampert's Upper West Side party. Kotik began his career at age 11, performing in Warsaw, Łódź, Vilna, and Eyshishok. He continued to perform in the ghetto for a starving audience. According to Kotik, this is much better than performing for corpses in New York.

> I met a man who ran a Rumanian restaurant in a cellar. He called it Night-Spot Cabaret. Jewish ex-truck drivers go there with their *shiksehs*. Every one of the men is over seventy. They all have wives and grandchildren who are already professors. The women wear expensive mink coats and Yasha Kotik has to amuse them. My specialty is that I speak a bad English and throw in Yiddish words. And that's what I get for saying no to the gas chambers, for refusing to lie down and die for Comrade Stalin in Kazakhstan. Just my luck, I've developed arthritis here in America and my heart is beginning to act up.[29]

In the Yiddish version Kotik mentions Irish and Yiddish song titles and characterizes the women as whores (*zoynes*). The following excerpt exemplifies Singer's standard translation procedure of cutting out or toning down offensive language and of universalizing national, ethnic, and religious differences:

> I met a man who ran a Rumanian restaurant in a cellar. He called it Night-Spot Cabaret. Jewish ex-truck drivers go there with their Irish *shiksehs*. Every one of the men is over seventy. They all have wives and grandchildren who are already professors. They ask for the song "A Letter to Mama" and she wants "When Irish Eyes Are Smiling." The whores are dressed in expensive mink coats and Yasha Kotik has to amuse them. My whole power is that I speak a bad English and throw in Yiddish words. And that's what I get for saying no to the gas chambers, for refusing to lie down and die for Comrade Stalin in Kazakhstan. Just my luck, I've developed arthritis here in America and my heart is beginning to act up.[30]

Kotik is the embodiment of Yiddish humor as a survival strategy through a forty-year career in the Yiddish theater. Masha characterizes him as a *lets* (a clown) and a *payats* (buffoon). Lacking the authenticity of his Yiddish speech, Kotik's comedy routine does not succeed with an elderly, mostly female American Jewish audience. Kotik's performance—his blend of bad English and a few Yiddish phrases—has been stripped of its Yiddish authenticity.

In the old country Kotik's jokes literally saved him from the gas chambers and the gulag, first in the original Yiddish version, followed by the English translation:

> It was said he told jokes while digging his own grave. He made the Nazis laugh and saved himself. Later he scolded the Bolsheviks. He had overcome countless perils with his clowning, gallows humor and comic antics.[31]

> It was said he told jokes while digging his own grave and the Nazis had been so amused by him that they let him go. Similarly, his buffoonery also stood him in good stead with the Bolsheviks. He had been able to overcome countless perils with his gallows humor and comic antics.[32]

Kotik is man of action and a comedic genius who survived the war against the most implausible odds. Broder, in contrast, survived by hiding in a hayloft in his Polish hometown thanks to his Polish maid Yadwiga, who fed and cared for him. Broder is an intellectual, a former university student who reads Plato and Psalms in their original languages. As Nathan Pesheles astutely characterizes Herman, "To me you look like a nothing."[33] It is Herman the *luftmentsh* (a person who subsists on nothing) whom Masha marries, dumping Kotik, her lover in the displaced persons camp. Kotik asks Masha, "What, for example, does he have that I don't? I want to know." She answers, "He's a serious person and you're a pain in the neck."[34]

Herman Broder becomes the gravitational center in this farce that pokes fun at both the Holocaust survivors and the American-born Jews. Herman and his three wives, Masha, Yadwiga, and Tamara, survivors in their 20s and 30s, are the vanguard of transgressive social mores that shake up the staid American conformity in 1948–1949, the novel's narrative time frame. Published in English book form in 1972, at the height of the hippie movement's gospel of free love, the novel replaces the conventional representation of the passive, long-suffering Holocaust survivor with Herman and Masha, representatives of antinomian sexual and social behavior among the Jewish high society of the Upper West Side. In Pesheles' words: "These greenhorns know how to live. With us Americans, when you get married, you stay that way, whether you like it or not. Or you get divorced and pay alimony, and if you don't pay, you go to prison."[35]

Each of the three women in Herman's life resides in a different borough characterized by distinct socioeconomic, cultural, and linguistic features. Yadwiga and Herman live on Coney Island, home to a Jewish refugee community and surrounded by an American amusement park of make-believe and leisure. Yadwiga is the stereotypical Polish peasant woman, the *shikse*—innocent, illiterate, truthful. Like Sarah/Wanda in *The Slave*, she converts to Judaism and bears Herman's child. Herman serves as the illiterate Yadwiga's liaison to American society and as the conduit to their Polish past, reading to her the letters that she receives from her family in Poland.

The Yiddish survivor community is represented by Masha, Herman's lover, and her mother Shifra Puah in the Bronx. The Yiddish press is the other locus through which Herman contacts his wife Tamara, who he thought had been killed in the war. Tamara and her pious uncle and aunt, survivors from Eastern Europe, reside on the Lower East Side, the old Jewish immigrant neighborhood. The English-speaking world is located on the Upper West Side, where Rabbi Lampert throws a party for a multilingual gathering of Jewish intellectuals. In contrast to Coney Island and the Bronx, Rabbi Lampert's Upper West Side apartment situates him among the American Jewish intellectual elite.

Unlike Yasha Kotik, who must rely on his nonverbal acrobatic antics as a clown and stand-up comedian, Herman's multilingual verbal dexterity in Polish, Yiddish, Hebrew, German, and English enables him to deceive and trick the three women partners as well as Rabbi Lampert. Most of the Yiddish novel's humor derives from its multilingual play and the absurd incompatibilities of characters transplanted from prewar "Yiddishland" to the boroughs of New York. In contrast to Gimpel the Fool, Herman is no innocent and simpleminded character who ends up becoming a storyteller. He is the quintessential *nar* (deceptive fool), who creates his own Chelm (fools' town). Herman's manipulating comedy is highlighted when he speaks to Yadwiga in Yiddish.

> He started talking to Yadwiga in Yiddish.—Alone, with the queen of Sheba. I'm as much a book salesman as you are a rabbi's wife. If it wasn't for the rabbi, that thief, we would both have had to starve [*geleygt di tseyn in beytl*]. He is full of money and throws pennies at me. She, moreover, in the Bronx, is a sphinx. That I don't go insane is a miracle from heaven. Pif-pif.[36]

The same passage in *Enemies*:

> He started talking to Yadwiga in Yiddish. "Alone. That's what you think! I'll be eating with the Queen of Sheba. I'm as much a book salesman as you're the Pope's wife! That faker of a rabbi I work for—still, if it weren't for him we'd be starving. And that female in the Bronx is a sphinx altogether. What with the three of you, it's an absolute miracle I haven't gone out of my mind. Pif-pof."[37]

The Yiddish expression *geleygt di tseyn in beytl* ("to starve," or literally, "to put the teeth in the purse") has been simplified to "we'd be starving" in translation. The reference to the rabbi as a *marvikher* (a thief) who exploits Herman economically has been deleted in the English. Moreover, the Yiddish joke about Yadwiga as a *rebbetzin* has been replaced with "the Pope's wife" with no Jewish humorous punch. Again, the sharper, unsparing directness of the Yiddish has been toned down in the portrayal of Rabbi Lampert's exploitation of a newly arrived Jewish war refugee. By using a distinctly Christian expression, the English version universalizes the novel to reach a mostly non-Jewish readership.

The love story of Herman and Masha ends in tragedy when Masha commits suicide. In the novel's denouement, Yadwiga and Tamara bring up the Yadwiga's newborn baby Masha named after Herman's deceased lover, with support from Rabbi Lampert. The Yiddish ghost world of Holocaust survivors associated with the passionate love affair between Herman and Masha is doomed to extinction. By the novel's end, Herman disappears and becomes one with his identity as a ghostwriter. The Jewish American future belongs to Rabbi Lampert with his vulgarity, materialism, and sentimentality. Lampert has built a career as an intellectual operator who translates and markets Broder's original Yiddish and Hebrew writing under his own name in English journals. Similarly, Singer's artistic work in America is built on lies and deception and looks a lot like Rabbi Lampert's. Singer's ambivalence about his success in marketing his work in English translation is articulated in the character of Rabbi Lampert.

On a metaphorical level the enemies of the novel's title also represent the incompatibility of the Yiddish ghost world and the Jewish American reality. This is depicted humorously in Masha and Herman's alienation in the Jewish bungalow colony among the Catskills families. Their alienation in the Jewish American middle-class idyll of the summer resort signifies that their Old World Yiddish identity is completely at odds with the forward-looking American industriousness of Rabbi Lampert.

The 1989 film version of *Enemies*, directed by Paul Mazursky, who makes a cameo appearance as Leon Tortshiner, one of Masha's lovers, heightens the novel's comedy and farce. Particularly successful are the film's slapstick and other forms of comedy. The characters come to life in the film's authentic recreation of the Jewish neighborhoods on the Lower East Side, the Bronx, and Coney Island. The film was made for a mainstream American audience, so the Jewish content is primarily presented in formulaic ways, such as the Jewish wedding ceremony of Masha and Herman and the Jewish summer retreat in the Catskills. The Jewish refugees in the film speak English with stereotypical Yiddish accents, but there is almost no trace of their mother tongues. *Sonim*'s subtle and *Enemies*' cruder use of multilingualism, woven into the characters' speech patterns, have been erased in the film. The movie begins with Herman reading the *New York Times* in the bathtub, a strange choice for a Jewish survivor in the late 1940s, who most likely would have read a Yiddish newspaper. The film completes the transfer of *Sonim* into *Enemies* by Americanizing its language, style, and humor.

In *Enemies* Singer spun yet another yarn in the ghost story genre. The key to *Enemies*' popular success as a book and a film adaptation is the way in which Singer took inspiration from Sholem Aleichem–style tragicomedy and farce. In writing, translating, and editing *Enemies*, Singer deepened his artistic exploration of the plight of Holocaust survivors in America as a universal human predicament while infusing it with the Jewish humor of laughter through tears. The storyteller Gimpel the Fool and the ghostwriter Herman Broder represent two types of fools: the simpleminded (*tam*) and the deceiver (*nar*) in pursuit of *luft parnoses* (castles in the air professions). They embody the subaltern reality of Singer's Yiddish diaspora of survivors in postwar New York.

Enemies demonstrates that Singer successfully mastered the rich modalities of Jewish American humor while remaining deeply connected to the world of Yiddish-speaking survivors. By making his own split personality as a bilingual writer the humorous crux of *Enemies*, Singer cast his lot with the world of American entertainment. This paid off both artistically and commercially, as evidenced by the popularity of both the book and the film adaptation.

Singer skewered the sacrosanct image of Holocaust survivors in his tragicomic portraits of Herman, Masha, and Tamara. In contrast, Yasha Kotik, the authentic voice of heroic resistance during the Holocaust and the gulag, is depicted as a loser, a pathetic stand-up comedian performing in bad English for mostly elderly American-born Jews. Singer did not resurrect the Yiddish-speaking ghosts in New York in their own tongue; instead, he translated them into the Jewish American farce *Enemies*.

Notes

1. The author used the name Yitskhok Bashevis in his Yiddish book and journal publications in addition to the pseudonyms Yitskhok Varshavsky and D. Segal in his journalistic writing in the *Forverts*. He used Isaac Bashevis Singer or I. B. Singer in his English publications.
2. Isaac Bashevis Singer, "Concerning Yiddish Literature in Poland," trans. Robert Woolf, *Prooftexts* 15 (1995): 120. Originally published in *Tsukunft* 48, no. 8 (August 1943): 468–475.
3. Singer's key short stories with an American setting and combining the ghost story and Holocaust survivors are "Mayse tishevits" (The Last Demon; Yiddish, 1959; English, 1964), "Di khasene in Brownsville" (A Wedding in Brownsville; Yiddish, 1962; English, 1964), "Di forlezung" (The Lecture; Yiddish, 1965; English, 1968), and "Di kafeterye" (The Cafeteria; Yiddish, 1968; English, 1970). *Shadows on the Hudson*, serialized in the *Forverts* twice weekly between January 1957 and January 1958, takes place between December 1947 and November 1949 in New York. In the early 1950s, before Singer became widely known in English translation, he wrote the novel *Farloyrene neshomes* (Lost Souls). According to Chone Shmeruk, the novel was retrieved from Singer's archive for serialization in the *Forverts* in 1981–1982 and first published in English posthumously in 1994 with the title *Meshugah*. Chone Shmeruk, "The Perils of Translation: Isaac Bashevis Singer in English and Hebrew," in Ezra Mendelsohn, ed., *Literary Strategies: Jewish Texts and Contexts—Studies in Contemporary Jewry XII* (Oxford, UK: Oxford University Press, 1996), 231.
4. See Jan Schwarz, *Survivors and Exiles: Yiddish Culture After the Holocaust* (Detroit: Wayne University Press, 2015).
5. See Jan Schwarz, "The Lost Souls of *Meshugah*: Textual Transmission of Isaac Bashevis Singer's Work in Post-War New York," in Uzi Rebhun, ed., *Studies in Contemporary Jewry 31* (New York: Oxford University Press, in press).
6. "Der toyter klezmer," *Forverts*, 2, 3, 9, 10, 16, 17, 23 September 1966. The story was published as a whole in *Mayses fun hintern oyvn* (Tel Aviv: Farlag Y. L. Perets 1971) and translated into English in *The Seance and Other Stories* (New York: Farrar, Straus & Giroux, 1968).
7. I. B. Singer, *The Collected Stories* (New York: Farrar, Straus & Giroux, 1982), 217.
8. Singer, *Collected Stories*, 239.
9. I. B. Singer, *Enemies, A Love Story* (New York: Farrar, Straus & Giroux, 1972), 202.

10. Singer, *Enemies*, 188.
11. Singer, *Enemies*, 193.
12. See David Roskies, "Found in America: Sholem Asch and I. B. Singer," in Nanette Stahl, ed., *Sholem Asch Reconsidered* (New Haven, CT: Yale University Press, 2005), 239–48.
13. Yitskhok Varshavsky [I. B. Singer], obituary for Sholem Asch, *Forverts*, 12 July 1957.
14. Varshavsky, obituary for Sholem Asch.
15. Isaac Bashevis Singer, *The Slave*, trans. Isaac Bashevis Singer and Cecil Hemley (New York: Farrar, Straus & Cudahy, 1962); published in Yiddish as *Der knekht* (New York: Tsiko farlag, 1967).
16. The main family novels before *Enemies* were *The Family Moskat* (1950) and *The Manor* and *The Estate* (1967–1968).
17. See Joseph Sherman, "Translating 'Shotns baym hodson' (Shadows on the Hudson): Directly Encountering Isaac Bashevis Singer's Authorial Dualism," in Hugh Denman, ed., *Isaac Bashevis Singer: His Work and His World* (Leiden: Brill, 2002), 49–81.
18. Singer published human interest stories under the pseudonyms Yitskhok Varshavsky and D. Segal. The human interest stories in the Yiddish press that Singer's older brother I. J. Singer (1893–1944) published in the late 1920s under the pseudonym G. Kuper became the inspiration for Singer's autobiographical vignettes "Mayn tatns bezdn shtub" (My Father's Rabbinical Court) and "Mentshn af mayn veg" (People on My Road) in the 1950s. These vignettes portray the incredible melodrama of people in the poor section of Krochmalna Street in Warsaw narrated from Singer's child's perspective in his father's rabbinic court. See Eddy Portnoy, *Bad Rabbi and Other Strange and True Stories from the Yiddish Press* (Stanford, CA: Stanford University Press, 2017), ch. 11, "The Strange Case of Gimel Kuper."
19. Rebecca Walkowitz's concept of the "born-translated" novel can serve as a useful characterization of Singer's process of translating the Yiddish serialized version into English: "In born-translated novels, translation functions as a thematic, structural, conceptual, and sometimes even typographical device. These works are *written for translation*, in the hope of being translated, but they are also often *written as translations*, pretending to take place in a language other than the one in which they have, in fact been composed." Rebecca Walkowitz, *Born Translated: The Contemporary Novel in an Age of World Literature* (New York: Columbia University Press, 2015), 4.

20. Neugroschel, Sloan and Shevrin letters, Isaac Bashevis Singer Papers, Harry Ransom Center (HRC), University of Texas, Austin.
21. Elizabeth Shub Collection of Isaac Bashevis Singer Papers, HRC.
22. "Herman Broder hot kloymersht geton farn rabay vos yener hot gerufn 'risoyrtsh'; in emesn hot er farfast zeyne bikher, zayne eyseyen far di yudaistishe shurnaln, afile zayne redes. Herman hot alts geshribn in hebreish, oder in yidish, ober emets hot ibergezetst di shraybekhtser in English. A driter hot redagirt, a ferter hot gemakht der rabay 'publisiti.' Der rabay hot fardint groyser gelter" (*Forverts*, 18 February 1966, p. 3).
23. Singer, *Enemies*, 21.
24. "Di parnose zayne iz azoy oysterlish un krum, vi alts vos s'pasirt mit im. Er iz gevorn a 'gayst-shrayber' bay a rabay. Fun ale luft-parnoses vos yidn zukhn zikh oys, iz gefaln oyf zayn, Hermans goyrl di same luftikste . . . er hot geshribn vegn zakhn, vos er hot in zey nisht gegloybt . . . er hot oykh tsugezogt a besere velt un a likhtike tsukunft—in gan-eydn" (*Forverts*, 18 February 1966, p. 2).
25. Singer, *Enemies*, 19.
26. *Forverts*, 18 February 1966, p. 3.
27. "Er hot itst geleynt dem ksav-yad un zikh gekrimt. Er, Herman, hot gehandlt mit got vi Terakh mit di getsn. Herman hot gehat far zikh eyn farentferung: yene vos hern zikh tsu tsum rabay's droshes oder vos leyenen zeyne eseyen, zenen oykh nisht erlekh. Dos gantse modern yidishkeyt iz eyn groyse system fun gegenzaytike opnareray" (*Forverts*, 19 February 1966, p. 3).
28. Singer, *Enemies*, 19.
29. Singer, *Enemies*, 222.
30. The original Yiddish is: "S'hot zikh opgezukht a yid vos hot a rumenisher restoyrant in a keler un er ruft es: nakht local cabaret. S'kumen ahin gevezene balegoles un zey firn mit zikh ayrishe shikses. Yeder balguf iz nit veyniker fun zibetsik. Zey hobn alte vayber un eyniker profesorn. Er heyst shpiln 'A brivele der mamen' un zi vil: 'When Irish Eyes Are Smiling.' Men hot ongeton zoynes in mink-futers un Yashe Kotik darf zey freylekh makhn. Der gantser koykh mayner ligt derin vos ikh red shlekht english un varf arayn yidishe verter. Ot dos iz mayn loyn far nisht veln geyen in gazkamer un far opzogn zikh tsu shtarbn baym khaver Stalin in Kazakhstan. Ikh hob shoyn mit mazl bakumen artretis in amerike un soharts hot ongehoybn unterfonfen far a tsulog" (*Forverts*, 25 June 1966, p. 2).
31. Singer, *Enemies*, 219.
32. The original Yiddish is: "Er zol hobn gezogt vitsn bay grobn doz eygene keyver. Er hot lakhndik gemakht di natsis un azoy zikh geratevet. Shpeter hot er arayngezogt

di bolsyevikes. Er hot ibergekumen umtsolike farn mit zayn letsones, galgenhumor, payatishe shtik" (Forverts, 24 June 1966, p. 2). For a different reading of the Yasha Kotik episode, see Miriam Udel, *Never Better! The Modern Jewish Picaresque* (Ann Arbor: University of Michigan Press, 2016), 78–90.

33. Singer, *Enemies*, 229.
34. Singer, *Enemies*, 220. The original Yiddish is: "*Vos a shteyger kedoyme lemoshl hot er vos ikh hob nisht? Aderabe, ikh vil oykh visn!* . . . —*Geblibn a blazen—hot Mashe geredt—er iz an ernshter mentsh un du bist a farshlepte krenk*" (*Forverts*, 24 June 1966, p. 6).
35. Singer, *Enemies*, 223. The original Yiddish is: "*Di grine veysn vi zikh aoyntsuordenen. Bay undz Amerikaner, az m'hot khasene ligt men vi m'zogt ayngeleygt. Me tsolt alimony un aldos iberike. M'geyt in prison oykh*" (*Forverts*, 25 June 1966, p. 2).
36. "*Er nemt redn tsu ir in yidish.—Aleyn, mit der malke sheba. Ir handlt azoy mit bikher, vi du bist a rebetsn. Ven nisht der rabay der marvikher, voltn mir beyde geleygt di tseyn in beytl. Er iz ongeshtopt mit gelt un mir varft er tsu di penis. Yene, vider, in di bronks, iz a sfinks. Vi azoy ikh ver nisht khoser-deye iz a nes fun himl. Pif-pif*" (*Forverts*, 12 February 1966, p. 2).
37. Singer, *Enemies*, 13.

"A Ring of Fire"

Humor and the Holocaust

Stephen J. Whitfield

> The author greatly appreciates the help of Steve Krief, Joel Rosenberg, and Avihu Zakai.

IN A GROTESQUE WAY, the Holocaust can be said to have been framed in hilarity—as well as in the claims of laughter. On January 30, 1939, on the sixth anniversary of the Nazi seizure of power, Hitler told the Reichstag, "I have very often in my lifetime been a prophet. . . . It was in the first instance the Jewish people who received only with laughter my prophecies," which included the prospect of a "solution" to the "Jewish problem." But by 1939 "this once hollow laughter of Jewry in Germany has meanwhile already stuck in the throat."[1] The Reichstag representatives are reported to have laughed. And then the Führer warned that "if international finance Jewry . . . should succeed in plunging the nations once more into a world war," the consequence would be "the annihilation [*Vernichtung*] of the Jewish race in Europe!" Two years later, half a year before Operation Barbarossa and almost a year before Pearl Harbor, Hitler referred to "the hint which I gave already once before, on September 1, 1939, in the German Reichstag—that should the world be plunged into a general war, Jewry as a whole will have played out its role in Europe. They can laugh at this today, just as they laughed at my prophecies before. The coming months and years will prove that here too I saw correctly."[2] And after the Final Solution had become horrifically close to achievement, *Obersturmbannführer* Adolf Eichmann boasted of his role in "the death of five million Jews" or "enemies of the Reich," enabling him to foresee that "I will jump into my grave laughing."[3]

Perhaps such statements should be included among the many mysteries of human life: that the most systematically horrific of crimes cannot be entirely detached from expressions of humor. Perhaps one inescapable inference is the moral neutrality of merriment. Whatever its value, it is not inherently good; nor is it to be prized in all circumstances. It is not necessarily liberating or redemptive. Consider another piece of evidence from 1939, when the Third Reich conquered Poland. A famous photograph shows grinning German soldiers who have just murdered the six brothers of an observant Jew, who is shown praying over their corpses. He knows in a moment that he will be next. The depiction of such ineffable cruelty is heightened by the enjoyment of the soldiers. Nor can it be irrelevant that Hitler "could laugh loudly, with abandon, sometimes literally writhing with laughter. . . . But it was always laughter at the expense of others," according to Albert Speer, the Reich minister of armaments and war production. "Hitler had no humor. He left joking to others," but he could also make "fun of his closest associates with striking frequency."[4]

Philosophers understand how integral cruelty has been to amusement. Dropping by the "games" in the Colosseum, Seneca watched lions starved so that they could "slaughter" defenseless men in the arena; such "butchering," he noted, was designed for the "merriment" of the spectators. Even when in the form of verbal humor, what is its dynamic? To Henri Bergson, the intention of humor—or at least what passes for jokes—is "to humiliate. . . . Its function is to intimidate by humiliating," he wrote in *Le Rire* (1900). Add Freud to this litany. "Tendentious jokes" or wit can slip past the censor of the superego to express the sort of aggression that courtesy and civility prohibit, he wrote in *Der Witz* (1905).[5]

In the United States the tradition of "Southwestern" humor, which became the marrow of the nation's humor, is striking for its sadism, for its habit of mocking the helpless. The tall tales relayed around campfires were "sickeningly violent, exaggeratedly cruel," often at the expense of the slaves and indigenous peoples, one scholar has emphasized. William Keough, the author of a study that is aptly titled *Punchlines*, generalizes that "American humor is violent—and often sexist, racist, brutal, and disgusting as well." Such deflation aims at "violation—not just of the body, but of rights and dignity as well."[6] Huckleberry Finn notes the guffaws of the mob when the Duke and the Dauphin are tarred and feathered and run out of town.

Or take the plague that struck in the 1980s. The manifestations of AIDS included *Pneumocystis carinii* pneumonia, which floods the lungs until the patient drowns; cryptosporidiosis, in which a parasite invades the gastrointestinal tract until starvation becomes terminal; and toxoplasmosis, which quickly transforms the young into Alzheimer's sufferers. Yet as late as 1986, after hundreds of thousands had died under such harrowing conditions, President Reagan laughed in public at a coarse joke about AIDS.[7] These instances of mirth at the misfortune of others could easily be extended, allowing Nazis to cite a considerable lineage in finding the ordeal of their Jewish victims amusing.

There is something nevertheless singular about the implementation of the Final Solution. "Auschwitz is as important as Sinai," Elie Wiesel once claimed.[8] This symmetry is dubious: For the pious, this is not so and perhaps even smacks of blasphemy; and for the unbeliever, the Decalogue and the Covenant are not divine interventions but are cast in mythic origins, in contrast with the all-too-human creation of the camps. But Wiesel's assertion does reinforce the warning that the Holocaust, no matter where it is located on the historical continuum of horror, must be treated warily. The massacre of half of European Jewry constitutes a test for "the limits of representation" and indeed whether they can be stretched. This particular aspect of the broader political and military challenge that Nazism posed emerged as early as 1933. No Austrian satirist was quite as gifted or as adroit in converting language into both an object and a weapon as Karl Kraus. Yet he wrote, in the first sentence of *Die Dritte Walpurgisnacht*, "Mir fällt zu Hitler nichts ein" ("I cannot think of anything to say about Hitler").[9]

Even now the character of Hitler's crimes can still evoke a grisly fascination with the personality who inspired them. Although Stalin matched him in depravity, Hitler incarnated evil. But the deeper mystery has not yet been pierced: how this apparently banal figure, veering toward the ridiculous in the nullity of his character and the ferocity of his obsessions, this erstwhile corporal whom his regimental adjutant during the Great War deemed unfit for promotion to sergeant, made himself the undisputed master of one of Europe's most advanced nations and then put into effect the most monstrous blot on Western civilization. The earliest extant document of Hitler's political life promised "the elimination of the Jews altogether" (September 16, 1919), and the final words of his "political testament" (April 29,

1945) admonished Germany to maintain "an implacable opposition to the poisoners of all people, international Jewry." In between, whether haranguing parliamentarians or officers, Hitler relished the role of prophet in anticipating the obliteration of "this pestilence."[10] Of course, the reduction of Kraus to exasperated silence occurred nearly a decade before the Wannsee Conference. The menace that Nazism posed—first to his native Austria and then to the rest of Europe—makes his reticence seem inadequate and even a kind of complicity.

This unprecedented threat to the Jews, and to Western civilization itself, required its embattled defenders to break that silence, marshaling even humor to target the Third Reich and Hitler himself. A trio of cinematic comedies demonstrated how they might be ridiculed: *The Great Dictator* (1940), *To Be or Not to Be* (1942), and *The Producers* (1968). These films generated unease upon their release: Could the genre itself do justice to what Nazism meant? Could a tradition stretching back to Aristophanes be adapted to take on a totalitarian power that was fiendishly devising a solution to the "Jewish problem"? Against that "solution," how effective could a movie be? Although the designation of "classic" status is too promiscuously bestowed, these three films belong on the fairly short list of enduring comedies. On August 22, 2017, for example, the British Broadcasting Corporation released the results of a poll taken of an international group of 253 film critics. This BBC Culture poll ranked Ernst Lubitsch's *To Be or Not to Be* thirteenth among the greatest comedies of all time. Charles Chaplin's *The Great Dictator* ranked sixteenth, and Mel Brooks's *The Producers* came in at a respectable fortieth place.[11] All three works include characters based on or purporting to be the Führer and rubbed against the limits of representation as well.

The Great Dictator

Confronted with evil, the popular arts sometimes get ahead of their betters. The lowbrow gossip columnist Walter Winchell alerted his readers to the menace of Nazism before the mandarin pundit Walter Lippmann did. In mocking the Third Reich on screen, Charlie Chaplin lost the race to the silly Jewish clowns who called themselves the Three Stooges.

On January 19, 1940, while the Reich and the Soviet Union were allied, while the blitzkrieg was almost half a year away, Columbia Pictures released

You Nazty Spy, in which Moe Howard played Dictator Hailstone (a former paperhanger), Larry Fine served as Minister of Propaganda Pebble, and Curly Howard fancied himself Field Marshall Gallstone. Set in the Kingdom of Moronica, this nineteen-minute quasi-parody of Warner Brothers' *Confessions of a Nazi Spy* (1939) ridicules a regime that brandishes as its official insignia a swastika formed by crossed serpents. The targets include book burnings, the conquest of neighboring lands, the imprisonment of political foes, and the dictator's moustache. The storm troopers resemble Keystone Kops. The trio that made 260 films for Columbia with such titles as *Wee Monsieur* and *Loco Boy Makes Good* thus went political in the shadow of the fascist threat. On July 4, 1941, more than five months before Pearl Harbor, the Stooges reprised their roles with the release of *I'll Never Heil Again*. Curly tells Moe in the sequel that "we bombed 56 hospitals, 85 schools, 42 kindergartens, 4 cemeteries, and other vital military objects." (Not on that list, of course, are concentration camps, which were notorious and feared from virtually the dawn of the Third Reich.) Axis expansion meant that more regimes needed to be spoofed, so that the trio leading Moronica competes for the globe with Italy, Japan, and even Spain. They treat the globe as though it were a basketball. The introductory title card for *I'll Never Heil Again* reads "The characters in this picture are all fictitious. Anyone resembling them is better off dead."[12] The interest that the Three Stooges nevertheless generated for their two-reelers was no match, of course, for *The Great Dictator*.

Well before *The Great Dictator* went into production in early September 1939 (barely a week after the invasion of Poland), the Third Reich had banned the re-releases of Chaplin's oeuvre. Perhaps the prohibition was due to the allegedly communistic slant of his 1936 feature, *Modern Times* (working title: *Masses*). Perhaps the Nazis assumed that his ancestors were *Untermenschen*. After all, the regime had produced a propaganda volume titled *Juden sehen dich an* (Jews Are Looking at You), which offered unflattering portraits, including one of Chaplin. Chaplin was called a "little Jewish acrobat, as disgusting as he is tedious." Chaplin himself had gallantly refused to deny publicly that he was Jewish; to do so, he believed, would suggest something shameful and would merely "play into the hands of anti-Semites." Perhaps the Nazis also feared that the Tramp's moustache might make the Führer look ludicrous.[13] It remains a historical oddity that the most enchanting of comedians and the most lethal of despots were indissolubly linked. One had played a tramp; the other had been one. Chaplin, who had become by the end of World War I the most famous person in the world, and Hitler, who became during the subsequent war the most notorious tyrant in history, were born within four days of one another, in 1889.

As though to rebuke the silence that Kraus had earlier imposed on himself, Chaplin decided to make his first talkie; it was also the first film that he began with a completed script.[14] He made *The Great Dictator*, he claimed, "for the Jews of the world";[15] and no one else in Hollywood had the power to do so. Chaplin had his own studio and spent his own money (in this case $1.5 million); and the distributor of *The Great Dictator*, United Artists, was a company that he had helped to found. Although he remained subject to the rules (and whims) of the industry's self-censorship, Chaplin's autonomy was exceptional. He could thus enact an idea that came from the Hungarian Jewish émigré Alexander Korda. In 1937 Korda suggested that because Chaplin and Hitler had similar moustaches, the comedian "should do a Hitler story based on mistaken identity. . . . I could play both characters," Chaplin recalled. "As Hitler I could harangue the crowds in jargon and talk all I wanted to. And as the tramp I could remain more or less silent."[16] Chaplin's best friend in Hollywood, Douglas Fairbanks Sr. (and a partner in United Artists), sensed the value of such a film, based on "one of the most fortuitous tricks in the history of civilization—that the greatest living villain in the world and the greatest comedian should look alike." But could mirth be deployed against despotism? "I'm the clown," Chaplin asserted, "and what can I do that is more effective than to laugh at those fellows who are putting humanity to the goose step?"[17]

Chaplin, who made no films between 1936 and 1940, had begun writing *The Great Dictator* in the month of the Munich crisis, in September 1938. Although some in Hollywood tried to dissuade him from making the film, among those encouraging him was President Roosevelt. The film premiered in New York City in October 1940 and played to packed houses for fifteen weeks. It did extremely well in London too, during the Battle of Britain. *The Great Dictator* was of course banned in Nazi-occupied Europe, nor was it shown in several South American countries or in the Irish Free State; yet no previous film of Chaplin's had racked up higher grosses. After the war the Federal Republic of Germany and Italy demonstrated their commitment to democracy, yet United Artists did not release *The Great Dictator* in those nations until 1958. Spain had to wait until 1976, a year after the death of Francisco Franco. But it is possible that at least one German saw the film soon after its release in the fall of 1940. Some inconclusive evidence exists that Hitler saw *The Great Dictator* one night, in solitude, and then watched it again, alone, the following night.[18] If he did screen the film, his reaction is unknown.

Hitler would have seen a film that starts in the Great War and ends with the invasion of a peaceful neighbor, Osterlich, and that oscillates between "People of the Palace" and "People of the Ghetto." Adenoid Hynkel, the dictator of Tomania, is referred to as Der Phooey and serves as the leader of the Double Cross Party. Tomania's minister of war is named Herring (conflating Hermann Goering). Played by Jack Oakie, Benzino Napaloni serves as dictator of Bacteria; its capital is Aroma. A top aide to Hynkel is the minister of propaganda, named Garbitsch, who announces to a mass rally that "each man will serve the interests of the state with absolute obedience. . . . The rights of citizenship will be taken away from all Jews and other non-Aryans. . . . It is the duty of all true Aryans to hate and despise them."[19] Persecution and violence, or the fear of such atrocities, permeate *The Great Dictator*, which even goes inside a concentration camp. The People of the Ghetto include Hannah (the name of Chaplin's own mother), played by Paulette Goddard, née Marion Goddard Levy (her father was Jewish). "Life could be wonderful if people would leave you alone," Hannah declares. "Wouldn't it be wonderful if they stopped hating us? If they'd leave us alone . . ."[20] These lines sound banal and simplistic, and yet they convey an important historical truth about the experience of the Diaspora. The yearning to be left alone—to live out one's life and to practice one's faith—has indeed been a yearning too often denied over the course of roughly two millennia.

Hannah represents the romantic interest of the ghetto's barber, who rarely speaks and who is the look-alike of the dictator. To have made the chief Jewish character a barber might in retrospect remind viewers of *Shoah* (1985), although Chaplin's choice of this particular occupation was coincidental rather than prescient. Nevertheless, no segment of that documentary may be more harrowing than Claude Lanzmann's interview with Abraham Bomba, the barber whom he tracked down in Tel Aviv and persuaded to recall what it was like to cut the hair of those destined moments later for the gas chambers of Treblinka.[21] It was also Lanzmann who insisted on the singular difficulty of coming to terms with the Holocaust, which "erects a ring of fire around itself. . . . There are some things that cannot and should not be represented."[22] No one expressed more concisely the need to secure the meaning and memory of the Holocaust from those who would cheapen it. Chaplin's film does not violate Lanzmann's credo. "Had I known of the actual horrors of the German concentration camps," Chaplin famously wrote in his autobiography, "I could not have made *The Great Dictator*. I could not have made fun of the homicidal insanity of the Nazis."[23] Chaplin was clearly referring to the extermination camps, where the Final Solution was realized during the war, rather than to camps such as Dachau and Buchenwald, where political prisoners and pacifists as well as Jews were sent. Only after the publication of Chaplin's autobiography did the distinction within *l'univers concentrationnaire* become a staple of the historiography of the Holocaust.

The comic episodes are nevertheless rightly admired. They include Hynkel and Napaloni competing with one another like mediocre vaudevillians to sit higher in his respective barber's chair, or Hynkel's iconic dance with the globe, which finally bursts, as though the aim of world conquest will be futile. (That particular scene took Chaplin three days to film.) With exquisite timing, the barber shaves a customer to the tune of Brahms's "Hungarian Dance No. 5." Somewhere between the comic and the chilling is the harangue that Hynkel delivers, for which Chaplin prepared by watching newsreels of Hitler's speeches. What Der Phooey declaims is gibberish; look who's talking. And when the microphones wilt, an interpreter explains that the dictator of Tomania has just mentioned the Jews. This scene marks the first time that Chaplin spoke at any length on the screen, and the speech was entirely improvised.[24]

Far more problematic is the final speech, which the barber—mistaken for Hynkel—first hesitantly and then passionately delivers at a mass rally. This plea for tolerance and brotherhood runs nearly six minutes long; Chaplin—auteur rather than barber—addresses the camera directly. Filmed in late June 1940, a week after the French surrender to the Third Reich,[25] this exhortation to soldiers that they not be used as cannon fodder matched the foreign policy of the Soviet Union, which was then allied with

Germany and opposed American intervention on behalf of Britain. But the real problem with that speech is its illogic. Given the brutality that *The Great Dictator* exposes, shouldn't Chaplin have called for vigorous military resistance—rather than desertion or defection—to liberate occupied Europe? Shouldn't he have appealed for something more demanding than such common virtues as "kindness and gentleness" or the assertion of political will rather than an evocation of private attributes?[26] For an analogy in American domestic politics, consider the consistency with which Republican politicians have reacted to mass shootings by offering prayers rather than trying to limit access to guns. In 2017, when the majority whip of the House of Representatives, Steve Scalise, returned from convalescence after getting shot on a baseball diamond and reporters asked about the mass shooting in Las Vegas, he averred that "in the face of unspeakable evil, our whole nation must respond with countless acts of kindness"—rather than with, say, gun control legislation.[27]

The Great Dictator demonstrates the possibilities of derision that Nazism presented. To be sure, the gas chambers that would accelerate the process of mass murder had not yet been built; the first were used at Chelmno in early December 1941. It is nevertheless impossible to watch this film without an awareness of the fate of mostly friendless Jews. *The Great Dictator* therefore invites appreciation of the effort of a cinematic artist to decry, through his art, the persecution that would be the immediate prelude to the Final Solution. Chaplin cannot be expected to have foreseen the intensity of the German drive to exterminate European Jewry. He lacked what Henry James, in a different context, called "the imagination of disaster." But by juxtaposing palace and ghetto, *The Great Dictator* does suggest a link between the impulse for aggression and the animus of antisemitism. The Double Cross Party is shown to be motivated by "an imbecilic fanaticism," François Truffaut wrote, while "the persecuted are shown with a furious appetite to live." With Chaplin's double role, both tendencies, Truffaut explained, "had to be brought together in the same film."[28]

Not until after the war did it become obvious that Nazis waged the war against the Jews no less seriously than their quest for *Lebensraum*. *The Great Dictator* was released too early for Chaplin to face the challenge of applying comedy to the genocidal impulses of a modern state. But his next film would enable him in some small measure to rectify that omission.

In *Monsieur Verdoux* (1947) the protagonist is eventually put on trial for murdering middle-aged women. But Henri Verdoux turns the tables on his accusers and calls out their hypocrisy. Announcing that the body count of nation-states is far greater than his own, this lady-killer faces the guillotine by acknowledging that, "as a mass murderer, I am an amateur by comparison."[29]

To Be or Not to Be

Although lacking the independence that Chaplin enjoyed, Ernst Lubitsch nevertheless cut a distinctive figure. He may have been Europe's most famous director before getting summoned to Hollywood in 1922; and upon becoming the head of production at Paramount Pictures, Lubitsch was unique: the only major director in the history of the industry to run a large American studio. The films of no other studio director were more exempt from tampering from above,[30] perhaps because, in the opinion of Jack Benny, Lubitsch was "the greatest comedy director that ever lived."[31] (Greater than Chaplin?) Born in Berlin to a Jewish family, Lubitsch was sensitive to the fragility of Jewish life in Europe, even from his new home in America. As early as 1933, he was soliciting funds for the United Jewish Appeal and later helped sponsor the Hollywood Anti-Nazi League.[32] Lubitsch had already contributed to the formation of Jewish culture when he urged Warner Bros. to scoop up the rights to what would become the most influential of the American Jewish stories that Hollywood ever told: *The Jazz Singer* (1927). He himself appears to have concocted the original story for *To Be or Not to Be*; and his collaborator, Melchior Lengyel, modestly disclaimed credit for having exerted much input: "Writing for Lubitsch is just *kibitzing*."[33] The screenplay happens to be credited to Edwin Justus Mayer, whose merely workmanlike screenwriting career further warrants the assumption that Lubitsch's role was dominant.

Yet, however credits for the film are retrospectively allocated, the travails of a Polish acting troupe under German occupation are maddeningly difficult to recount. Indeed, "an hour later, or even if you've just seen it for the sixth time, I defy you to tell me the plot of *To Be or Not to Be*," Truffaut admitted. "It's absolutely impossible."[34] Co-produced by the ubiquitous Alexander Korda and released through United Artists, *To Be or Not to Be* opened on March 6, 1942. Two months earlier, the enchanting Carole Lombard, who was given top billing, had been killed in a plane crash. Having done the planning and production of the film before the United States entered the war, Lubitsch claimed that he wanted to expose "the miseries of Poland." A non-Jew had made *The Great Dictator* for the world's Jews. By contrast a Jew launched a satiric assault on Nazism not explicitly for the sake of his own threatened and slaughtered people but to affirm Polish sovereignty. The vulnerability of one segment of the population is thus downplayed, though the horror inflicted on Polish Jewry is not entirely effaced. The farce that is nevertheless at the heart of *To Be or Not to Be* struck some reviewers as a rather peculiar way to awaken sympathy in American audiences. "A lapse of taste" and "a callous comedy" were among the complaints; and the *New York Times* reviewer found himself "unable even remotely to comprehend the humor."[35]

For instance, the film opens with the Führer, strolling in Warsaw amid cries of "Heil, Hitler," responding with a rather self-deprecatory "Heil, myself." He turns out to be a Polish actor named Bronski pretending to be Hitler in order to ascertain how effective he might be in the stage production of an anti-Nazi play titled *Gestapo*. Audiences in America might not have been amused. But a couple of other examples signal the deeper problem that disturbed critics. A running joke in *To Be or Not to Be* is the vanity of Joseph Tura (Jack Benny), who keeps referring to himself as "that great actor" and even "that great, *great* Polish actor." Dressed up as a Nazi, Tura asks an oafish German colonel, known as "Concentration Camp" Ehrhardt, if he has heard of him. "I saw Joseph Tura on the stage once," goes the reply. "What he did to Shakespeare, we are doing to Poland." Admittedly, as film critic Richard Corliss noted, "There *is* a certain audacity in the equation of bad acting with genocide."[36] Rehearsing *Gestapo*, which the occupiers will quickly ban, the Polish troupe is well aware of what the subjugation of their country portends. Tura's wife, Maria (Carole Lombard), nevertheless cheerfully shows off the gorgeous dress that she will wear "in the concentration camp scenes." When Tura, this time pretending to be "Concentration Camp" Ehrhardt, meets Professor Alexander Siletsky, a spy for the Germans who has faked an identity as a Polish patriot, the faux colonel takes jocular pride in his nickname: "We do the concentrating, and the Poles do the camping."[37] The vanity that is being spoofed, so Lubitsch suggests, is no monopoly of theatrical folk; but such lines must have been chilling in 1942 and can be unsettling in retrospect as well.

So can a comedy about the bombing and subsequent occupation of Warsaw be viable? That is the question.

One answer is that, although *To Be or Not to Be* is punctuated with many farcical elements, the underlying horror of what German domination entails is never absent. The footage of what aerial bombardment can do to a city looks authentic and is certainly not played for laughs. Members of the Polski Theater listen on the radio to Hitler, and the hysterical voice is not Charlie Chaplin's. Even though the subject of the film is Polish subjugation, the helplessness of the Jews is not ignored. No one mentions them, but because the Polski Theater casts so many actors who overdo their roles, Greenberg (Felix Bressart) tells one of his colleagues, "What you are, I wouldn't eat."[38] The riposte ("I resent your calling me a ham!") was hardly necessary to establish Greenberg's ethnicity, though the film was released in the era that Henry Popkin first identified as the near-elimination of Jewish characters and Jewish names from the American screen. They had largely vanished (making *The Great Dictator* a striking exception). Greenberg gives Lubitsch's comedy its moral ballast, however. Played by an actor from East Prussia, the unassuming and poignant Greenberg barely utters more than twenty lines throughout *To Be or Not to Be*,[39] but he incarnates the terrible precariousness of Jewish life in 1942.

Rather than serving as a mere extra, a spear carrier, Greenberg dreams of playing Shylock, and three times utters his vindication of his own humanity. The third time, surrounded by German soldiers protecting the Führer during an official visit to Warsaw, Greenberg implores the Nazis, "Aren't we human? Have we not eyes? Have we not hands, organs, sense, dimensions, affections, passions?" He continues, "If you prick us, do we not bleed? If you tickle us, do we not laugh? If you poison us, do we not die? If you wrong us, shall we not revenge?" These famous lines have, of course, been slightly, subtly altered, so that the word "Jew" in Shakespeare's text has been excised.[40] Greenberg could therefore be speaking for his fellow Poles or for embattled humanity itself under the Nazi boot; but it seems undeniable that he is speaking for his fellow Jews as well. "What a Shylock you would have made!" another actor in the troupe exults, further expressing the wan hope that "we can carry spears again." The year 1942 marked the apogee of the German domination of the continent. Nine out of every ten Polish Jews would perish in the Holocaust, so that the odds of a real-life counterpart to an actor like Greenberg carrying a spear again, much less performing in *The Merchant of Venice*, were staggeringly remote. *To Be or Not to Be* nevertheless ends happily, with members of the troupe finding refuge in Shakespeare's own homeland. But film scholar Joel Rosenberg noticed that one of the Polish actors is missing: Greenberg.[41]

Yet it is Greenberg who makes the claim that in effect justifies *To Be or Not to Be*: "A laugh is nothing to be sneezed at." He is too morose, too beleaguered to laugh; "he has little to laugh about," as Rosenberg states in his astute analysis of the film. But on five different occasions, Greenberg makes the case for the value of comedy.[42] Indeed, whatever mirth Lubitsch's film generates is likely to be a nervous laughter, the sort of response that might well disturb the viewer even as it is exhilarating. Perhaps what ensures the artistic integrity of the movie is the sheer intricacy of the plot. What amazed Truffaut were the layers of concealment, the playacting that seems to confuse Nazis and Poles, spies and patriots, invaders and actors, so that even the most harmless of citizens—such as the members of the Polski Theater—can transform themselves into heroes. The artifice keeps the reality of suffering far enough away and somehow contrives to be so tactful that the frivolity does not offend.

Here the casting of Jack Benny helped. A beloved figure in vaudeville, Benny became a popular radio comedian by making himself rather than his stooges the butt of humor. He thus revolutionized the sitcom and deserves recognition as the Robespierre of radio comedy. But Benny was not much of an actor. He would have been manifestly inadequate as Hamlet. He is first seen in a Nazi uniform, saying "Heil, Hitler" (which in the course of the film he says five more times).[43] Not that the former Benjamin Kubelsky could have passed for a German; hailing from Waukegan, Illinois, he does not seem much like a Pole either. But Lubitsch wrote the screenplay with Benny in mind,[44] perhaps understanding that the comic dimension would not become too cringingly close to what German occupation meant for Poland.

Lubitsch had already satirized the Soviet Union with *Ninotchka* (1939), which reveals the mistrust, fear, and bleakness of life in Moscow. *To Be or Not to Be* constitutes an even more daring cinematic approach to the other version of totalitarianism, which is why he may have scattered too much black humor for audiences in 1942 to accept or absorb. The film did not catch fire at the box office, and United Artists wrote off *To Be or Not to Be* as a loss.[45] But the film managed, in the form of a perfectly paced comedy, to condemn the violation of Polish independence while still alluding to the ineffable plight of European Jewry.

Interregnum

Historians agree that what came to be called "Holocaust consciousness" is a postwar phenomenon. Lanzmann had belonged to a Communist resistance group during the war and won a decoration while fighting for the Maquis; after the release of *Shoah*, he was asked when he had learned of the systematic destruction of European Jewry. "Like everybody," he replied, "after the war. But this was an event of such scope and magnitude that nobody could immediately grasp the meaning."[46] The centrality of the Holocaust to the Western understanding of Nazism and of World War II can be dated no earlier than the middle or end of the 1960s, with two events in Israel—the trial of Adolf Eichmann and the Six-Day War—accelerating and reinforcing such awareness. Even the author of the most influential revisionist account of the genesis of Holocaust consciousness, Hasia R. Diner, does not deny the dramatic increase in representations of the Holocaust and the efforts to memorialize its victims by the end of the 1960s. Instead, her book shows the extent to which the internal institutions of American Jewry reckoned with the calamity and largely ignores the larger discourse in the nation's civic culture and popular arts.[47]

During those years the Cold War converted an enemy into an ally. Because the Federal Republic of Germany became integral to the Western alliance, the process of denazification (which was never very serious) was rapidly terminated and sensitivities had to be respected. Thus, when *Casablanca* (1942) was shown a decade later for the first time in West Germany, the film was heavily edited so that all the jokes told at the Nazis' expense were cut.[48] They nevertheless remained of interest to satirists—a task that Jews in particular assumed. For example, with the immediate past scrubbed for the sake of postwar geopolitics, the consoling myth of "the good German" made a tempting target. The Galician-born director and co-scenarist Billy Wilder, whose mother had perished at Auschwitz, mocked that myth in *One, Two, Three* (1961), when the experience of having been in "the underground" turns out to be nothing more heroic than taking the Berlin subway. In 1969 the Canadian Mordecai Richler turned up the heat in his novel *Cocksure*, which locates a British gentleman who, after the war, "had collected case histories and compiled a book, elegantly produced if necessarily slender, about all the charitable little acts done by Germans for Jews during the Nazi era. Here a simple but goodhearted sergeant offers spoonfuls of marmalade to Jewish children before they are led off to the gas chambers, somewhere else a fabled general refuses to drink with Eichmann or a professor quotes Heine right to a Nazi's face."[49] Woody Allen's "The Schmeed Memoirs" (1971) parodied the rationales of "the good German" who kept his head down. "I have been asked if I was aware of the moral implications of what I was doing," the Führer's clueless barber (!) recalls. "As I told the tribunal at Nuremberg, I did not know that Hitler was a Nazi. The truth was that for years I thought he worked for the phone company. When I finally found out what a monster he was, it was too late to do anything, as I had made a down payment on some furniture."[50]

One "good German" even became pivotal to the space race during the Cold War. He was not directly associated with the war against the Jews, though Wernher von Braun did belong to the SS and had used slave labor at his rocketry complex at Peenemünde. With the Holocaust itself off limits to satirists, he served nicely, as in Tom Lehrer's ditty about the "widows and cripples in old London town / Who owe their large pensions to Wernher von Braun." He had become the "big hero" who "learned to count backward to zero."[51] As Dr. Strangelove (Peter Sellers), who serves as scientific adviser to the president in Stanley Kubrick's eponymous black comedy, von Braun was lampooned as still a fervent Nazi. Kubrick threw elements of two Jewish strategists of deterrence, Herman Kahn and Henry Kissinger, into the portrayal of Dr. Strangelove as well. In 1960 Columbia Pictures released a biopic of von Braun, omitting the less savory aspects of the rocket engineer's career, titled *I Aim at the Stars* (1960). Mort Sahl is generally credited with suggesting an apt subtitle: *But I Hit London*. Although von Braun, who had developed the V-2 rocket, died before his complicity with Nazism was fully exposed, the secretary-general of the United Nations and president of Austria, Kurt Waldheim, was less lucky. He was forced to defend or correct his significant memory problems (including his length of service in the Wehrmacht), leading to wisecracks about "Waldheimer's disease." Such forgetfulness provoked the stand-up comedian Robert Klein to have Waldheim recall, "It vas 1941. I vas in Vienna. I vas drinking a cup of café *mit Schlag*. Suddenly it vas 1946."⁵²

For Jewish humorists and comedians, as for Jewish novelists, Nazism had to be rendered separable from the Holocaust itself. If the Holocaust was the subject, it could not be deemed funny; and if the point was to be funny, it couldn't be about the Holocaust. That wall was rarely breached. No comic novelist was more prodigiously gifted than Philip Roth. But when he decided to tackle the Holocaust, however peripherally, in *The Ghost Writer* (1979), the novella that he published is not a comic one. The French Jewish novelist Romain Gary imagined the dybbuk of a veteran of the Yiddish burlesque stage, murdered in Auschwitz in 1943, haunting his executioner in *The Dance of Genghis Cohn* (1968). Whatever its rather ambitious intentions, that novel is not funny either. An even stronger case for the persistence of this pattern was the film by a successor to the Three Stooges: Jerry Lewis. No stranger to tastelessness, Lewis had starred one day after Yom Kippur (the Day of Atonement) in 1959 in an NBC version of *The Jazz Singer*, in which he sang Kol Nidre (perhaps the most stirring prayer in Jewish liturgy, in which Jews ask God to release them from vows made in the previous year) in blackface. The slapstick that made him famous also elevated him, especially in France, to the rank of genius. (Perhaps 50 million Frenchmen *can* be wrong.) Lewis's admirers included his fellow auteurs Truffaut, Jean-Luc Godard (who considered Lewis an even greater comic artist than Chaplin), and Louis Malle. When Lewis died in 2017, it was front-page news in the daily newspaper *Libération*.⁵³ Speculation remains rife over his decision, more than half a century earlier, to take on the subject of the Holocaust.

The movie that Lewis planned to direct explored the predicament of a circus clown, Karl Schmidt, whom the SS forces to lead unsuspecting children into the gas chambers. The tale that inspired the film made the clown a non-Jew who is sent to Auschwitz after making the mistake of satirizing Hitler. Lewis turned Schmidt into a Jew and intended to play the lead. Lewis's research was diligent. "I went to Belsen, Dachau, and Auschwitz," he recalled. "I saw the killing camps, the sprinklers which unleashed Zyklon B, and I saw the nail scratchings on the walls."⁵⁴ *The Day the Clown*

Cried (1972) was shot partly in Paris and partly in Stockholm (where one of Ingmar Bergman's favorite actresses, Harriet Andersson, was cast). Filming the final scene "terrified" Lewis: "I stood there in my clown's costume, with the cameras ready. Suddenly the children were all around me, unasked, undirected, and they clung to my arms and legs, looking up at me so trustingly. . . . I thought, 'This is what my whole life is leading up to.'"[55] No cinematic culmination transpired, however. Lewis never finished post-production and got ensnarled in disputes over the legal rights to make the film at all. *The Day the Clown Cried* has never been released,[56] and whether it might have been a masterpiece may never be known. But it would not have been a comedy (any more than *Pagliacci* is a comedy); not even Lewis dared to cross that ring of fire.

The comedian who breached that barrier was, predictably, Lenny Bruce. In his nightclub act he could pretend to be a salesman, offering customers "a Volkswagen pickup truck that was just used slightly during the war carrying the people back and forth to the furnaces." (There was of course no "back," only "forth.") Before the malignant eruption of Holocaust denial posed a challenge to morality and memory and law, Bruce could hold up a fake newspaper blaring the headline "Six Million Jews Found Alive in Argentina." (Quite a card, that Lenny Bruce.) "Adolf Eichmann," a routine done in a German accent, announced, "My defense: I vas a soldier." (He wasn't; Eichmann belonged to the SS.) Channeling Eichmann, Bruce could claim to have seen Jews "turned into soap" (a process that never in fact happened). He also invited audiences to wonder if the crimes of the man in the glass booth were worse than unleashing atomic weaponry to kill "enemies at long distance." "Hiroshima *auf Wiedersehen*," he snarled. (If such a moral calculus is to be considered at all, the differences between the two lethal policies should be self-evident. Beginning at Guernica, all sides capable of bombing civilian populations did so; the Final Solution, however, was unprecedented.) Even outside the setting of a nightclub, Bruce somehow identified with the former *Obersturmbannführer*. In 1964, when a conviction for a misdemeanor (obscenity) might have led to incarceration on Rikers Island, Bruce told Judge John M. Murtagh, "I realize I come back before this court as Eichmann before a Jewish judge."[57] By then, however, the career of a lifetime was scuttled; he was moving into terrain entirely of his own. "I'm not a comedian," he proclaimed. "I'm Lenny Bruce."[58]

The posthumous influence that he exerted on other stand-up comedians has nevertheless been formidable. They have often wanted to be like him, rather than like, say, Sam Levenson. *The Sick Humor of Lenny Bruce* (1959), his first solo album, does exhibit a certain prescience and shrewdness. In "Hitler and the MCA," two German talent agents circa 1930 discover Hitler painting the walls at the office of the Music Corporation of America (MCA) while conducting auditions for the role of a new dictator ("Der Kaiser is oudt, he's haddit"). The house painter is recruited, and a star is born. Show business and politics, so goes the premise, are not easy to distinguish; and how they reach and manipulate the mass mind can disclose all sorts of troublesome similarities.[59] The world that Bruce knew best, however, and indeed the only world he knew, was not the web of civic institutions or the ways by which the consent of the governed is consolidated or blocked, but entertainment. Which brings us to Mel Brooks.

The Producers

The father of Mel Brooks (né Kaminsky) was born in Danzig, and the comedian's mother was born in Kiev. Those cities would become among the coordinates of World War II in which Brooks served in Europe. Early in the postwar era, he became a television writer and, like Chaplin earlier, had to educate himself. On his own Brooks read Gogol ("*Dead Souls* is a masterpiece"), Tolstoy, and Dostoevsky, novelists who "made me realize it's a bigger ball park than the *Bilko* show. Right from the moment I read them, I knew I wanted to achieve more than Doc Simon and Abe Burrows did. I wanted to be the American Molière."[60] (That sobriquet belongs instead to Doc Simon's younger playwright-brother Neil; but Brooks's ambition is laudatory.)

Restless while writing for television, Brooks conceived of a novel about "two schnooks" who concoct a Broadway scam—a deliberate flop to enable the pair to take the money and run from the bilked backers of the show. What failure could be more surefire than a musical that would celebrate Nazism? So the novel—and the certified, guaranteed loser of a Broadway play within it—was to be called *Springtime for Hitler*. Brooks then changed it to a screenplay, which took him about nine months to write. Then he decided to direct it, "in self-defense." Universal Studios was agreeable, but there was a catch: The film had to be titled *Springtime for Mussolini*. Brooks told the studio, "I think you missed the point."[61] Next, at Avco-Embassy, Joseph E. Levine warned the would-be director-screenwriter that no Jewish exhibitor would put the Führer's name on the marquee. So Brooks reluctantly settled for an anodyne title, *The Producers*.[62] Although Brooks would win an Oscar for the Best Screenplay of 1968, the reviewers who panned the film included such heavyweights as Renata Adler, Pauline Kael, Stanley Kauffmann, and Andrew Sarris. Somehow they experienced no catharsis watching a movie about a musical about the Third Reich. Perhaps even worse were the box office returns, especially west of New York—as Brooks quipped, *The Producers* "couldn't get across the George Washington Bridge."[63]

It took four years for the film to become profitable; and by then its loony centerpiece, consisting of the scenes from the musical, was on its way to becoming a comic classic. In the movie, *Springtime for Hitler* is based—quite loosely, presumably—on the unproducible play of the same name written by a goofy and unrepentant Nazi, Franz Liebkind. It is directed by the flamboyant transvestite Roger De Bris, who is fascinated to learn that Hitler had been the leader of Nazi Germany. De Bris's "private secretary" is Carmen Giya, who is the director's "aide-de-camp" (as Robert Brustein put it).[64] The hippie actor playing Hitler (Dick Shawn, who was Jewish) is named Lorenzo Saint DuBois (initials: L. S. D.). A chorus of dancing Storm Troopers in jackboots, filmed from above as though performing in a Busby Berkeley musical, croon the lilting title song, "Springtime for Hitler," in the formation of a swastika. Somehow a phrase like "over the top" doesn't seem adequate as a description of the explosively hilarious wackiness. To have accused *The Producers* of bad taste would have been beside the point, because bad taste is the very subject of the film. By intent and in content, *The Producers* is zanily overstated.

Yet for all the shocks it administers, the words *Jew* and *Jewish* are not heard on the soundtrack, though producer Max Bialystock (Zero Mostel) and his accountant, Leo Bloom (Gene Wilder), are quite obviously of that persuasion. Brooks thus takes delight in spoofing Nazis but stays completely clear of any reference to what they actually did to his co-religionists. He avoids juxtaposing humor and the Holocaust. Such uncharacteristic tact may help account for Brooks's evident admiration of *To Be or Not to Be*, which he remade—quite pointlessly—in 1983. Brooks also paid a sort of tribute to the tradition that Chaplin personified. Chaplin had made his last silent feature in 1936, exactly four decades before Brooks released *Silent Movie* (1976). But Brooks preferred to return to his own greatest triumph, transforming *The Producers* into a Broadway musical in 2001. This time the critics were rapturous; the show would also win a dozen Tony Awards. Audiences were willing to spend an unprecedented $100 to buy seats for "a gay romp with Adolf and Eva," with the former singing a solo called "Heil to Me." "Heil myself. Heil to me," the actor playing Hitler says, stealing shamelessly from *To Be or Not to Be*. When the two scam artists (Nathan Lane and Matthew Broderick) first meet Franz Liebkind, the startled playwright assures them, without prompting, "I vas never a member of the Nazi Party. I am not responsible. I only followed orders." What the Führer thought of *The Great Dictator* in 1940 will never be known. But Barry Blitt illustrated a cover for the *New Yorker* (May 7, 2001) that shows a scowling Hitler in the audience, while everyone around him is convulsed with laughter.

Five years later, when the 1968 film finally opened in Berlin, a reviewer for *Stern* reported that "people were applauding after the press screening. Some said there should have been more scenes from the *Springtime for Hitler* musical." In the spring of 2009, when the 2001 musical opened in Berlin, the *Berliner Morgenpost* asked, "Should one be allowed to laugh about Hitler?" The answer that came from the *Berliner Zeitung* was exculpatory: "People in Tel Aviv laughed." Some deference to sensitivities was nevertheless adopted in Berlin, where the swastikas that were displayed on Broadway were replaced by pretzels.[65] Universal adapted the Broadway musical for the screen in 2005. The movie recouped only $19 million of its $45 million cost,[66] an indication of diminishing returns. If the definition of humor can be reduced to "tragedy plus time," perhaps that time was expiring.

Yet Brooks himself defended *The Producers* in its various manifestations by insisting that "you can bring down totalitarian governments faster by using ridicule than you can with invective." He added that "if you stand on a soapbox," you miss the "only one way to get even" with Hitler. "You have to bring him down with ridicule."[67] This is delusionary. Ridicule didn't work when Hitler was alive and dangerous. *The Great Dictator* didn't bring down Hitler, nor did searing works like Picasso's *Guernica* (1937) or Brecht's *Furcht und Elend des Dritten Reiches* (1935–1938). Only military power, at an incalculable cost, could do so. Nor are gales of laughter likely to neutralize the enduring vestiges of neo-Nazism. Whether any work of art in any medium can satisfactorily capture the depravity of the Third Reich is an open question, or at least not a soluble one; and even whether memoirs and other first-person accounts of the Holocaust can do so is at least debatable. But it is doubtful whether anyone's life during those years was lengthened as a result of the release of comedies that were, like Chaplin's and Lubitsch's, among the greatest ever.

The obligation not to dishonor the memory of the victims of Nazism may, however, require brushing back against the transgressive tendencies to which even—or especially—the best satire is prone. Jokes can push up against the boundaries of decency and dignity. Perhaps, as Freud suspected, humor stems from a psychic need to discharge antisocial desires—to demean or to traduce the humanity of others. Such impulses, such violations of conscience, are proscribed outside the precincts of comedy. Therefore the expressiveness and creativity that mark humor at its best may be incompatible with the quest to acknowledge the catastrophe that befell European Jews or with the duty to grieve for them.

The indispensable need for comedy—even boundary-defying comedy—is compatible with the obligation, inherent in civilization itself, to acknowledge the degenerate barbarism that Nazism entailed. Fortunately, historical scholarship can be enlisted as an ally on the side of remembrance. Nazi Germany was certainly a "racial state," historian Dan Stone has recently declared; but its character cannot be reduced to or held synonymous with the policies of antisemitism, much less with the Final Solution itself. The ideological scope of Nazism was not unlimited, Stone warns, so that "the significance of race to the structure and functioning of the Third Reich [was] exaggerated."[68] One inference from his claim can thus be drawn: Nazism need not be fully equated with the lethal consequences of its racial hatred. Holocaust humor can thus be separated from satire of the Nazis. The latter makes it possible to honor the memory of the victims, whereas the former remains ethically problematic. The three comedies discussed here kept the systemic horror of the Holocaust offscreen and implicitly recognized the value of the taboo that prohibits the mockery of the murdered. Even when laughing at what the Reich represented, these films thus offer a critique that is both liberating and humane.

Notes

1. Ian Kershaw, *Hitler, 1936–45: Nemesis* (New York: Norton, 2000), 152–53.
2. Norman Cohn, *Warrant for Genocide* (New York: Harper & Row, 1967), 190.
3. Hannah Arendt, *Eichmann in Jerusalem: A Report on the Banality of Evil* (New York: Viking, 1964), 46.
4. "Kiddush Ha-Shem," *New Jewish Encyclopedia*, ed. David Bridger (New York: Behrman House, 1962), 268; Albert Speer, *Inside the Third Reich: Memoirs*, trans. Richard and Clara Winston (New York: Macmillan, 1970), 94, 123.
5. Will Durant, *Caesar and Christ* (New York: Simon & Schuster, 1944), 387; Henri Bergson, "Laughter," in Wylie Sypher, ed., *Comedy* (Baltimore: Johns Hopkins University Press, 1980), 150, 187, 188; Sigmund Freud, *The Basic Writings of Sigmund Freud*, ed. A. A. Brill (New York: Modern Library, 1938), 692–98.
6. Kenneth S. Lynn, *Mark Twain and Southwestern Humor* (Boston: Little, Brown, 1960), 30; William Keough, *Punchlines: The Violence of American Humor* (New York: Paragon House, 1990), xi, xxii.
7. Andrew Sullivan, "A Right to Live," *New York Times Book Review*, 27 November 2016, p. 22.
8. Naomi Seidman, "Elie Wiesel and the Scandal of Jewish Rage," *Jewish Social Studies*, n.s., 3, no. 1 (1996): 2.
9. Harry Zohn, *Karl Kraus* (New York: Frederick Ungar, 1971), 127.
10. Eberhard Jäckel, *Hitler's Weltanschauung: A Blueprint for Power*, trans. Herbert Arnold (Middletown, CT: Wesleyan University Press, 1972), 48, 59, 66.
11. "The 100 Greatest Comedies," www.bbc.com/culture/story/20170821-the-100-greatest-comedies-of-all-time [accessed 23 August 2017].
12. Quoted in Lawrence J. Epstein, *The Haunted Smile: The Story of Jewish Comedians in America* (New York: Public Affairs, 2001), 100–101; Ken Sutak, *Cinema Judaica: The War Years, 1939–1949* (New York: Hebrew Union College, Jewish Institute of Religion Museum, 2012), 11, 29–30; and David Marc, "The Three Stooges," *Shmate: A Journal of Progressive Jewish Thought* 1 (summer 1983): 22.
13. J. Hoberman, "The First 'Jewish' Superstar: Charlie Chaplin," in J. Hoberman and Jeffrey Shandler, eds., *Entertaining America: Jews, Movies, and Broadcasting* (Princeton, NJ: Princeton University Press, 2003), 34–39; Jeffrey Vance, *Chaplin: Genius of the Cinema* (New York: Harry N. Abrams, 2003), 225, 228, 234, 240.
14. David Robinson, *Chaplin: His Life and Art* (New York: McGraw-Hill, 1985), 489.
15. Charles Chaplin, *My Autobiography* (New York: Simon & Schuster, 1964), 392; Vance, *Chaplin*, 236; Kenneth S. Lynn, *Charlie Chaplin and His Times* (New

York: Simon & Schuster, 1997), 395; Steven J. Ross, *Hollywood Left and Right: How Movie Stars Shaped American Politics* (New York: Oxford University Press, 2011), 37, 38.

16. Chaplin, *My Autobiography*, 391–92.
17. Garson Kanin, "Paradoxical Sir Tramp," *New York Times Book Review*, 10 November 1985, p. 60; and Vance, *Chaplin*, 236.
18. Vance, *Chaplin*, 236, 237, 246, 250; Joyce Milton, *Tramp: The Life of Charlie Chaplin* (New York: Harper Collins, 1996), 381; Lynn, *Charlie Chaplin*, 404; Glenn Mitchell, "*The Tramp and the Dictator* Reviewed," in Frank Scheide, Hooman Mehran, and Dan Kamin, eds., *Chaplin: The Dictator and the Tramp* (London: British Film Institute, 2004), 51.
19. Vance, *Chaplin*, 241.
20. Vance, *Chaplin*, 240.
21. Claude Lanzmann, *Shoah: An Oral History of the Holocaust* (New York: Pantheon, 1985), 111–17.
22. Geoffrey H. Hartman, "The Cinema Animal," in Yosefa Loshitzky, ed., *Spielberg's Holocaust: Critical Perspectives on Schindler's List* (Bloomington: Indiana University Press, 1997), 63.
23. Chaplin, *My Autobiography*, 392.
24. Milton, *Tramp*, 377, 378; Robinson, *Chaplin*, 499.
25. Milton, *Tramp*, 380; Lynn, *Charlie Chaplin*, 400.
26. Chaplin, *My Autobiography*, 399.
27. Annie Linskey, "Don't Expect Congress to Take Action on Mass Shootings," *Boston Globe*, 3 October 2017, p. A1.
28. Henry James, *Letters to A. C. Benson and Auguste Monod*, ed. E. F. Benson (New York: Charles Scribner's Sons, 1930), 35; François Truffaut, *The Films in My Life*, trans. Leonard Mayhew (New York: Simon & Schuster, 1978), 55, 56.
29. Milton, *Tramp*, 453.
30. Scott Eyman, *Ernst Lubitsch: Laughter in Paradise* (New York: Simon & Schuster, 1993), 15.
31. Eyman, *Ernst Lubitsch*, 293.
32. Eyman, *Ernst Lubitsch*, 249, 311.
33. Eyman, *Ernst Lubitsch*, 290.
34. Truffaut, *Films in My Life*, 52; Joel Rosenberg, "Shylock's Revenge: The Doubly Vanished Jew in Ernst Lubitsch's *To Be or Not to Be*," *Prooftexts* 16 (September 1996): 234.
35. Eyman, *Ernst Lubitsch*, 301, 302.

36. Richard Corliss, *Talking Pictures: Screenwriters in the American Cinema* (New York: Penguin, 1975), 305.
37. Epstein, *Haunted Smile*, 102.
38. Rosenberg, "Shylock's Revenge," 212.
39. Henry Popkin, "The Vanishing Jew of Our Popular Culture: The Little Man Who Is No Longer There," *Commentary* 14 (July 1952): 46–55; Rosenberg, "Shylock's Revenge," 209.
40. Gerd Gemünden, "Space Out of Joint: Ernst Lubitsch's *To Be or Not to Be*," *New German Critique* 89 (spring–summer 2003): 71–73.
41. Sutak, *Cinema Judaica*, 36–37; Thomas Doherty, "Hollywood's Other Great Anti-Nazi Movie," *Tablet*, 14 July 2017, http://www.tabletmag.com/jewish-arts-and-culture/235331/hollywood-anti-nazi-ernst-lubitsch [accessed 14 July 2017]; Annette Insdorf, *Indelible Shadows: Film and the Holocaust* (New York: Random House, 1983), 61; Rosenberg, "Shylock's Revenge," 235.
42. Rosenberg, "Shylock's Revenge," 219, 222.
43. Epstein, *Haunted Smile*, 101.
44. Irving A. Fein, *Jack Benny: An Intimate Biography* (New York: G. P. Putnam's Sons, 1976), 86.
45. James Harvey, *Romantic Comedy in Hollywood from Lubitsch to Sturges* (New York: Knopf, 1987), 481; Gemünden, "Space Out of Joint," 77.
46. Claude Lanzmann, interview with Edward Grossman, "Magnificent Obsession," *Jerusalem Post Magazine*, 27 June 1986, p. 8.
47. Hasia R. Diner, *We Remember with Reverence and Love: American Jews and the Myth of Silence After the Holocaust, 1945–1962* (New York: New York University Press, 2009), 372–75.
48. Noah Isenberg, *We'll Always Have Casablanca: The Life, Legend, and Afterlife of Hollywood's Most Beloved Movie* (New York: Norton, 2017), 156–57.
49. Mordecai Richler, *Cocksure* (New York: Bantam, 1969), 30.
50. Woody Allen, *Getting Even* (New York: Warner Paperback Library, 1972), 22.
51. Tom Lehrer, *Too Many Songs by Tom Lehrer* (New York: Pantheon, 1981), 124.
52. Epstein, *Haunted Smile*, 225.
53. Shawn Levy, *King of Comedy: The Life and Art of Jerry Lewis* (New York: St. Martin's, 1996), 241–43; Agnès C. Poirier, "Why France Understood Jerry Lewis as America Never Did," *New York Times*, 21 August 2017, p. C5.
54. Epstein, *Haunted Smile*, 123; Levy, *King of Comedy*, 377.
55. Levy, *King of Comedy*, 378–79.

56. Levy, *King of Comedy*, 380; Chris Fujiwara, *Jerry Lewis* (Urbana: University of Illinois Press, 2009), 8.
57. Quoted in Epstein, *Haunted Smile*, 171; and in Ronald K. L. Collins and David M. Skover, *Lenny Bruce: The Fall and Rise of an American Icon* (Naperville, IL: Sourcebooks, 2002), 145, 293.
58. Keough, *Punchlines*, 173; Collins and Skover, *Lenny Bruce*, 23.
59. William Karl Thomas, *Lenny Bruce: The Making of a Prophet* (Tucson: Media Maestro, 2000), 38, 40, 111; J. Hoberman, "When the Nazis Became Nudniks," *New York Times*, 15 April 2001, p. 24; Kirsten Fermaglich, "Mel Brooks' *The Producers*: Tracing American Jewish Culture Through Comedy, 1967–2007," *American Studies* 48 (winter 2007): 62.
60. Brad Darrach, "Playboy Interview: Mel Brooks," *Playboy* (February 1975): 61.
61. Darrach, "Playboy Interview: Mel Brooks," 63.
62. Kenneth Tynan, *Show People: Profiles in Entertainment* (New York: Simon & Schuster, 1979), 245; Ralph Rosenblum and Robert Karen, *When the Shooting Stops . . . the Cutting Begins* (New York: Penguin, 1980), 195.
63. Hoberman, "When the Nazis Became Nudniks," 1; Darrach, "Playboy Interview: Mel Brooks," 64.
64. Tynan, *Show People*, 247; Robert Brustein, "A Delayed Revenge on Hitler and Hollywood," *Forward*, 24 January 2003, p. 11.
65. "No Comment Department," *New Yorker*, 82 (31 July 2006): 81; Michael Kimmelman, "The Führer Returned to Berlin, This Time Saluted Only by Laughs," *New York Times*, 18 May 2009, p. C1; Nathan Burstein, "Mel Brooks's 'Nazis' March on Berlin," *Forward*, 24 April 2009, p. 2.
66. Fermaglich, "Mel Brooks' *The Producers*," 80.
67. Maurice Yacowar, *Method in Madness: The Comic Art of Mel Brooks* (New York: St. Martin's, 1981), 81; Leon Wieseltier, "Less Than Zero," *New Republic* 224 (28 May 2001): 50.
68. Dan Stone, "Nazi Race Ideologues," *Patterns of Prejudice* 50 (September–December 2016): 446, 448.

BREAKING TABOOS

Nebbishes, New Jews, and Humor

The Changing Image of American Jewish Masculinity Post-Holocaust

Jennifer Caplan

> I would like to thank my research assistant Kira Stern for her invaluable help in composing this essay, as well as Deborah Barer, Barry Gittlen, Sarah Oliver, and Carl Yamamoto for their guidance.

"If God exists, why is there so much evil in the world? Why were there Nazis?"

"How the hell do I know why there were Nazis? I don't know how the can opener works."

Hannah and Her Sisters

LAURA LEVITT ONCE WROTE, "No event informs the narrative of 20th-century Jewish history more than the Holocaust."[1] That the Holocaust altered every facet of Jewish life, both in Europe and abroad, is as close to an inarguable statement as might exist when discussing Jews. In this essay I focus on one particular element of Jewish life: the presentation and reception of Jewish masculinity. I argue that in the decades following World War II many prominent Jewish performers, specifically comedians, presented differing and sometimes competing versions of modern Jewish masculinity, all of which owed something to the lasting psychosocial impact of the Holocaust. The Holocaust left Jews desperate to escape the conception of them as consummate victims, and throughout the 1950s and 1960s Jewish writers, artists, and performers all sought to put forth new narratives of Jewish strength and agency. Few went as far as Leon Uris and the Jewish superheroes he created for *Exodus*, but many if not most Jewish artists of the postwar period ended up establishing new visions of Jewish strength and power. In addition, because of the specific ways in which World War II and the Holocaust altered the American landscape for Jews, Jewish men in particular found themselves with a much more open field on which to play out their construction of gender. I focus on Lenny Bruce and Woody Allen to highlight two poles of this new Jewish masculinity and show not only the cultural forces that made their seemingly opposite portrayals possible but also the ways in which they each sought to counter pre-Holocaust conceptions of Jewish masculinity with their unique types of subversions.

Long-standing images of Jews as passive and helpless pushed some Jews to embrace hypermasculine or athletic Jewish heroes, whereas others felt more comfortable with an acerbic wit or ironic barb, especially when pointed at antisemites or others seen as obstacles to Jewish success. Both approaches, however, had the Holocaust in their DNA, because they were both attempts at an "I'll never be passive again" mentality (with apologies to Scarlett). The two visions of Jewish masculinity that I discuss here are therefore much more closely linked than they might appear. If you are still seeing Nazis as the enemy (and both Bruce and Allen at times use Nazis in their humor), then you fight them with whatever you have, whether that is physical strength, intelligence, sarcasm, or slapstick.

The Holocaust and humor have often overlapped. Before, during, and after the Holocaust, Jews made jokes about Nazis, about Hitler, and about antisemitism. Mel Brooks famously said of Hitler, "You have to bring him down with ridicule, because if you stand on a soapbox and you match him with rhetoric, you're just as bad as he is, but if you can make people laugh at him, then you're one up on him. It's been one of my lifelong jobs—to make the world laugh at Adolf Hitler."[2] That approach became one of the ways Jewish comedians in the 1950s and 1960s could reassert themselves as human beings and (largely) as men.[3] Bruce and Allen represent the many different ways comedians performed their idea of what a Jewish man is, or should be, and in doing so, they won their "posthumous victories" over Hitler and the antisemitic establishment that had sought to demean and define Jewish men (and women) for so long.

Pre-Holocaust Jewish Masculinity

American antisemitism was at an all-time high in the years between World War I and World War II. As Eric Goldstein argues, "Jews increasingly became a target for those nervous about the direction of modern American culture.... By the early 1920s, Jews were held responsible for a variety of the country's modern evils."[4] Jews were seen, by some, as the most dangerous group in America because they could so easily "pass" and therefore infiltrate American life. Gender theorist Michael Kimmel argues that in the early twentieth century Jews were seen as "less manly. The Jew was effeminate, bookish, and conniving; he got his way insidiously by passing himself off as a real man, and thereby sabotaging the purity of the race."[5] After World War II, however, much of this anti-Jewish sentiment was quieted, though not eliminated. The new image of the Jew, as the perfect victim of Hitler and the Final Solution, may have evoked pity more than suspicion, but it was just as damaging. This sense of Jews as weak, fearful, ineffective, and unable to defend themselves interacted with much, much older images of Jews, especially Jewish men, as weak, effeminate, and passive.[6] This was especially frustrating to the many Jewish men who served in World War II. As Deborah Dash Moore writes, "Fighting for their country empowered American Jews. In the armed services they came to identify with America and its ideals."[7] Jews who saw themselves as patriotic Americans were faced with the pervasive idea that American involvement in World War II was a result of Jews' inability to defend themselves or fight on their own.

Simultaneously (and seemingly incommensurately) Jewish men were seen as being lascivious seducers of innocent Gentile women. This image of Jewish men as sexually dangerous was part of the racialization of Jews during the Progressive Era in the United States. Journalist Tom Watson wrote in 1915 that "the black man's lust after the white woman is not much fiercer than the lust of the licentious Jew for the gentile."[8] Jews were seen as seducers of white women through their sneakiness, their wiliness, or often through their money. When one pushes this a little harder, it becomes clear that the tension between the sexually threatening Jew and the emasculated Jew is less than it originally appeared. Unlike the way black masculinity was being conceived—that is, as physically powerful—Jewish men were seducing women through "softer" means, such as money and trickery. Both types of men were a threat, but the Jewish threat was sometimes viewed as more perfidious, because it was harder to spot. Jewish men were thought of as inherently untrustworthy, especially around women, because they were such skilled manipulators.

One popular embodiment of this stereotype can be seen in the characters portrayed by Julius (aka Groucho) Marx. Each of the Marx Brothers had a distinct, larger-than-life personality that took them from vaudeville to Hollywood. Chico was the felonious immigrant, Harpo was a mute and child-like clown, and Groucho was the suave, fast-talking con man who spent the film trying to seduce some heiress or wealthy widow, usually played by the very non-Jewish Margaret Dumont. The Marx Brothers were among the most famous and prolific film stars of the 1930s, producing nearly a film a year, so many Americans saw and experienced their performances. Groucho, as the leader, seemed to embody the exact stereotype Watson and others had been warning people about. He was slick, erudite, and urbane and dazzled Gentile women through his facility with language and manipulation. Take, for example, the opening of *Duck Soup* in which Groucho's Rufus T. Firefly meets Dumont's Mrs. Teasdale.

> FIREFLY: Not that I care, but where is your husband?
> MRS. TEASDALE: Why, he's dead.
> FIREFLY: I'll bet he's just using that as an excuse.
> MRS. TEASDALE: I was with him to the very end.
> FIREFLY: Hmmph. No wonder he passed away.
> MRS. TEASDALE: I held him in my arms and kissed him.
> FIREFLY: Oh, I see. Then, it was murder. Will you marry me? Did he leave you any money? Answer the second question first.
> MRS. TEASDALE: He left me his entire fortune.
> FIREFLY: Is that so? Can't you see what I'm trying to tell you? I love you! [jumps into her arms]
> MRS. TEASDALE: Oh, your Excellency!
> FIREFLY: You're not so bad yourself.[9]

In the performance of the scene Groucho speaks so quickly that Mrs. Teasdale can hardly catch her breath between his questions and professions of love. He spins her around with his rhetoric and attempts to seduce her through his frenetic speech. Despite conforming to some of the most insidious antisemitic tropes of their era, the Marx Brothers were, nonetheless, actually quite subversive. They included little hints of Jewish references in an era when the censors were eagle-eyed for any hint of religion, politics, or sex. Groucho has been described as "the eternal outcast, removed from his working-class background, but retaining a proletariat disdain for elite behavior. His battle cry, 'Whatever it is, I'm against it,' can be seen as both an attack on unduly held power and as anarchic expression of distrust of any form of social or political organization."[10] They demonstrated a sort of guerilla class warfare in which the ragtag brothers always prevail over the wealthy (and WASPy) establishment.[11]

Therefore, while the rest of the country was becoming more "manly" as the phenomenon of muscular Christianity spread, "American Jews were far less invested in physical strength and ruggedness, spent much less time and energy complaining about women and the 'feminization' of religion, and rarely embraced the 'barbarian virtues' that Teddy Roosevelt, G. Stanley Hall, and others trumpeted as essential for American men."[12] Groucho's portrayal is in some ways a "if you can't beat 'em"–type compromise. "Be what they expect you to be," his performance seems to say, "because then they won't notice when you tweak their noses." Muscular Christianity and, moreover, the subtle influence of Christian hegemony, put Jews in a position where they could never quite seem to match mainstream gender expectations. Jewish familial and religious expectations were simply at odds with Christian trends. Family religion had become primarily a (Christian) woman's obligation as early as the Second Great Awakening. It was up to the wife to keep her husband's soul protected and to drag recalcitrant children to church on Sundays. But rabbis worried that this trend would have disastrous results on the Jewish home. Jenna Weissman Joselit recounts an interwar rabbi who "roundly criticized the Jewish father for his inattentiveness. . . . The decision to leave matters of faith and ritual entirely in the hands of one's wife was sure to have a chilling effect on the next generation, especially in the case of young boys. . . . Fathers, faced with the prospect of an entirely feminized Judaism, were exhorted to assume their rightful place in the pews of the synagogue and at the Sabbath dinner table."[13] Jewish and Christian family values were therefore at odds. Jewish religious leaders believed the feminization of Judaism would come from men not being involved enough with child rearing and the religious lives of their families, whereas the dominant trend was toward fathers who spent increasingly little time with their children or in church. "Buried even deeper than the political, military, and economic policies and actions of Christian institutions and individuals there seems to be a dominant Christian worldview which has shaped Western culture so profoundly that it is difficult to delineate fully," according to Paul Kivel.[14] Because of this subtle yet pervasive Christian hegemony and the growth of a certain masculine ideal associated with the American Christian, Jews were relegated to a second-class masculinity that was in most ways seen as opposed to rugged American manliness.

Naomi Seidman further describes the complicated relationship between Jewish men and Western idealized masculinity that Kivel and others are trying to articulate. Seidman argues that the primary method of countering anti-Jewish stereotypes was not to claim that Jews were every bit as manly as their Christian counterparts but instead to rethink what was valuable in the performance of masculinity: "Thus, what appeared as a pathetic lack of virility, an inability or unwillingness to work productively and provide for one's family, or (in Freud's Vienna) an incapacity for 'scientific objectivity,' is now marked as a coherent value system, in which nonviolence, early marriage, and Torah learning are prized over and against heroic, romantic (or celibate), and economic Christian/European ideals of masculine behavior."[15]

For obvious reasons, this perceived "pathetic lack of virility" did not sit well with many Jews. During the roughly two decades immediately following the end of World War II two primary camps emerged in American Jewish popular culture that attempted to disrupt this passive image of Jewish masculinity in different ways. One was hypermasculine, and the other was emphatically not. Comedy clubs may not have been where scholars were arguing over the theological soul of Judaism, but they were where some people were getting their cues about what it meant to be an American Jew, specifically, a male one. David Kaufman argued that "a newly assertive Jewishness had entered the American public sphere, fostered by the radical notion that one could succeed in America, could become an insider—*as an outsider*, that is, while retaining one's identity as a Jewish *other*. This pointed message was conveyed by a specific medium: the public images and popular representations of certain famous Jews."[16]

Post-Holocaust Jewish Masculinity

Judaism has long had a different and more complicated relationship to gender than much of the rest of the West. According to Kaufman, "Manhood is a fraught subject for Jews, torn between traditional Jewish ideals of male gentility and scholarliness on the one hand, and modern Western ideals of male power and competitiveness on the other."[17] Not only have Western anti-Jewish sentiments frequently resulted in depictions of Jewish men as effeminate and Jewish women as excessively masculine, but Judaism, religiously, has a more polyvalent notion of gender than many would credit an ancient monotheistic tradition with having. As antisemitism shifted from public and blatant to subtle and behind-the-scenes, comedians used many techniques to continue to keep Jews and "Jewish sensibilities" in the spotlight.[18] Stand-up comedy was also changing, from the old "Take my wife, please" joke tellers and one-liners to hipsters and cool cats who were basing their performances on politics and current events and who told stories instead of jokes.

One of these new comedians was Lenny Bruce, who began performing in nightclubs in 1957. His brash, gutter-dwelling, violent performance of masculinity is a sort of admixture of Leon Uris's heroic *Exodus*-type Jewish man and Norman Mailer's "white negro" hipster figure. As Uris said in 1958, "We Jews are not what we have been portrayed to be. In truth, we have been fighters."[19] Bruce takes the aggressive fight of Uris and combines it with what Mailer called "the American existentialist" in his 1957 manifesto. Mailer's "white negro" is

> the hipster, the man who knows that if our collective condition is to live with instant death by atomic war, relatively quick death by the State as *l'univers concentrationnaire*, or with a slow death by conformity with every creative and rebellious instinct stifled (at what damage to the mind and the heart and the liver and the nerves no research foundation for cancer will discover in a hurry), if the fate of twentieth century man is to live with death from adolescence to premature senescence, why then the only life-giving answer is to accept the terms of death, to live with death as immediate

danger, to divorce oneself from society, to exist without roots, to set out on that uncharted journey into the rebellious imperatives of the self.[20]

Bruce is aggressive and doesn't back down from a fight, but he is also part of this existentialist underground described by Mailer. Mailer's reference to the "concentration universe" is particularly telling here. Mailer demonstrates that the image of the concentration camp, and its expansion into the universe of oppression, highlights the way the Holocaust is there, lurking in the background of this countercultural mind-set. Mailer's white negro is rebelling not only against the idea that a Jewish man must be a certain type of meek intellectual but also against the entire modern mechanization of death and the anomie of contemporary existence. Mailer did not have Bruce specifically in mind when he wrote his essay; the timing does not really allow for that possibility. But Bruce is nevertheless just the type of antisocial, anticonformist urbanite Mailer is describing.

On the other end of the spectrum is Woody Allen's "new nebbish" type. Traditionally, the nebbish was nothing anyone would be proud to be, but Allen's version of the nebbish managed to be a sexually successful Everyman-type hero.[21] He may still be a victim of circumstance, but he is not pathetic in the same way Jews were perceived to be immediately after World War II.[22] Allen's persona was neither aggressive nor hip. He was generally rumpled, out of step, awkward, and milquetoast. But he was smart, sardonic, persistent, and, most important, funny. Funny became the new sexy, and the idea that "a good sense of humor" is what women really want made comedians rush in where previously only leading men dared to tread. Both ends of the spectrum demonstrate the way that Jewish comedians in the 1950s and 1960s were attempting to redefine what it meant to be both masculine and Jewish in America.

Bruce and Allen's Performative Masculinity

In his routine "The Difference Between Men and Women," Bruce talks at length about what men are.[23] The best-known recording of this routine comes from Bruce's Berkeley concert in December 1965 (although the recording was not released until several years later). Bruce died less than a year after this performance, and as with many of Bruce's late-career performances, it is a mixture of what is clearly a planned and rehearsed central idea over and through which he wanders and meanders in a semi-improvisational, at times rambling manner. Men, in Bruce's routine, are both physically and sexually aggressive. The routine discusses blood and grievous injury and sex all in the same breath. It is actually an intervention into many of the oldest images of Jewish masculinity and sexuality. The male character in Bruce's routine is aggressively sexual, even at the expense of bodily harm or pain. The Jewish lech woos women away through guile and manipulation, but Bruce's man is all action, with no subtlety or wooing in sight. Bruce maintains that "no guy ever cheated on his wife" because cheating, he argues, is an emotional act. It involves "kissing and hugging and LIKING SOMEBODY"; to cheat, you must have feelings. Men, he is arguing, have no feelings when it comes to sex and will simply take any opportunity, no matter how inopportune, for sexual gratification.

Although in his routine Bruce is discussing men, and not Jewish men per se, that it is a Jewish male body standing in front of the audience speaking these words is not without meaning. Bruce is performing a similar sort of subversion to what Groucho had done decades before; he is leaning into the image of the lascivious and hypersexual Jew but doing it in a way that denies the antisemite the power to use those qualities against him. Sander Gilman, in his classic *The Jew's Body*, argues that the mark of circumcision, common now but until a few decades ago seen by many non-Jews as a form of genital mutilation, made "the Jew the representation of the male as outsider, the act of circumcision marking the Jewish male as sexually apart, as anatomically different."[24] Gilman goes on to say that throughout the early modern period there was "constant and purposeful confusion" between circumcision and castration.[25] What this has created, over time, is a cultural sense of unease with Jewish bodies, especially Jewish male bodies. Bruce's presentation of manhood only heightens that unease through its transgressive violence.

Bruce calls men animals, saying that even lying bleeding in an ambulance, limbs severed and semiconscious, a man will become sexually aroused by a nurse's uniform and attempt to make sexual advances on her. Although what Bruce is projecting is hardly what we might call a healthy or enlightened sexual attitude, it is nevertheless subversive in its refusal to conform to existing societal expectations of Jewish sexuality. Men on a desert island, Bruce says, will "do it to mud." This evokes not only subversive sexuality but also Mary Douglas's ideas about purity and impurity. Douglas argued that "ideas about separating, purifying, demarcating, and punishing transgressions have as their main function to impose system on an inherently untidy experience. It is only by exaggerating the difference between within and without, above and below, male and female, with and against that a semblance of order is created."[26] Bruce is intuitively tapping into the very taboo crossing that Douglas wrote about. Sex and mud are both transgressive, and they make a society (and those members of a society who are concerned with maintaining the status quo) feel vulnerable and uneasy, because sex and mud together are messy and out of place. Mud has its place, and sex has its place, but their place is not together and this sort of pollution upsets a well-balanced society.[27]

Judith Butler writes about the problems created when bodies transgress sexually, or disrupt society's notions of what is proper, or safe, sexual activity. In *Gender Trouble* she argues that "the construction of stable bodily contours relies upon fixed sites of corporeal permeability and impermeability.... The deregulation of such exchanges accordingly disrupts the very boundaries that determine what it is to be a body at all."[28] By combining aggressive Jewish male sexuality with transgressive sexual encounters, such as those involving blood, severed limbs, broken glass, or mud, Bruce evokes images that are, in a word, icky. But they are icky in specific ways. Douglas and Butler are arguing that there are primal taboos, especially around sex and pollution, that hold us together as a civilization. And when Bruce smashes through them so completely, he creates a sense of titillation and danger to which his audience responds positively.

At the end of the routine Bruce even begins to subvert heteronormativity itself to some extent. His final binary comparison is that men are like dogs and women are like cats. Women end a relationship, and that is it. It is over. Men, he says, don't get that. Men are like dogs you can yell at or even beat and they will keep slinking back to you with their tail between their legs. Women, he says, are like cats because you can look at one cross-eyed and you'll never see it again. So in the end Bruce says that women actually want men who act like women, who can understand the emotional side of relationships, and that when that ends, the relationship ends. In the final seconds of the bit Bruce brings up the possibility that masculinity, at least as he is constructing it, may not even be a useful or desirable attribute.

Similarly, in his Carnegie Hall concert in 1961, Bruce talks about the difference between the way "faggots" and "dykes" are perceived.[29] Faggot comedians, he claims, are well known. He says that because of people like Milton Berle, who does "heavyweight transvestite humor," gay men have been introduced to small town America.[30] "So they're all hip to faggots in these towns," Bruce says, "but they're not hip to dykes! Consequently, in these towns lesbians get away with murder, because the townspeople are not aware of them!" Lesbians, he claims, fly under the radar as "tomboys" or women who can hit a baseball as well as a man. He does not seem to be using either "faggot" or "dyke" as a pejorative term, and it is unclear whether the audience takes them as such. The use of "faggot" here appears to be as much in the service of disruption and provocation as any actual homophobic agenda. Bruce even goes as far as to say that the definition of "homosexual" needs to be clarified, because if it is anyone who has engaged in homosexual behavior, then all men are homosexual. "Men," he says, "are carnal. You put a guy in the joint for fifteen years, he'll schtupp anything; mud!" As in "The Difference Between Men and Women," Bruce focuses on the transgressive and nonspecific nature of men's sexual desires. He ends up circling a sort of Butlerian performance of gender that involves men behaving more like women and women behaving like men. Throughout his relatively short career, Bruce devoted a lot of energy to subverting the categories of men and women, gay and straight, through both sexual relationships and gender presentation. Bruce spent most of his career in a culturally liminal state somewhere between Mailer's late 1950s "white Negro" and the "free love" counterculture of the late 1960s and 1970s. Bruce's brief career, therefore, is one of our best case studies into how the Baby Boom generation pushed further and further away from the ethics of their World War II–era parents.

Bruce was not performing his subversion in a vacuum. This period of the late 1960s saw several performers rise to prominence, and they all performed interventions into the traditional narrative of Jewish masculinity. No one is a better example of the curious embracing and reimagining of the nebbish that was happening in the 1960s than Woody Allen. The reimagining of the nebbish was more revolutionary than it might seem because the traditional nebbish was ontologically a loser. He was a cautionary tale. He was a warning to Jews that if they give up their political autonomy, they will become beasts of burden for European heads of state, who will only use and abuse them. The nebbish is one of the stock types of Yiddish literature, along with characters such as the *schnorrer, gonif, schlemiel,* and *schlimazel,* and in their original Yiddish literary form none of these characters were remotely aspirational.

But in the 1960s several Jewish performers and writers began to present new nebbishes, who, while still being weak, effeminate, intellectual, and ineffectual, could nevertheless be sexually successful and able to seduce women who would seem far out of their league. *Annie Hall* obviously gets held up as the nebbish's finest hour, but he was just as present in the writing of Philip Roth, the comedy of Jerry Stiller, or any of those who followed in the 1970s and 1980s, from Paul Reiser to Richard Lewis to Jerry Seinfeld. The dominant trend in trying to reclaim Jewish male sexuality was to lean into the nebbish type while also creating a space where the little guy gets the girl. In some ways, although this was and is an ongoing trend, it is an easier stance to take than the one Bruce took. It is able to acknowledge and even reify certain stereotypes to therefore fight a one-front war, so to speak. These men can still be neurotic, awkward, uncomfortable, and even unattractive, but something in their wit and their mind attracts women, especially non-Jewish women, anyway. In fact, this is not far from coming out and acknowledging that Tom Watson's antisemitic screed from 1915 was actually correct. These Jewish men *are* coming for Gentile women; they are just wooing them with subtle wiles and not physical prowess.

Allen created a persona who was able to highlight his own nebbish qualities while still coming out on top. Allen used to tell a joke during his stand-up routine about how he got hired to do a vodka ad. He describes the company as originally trying to get Noël Coward, who was busy removing the music and lyrics from *My Fair Lady* to turn it back into *Pygmalion.* They then tried to get Laurence Olivier and Haleloke (Kahauolopua), and eventually found their way to Allen. "And," he says "you know how they got my name? It was on a list in Eichmann's pocket when they picked him up."[31] Allen's ability to both mock himself and, in a subtle way, evoke the

Holocaust itself while still highlighting the fact that he ended up in this "big ad" (it was a magazine campaign for Smirnoff) is precisely emblematic of what the new nebbish is all about. He is simultaneously a winner and a loser. He ends up booking the ad, but at the same time he is clearly distinct from "them" in the story, and "they" seem to have the power. The "they" who "picked up" Eichmann would be Mossad, the sort of muscular and heroic Jews to whom Allen stood in diametric opposition, while the "they" who got his name seem to be the important people at the ad agency. Although Allen is not a hipster, Mailer's thesis that the Holocaust had irrevocably changed and perhaps even scarred society as a whole can be seen in the way Allen is joking about it twenty years after the end of the war and five years after the Eichmann trial. Ongoing Jewish vulnerability is still there, lurking in the background of Allen's premise. Whether the joke was in poor taste is for others to decide, but Allen's inability to look at something as simple as his name being on a list in non-Holocaust terms indicates the "psychic havoc of the concentration camps."[32]

One of the most famous scenes in Allen's film repertoire, the "Easter dinner scene" from Annie Hall, displays both the ambivalence Allen has about himself compared to idealized Gentile masculinity, and the residual feeling of otherness and difference he has absorbed. In this scene he is having dinner with Annie Hall's family. Her parents do not even have names beyond Mom and Dad, and her grandmother is called simply Grammy Hall. Only Annie's psychopathic brother Duane has a name. While the family goes on about swap meets and Grammy's "dynamite ham," Allen's character Alvy imagines himself through their eyes. And despite being dressed in a dress shirt and slacks and eating and enjoying Grammy's dynamite ham, he imagines that they see him as a stereotypical Eastern European Hasid. He goes so far as to do a fourth wall–breaking side-by-side comparison between dinner at his family's house and the Hall house. He imagines his family as loud, rude, disrespectful, and overbearing compared to the quiet, polite Halls. Even in what some have called a self-loathing depiction of Jews, Allen pushes against the post-Holocaust image of passivity and victimhood. His family may compare unfavorably to the Halls, but they are not the meek ones.

Where Allen overlaps most with Bruce's gender differentiation is in another scene from *Annie Hall*. In this side-by-side overlapping scene Annie and Alvy are visiting their respective therapists. Annie's scene takes up only about one-third of the screen, and only Annie is visible. Alvy's scene takes up the other two-thirds of the screen, and we can see both Alvy lying on the couch and his therapist sitting in a chair. Even the spaces seem differently gendered; Annie's therapist's office is white and modern with colorful metal and cloth furniture, whereas Alvy's is all dark wood and leather. At one point their therapists ask them about how often they have sex. Alvy responds first, saying, "Hardly ever, maybe three times a week," and then Annie replies "Constantly, I'd say three times a week." Here Allen is presenting a face of Jewish masculinity that is similar to Bruce's presentation. Both of them are saying that men, and in their cases specifically Jewish men, not only have voracious sexual appetites, but also that they can and do land sexual partners who are described in desirable and implicitly non-Jewish terms.

A final example from *Annie Hall* comes from an early meeting between Alvy and Annie. If the therapy scene showed the places where Bruce and Allen overlapped, the balcony scene shows how far apart they could also be. Alvy and Annie are having a glass of wine and making uncomfortable small talk. Annie tells Alvy that he is what her Grammy would refer to as "a real Jew." Alvy, naturally, is a little unsure what to make of that, so he mutters a sort of noncommittal "Oh. Thank you," to which Annie replies, "Yeah, well, she hates Jews. She thinks they just make money, but let me tell you, I mean she's the one, yeah, is she ever." At this point Bruce's tough guy persona would likely fight back against such blatant antisemitism. Alvy, however, just shrugs and changes the subject. He neither stands up for himself nor defends Jews as a group. He does, however, successfully seduce Annie and begin a serious, though ultimately unsuccessful relationship. Alvy Singer is really the prototype for the new nebbish. Although he does not find lasting love with Annie, he nonetheless carries the film, and even though his nebbish-like qualities are often highlighted for laughs, they are also used to give the character depth and to give the audience someone to relate to. Instead of the nebbish being someone the viewer must strive not to be, he becomes someone with whom the audience could identify, and viewers could therefore feel empowered to take pride in their own nebbishness rather than feel ashamed of their perceived passivity.

Both Allen and Bruce found ways to undermine or subvert the ongoing stereotype of Jewish passivity throughout their comedy careers. Bruce, ever the provocateur, often performed a routine about the old charges of Jewish deicide. He wants to clear the air, he says, "Yes, we did it. I did it, my family. I found a note in the basement. It said: 'We killed him. Signed, Morty.' And a lot of people say to me, 'Why did you kill Christ?' 'I dunno . . . it was one of those parties, got out of hand, you know.' We killed him because he didn't want to become a doctor, that's why we killed him."[33] This is similar to the Nazi scene from Allen's *Manhattan*, in which Isaac, played by Allen, mentions a Nazi demonstration in New Jersey and suggests they get some people together "with bricks and baseball bats and really . . . explain things to them." The other guests at the party, all seemingly WASP-ish Gentiles, instead want to discuss the "devastating satirical piece on [the demonstration] on the op-ed page of the *Times*." When Isaac suggests that bricks and bats might be more effective, a female guest tells him that "really biting satire is always better than physical force." Isaac retorts: "No, physical force is always better with Nazis. It's hard to satirize a guy with shiny boots." Just as Bruce inverted an antisemitic stereotype by claiming credit for the crucifixion, Allen is painting Jews as the ones ready to resort to anti-Nazi violence while the non-Jews in the room want to sit around writing op-eds and barbed satires. This is where their gender performativities come closest to each other; although they take different routes, both Bruce and Allen present a vision of Jewish masculinity that takes action and is willing to fight dirty.

Bruce and Allen were shaped by a combination of post-Holocaust Jewish visibility and Zionist "tough Jew" notions of power and virility. In the 1950s and 1960s, Zionism experienced a specific moment of growth and cache. The image of Jewish pioneers taming the desert and carving out a place in an inhospitable environment became part of the Jewish answer to muscular Christianity, though Zionism at that point was still not accepted across the mainstream of American Judaism. But Uris's *Exodus* had a profound effect on many people. It presented Zionists as strong, noble, adventuresome, and (especially with the release of the film version in 1960), attractive. American Jews no longer had to feel as though Dickens's Fagin or Shakespeare's Shylock were their primary representations on film or the page; Paul Newman made for a much more desirable avatar. That upswing in Zionist sentiment met the seemingly unbelievable victory Israel won in the Six-Day War. The introduction of mid-1960s political attitudes that came with Zionism and Israel widened the gap between Bruce and Allen and created more and more space for a variety of Jewish masculinities to exist.

Conclusion

Jewish feminist writers such as Laura Levitt, Miriam Peskowitz, Jenna Weissman Joselit, and Melanie Kaye/Kantrowitz have all written powerfully and at length about the ways in which Judaism, feminism, and womanhood have interacted. Jewish masculinity has been less extensively studied, though Sarah Imhoff's *Masculinity and the Making of American Judaism* is an excellent analysis of American Judaism before World War II. In this essay, focused as it is on the specific moment after World War II, when so much was changing for Jews socially, politically, and economically, I have attempted to bring the conversations about feminism and gender to bear on what was becoming the most prominent and popular expression of "Jewish sensibilities": comedy.[34] In a sense I see this essay as continuing the themes of Imhoff's work; she demonstrates the narratives of Jewish masculinity that were subverting stereotypes in the early twentieth century, and Bruce and Allen pick up several of those same threads, although they pull them in different directions than most of Imhoff's interlocutors. This highlights what Judith Butler is saying when she writes about gender as a performance. If gender is a performance, what better way to look at that performance than through those who are consciously performing? It may be an unconscious process to most of us, but as Butler says, "What we take to be an internal essence of gender is manufactured through a sustained set of acts, posited through the gendered stylization of the body."[35] Although it is difficult to assign intentionality to unconscious acts, performers such as Bruce and Allen carefully chose and crafted every element of their performance, from their mien to their speech to their wardrobe, and that includes the specific incarnation of Jewish masculinity they presented. They were truly performing gender, as well as performing comedy, and in doing so they became the face(s) of American Jewish culture.

What emerged was a clear sense that Jews, especially Jewish men, needed to take control of the narrative surrounding them and shape their own image. After the Holocaust few people wanted to continue to be seen as passive victims, which were also qualities that have traditionally been gendered as feminine. There was, however, no consensus about what the new narrative should be. Lenny Bruce operated in an aggressive style, cursing, pushing boundaries, breaking the law, and offering no apologies. Woody Allen reinvented the nebbish, keeping the nebbish's smallness, his awkwardness, and his intellectualism but imbuing him with a sexual prowess and ability to outwit or out-talk more traditionally "masculine" Gentiles.

The performance of Jewish masculinity after the Holocaust may have been complicated in the sense that many social and psychological factors contributed to the ways in which these different comedians chose to proclaim their own maleness. But it is also simple. The way Jews were thought of, looked at, and written about after the Holocaust was understandably intolerable to many Jews. Comedians were not the only ones to notice. Leon Uris obviously did. Contemporary dramatic films such as *Defiance* show that there remains an interest in reclaiming the story of Jews during the Holocaust. Jews were not even the only ones to notice. Quentin Tarantino's *Inglorious Basterds* can be read as a Jewish revenge fantasy. But as David Kaufman notes, it was the performance of masculinity that these popular Jewish performers took on that had the greatest impact on how Americans, Jewish and not, thought about Jewish men.

This makes Bruce's sort of gender play feel, in hindsight, even more dangerous. His insistence on a portrayal of aggressive sexual urges, barely restrained and unpredictable kinetic energy, and a physical presence that felt as though it could go off like a volcano at any moment forced audiences absolutely away from the stereotypes that his contemporary nebbish brethren were willing to accept. Christy Burns wrote that Bruce's was the type of humor that goes "against the springboard of social propriety, retrieving such sources of bodily embarrassment as shit, snot, and gaseous expulsions to produce a comic cringe. Despite the claim that postmodernism has exhausted the limits of scandal," she continues, comics like Bruce "continue quite arguably to attain a high level of the comic grotesque." Here we hear Burns echoing Mary Douglas and Judith Butler by seeing Bruce's comedy as specifically transgressive of social norms regarding bodies, boundaries, interiority and exteriority, and general propriety.

But what became the dominant narrative of Jewish masculinity in the post-Holocaust period was the new nebbish, so ultimately one could say that

Bruce's intervention into Jewish sexual stereotypes was less successful than Allen's. I would push back against that notion, however, and say that Bruce's presentation of himself as a different kind of man—and his comedy that portrays men in an unflattering but non-nebbish light—was one of the stepping-stones that allowed the new nebbish to develop and become dominant. Allen's persona owed something to Bruce's, in that Bruce created the space to allow for unapologetic performances of Jewish masculinity, especially ones that in various ways went against the mainstream Western or American notion of what it meant to be a man.

The pervasive image of Jew-as-victim was unpalatable to most American Jews after World War II, and they gravitated strongly toward those artists who were presenting alternative visions of Jewish identity. From Uris to Mailer to Bruce and Allen, American Jews were given models of Jewish success and ways that Jews, especially Jewish men, could be desirable and powerful even when they did not match the all-American physical ideal. Although Bruce and Allen did not often discuss the Holocaust directly in their acts, they undeniably represent elements of post-Holocaust American Jewish identity. Bruce once famously went onstage with a specially printed newspaper that said "Six Million Jews Found Alive in Argentina," and he occasionally joked about selling used Volkswagens, "just used slightly during the war, carrying people back and forth to the furnaces."[36] Allen occasionally joked about Nazis or included sight gags, such as the one in *Zelig* where the protagonist accidentally ends up as part of Hitler's entourage. The Holocaust did not need to be a primary topic of Bruce's and Allen's stand-up routines in order to be a major influence on them as performers, and nowhere is that more evident than in their participation in the reshaping of American Jewish masculinity in the postwar period.

Notes

1. Laura Levitt, *American Jewish Loss After the Holocaust* (New York: NYU Press, 2007), xiii.
2. "Mel Brooks on Anti-Semitism," CBS News, 12 April 2001, https://www.cbsnews.com/news/mel-brooks-on-anti-semitism/ [accessed 24 April 2019].

3. There were, of course, Jewish women performing comedy in this era as well. Belle Barth is a particularly good example. And women comics' subversion of both traditional and stereotyped Jewish femininity is no less important than what the men were doing. Several good books and essays exist on these women. See, for example, Joyce Antler, "One Clove Away from a Pomander Ball: The Subversive Tradition of Jewish Female Comedians," *Studies in American Jewish Literature* 29 (2010): 123–38; and Sarah Blacher Cohen, "The Unkosher Comediennes: From Sophie Tucker to Joan Rivers," in Sarah Blacher Cohen, ed., *Jewish Wry: Essays on Jewish Humor* (Bloomington: Indiana University Press, 1987), 105–24. See also the 2018 biography of Sophie Tucker: Lauren Sklaroff, *Red Hot Mama: The Life of Sophie Tucker* (Austin: University of Texas Press, 2018).
4. Eric L. Goldstein, *The Price of Whiteness* (Princeton, NJ: Princeton University Press, 2008), 122.
5. Michael Kimmel, *Manhood in America* (New York: Oxford University Press, 2012), 68.
6. For a particularly good overview of this particular image, see Irven Resnik, "Medieval Roots of the Myth of Jewish Male Menses," *Harvard Theological Review* 93, no. 3 (2000): 241–63.
7. Deborah Dash Moore, *American Jewish Identity Politics* (Ann Arbor: University of Michigan Press, 2008), 32.
8. Tom Watson, "The Leo Frank Case," *Watson's Magazine* 20 (January 1915): 143.
9. *Duck Soup*, Paramount Pictures, 1933.
10. Leonard Helfgott, "Groucho, Harpo, Chico, and Karl: Immigrant Humor and the Depression," in Leonard Greenspoon, ed., *Jews and Humor* (West Lafayette, IN: Purdue University Press, 2011), 113–14.
11. Helfgott, "Groucho," 113–14.
12. Sarah Imhoff, *Masculinity and the Making of American Judaism* (Bloomington: Indiana University Press, 2017), 16.
13. Jenna Weissman Joselit, *The Wonders of America* (New York: Hill & Wang, 1994), 87.
14. Paul Kivel, "The Everyday Impact of Christian Hegemony," in Michael Kimmel and Abby Ferber, eds., *Privilege* (Boulder, CO: Westview Press, 2017): 141.
15. Naomi Seidman, "Theorizing Jewish Patriarchy *in extremis*," in Miriam Peskowitz and Laura Levitt, eds., *Judaism Since Gender* (London: Routledge, 1997), 40.
16. David Kaufman, *Jewhooing the Sixties* (Waltham, MA: Brandeis University Press, 2012), 41.

17. Kaufman, *Jewhooing the Sixties*, 58.
18. Joseph Telushkin, *Jewish Humor* (New York: William Morrow, 1992), 16.
19. Paul Breines, *Tough Jews* (New York: Basic, 1990), 54.
20. Norman Mailer, *The White Negro* (San Francisco: City Lights, 1957), unpaginated.
21. See Jennifer Caplan, "The Nebbish in Popular Culture, Or How the Underdog Can Win," *Journal of Modern Jewish Studies* 16, no. 1 (2017): 138–52.
22. Somewhere in the middle of the spectrum sits Mort Sahl. Sahl was a friend and performance partner of Bruce and a mentor to Allen. He shared some of Bruce's brash aggression, but he was aggressively intelligent, ranting about politics and current events more than Bruce's favorite topics of religion and sex. He was also Allen's mentor, and Allen included Sahl's wife performing a striptease at the end of his first film, apparently as a favor to Sahl if the text that scrolls over her increasingly undressed body is to be believed.
23. Lenny Bruce, *The Berkeley Concert Album* (Transatlantic Records, 1969).
24. Sander Gilman, *The Jew's Body* (New York: Routledge, 1991), 119.
25. Gilman, *Jew's Body*, 119.
26. Mary Douglas, *Purity and Danger* (New York: Routledge, 2002), 5.
27. It is interesting to note the way that social standards about these sorts of transgressions change. When Bruce brought sex and mud together, it was titillating and boundary-pushing but not remotely considered one of his most objectionable statements. Compare that to the reaction to Larry David's *Saturday Night Live* monologue in November 2017 during which he talked about concentration camp pickup lines. The public response to that was swift and overwhelmingly (but not unanimously) negative. David brought the sexual into contact with the impure or profane in a way the public was not willing to accept.
28. Judith Butler, *Gender Trouble* (New York: Routledge, 2015), 180.
29. Lenny Bruce, *The Carnegie Hall Concert* (Blue Note Records, 1995).
30. Although Berle's cross-dressing was a well-known part of his act, Berle was not openly homosexual. He was married to several women, and in his 1974 autobiography he writes in detail about the many women with whom he had sexual relationships. Either Bruce is assuming things about Berle's sexuality based on his cross-dressing, or else he is speaking based on rumors he may have heard. Regardless, my intent here is not to assert anything about Berle's sexuality and only to use Bruce's routine to further demonstrate the way Bruce constructed ideas of masculinity.
31. Woody Allen, "The Vodka Ad," *The Dean Martin Show*, 23 November 1967.

32. Mailer, *White Negro*.
33. John Cohen, ed., *The Essential Lenny Bruce* (New York: Bell, 1970), 30. Compare to the recorded version on *Lenny Bruce: Let the Buyer Beware*, disc 4, cut 11 (recorded 1963).
34. Telushkin, *Jewish Humor*, 16.
35. Butler, *Gender Trouble*, xv.
36. Lawrence Epstein, *The Haunted Smile* (New York: Public Affairs, 2001), 171.

"We're Safe Here, but Poland Is a State of Mind"

The Exploitation of Holocaust Consciousness in Jewish Fiction and Memoirs

Jarrod Tanny

THE IDEA OF HOLOCAUST humor makes people cringe. At first glance it seems frivolous, distasteful, and blasphemous, making light of what has been consecrated as the greatest tragedy of the twentieth century. Yet Holocaust humor has become an important component of Holocaust memory, and numerous writers, including Mordecai Richler, Romain Gary, Shalom Auslander, Gary Shteyngart, and S. Hanala Stadner, have invoked levity rather than solemnity to comprehend and cope with the inherited suffering that is now the collective patrimony of the Jewish people. Stadner, the child of survivors, quipped, "My parents survived Hitler. I survived my parents. Going through the Holocaust made them cranky."[1] Stadner grew up searching for Goebbels and Göring under her bed, even though her family home in Montreal, Canada, was separated from Auschwitz by thirty years and thousands of miles. But Poland is not a place on the map, it "is a state of mind,"[2] she muses, much like the British novelist Howard Jacobson, who came of age "somewhere between the ghettos and the greenery of North Manchester, with 'extermination' in my vocabulary and the Nazis in my living room."[3] In 1987 Terrence Des Pres asked whether "Holocaust laughter" is possible.[4] By using multiple literary genres, including novels, short stories, and memoirs, such writers show that Holocaust humor is not only possible but also perhaps therapeutic, particularly because the proliferation and sacralization of Holocaust consciousness through museums and film have rendered laughter taboo. What often appears to be an insolent misuse of catastrophe is in fact a subtle critique of the ways in which the catastrophe has been commodified and commemorated. Their witty and ironic writings form an alternative narrative to the homogenized gravitas of publicly sanctioned Holocaust memory.

The Origins of Holocaust Laughter

The production of humor involving the Nazis and Adolf Hitler began during World War II, before the full horrors of their crimes against humanity and the Jews came to light. Charlie Chaplin famously mocked Hitler in the 1940 film *The Dictator*; that same year, the Three Stooges produced a film short called *You Nazty Spy!*[5] Theodor Reik notes that there was even room for levity by those on the battlefield. He describes how a soldier's magazine held a contest during the war for the most suitable punishment for Hitler. First prize went to an American Jewish soldier stationed in Italy, who proposed that "he should live with my in-laws in the Bronx."[6] Some evidence indicates that Jews used humor during the Holocaust to cope.[7] Although the often defiant yet dark humor of Holocaust victims may have been worlds apart from the slapstick of the Three Stooges, these instances demonstrate that comedy can be alleviating and even redemptive in moments of extreme tribulation.

But it was not until the early 1960s that Jewish comics tackled Nazism, and the way they broached the topic speaks volumes about the place of the Holocaust in popular consciousness, particularly in the United States. The now classic 1960 comedy recording *2000 Years with Carl Reiner and Mel Brooks* has a track titled "The Peruvian," in which a journalist (Carl Reiner) interviews an Argentinian coffee planter of alleged "Peruvian Indian" descent (Mel Brooks) who turns out to be a Nazi in hiding. He is ultimately unmasked by his confusing biography, his German accent, and an inadvertent diatribe on how they "crushed France in twenty-seven days." The early 1960s also witnessed the iconoclastic Lenny Bruce going on stage with a newspaper whose headline read "Six Million Jews Found Alive in Argentina."[8] The use of Argentina in these two bits was not accidental, as numerous Nazis had fled to South America, and in 1960 Israeli agents captured Adolf Eichmann in Argentina and brought him to trial in Jerusalem.[9]

More humor involving the Nazis was produced throughout the 1960s, in film, on TV, and in literature, culminating in Mel Brooks's 1968 film *The Producers*. But most of this humor, including *The Producers* and the television series *Hogan's Heroes* (1965–1971), was about Nazis, not about the Holocaust. "Any understanding of the Shoah," writes Sander Gilman, "must acknowledge that its meaning and function has changed over the fifty years since it occurred. The murder of the Jews moved from being one aspect of the crimes of the Nazis to being their central, defining aspect over half a century."[10] Gilman argues that the zany Nazis incarcerating Allied POWs on *Hogan's Heroes* did not imply the Holocaust, because the Jewish Holocaust had yet to be sanctified—through scholarship, literature, film, and television—as the greatest crime against humanity and, accordingly, as the essence of Nazism. This unstated absence of the Jewish Holocaust from televised Nazism was not lost on *Mad Magazine*, which satirized *Hogan's Heroes* in a 1967 issue. The comic included graphic images of skeletal inmates incarcerated at Buchenwald laughing about "the latest gag we're gonna pull on the guards over at the *Crematorium*. Boy it's a *hot* one,"[11] thereby lampooning the *Hogan's Heroes* narrative of erasure. Perhaps this is what Lenny Bruce had in mind with his satirical newspaper headline: The extermination of 6 million Jews was not part of public discourse.

Mad Magazine and Bruce were not the only ones who noticed the absence of Holocaust consciousness. S. Hanala Stadner recalls watching *Hogan's Heroes* as a child, laughing at the antics of Sergeant Schultz, "the Nazi you hate to love," when her mother walked in and casually observed, "If only da Germans ver so stupid! My sister would still be alive."[12] Stadner was shocked into silence as it dawned on her that these are "the same people who brought us genocide by gas chamber. . . . Somewhere down the road from Hogan's kooky camp . . . is Dachau."[13] Stadner's distinct vantage point—the child of survivors—complicates the apparent decoupling of the Shoah from the Third Reich in the quarter-century following the war. For the victims and their children, Nazism was the Final Solution by definition, and the swastika symbolized razed shtetls, Einsatzgruppen, and crematoria, even if their new neighbors in their new homeland thousands of miles away from Poland's gas chambers did not see Nazism in that light. Holocaust consciousness had yet to proliferate.

But it did proliferate in the ensuing decades, with most scholars citing the 1978 TV miniseries *Holocaust* and the 1993 film *Schindler's List* as the crucial turning points.[14] Museums were opened, Holocaust studies grew as an academic field, and the Holocaust became the yardstick against which all war crimes were measured, "an ethical touchstone, demanding moral accounting not only for the atrocity that bears its name, but also for other atrocities," as Jeffrey Shandler puts it.[15] The victims had hitherto evoked relative indifference and pity, but they came to elicit profound interest. Those who perished, like Anne Frank, were revered as tragic heroes, and those who survived, like Elie Wiesel, were elevated to divine stature, engendering what Peter Novick calls "the cult of the survivor as secular saint."[16] And it was also in this period that Holocaust humor proliferated. *Mad Magazine*'s 1967 comic was among the first to inscribe in print the Holocaust into Nazism through humor, but others followed. Such levity is neither the product of ignorance nor an attempt to trivialize Jewish victimhood. Most of these works constitute a serious quest to understand the Holocaust's significance and the political, psychological, cultural, and theological consequences of its consecration. Comedy developed into a device for exploring and confronting what had become the sacred ground of Jewish catastrophe.

The Lord, Our God, Mr. Holocaust

Throughout history Jews have turned to God for answers during times of persecution, whether it was in response to the massacres of the Crusades, the expulsion from Spain, or the Holocaust. In *Night*, Elie Wiesel describes how he lost faith in God for his apparent abandonment of the Jews; God still existed, but he either ceased to care or "chose us from among all the nations to be tortured day and night, to watch as our fathers, our mothers, our brothers end up in the furnaces."[17] In Auschwitz a group of rabbis put God on trial for abandoning the Jews and pronounced him guilty.[18] And in the ensuing years some theologians grappled with God's lack of intervention to save the Jews, concluding that he broke the covenant with his people, and the contract needed to be renewed.[19]

Whereas some tackled God's role in the catastrophe with solemnity, others used humor. In *Me of Little Faith*, comedian Lewis Black contemplates the veracity of the Bible in the context of the Holocaust.

> Is the Bible absolutely true? Is it truly the word of God? ... But, even if the Bible is a dead-on accurate transcription

of God's words, it's rather shocking that God only had two books in him, the Old and the New Testament. I've actually written two books and I am sure God would have written more than me.... That was all he had to say to us? You think he would have put out at least a pamphlet in response to the Holocaust. And if not a pamphlet, a couple of well-placed fireballs, for crying out loud. This is the Supreme Being we're talking about, who whacks Sodom and Gomorrah and turns Lot's wife to salt, and Hitler doesn't get so much as a twisted ankle? It seems a little suspicious to me.[20]

Although Black is a secular American Jew, his musings are not so different from what Shalom Auslander heard from the Orthodox rabbis at the New York yeshiva he attended: "My rabbis taught me that it was wrong to say God caused the Holocaust; that He had simply, in 1938, turned His head. He looked away. What? Huh? Geno . . . really? Shit, I was in the bathroom. Not a murderer, just an accessory."[21]

But neither Black nor Auslander is convinced of God's apathy. Black speculates that if the Bible's God of vengeance is real, then "I am fucked. And then I'm fucked for saying fuck. And I say it a lot. It's not really a word to me, it's a comma."[22] Auslander has his doubts as well, and he wonders if he should fear for his safety because he writes irreverent blasphemous stories for a living, and his "teachers told me that it is a sin punishable by death from above for a Jew to embarrass the Jewish people, which I am concerned these stories do. But I take a deep breath and remember that Aaron Spelling's doing okay, and if he's not an embarrassment to the Jewish people, I don't know who is."[23] But the God of his childhood keeps creeping back into his consciousness, and he spends his days petrified that "*this* God . . . Mr. Vengeance . . . Mr. Flood the Earth . . . Mr. Holocaust" is out to get him.[24]

Jewish humorists want to blame God for the Holocaust, seeing the Shoah as not merely an unjustifiable calamity but the culmination of 3,000 years of relentless calamity thrust upon the Chosen People. And they are intent on holding their parents, teachers, and communal leaders accountable for transmitting this message. In Canadian writer Mordecai Richler's 1971 novel *St. Urbain's Horseman*, a rabbi in Germany tells Jacob (Jake) Hirsch, the protagonist, how Jake's cousin, a Jewish gangster who fled Montreal allegedly to hunt Nazi war criminals, showed up drunk at services to confront him.

> You know, rabbi, he said, you're right. The Lord is our God, and the Lord is One. But do you know why, rabbi? It is because our Lord has such a tapeworm inside him, such a prodigious appetite, that he can chew up six million Jews in one meal. And if the Lord, our God, were Two. What then? Twelve million. Who had them to spare at the time? So, the Lord our God is One, because Two we couldn't afford.[25]

For Shalom Auslander, the connection between God and the Holocaust is inculcated during childhood, as he sardonically suggests in one of his (blasphemous) stories, "Holocaust Tips for Kids."

> Rabbi Brier says that the Holocaust happened because the Jews assimilated.
> That's also why Hashem made the Jews slaves in Egypt.
> And why He let the Holy Temple be destroyed by the Romans. . . .
> Assimilating is when you stop being Jewish, like Woody Allen.
> My mother says Woody Allen is a self-hating Jew. . . .
> My mother says nose jobs are for people who are ashamed to be Jewish.
> If you put double-sided tape around the top of your penis and pull the skin up around it, you can tell the Nazis that you're not a Jew.
> *During the Inquisition, thousands of Jews were murdered simply for refusing to convert to Christianity.*
> "And now," says Rabbi Brier, "you're going to violate the Shabbos?"[26]

Written as a long series of aphorisms, "Holocaust Tips for Kids" grotesquely suggests how children may pick up bits and pieces of what their elders say, mentally reconstructing these snippets into one horrific narrative of an omnipotent yet angry God who threw his people under the proverbial bus when the Nazis came, and it follows that, should they come back, he will do it again.

Holding God accountable for the Holocaust is in keeping with much of Jewish humor, which is rooted in the paradox of exile: The Jews are God's chosen people, yet he perpetually forsakes them, leaving them to suffer expulsions, pogroms, and blood libels.²⁷ Since the nineteenth century Jewish humorists have used this trope, which could be called the irony of divinely ordained abandonment, and it can be found in classic Yiddish literature of the nineteenth century (most notably in Sholem Aleichem's stories), twentieth-century American fiction (such as Philip Roth's novels), the films of Woody Allen, and Larry David's *Curb Your Enthusiasm*. Much as Sholem Aleichem's Tevye jokes about his people's special selection for poverty and pogroms, while "God is still snoozing away in bed,"²⁸ while God keeps himself busy by inventing "a new calamity, a new catastrophe, a new disaster"²⁹ to try out on Tevye, Lewis Black, Shalom Auslander, and Mordecai Richler search for the hand of God in the Holocaust. But whereas Tevye cannot see past his imagined creator, Black, Auslander, and Richler unpack the theology and blame the messenger. They are challenging the custodians of Judaism because their explanation for the murder of 6 million Jews by Nazi Germany is inadequate.

Guilty unto the Tenth Generation

The Holocaust occurred in a predominantly secular age and, accordingly, the place of God in Holocaust consciousness—and by extension in Holocaust humor—pales in comparison to the place of the perpetrators. We "are forbidden to give Hitler posthumous victories," famously enjoined Emil Fackenheim, calling on Jews to ensure the continuity of their religion and peoplehood.³⁰ Although Fackenheim's maxim is about looking ahead, not looking back, it has contributed to what Peter Novick calls a culture of "*Trotzjudentum*, 'Jewishness out of spite,'" and has led to the elevation of "the Holocaust as [the] central symbol of Jewishness" in the last quarter of the twentieth century.³¹ To be Jewish is to remember the Holocaust, and to remember the Holocaust is to never forget who conducted it and to hold them accountable.

This desire to hold the Germans collectively responsible—notwithstanding West Germany's postwar reparations, the Nuremberg trials, and Konrad Adenauer's 1951 acceptance of the nation's guilt before the Bundestag—is frequently voiced in Jewish fiction and memoirs. In Richler's *St. Urbain's Horseman*, Jake's Gentile British wife, Nancy, confronts her husband over his obsession.

> How, Jake was asked again and again, as if it were perverse of him, could he still hate the Germans?
> —Easily.
> —Now look here, Nancy would reason sweetly, can you hate Günter Grass?
> —Without any trouble whatsoever.
> —Brecht?
> —Unto the tenth generation.
> Which Nancy, barely seven years old on V-E Day, could not comprehend.[32]

German culpability, and the Jew's inherent right to mock each and every German for his culpability, is a theme that repeatedly comes up in Richler's novels. In *Joshua Then and Now*, the main character, a Jewish playwright who, after marrying into a prominent Canadian family, comes to believe that a whiff of antisemitism lurks behind their circle of friends' polite yet probing verbal exchanges with him, relishes the opportunity to mock a German guest at one of their parties.

> The guest of honor was a visiting German industrialist looking for investment opportunities.
> "Tattoo credit cards," Joshua said, grinning.
> "I beg your pardon?"
> "The big problem with credit cards, as I understand it, is that people lose them or they are stolen. Think of what you could do to cut down overhead if you were to tattoo the serial number on a client's arm. . . . Of course, . . . it would be

necessary to test such an idea in the field. Germany, I think, would be ideal. You already have so many of the required technicians."[33]

The belief in collective guilt gives the offended Jew the right, perhaps even the obligation, to imply the Holocaust whenever a German enters the room.

Mordecai Richler's two protagonists (along with Richler himself, who was born in 1931) are old enough to remember the war and the revelation of genocide; they can draw from the wellspring of childhood memories to justify rebuking and ridiculing Germans. But Jake's scriptural-sounding vow to never forget and never forgive proves to be prescient, and it can be seen in memoirs written in the twenty-first century. Tuvia Tenenbom, an American journalist of German Jewish descent who was born in 1957, proclaims his inheritance of the Holocaust when he flies to Germany to explore his roots and the legacy of his ancestors' destruction: "Three days later, my plane takes off. I beat the ash cloud. Members of my family got lost in the ashes of Europe, but I beat the ash cloud. I am an American hero. I will conquer Europe! Germany will lie at my feet like an open book. This is the plan, the immediate plan."[34]

Similarly, Rebecca Schuman, a journalist for *Slate* who went to Germany in 1995 as a college exchange student, could not mentally separate her host family from the crimes of Hitler, seeing the Holocaust as a legitimate excuse for her occasionally bad behavior as a house guest.

> I may have committed my share of minor infractions in their house, but fuck if I wasn't going to remind them that they were almost certainly the direct descendants of people who had either passively or actively participated in the genocide of the tribe with which I selectively identified.... Suddenly snubbing your midday soup and ringing that buzzer in the middle of the night doesn't seem so bad, does it? They didn't need to know that I hadn't set foot in a synagogue since 1986.[35]

As far as Schuman was concerned, "My very presence in the Fatherland as a selective Jew was both a gift to the Volk and a stubborn reminder of my people's refusal to be exterminated in our entirety."³⁶ And to underscore the tenacity of collective memory, she titled this particular chapter of her memoirs "Lebensraum," sardonically writing that "rooming with Germans in their natural *Lebensraum* gives a person ample opportunity to remind them, in various subtle ways, how the Nazis perverted the word *Lebensraum* (among other things)."³⁷

Although of different backgrounds and generations, Richler, Tenenbom, and Schuman create similar comical scenes in their writings to explore the responsibility of the German people for the Holocaust. Their use of humor as a form of retribution is in keeping with tradition, given that Jews made jokes at the Germans' expense in the ghettos and concentration camps.³⁸ But what if the professional comedian himself could take on the Nazis? What if the weaponization of laughter could impose suffering on the Germans? Such is the theme explored by Romain Gary, a French writer of Eastern European Jewish descent, in his novel *The Dance of Genghis Cohn*, an imaginative tale about a Jewish comedian executed in Poland who comes back as a ghost to haunt the Nazi responsible for his death. Published in 1967, the novel is perhaps the first comprehensive literary exploration of how comedy could serve as a valuable tool for grappling with the Holocaust's legacy.

The novel begins with Cohn introducing himself as a comedian who "used to be well known on the Yiddish Burlesque circuit: first at the Shwarze Shikse in Berlin, then at the Mottke Ganeff in Warsaw, and finally in Auschwitz," thereby suggesting that the Holocaust was merely another venue for him to perform his shtick.³⁹ Cohn considers his stint at Auschwitz a success because he once "told a fellow inmate such a funny joke that he literally died laughing . . . the only Jew who ever died laughing in Auschwitz."⁴⁰ This infuriated the German guards because it meant they had lost control over choosing the time, place, and manner of an inmate's death, something that was repeated with Cohn's murder by an execution squad commanded by a German named Schatz. Cohn's execution haunts Schatz because, Schatz contends, "He wasn't like the others. *He fought back*" the moment the shots rang out by sticking out his bare ass and shouting, "*Kush mir in tokhes* [kiss my ass]."⁴¹ Jewish irreverence before Nazi aggression immediately troubles Schatz; it fills him with anxiety, nightmares, and, eventually the literal manifestation of Cohn in his consciousness. Cohn avenges his death by polluting his executioner's thoughts, living inside his head, forcing Yiddish words to come out of Schatz's mouth, and, "in the end," Schatz states, "I had to buy myself a Yiddish dictionary, so as to understand myself . . . *Rakhmones . . . Gevalt . . . Hutzpeh.*"[42] "So I wake him up and we have a little Yiddish lesson," Cohn explains to the reader. "We have a beautiful literature. Soon Schatzen will be able to read Sholem Aleichem in the original."[43] The Jew avenges the Holocaust by literally inscribing his humor, his language, and his culture's canonical comedic texts into the Nazi's mind, body, and conscience.

Gary's reworking of the dybbuk legend into the setting of the Holocaust is the ultimate act of Jewish vengeance, because, as Cohn points out, "For generations, the defenders of a racially pure Germany have called us Jews 'the enemy within,' and now at last they've succeeded in getting us truly inside them."[44] It suggests that the murdered Jews will haunt Germany and that the comedians will lead the way. They will be terrorizing them with Jewish laughter. But it is pure fantasy, much like Quentin Tarantino's 2009 film *Inglorious Basterds*, which tracks a covert unit of American Jewish soldiers in occupied France who hunt down and murder Nazis with extreme brutality. For Mordecai Richler's characters, vengeance remains unfulfilled. Notwithstanding Jacob Hirsch's obsession with his cousin, Joseph Hirsch, "the Horseman who once strode St. Urbain, bronzed as a lifeguard, trousers buckled tight against a flat stomach,"[45] tracking Mengele from Germany to the South American jungles, he knows it is just a dream. When in Munich, visiting the sites where Hitler built his power base, Jake is disillusioned that the phantoms of genocide are nowhere to be found.

> Gehenna, yes, the very lowest regions. The innermost circle. Fifteen kilometers to Dachau, no more. . . . Yet Jake slept very well indeed at his hotel and wakened with salubrious appetite. The rolls were delicious. So was the ham, so were the eggs. The coffee, the very best. The service, impeccable. Should he eat lunch at Humplmayr's, trying their fabled goose livers? Take a stroll in the English Gardens, perhaps? Look in at the Hofbrauhaus?[46]

But this was a journey of retribution, not a vacation.

> Jake spread the phone book on the bed and looked up "Goering." Four entries. There were no Eichmanns, but plenty of Himmlers.
> —Hello, Heinrich, what's cooking?
> —Ask a foolish question. The Jews, what else?
> Jake was back at the Bürgerbraukeller before ten in the morning, absolutely bewildered, unsure whether to be appalled or moved to see a sad little mouse of an army chaplain in a talith raise the holy scrolls aloft, before a makeshift sanctuary, in the very place where Adolph Hitler had fired his first two shots in the air.⁴⁷

The weight of the Holocaust oppresses the Jew, and mocking the Germans does not fully alleviate the burden. It does not erase the inherited trauma wrought by Auschwitz.

Sacralization and Its Discontents

The Dance of Genghis Cohn was published in 1967 and *St. Urbain's Horseman* in 1971, during what Peter Novick calls "The Years of Transition,"⁴⁸ when Holocaust consciousness had already been stimulated by the Eichmann trial but had not yet become the universal "referent point for collective suffering," as Alan Mintz puts it.⁴⁹ That the exponential increase in Holocaust museums, memorials, historiography, and films from the late 1970s onward occurred in tandem with an increase in Holocaust humor is not coincidental, because the sacralization of tragedy in the public sphere elicits a multiplicity of responses. Those who have chosen to use humor are doing so to come to terms with the impact of Holocaust memory on their lives.

It is also not surprising that the children of survivors (known as the Second Generation, or 2Gs) deployed humor in recalling their childhoods, because they were already dealing with the burden of the Holocaust before it became the historical baggage of the wider Jewish community.⁵⁰ According to S. Hanala Stadner, "I didn't go through the Holocaust; the Holocaust went through me. And it likes to talk about itself. I don't try to bring it up, it comes up. Like bad clams. Just the sight of a swastika gives me a hot flash. It's like swallowing horseradish."[51] She insists that she is the product of "bad *heir* conditioning," because her parents, "Ma and Pa Holocaust," throw the extermination of European Jewry in her face whenever she approaches them with a problem: "'You're *scared*? Vhat, is a Nazi chasing you? Do you live in a hole in da ground? Did your family die in da gas chambers?' Yes, technically," she muses, "and the ones still alive are in no state to raise children."[52] "Without the Holocaust I would not be who I am," writes Bernice Eisenstein in her graphic novel *I Was a Child of Holocaust Survivors*. "It has seared and branded me with its stippled mark on my forearm and pulled me into its world, irrevocably, as its offspring."[53] For Sonia Pilcer, a perpetual sense of guilt hangs over her, especially because her path to becoming a professional writer necessitated a stint penning shlock for an entertainment tabloid: "It started like a migraine. The blue haze before the assault. Silent, cruel, insidious accusations. Did we survive the war for this? Sleaze? You think you're a real writer? Shlockmeister. Try standing in the freezing snow for two hours without shoes."[54]

The Second Generation's inheritance of the Holocaust—and its attendant feelings of guilt, trauma, and bitterness—ineluctably radiated outward to Jewry writ large as Holocaust consciousness expanded in the United States and in other Western countries, including Canada and the United Kingdom. In British author Howard Jacobson's 2006 novel *Kalooki Nights*, the protagonist, a secular Jewish cartoonist named Max Glickman, mulls over his ascribed victimhood.

> By any of the usual definitions of the word *victim*, of course, I wasn't one. I had been born safely, at a lucky time and in an unthreatening part of the world, to parents who loved and protected me. I was a child of peace and refuge.... But there was no refuge from the dead. For just as sinners pass on their accountability to generations not yet born, so do the sinned against. "Remember me," says Hamlet's father's ghost, and that's Hamlet fucked.[55]

For Lewis Black, inculcation began at the age of 10 in Sunday school.

> The names of the camps were pounded into my head, like a train schedule to hell: Treblinka, Bergen-Belsen, Auschwitz, Dachau. I don't think it was really very healthy for me to be viewing that footage in the innocence of my youth. No, not good at all. By the time I was twelve, I felt like I had seen every Jew killed about eight times over. Combine this with a reading list on the subject, and I am amazed I can walk without braces on my legs or a breathing apparatus trailing behind me on wheels.[56]

For Shalom Auslander, the Holocaust followed him wherever he went. "The traffic light is still red," he writes in his memoirs, "and my mind wanders. It wanders into the graveyard, it strolls into the morgue, it meanders into Bergen-Belsen."[57] As an Orthodox Jew, Auslander received his Holocaust education in conjunction with the fear of God, "Mr. Holocaust," who would punish him in the next world for the sins committed in this one, including the sin of masturbation. "When I was young," writes Auslander, they told him the angels would force him to watch "hundreds of thousands of Jews, praying and studying, Jews that would have been born if I hadn't killed them, wasted them, mopped them up with a dirty sock during the hideous failure of my despicable life." Doing the math, Auslander estimates that "there are roughly 50 million sperms in every ejaculate; that's about nine Holocausts in every wank. I was just hitting puberty when they told me this, or puberty was just hitting me, and I was committing genocide, on average, three or four times a day."[58] The oversaturation of Holocaust education imprisons the Jew's consciousness, damages his psyche, and corrupts his sexuality.

Auslander continues to explore the collective trauma wrought by the Holocaust in his 2012 novel *Hope: A Tragedy*. The main character, Solomon Kugel, is brought up thinking his mother went through the Holocaust, when in reality she was born in Brooklyn in 1945.[59] When Kugel was 8 years old, his mother came to his bedroom with a picture book and a lamp shade, and she "brushed the hair from his brow, and told him that it was time he learned about a terrible place known as Buchenwald."[60] Flipping through the book, which was called *The Holocaust*, she showed him photo after photo "of mass graves, starved prisoners, piles of naked corpses," saying,

"That's your uncle . . . That's your grandfather's sister . . . That's your cousin's father."[61] Perplexed yet inquisitive, Kugel asked why she brought him a lamp shade.

> That, she said with a sigh. That's your grandfather.
> Then she buried her face in her hands and wept. . . .
> Kugel held the lamp shade in his hands and turned it over.
> This is Zeide? he asked.
> Mother nodded, composed herself.
> You see what they do to us? she said. There's no peace, no peace. Wherever we go, wherever we hide. Terror and more terror and more terror.
> It says Made in Taiwan, Kugel said.
> Mother looked at him, disappointment and anger in her tear-stained eyes.
> Well, they're not going to write Made in Buchenwald, are they? she snapped.
> No, said Kugel.[62]

But even after learning the truth, Kugel decides to humor his mother, because he realizes she has co-opted this trauma into her identity to cope with her husband's abandonment of the family. "She seemed to need the war, and he was pleased to be able to give it to her. At last there was something other than hate that young Kugel could give the mother he so adored: he could give her suffering."[63]

Perhaps Kugel's mother *chose* to become a survivor because the proliferation of Holocaust consciousness beginning in the 1970s engendered the sanctification of the victims, a fundamental shift from how they had been viewed in previous decades. "Survivors' wartime experiences were," writes Jeffrey Shandler, "largely regarded as something they should overcome and put behind themselves."[64] But in time there arose what Alvin Rosenfeld calls "a new mystique of 'victimization.'"[65] More than anyone else, Anne Frank was transformed into the martyred saint of the Holocaust, becoming the subject of a museum, countless plays, biographies, fiction, music, films, and websites, including an entire project dedicated to the restoration, preservation, and celebration of the tree made famous in her diary.[66] The Holocaust victim became American Jewry's patron saint: heroic, flawless, existing outside time and space.

But the veneration of victimhood is ultimately a burden to those who must deal with the victims. Although Solomon Kugel may be able to handle his mother's imaginary Buchenwald narrative, he is crushed by the weight of the Holocaust when he discovers an elderly woman living in his attic who claims to be Anne Frank. The elderly Frank refuses to leave, insisting that after the war and the critical acclaim of her diary she approached the publisher, who "held up a copy of that goddamned diary, with that goddamned smiling child on the goddamned cover, and said, They don't want you. They want *her*."[67] The elderly Frank is everything a venerated saint is not: She is obnoxious and demanding, emits noxious odors, and regularly urinates and defecates into Kugel's heating ducts. But Kugel understands that he is the one who is prisoner to the Holocaust, not Anne Frank. He imagines the newspaper headlines should he call the cops:

LOCAL MAN EVICTS ANNE FRANK.
Jew Drops Dime on Holocaust Survivor.
Brutalized by Nazis, Tossed Out by a Jew:
One Survivor's Tragic Story of Something.[68]

Kugel "would forever be known as the person—the *Jewish* person—that reported Anne Frank to the authorities."[69] Even worse, he imagines his mother's reaction.

> My own son, she would say, ratting out Anne Frank.
> You had to call the police, she would say. What's the matter, you didn't have Dr. Mengele's number? He doesn't make house calls?
> You want Elie Wiesel's address? Maybe you could turn him in, too?[70]

Auslander cleverly inserts the Holocaust into the traditional narrative of Jewish humor because the imagined wrath of Mother Kugel reflects the stereotype of the guilt-tripping Jewish mother; she can blame her son for everything, including his complicity in the Final Solution. As a mother, as a Jew, as an alleged survivor, she claims ownership of the Holocaust; she, along with the old woman in the attic, is entitled to use the extermination of 6 million Jews to get what she wants.

There's No Business Like Shoah Business

The Jews have been emotionally scarred through the proliferation of Holocaust memory. "Never again" means always remember—with guilt—that it could have been you, as a Jew, in the gas chambers of Auschwitz. Shalom Auslander's Anne Frank, an elderly, bitter, unattractive squatter who pollutes someone else's space through her filthy language ("Blow me, said Anne Frank," to Kugel)[71] and her bodily functions, is not an attack on Anne Frank; it is satirical commentary on the ways in which the weight of Holocaust consciousness perversely consecrates the Nazis' human victims and unfairly burdens future generations of Jews with an inherited responsibility of remembrance. But there is a flip side to the Holocaust as burden, and that is the Holocaust as entitlement: Inheritance is a birthright; it denotes ownership, "certification as (vicarious) victims," as Peter Novick puts it, "with all the moral privilege accompanying such certification."[72] "The Judaism I had received," writes the French philosopher Alain Finkielkraut, "was the most beautiful present a post-genocidal child could imagine. I had inherited a suffering to which I had not been subjected, for without having to endure oppression, the identity of the victim was mine."[73]

Where some of the Second Generation feel the Holocaust as oppression, others see it as opportunity. Bernice Eisenstein understood this at an early age.

> Because I am your child—someone who learned there was no limit to how much you can socially trade on this stuff: Hey man, I'm different than you are. My parents were in Auschwitz. What do you have that could top that one? I knew I could throw that line out anywhere, anytime—in a sandbox, for instance. Can I play with your shovel and pail? No? Well, my parents were in Auschwitz. . . . Out on dates: I'm not like the other girls you date because my parents . . .

> It was a paragon of non sequiturs, and I would trade on its cachet, shamelessly it seems to me now . . . it was a way of staking claim to my position in the world.[74]

"I was a medium, Houdini of the Holocaust," writes Sonia Pilcer. "I strove for recognition . . . the Holocaust was mine—except for the survivors. It was an exclusive club. No Johnny-come-lately academic, theologian, or artist should be allowed to cash in on my private cache of suffering and obsession."[75] Where Pilcer sees the Holocaust as "the gift of light and life," Eisenstein contends that "the Holocaust is a drug and I have entered the opium den" and that her parents, unwittingly, are the drug dealers.[76]

Pilcer and Eisenstein cashed in on their entitlement, but they failed to understand that the club was not exclusively theirs, because the proliferation of Holocaust consciousness opened membership to each and every Jew, unto the tenth generation, as Richler's Jacob Hirsch would likely put it. Hence the exploitation of Holocaust memory by Jewish interest groups, which can be seen in Mordecai Richler's final novel, *Barney's Version*, published in 1997. After gallivanting aimlessly around Europe, Barney Panofsky decides to become a respectable Jew, "to infiltrate the Jewish establishment, set on qualifying as a pillar, or at least a cornice . . . [by volunteering] to work as a fundraiser for United Jewish Appeal," where he is delegated with the task of raising money for Israel.[77] As a novice, Barney is coached by a seasoned fundraiser, a man named Irv Nussbaum, who explains why the decline in antisemitism is bad for business.

> Don't get me wrong. I'm against anti-Semitism. But every time some asshole daubs a swastika on a synagogue wall or knocks over a stone in one of our cemeteries, our guys get so nervous they phone me with pledges. So things being how they are this year, what you've got to do is slam-dunk your target about the Holocaust. Shove Auschwitz at him. Buchenwald. War criminals thriving in Canada to this day. Tell him, "Can you be sure it won't happen again, even here, and then where will you go?" Israel is your insurance policy, you say.[78]

But it is a paradoxical situation, because, as Nussbaum later contends, "The lasting problem with the Holocaust is that it made anti-Semitism unfashionable."[79] The more antisemitism disappears, the more important Holocaust consciousness becomes.

And it is striking how in the 1990s, when antisemitism—in America at least—seemed to have all but disappeared, Holocaust commemoration increased markedly, with 1993 being the pivotal year. *Schindler's List* was released and quickly canonized as The Holocaust Film, and the United States Holocaust Memorial Museum opened its doors in the heart of Washington, D.C., to millions of Holocaust travelers. The film and the museum are emblematic of the Holocaust's simultaneous sanctity and commercialism; it is a spectacle for audiences to consume, carefully manufactured and curated to elicit reverential responses. "There's No Business Like Shoah Business" is an often-heard and incisive quip of uncertain origins, used by Jews and antisemites alike to criticize the growth of the Holocaust industry.[80] One may speak of Holocaust memory as part performance, part commodity, and it is a theme that is tackled humorously in Holocaust literature.

Perhaps the Holocaust has always been spectacle, a question raised by Melvin Jules Bukiet, also a member of the Second Generation, in his 1996 novel *After*. The novel follows the escapades of some disreputable survivors, who, upon liberation, undertake numerous fraudulent activities to enrich themselves. Confined to displaced persons camps in the aftermath of the Allied victory, the survivors, still imprisoned behind barbed wire, are subjected to an onslaught of photographers lining up to document the human residue of Nazism. Rather than being outraged at this voyeurism, Isaac, a master dissimulator, quickly learns to give them the show that they want: debility, servility, and anguish. "Once, before, I was in the Cracow Zoo," Isaac tells his companion. "The monkeys they learned what the people liked, whatever it was, begging, swinging from the bars, so they would do that to earn a peanut. Not so different, hey."[81] The pitying journalists ply them with American dollars, foreshadowing the survivor's sanctification and his exhibition as museum artifact.

The deceptive role of museums in shaping Holocaust consciousness (as opposed to Holocaust consciousness shaping museum exhibits) is taken up by Gary Shteyngart, an American writer born in the USSR, in

Absurdistan, a novel about a Russian Jew who, after spending time in the United States, crafts an academically dubious proposal to set up an Institute for Caspian Holocaust Studies. His proposal states, "The Holocaust, when harnessed properly as a source of guilt, shame, and victimhood, can serve as a remarkable tool for Jewish continuity."[82] The envisioned museum will speak to Jewish trauma through its architecture, "a giant broken matzoh, in reference to the tragedy that befell our people" in Egypt.[83] The exhibition halls will include "Holocaust for Kidz," because "studies have shown that it's never too early to frighten a child with images of skeletal remains and naked women being chased by dogs across the Polish snow"; "The 'Think It Can't Happen Again?' Annex," a "daring conceptual space [that] will feature dozens of French Arab youths throwing rocks at passing museum goers, threatening, 'six million more'"; and "The Tent of Consent," where "Jews of reproductive age . . . will show Hitler and his goons just where they can stick their Final Solution."[84] One of the envisioned outcomes outlined in the proposal is that "twenty thousand Jewish children will learn that it's somehow their fault."[85]

Holocaust consciousness is a tool; it can be used to advance one's agenda, whether laudable or ignoble. Bernice Eisenstein discovered this as a child, which is why she always got the best spot in the sandbox. For all her anger, Auslander's Anne Frank knows this, which is why she is not surprised when Kugel tells her he will not call the cops on her, and she has no compunction in casually handing him a shopping list.[86] Kugel knows this too, and he believes he can beat Anne Frank at her own game by weaponizing the symbols of the Holocaust. "How difficult could it be to get an elderly Holocaust survivor out of your house?" Kugel wonders. "He'd play Wagner. He'd get a German shepherd. When the UPS man had gone, he'd tell her it had been a man from the Gestapo, asking a lot of questions. A lot of questions."[87] But Kugel fails to beat Anne Frank, because in a culture of victimhood there is always a hierarchy of suffering, and the sanctified victim will always win, even if she is a foul-mouthed putrid trespasser who defecates in the heating ducts.

Conclusion: Serious Laughter

In one of her few moments of clarity, Auslander's Anne Frank explains her position on Holocaust memory and, by implication, the deification of the diary's version of Anne Frank: "I think never forgetting the Holocaust is not the same thing as never shutting up about it."[88] Frank is echoing a point made by Alvin Rosenfeld on the oversaturation of Holocaust memory. Rosenfeld insists that "the very success of the Holocaust's wide dissemination in the public sphere can work to undermine its gravity and render it a more familiar thing. . . . Made increasingly familiar through repetition, it becomes normalized."[89] On the surface it may seem as though Holocaust humor is contributing to this normalization, by mocking the sacred, by trivializing the horror, by exploiting the memory. But well-crafted Holocaust humor interrogates the ways in which we have chosen to commemorate atrocity and what impact such commemoration has on survivors, their children, and the Jewish community as a whole. It also raises questions about how we deal with collective responsibility, how "never again" may affect the way we view the descendants of the perpetrators and the bystanders who watched the Jews die. Holocaust humor destabilizes the standard narrative we receive through historiography, documentaries, and monuments. It is an alternative lens through which we can understand one of the greatest catastrophes of the twentieth century. Humor forces us to think seriously about genocide.

Notes

1. S. Hanala Stadner, *My Parents Went Through the Holocaust and All I Got Was This Lousy T-Shirt: A Near-Life Experience* (s.l.: Matter Inc., 2006), xv.
2. Stadner, *My Parents*, 7.
3. Howard Jacobson, *Kalooki Nights: A Novel*, Kindle ed. (New York: Simon & Schuster, 2006), loc. 67–68.
4. Terrence Des Pres, "Holocaust Laughter," in Terrence Des Pres, *Writing into the World: Essays; 1973–1987* (New York: Viking Penguin, 1991), 277–86.
5. *The Great Dictator*, directed by Charlie Chaplin (1940); *You Nazty Spy!*, directed by Jules White, 1940.
6. Theodor Reik, *Jewish Wit* (New York: Gamut Press, 1962), 49.

7. See, for instance, Steve Lipman, *Laughter in Hell: The Use of Humor During the Holocaust* (Northvale, NJ: Jason Aronson, 1991).
8. Lawrence J. Epstein, *The Haunted Smile: The Story of Jewish Comedians in America* (New York: Public Affairs, 2001), 171.
9. On the impact of the trial on Holocaust consciousness, see Peter Novick, *The Holocaust in American Life* (Boston: Houghton Mifflin, 1999), ch. 7.
10. Sander L. Gilman, "Is Life Beautiful? Can the Shoah Be Funny? Some Thoughts on Recent and Older Films," *Critical Inquiry* 26, no. 2 (2000): 281.
11. Larry Siegel and Jack Davis, "Hokum's Heroes / Hochman's Heroes (TV Satire)," *Mad*, no. 108 (January 1967): 8; emphasis in the original.
12. Stadner, *My Parents*, 59.
13. Stadner, *My Parents*, 59.
14. Alvin H. Rosenfeld, *The End of the Holocaust* (Bloomington: Indiana University Press, 2011), 254–55; Jeffrey Shandler, *While America Watches: Televising the Holocaust* (New York: Oxford University Press, 1999), ch. 6; Alan Mintz, *Popular Culture and the Shaping of Holocaust Memory in America* (Seattle: University of Washington Press, 2001), 26; Novick, *Holocaust in American Life*, ch. 10.
15. Shandler, *While America Watches*, xi.
16. Novick, *Holocaust in American Life*, 11.
17. Elie Wiesel, *Night*, Kindle ed. (New York: Straus & Giroux, 2006), 67.
18. See for instance, https://www.thejc.com/news/uk-news/wiesel-yes-we-really-did-put-god-on-trial-1.5056 [accessed 1 August 2017].
19. Peter Ochs, "Covenant," in Nicholas de Lange and Miri Freud-Kandel, eds., *Modern Judaism: An Oxford Guide* (New York: Oxford University Press, 2005), 290–300.
20. Lewis Black, *Me of Little Faith*, ed. Hank Gallo, Kindle ed. (New York: Riverhead, 2008), 124–25.
21. Shalom Auslander, *Foreskin's Lament: A Memoir* (New York: Riverhead, 2007), 27.
22. Black, *Me of Little Faith*, 124.
23. Auslander, *Foreskin's Lament*, 27.
24. Auslander, *Foreskin's Lament*, 136.
25. Mordecai Richler, *St. Urbain's Horseman*, Kindle ed. (Toronto: McClelland & Stewart, 1971), 277.
26. Shalom Auslander, "Holocaust Tips for Kids," in Shalom Auslander, *Beware of God: Stories* (New York: Simon & Schuster, 2005), 62–66; emphasis in the original.

27. See, for instance, Sarah Blacher Cohen, "Introduction: The Varieties of Jewish Humor," in Sarah Blacher Cohen, ed., *Jewish Wry: Essays on Jewish Humor* (Bloomington: Indiana University Press, 1987), 1–15.
28. Sholem Aleichem, "Today's Children," in Sholem Aleichem, *Tevye the Dairyman and the Railroad Stories*, trans. Hillel Halkin (New York: Schocken, 1987), 46.
29. Sholem Aleichem, "Today's Children," 75.
30. Emil Fackenheim, "Faith in God and Man After Auschwitz: Theological Implications," http://www.holocaust-trc.org/faith-in-god-and-man-after-auschwitz-theological-implications/ [accessed 1 August 2017].
31. Novick, *Holocaust in American Life*, 7.
32. Richler, *St. Urbain's Horseman*, 73–74.
33. Mordecai Richler, *Joshua Then and Now* (Toronto: McClelland & Stewart, 1980), 34.
34. Tuvia Tenenbom, *I Sleep in Hitler's Room: An American Jew Visits Germany*, Kindle ed. (New York: Jewish Theater of New York, 2011), 5.
35. Rebecca Schuman, *Schadenfreude, A Love Story: Me, the Germans, and 20 Years of Attempted Transformations, Unfortunate Miscommunications, and Humiliating Situations That Only They Have Words For*, Kindle ed. (New York: Flatiron, 2017), 76.
36. Schuman, *Schadenfreude*, 74–75.
37. Schuman, *Schadenfreude*, 57.
38. See Lipman, *Laughter in Hell*.
39. Romain Gary, *The Dance of Genghis Cohn* (New York: World, 1968), 3–4.
40. Gary, *Dance of Genghis Cohn*, 4.
41. Gary, *Dance of Genghis Cohn*, 22.
42. Gary, *Dance of Genghis Cohn*, 25.
43. Gary, *Dance of Genghis Cohn*, 24.
44. Gary, *Dance of Genghis Cohn*, 25.
45. Richler, *St. Urbain's Horseman*, 73.
46. Richler, *St. Urbain's Horseman*, 276.
47. Richler, *St. Urbain's Horseman*, 276.
48. Novick, *Holocaust in American Life*, pt. 3.
49. Mintz, *Popular Culture*, 26.
50. On the Second Generation, see Helen Epstein, *Children of the Holocaust: Conversations with Sons and Daughters of Survivors* (New York: Putnam, 1979).
51. Stadner, *My Parents*, xv.

52. Stadner, *My Parents*, xvi, 4, 35.
53. Bernice Eisenstein, *I Was a Child of Holocaust Survivors* (New York: Riverhead, 2006), 25.
54. Sonia Pilcer, *The Holocaust Kid* (New York: Persea, 2001), 10.
55. Jacobson, *Kalooki Nights*, loc. 74–78.
56. Lewis Black, *Nothing's Sacred*, Kindle ed. (New York: Gallery Books, 1967), 22–23.
57. Auslander, *Foreskin's Lament*, 8.
58. Auslander, *Foreskin's Lament*, 5–6.
59. Shalom Auslander, *Hope: A Tragedy—A Novel* (New York: Penguin, 2012), 67.
60. Auslander, *Hope*, 64.
61. Auslander, *Hope*, 64.
62. Auslander, *Hope*, 64–65.
63. Auslander, *Hope*, 69.
64. Shandler, *While America Watches*, 27.
65. Rosenfeld, *End of the Holocaust*, 50.
66. Rosenfeld, *End of the Holocaust*, 50. See also Barbara Kirshenblatt-Gimblett and Jeffrey Shandler, eds., *Anne Frank Unbound: Media, Imagination, Memory* (Bloomington: Indiana University Press, 2012). On Anne Frank's tree, see http://www.annefrank.org/en/News/Anne-Frank-Tree/ [accessed 1 August 2017].
67. Auslander, *Hope*, 60.
68. Auslander, *Hope*, 29.
69. Auslander, *Hope*, 30.
70. Auslander, *Hope*, 30.
71. Auslander, *Hope*, 27.
72. Novick, *Holocaust in American Life*, 9.
73. Alain Finkielkraut, *The Imaginary Jew*, trans. Kevin O'Neill and David Suchoff (Lincoln: University of Nebraska Press, 1994), 7.
74. Eisenstein, *Child of Holocaust Survivors*, 21–22.
75. Pilcer, *Holocaust Kid*, 87.
76. Pilcer, *Holocaust Kid*, 87; Eisenstein, *Child of Holocaust Survivors*, 20.
77. Mordecai Richler, *Barney's Version* (New York: Washington Square Press, 1997), 161.
78. Richler, *Barney's Version*, 161–62.
79. Richler, *Barney's Version*, 173.
80. The phrase has often been attributed to Abba Eban. See http://www.salon.com/2002/04/03/mirroring_evil/ [accessed 1 August 2017]. Moshe Waldoks, who is

one of the editors of *The Big Book of Jewish Humor*, and Lisa Lipkin performed a song with this line in a musical, *Taking the Shoah on the Road*. See http://www.utne.com/mind-and-body/holocaust-humor [accessed 1 August 2017].
81. Melvin Jules Bukiet, *After* (New York: Picador USA, 1996), 10–11.
82. Gary Shteyngart, *Absurdistan* (New York: Random House, 2006), 269.
83. Shteyngart, *Absurdistan*, 269–70.
84. Shteyngart, *Absurdistan*, 270–71.
85. Shteyngart, *Absurdistan*, 272.
86. Auslander, *Hope*, 53.
87. Auslander, *Hope*, 35.
88. Auslander, *Hope*, 266.
89. Rosenfeld, *End of the Holocaust*, 11.

"This Way to the Ovens, Señoras y Señores"

Holocaust Cartoons in Latin America

Ilan Stavans

It was at the end of the 1970s, while I was in my teens, when I first noticed that antisemitic cartoons would appear in the most prominent newspapers in my native Mexico. They were almost always in response to actions taken by the Israeli army against Egypt, Lebanon, Syria, and other Arab neighbors. My knowledge of world Jewish history was still quite limited and, even more, so was my understanding of Jewish life in the Spanish-speaking world, although I was part of it.

These cartoons—*caricaturas* in Spanish, a genre that in Latin American history and culture holds a special place and exerts significant influence—were created to instill hatred. The automatic response my friends and I had was to label them by-products of ignorance. I remember reading around that time the Spanish translation of a Polish book by Tadeusz Borowski called *This Way for the Gas, Ladies and Gentlemen* (1969), a collection of stories about the author's arrest by the Gestapo and his stay at Auschwitz. One of my friends, dismayed by the lack of response, used to play on its title, saying the *caricaturas* were an invitation for us to end up in a New World iteration of the crematoria. It was a time when Israel generated good will from the people in Latin America. Israel was seen as a bright, promising democracy and, with its thriving kibbutzim, an example of an entrepreneurial collectivism. The Israeli invasion of Lebanon in 1982 that enwrapped the massacres in the Sabra and Shatila camps was a few years away.

I do not believe the official response of the Mexican Jewish community to these cartoons was any different from mine. Ours was a small community, 30,000 people in a country that then had a population of 80 million. It was a minuscule minority, defenseless against these kinds of aggressions and careful to shy away from any form of self-affirmation in the public sphere. It was obvious to all of us, regardless of our age, that the stereotypes these cartoons promoted were neither transient nor innocuous and that they were the by-product of antisemitic groups within Mexican society not only fuming about Israeli politics but also intent on aborting Jews from its own midst.

As the decades have gone by, these insidious items have become quite pervasive. Looking back, the samples my friends and I came across in the 1970s were early manifestations of what feels like an orchestrated antisemitic campaign. Since then, the Palestinian cause has taken root in Latin America, which, outside the Middle East, holds the largest concentration of Palestinian refugees and their descendants. For instance, Chile has a community of 500,000 Palestinians. Indeed, not only Palestinians but also, in general, Arabs, a term widely used in the region to describe people of Muslim and Christian faiths from the Middle East and North Africa, have become an essential part of the overall population: Argentina has between 1.3 million and 3.5 million Arabs; and Mexico isn't too far behind, with 1.1 million.

In contrast, there are just 400,000 Jews in all the Latin American republics combined. The two countries with the largest concentration of Jews are Argentina, with 220,000, followed by Brazil with 180,000. Other countries, such as Colombia, Peru, Chile, Cuba, Guatemala, Venezuela, and the Dominican Republic, have smaller communities.

Politically, the Latin American left has aligned itself with the Palestinian cause, portraying Israel as a tool of Western colonialism against Arab civilization. The tropes the left indulges in in its rhetoric regularly link Israeli military actions with Jewish global domination. In this context, it is not surprising to come across, as I did in a major Brazilian newspaper in 2002, a *caricatura* of the entrance to a Nazi concentration camp where the German slogan *Arbeit macht frei* has been replaced with *Bem Vindo a Palestina*, Portuguese for "Welcome to Palestine." Or a portrait I saw more recently of revolutionary icon Ernesto "Ché" Guevara wearing a *keffiyeh*.

The disingenuous connection being emphasized in these cartoons is that the Arab-Israeli conflict and the Holocaust go hand in hand, the former being a continuation of the latter, and that Latin American Jews are auxiliaries of the Zionist machinery.

In the decades that followed, I would see the ways that these *caricaturas* not only poisoned public opinion but were also used as instruments of agitation. For instance, in Venezuela under the dictatorial regime of Hugo Chávez, the government would use *caricaturas* to align itself with Iran against Israel and to rally against the Jewish community in Caracas. Similar strategies were used by left-leaning governments in Ecuador, Bolivia, and Nicaragua.

Despite my deep love for Israel, I myself would eventually become critical of its diplomatic policies. Yet with age I would come to the realization that these antisemitic cartoons in Latin America were a symptom of a larger malady signaling a fraught side in Jewish-Hispanic relations. Starting in the 1980s, my instinct was to collect them, to build a reservoir through which to understand the fragile state of Jewish communities in the region. I have now gathered 250–300 items (including a handful from Spain). Most appeared in periodicals and on the internet after 9/11, when the so-called clash of civilizations between the West and the Arab world came to a boil.

The proper study of antisemitism globally requires an appreciation of the particular circumstances in which it is harbored. This means that not all antisemitic manifestations respond to the same historical factors. In Latin America it is possible to distinguish three varieties. The first dates back to the fifteenth century and is connected to the arrival of *cristianos nuevos* to the colonies. These New Christians and the crypto-Jews who were escaping the might of the Holy Office of the Inquisition were seen as part of a cohort whose mission was to take control of the resources of the New World, spread deviant views on Christianity, and proselytize for the Mosaic law.

The second variety of antisemitism unfolded at the end of the nineteenth century, as a series of waves of poor, Yiddish-speaking immigrants from the Pale of Settlement and French- or Ladino-speaking immigrants from the crumbling Ottoman Empire arrived in Argentina, Brazil, and other destinations. The belief was that they belonged to a concerted effort to, on the one hand, spread the gospel of communism across the Atlantic, and on the other, expand the net of money-hungry enterprises to tighten their grip on the entire plat. The antisemitic views attached to this period are connected with the *Protocols of the Elders of Zion*, Henry Ford's *The International Jew*, and other spurious propaganda.

This second variety culminated with the Shoah. Thousands of refugees made it to Latin American shores. So did ex-Nazi officers and other apparatchiks on the so-called "ratline". This parallel arrival gave rise to unavoidable contradictions. In such countries as Argentina, Brazil, Chile, Paraguay, and Bolivia, German immigrant communities harbored some individuals—for example, Adolf Eichmann and Josef Mengele—who had been instrumental in the genocide of 6 million Jews. These individuals lived in proximity with former inmates of Auschwitz and other concentration camps.

In part because of Latin America's small Jewish population and in part because of its remoteness from the scenes of World War II, the Shoah never became a full-fledged theme in its collective consciousness. Holocaust classics such as the *Diary of Anne Frank* and Elie Wiesel's *Night* are available in Spanish and Portuguese editions, but, with few exceptions, they are not part of the high school curriculum. The same might be said for films, such as Steven Spielberg's *Schindler's List*, that deal with the Shoah. They are distributed in commercial cinemas and through streaming services, yet they are not seen as essential tools to comprehend a major historical catastrophe. This explains why the Holocaust is regularly understood as a propaganda tool of Jewish groups who purportedly generate sympathy for their cause. Furthermore, in the second variety the Holocaust is presented as the quid pro quo whereby Jews after World War II were able to garner everyone's attention to create a state of their own in the Middle East.

And the third variety of antisemitism took shape in the 1970s, as the State of Israel went from being perceived as a benign entity that came about after the atrocities perpetuated by the Nazis during the Shoah to becoming an imperialist, colonial threat that worked in conjunction with the United States and other Western allies against the displaced Palestinian population in the Middle East and the Diaspora. The antisemitic motifs connected with this view established links between the Jew as moneylender, the denial of the Holocaust as a historical truth, Arab antisemitism, and the approach by the Israeli government to its Arab neighbors.

One of the barometers of this last variety of antisemitism in Latin America is the publication of political cartoons in newspapers, magazines, and other periodicals. These items deliberately erase the border between antisemitism and anti-Zionism. This juxtaposition is accomplished by repeatedly featuring traditional Diaspora Jewish types, such as a black-clothed, hunchbacked man with a long nose, a beard, and forelocks, carrying bags of money and displaying a conniving smile, or stern-looking male Israeli soldiers targeting their machine guns on defenseless Palestinian women and children.

It is important to remember that from its indigenous past onward, the cultures of Latin America have been image-driven. The Aztecs, Mayas, Quechuas, and other aboriginal empires had hieroglyphic-based alphabets. Their architecture, religion, and political cultures depended heavily on a distinct iconography. No surprise, then, that comic books, called *historietas* in Spanish, and graphic novels and other illustrated narratives play a decisive role in the way the population articulates its vision in everyday life. By the way, semantically *caricaturas* is the catchall term for subgenres such as *historietas*; that is, *historietas* are a form of *caricaturas*.

My purpose in this essay is to use *caricaturas* to explore the intersection of Holocaust memory and satirical humor used by non-Jews for antisemitic ends in Latin America. Humor in these *caricaturas* frequently relies on highlighting the falseness, insincerity, and outright hypocrisy of a particular current event. To bring a smile, ideas are turned upside-down, politicians are called out for being duplicitous, and government statements are decontextualized. It is essential, of course, for artists as well as editors to know their audience. The views expressed in political cartoons are an extension of the periodical's ideological stand. Consequently, the most significant form of antisemitic vitriol makes an outright connection between the Holocaust with the policies of the State of Israel. The logic is straightforward: David is now Goliath; that is, once the underdog, Jews have turned history on its head, going from being vulnerable targets to becoming the victimizer. In that sense, Palestinians are the new Jews. The line between antisemitism and anti-Zionism is thus erased.

To understand the metabolism of these cartoons, it is useful to put ourselves in the frame of mind of a newspaper opinion-page editor. The task is to be current, to comment on world events. The daily cartoon does it in a succinct, pungent way. That comment requires humor, because humor at first sight appears innocent. The cartoon also needs to reflect the publisher's ideological views. In Latin America, not even the most conservative media sympathize with Israel's policies toward its neighbors. This means that Israel is a frequent target of criticism. In that sense, cartoonists are spokespeople for larger forces.

It goes without saying that such an approach is not limited to Latin America. Such messages are also present in Europe, Africa, Asia, and, with singular emphasis, the Arab world. For example, in Barcelona, Spain, there is an adult *historieta* called *El Jueves (la revista que sale los miércoles)* that features a popular section, *DesHechos Históricos*, which is devoted to scrutinizing historical events through a sociopolitical lens. Launched in 1977, a couple of years after the death of General Franco and co-created by Josep Ilario (b. 1936), the creator of other magazines, for example, *Barrabás*, *Por Favor*, and *Interviú*, *DesHechos Históricos* currently has a staff of about thirty artists. The name (in itself a word suggesting a less-than-serious approach to the past) is a play on words that simultaneously means "unfactual events," "historical debris," and "historical happenings undone."

In 2016 *DesHechos Históricos* published a comic, signed by a pseudonymous "Don Julio,"[1] about Israeli policies toward Palestinians. It depicted Orthodox Jews and Israeli soldiers stating that Israel was exclusively for Jews, that Jews were set on financially controlling the world, and that the Holocaust was a fiction conveniently invented by Jews to advance their imperialist objectives.

The validity of the arguments made by "Don Julio" about Israeli-Palestinian relations was lost in his uneven-sided explanation of the conflict. A number of Jewish organizations in Spain publicly condemned the comic. But the creators orchestrated a campaign in which they accused their critics of being "a Jewish lobby" attempting to silence "factual opinions." Rather than an incident that might have been used to enlighten the shortcomings of a stubborn conflagration, *DesHechos Históricos*, on this occasion, chose to exacerbate the situation, purportedly using humor by means of exaggerated, stereotypical features as a tool to denounce Israel's colonialism. Spanish Jews and others who themselves are critics of Israel's excessive use of military force are automatically sidelined. There is no room for dissent.

• • •

This type of biased attack is just like those I remember from my teens in Mexico. As in *DesHechos Históricos*, the hatred in graphic form is not limited to the opinion pages. It shows up in graffiti on building walls and other sites. And it also manifests itself in native-grown *historietas*. One illustrator more than anybody else has come to personify this antisemitic drive. His full name is Eduardo Humberto del Río García (1934–2017), although he goes by Rius.

Not long ago, I wrote an essay on Rius's art in which I praised his style.[2] I compared his effort to an early version of Wikipedia, which at first sight was a model of affordable, easy-access encyclopedic information; Rius's *historietas* exposed his readership to a wide range of hefty topics. But the real point of comparison is the biased media available in the United States in the second decade of the twenty-first century. Rius's work was invariably partial, unfair, and prejudiced. His tours through history were infused with his subjective message. Still, he happened to be one of the most famous Latin American *caricaturistas* of the second half of the twentieth century. The author of hundreds of slim comics about all sorts of historical topics, his booklets sold hundreds of thousands of copies at corner newsstands on a weekly basis. Rius fine-tuned a technique: He would choose a lofty topic, for instance, birth control, Noam Chomsky, feminism, marijuana, or the Cuban revolution. With basic drawings and a pastiche of images borrowed from an assortment of sources accompanied by minimal text, he would proceed to offer a left-leaning disquisition. More than left-leaning, it was actually nihilistic. Nothing was sacred. This strategy proved to be successful even beyond Mexico. Rius's comic on Karl Marx, acquired by foreign publishers, became the international bestseller *Marx for Beginners* (1972), inaugurating a style that would become a pop culture staple in the United States, Europe, and elsewhere.

One of Rius's consistent targets was the Jews. A couple of his *historietas* dealt with themes connected with Jewish history, including the Holocaust. He described Jews as traitors to Jesus, whose guilt "pullulates" throughout history. He talked of usury, blood libels, and other "reprehensible behavior." References to Mexican Jews were tangential. Rius did not insert a chapter on the arrival of crypto-Jews to New Spain, as Mexico was called in the fifteenth century, escaping the Inquisition, although he did emphasize the campaign of "the Holy Office in the Iberian Peninsula to control Jews from ransacking all the gold from others." He did not depict anything about Yiddish-speaking Jewish immigrants from Russia, Poland, and other parts of Eastern Europe arriving in Mexico at the turn of the twentieth century, escaping pogroms.

But Rius did include comments on the financial crisis that Mexico was facing in the early 1980s, to which then-president José López Portillo responded by nationalizing the bank industry. In the media, Jews were targeted by López Portillo's administration for being *sacadólares*, moving their savings from Mexican banks to locations outside the country, therefore throwing the economy into further disarray. This was an activity that considerable portions of the bourgeoisie engaged in. Yet Mexican Jews were singled out. The president even intimated that he would publish a list of the top *sacadólares*, which he said included numerous Jewish surnames. With antisemitic acumen, Rius, an acerbic critic of the ruling PRI party, to which López Portillo belonged, highlighted the episode as another example of Jewish disloyalty and money laundering. Again, he played with the stereotype of the Jew as stingy, avaricious, and self-centered.

Another *historieta* by Rius, *Palestina: Del judío errante al judío errado* (Palestine: From the Wandering Jew to the Mistaken Jew), was about the Israeli-Palestinian conflict. This pamphlet was published after the Yom Kippur War, as international support for Israel progressively eroded. The good will that had surrounded the young Jewish nation since the 1950s took a U-turn. In Latin America this change manifested itself in the intelligentsia. Staunch supporters, such as Argentine writer Jorge Luis Borges, who visited Israel on a couple of occasions and was awarded the Jerusalem Prize, didn't budge. But a younger generation made tangible its disapproval of Israeli politics, especially when it came to military intervention in Lebanon and elsewhere. As in the case of *DesHechos Históricos*, the content included gross, one-sided generalizations that played into antisemitic tropes. There was no room for ambiguity, no balanced viewpoints, and no real historical analysis. Internal dissent in Israel with regard to its borders and the peace process was not explained. Israelis as a whole were guilty of genocide. Nothing in the material was subtle.

For the most part, Rius's work was made in Mexico for Mexicans. That is, it circulated within the nation's borders. In talking about him with friends from other Latin American countries, I am frequently struck by how unknown he is at the hemispheric level. In part this has to do with the dynamics of humor, which for the most part is produced for local consumption. By describing Jews as money-thirsty, Rius portrays himself as speaking truth to power, regardless of the gross generalizations he indulges in. That so-called courage, in the form of *caricaturas*, allows audiences to laugh at the way the "truth" of what is portrayed is supposedly left out of representations in the mainstream media. It is also based on a sense of pseudo-denunciations. Even when dealing with such large themes as antisemitism that reach beyond specific milieus, Rius's humor makes constant use of references that particular audiences will react to. Likewise, an Argentine, Colombian, or Venezuelan Rius would have been equally unknown to me as a Mexican reader of *historietas* in the 1970s. In other words, pop culture is always local, even in the age of globalization.

In Latin America, exceptions are transnational artists such as Joaquín Salvador Lavado (b. 1932), best known as Quino, the Argentine creator of the ever-popular Mafalda, a little girl who debuted as a cartoon character in 1963 and since then has become a staple of popular culture, reflecting on the anger the world around her generates. Quino's entrepreneurial publishing house, Ediciones de la Flor, marketed his art throughout the Spanish-speaking world, turning it into a popular icon of anti-establishmentarianism in the 1970s. Ideologically, Quino has always been rather balanced, attacking in equal measure right- and left-leaning regimes. He is known as a friend of Argentine Jews and not as a particularly strident critic of Israeli policies.

Quino serves as a segue to discuss a couple of cases of antisemitic *caricaturas* in Buenos Aires, arguably the capital of Latin American Jewry. An intriguing example took place in 2018, when, not long before the World Cup was about to kick off in Russia, Argentina's national team was scheduled to play a friendly game in Israel. But it canceled it in response to the Israeli military's reaction to Palestinian demonstrations in Gaza. Back home, the incident gave rise to a few antisemitic *caricaturas* published in newspapers and other printed media.

As I mentioned before, Latin America is a conglomerate of countries. It is therefore a mistake to approach each and every one of these cartoons as part and parcel of the same phenomenon being replicated across national lines. Although occasionally the countries behave as members of a consortium, they have unique characteristics that must be acknowledged in full in order not to make the type of blanket simplifications the cartoons themselves are guilty of.

The Buenos Aires neighborhoods that are traditionally known as Jewish are El Once and Villa Crespo, and the resort Punta del Este is a site that Jews frequent for vacation. It is not unusual to come across political cartoons in which Israel and these locations are linked in the artist's mind.

Buenos Aires is also the only place where a pogrom has ever taken place in the Americas. It is known as *Semana Trágica*, Tragic Week, and it took place on January 7, 1919. The city was also the stage, on July 18, 1994, for a terrorist attack against the AMIA (Asociación Mutual Israelita Argentina), the Jewish community center. The attackers killed eighty-four people and injured hundreds. Hamas and the Iranian government were implicated. The AMIA attack generated an enormous number of cartoons, a few of them linking the Nazi Holocaust to the policies of the Israeli government and its connections to the Argentine Jewish community.

What is striking, at least to me, is the scarcity of Jewish cartoons that respond to this campaign. Reactions are regularly performed in the form of official denunciations by members of the Jewish community. I do not know of a caricaturist who, as a national figure, assumed the role of countering this rhetoric. Yet there are indeed voices on the other side. In the Buenos Aires subway station where the AMIA is located, Estación Metro Pasteur, there is a mural in homage to the victims of the terrorist attack. It was commissioned by about a dozen *caricaturistas*. One of them is by Rep, aka Miguel Repiso. The text in his contribution uses the lyrics of a famous song called "La Memoria" (Memory) by León Gieco (2001). Each of the characters "sings" a stanza, in the style of "We Are the World." The character in Rep's depiction is called Gaspar, el Revolú, a man obsessed with his psychoanalytic sessions. In the mural the text reads, "Todos los muertos de la AMIA y los de la Embajada de Israel, el poder de las armas, la justicia que mira y no ve" ("All the dead of AMIA and the Israeli Embassy, the power of weapons, and justice that looks [at this carnage] but sees nothing.")[3]

Visibly, Gaspar, el Revolú, cries in the face of tragedy. His pain is a response to the hatred inflicted on that painful day. The fact that the image, one among several, is a *caricatura* on the wall—de facto, a mural—and that it was commissioned by and paid for with funds from the city of Buenos Aires might be taken as a rejoinder. The fact that Rep is not Jewish is significant. Still, these types of murals have not reduced the frequency of antisemitic cartoons in Argentine newspapers.

Shoah imagery in the region has at times been used for other purposes. In October 1979, *Humor*, a satirical Argentine journal intended for a middle-class audience, released an issue with cartoons about the Holocaust. They featured concentration camp inmates, obviously Jewish, as well as Nazi guards. The jokes made fun of the way Jewish bodies were used for soap and other types of industrial consumption. At one point, a male inmate with a number tattooed on his arm tells his wife that those using Jewish remains should be careful about cholesterol. In another image, one Nazi capo tells another to be patient because the tattooing still has a long way to go.

The artist's pseudonym is Catton. His real name is Raúl A. Bonato. The context in which these images appeared needs to be understood. The Argentine military junta was in power. This was the period known as *La guerra sucia*, the Dirty War. In that habitat, *Humor* was a magazine known for its dissent. The cartoons might have been designed to criticize the junta of its abusive policies. The Jewish community played it both ways during those years; a conservative portion was close to the military, and, likewise, a large segment of left-leaning Jewish youth were in the resistance and ended up paying the price. The number of Jewish victims among the *desaparecidos* was large.

Intriguingly, 1979 was also the year when Jacobo Timerman, a famous journalist who wrote the memoir *Prisoner Without a Name, Cell Without a Number* (1981) and who is known for his opposition to the military regime, used references to the Shoah in articles and speeches to describe the repressive strategies of the Argentine government. In addition, the TV miniseries *Holocaust*, which had been released in 1978, was scheduled to air, dubbed into Spanish, that year. According to logic, *Humor* and Timerman should have been on the same side. But the sheer fact that he was Jewish erased all ideological partnerships. He was often attacked as unpatriotic, even among left-leaning intellectuals.

The response from the Jewish Argentine community was strong. Letters to the editor denounced *Humor* as antisemitic. Yet those denunciations were quickly portrayed as an orchestrated effort by the Argentine Jewish lobby to silence dissent. Apparently, the consensus was that Zionism was a new incarnation of fascism. In fact, Zionism was a stepchild of Nazism, its ignominious justification of genocide having been revisited in such a way so that Jews, once victims, were now victimizers.

Another example: In 2012 the progressive Argentine newspaper *Página/12* published cartoons by artist Gustavo Sala depicting a DJ at a Nazi concentration camp. The inspiration was the British DJ David Guetta, whom Sala turned into David Gueto, meaning "ghetto." The cartoons were released on January 19, a day before the celebration of International Holocaust Day. The character David Gueto tells the camp inmates to start dancing, suggesting that when they are active, the production of soap is better. Once again, the cartoon was followed by a clamor. A number of international organizations openly manifested their official displeasure.

These reactions quieted down a few weeks later. The David Gueto narrative has become a rallying force on the internet, where it serves as inspiration to other antisemitic depictions whenever news cycles ignite public opinion. Sala's viewpoint is intrinsically Argentine. That is, he operates in a country where the Jewish community plays an active role in politics, business, culture, and sports. Unlike in Mexico, Peru, Colombia, and other countries in Latin America, in Argentina the Shoah is discussed relatively more often in schools, on TV, and in other media. Hence this type of humor is contextual.

A patient, meticulously researched history of Hispanic antisemitism, in particular, of antisemitism in the Spanish- and Portuguese-speaking Americas, is yet to be written. Until then, a cursive exploration of the tradition of anti-Jewish cartoons in the region must remain fragmented.

However, this fragmentation cannot hide the effect that these *caricaturas* have on their audiences. Not only do they sway public opinion in ways sought by their editors, but they also create a portrait of Jews that generates conflicted sentiments. Exposure to this pictorial tradition played a major role in shaping my identity as a Mexican Jew. For one thing, as soon as my friends and I began noticing these items, we realized the extent to which the small community we belonged to was vulnerable. I wouldn't say we were prone to hysterics. More than a few of us had family members who had perished in the Shoah. We also had relatives who lived in Israel, either since the creation of the state in 1948 or having made aliyah in the 1970s or later. For those and other reasons, we understood the risk that these manifestations posed.

That risk has intensified. The vision, inspired by the short stories of Tadeusz Borowski, of Jews in Latin America being taken to crematoria might have appeared innocuous at the time. Since 1992, when the Israeli embassy in Buenos Aires was the target of a terrorist attack, it has become clear that antisemitism, conflated with anti-Zionism, is on the rise. It might explode at any point. The AMIA tragedy a couple of years later is proof of that ascent. Latin American Jewry no longer lives on the periphery of Western civilization. It is part and parcel of a global realpolitik. After decades of dictatorship, only in the last couple of decades has democracy arrived in full swing in Latin America. One viewpoint is that these antisemitic *caricaturas* point to the fragility of civil discourse. A counterargument is that their existence actually emphasizes the vigor with which democracy flourishes in the region.

But it is still an immature democracy, in a constant state of fragile equilibrium. Over the course of the twentieth century its existence has been ratified by a drive toward pluralism. Aside from the Arab and Jewish minorities, dozens of other groups make their home in the region. They may have a different religious viewpoint. Or they might engage in cultural practices that are dissimilar to the mainstream. Stability and an open exchange of ideas depend on the well-being of any of these minorities, whose vulnerability is permanently at stake.

Just as any stereotypical portrait of Muslims or any other group would be, the humor exhibited in these cartoons is, needless to say, xenophobic. *Caricaturas* are expressions of a latent hostility toward Jews, an impetus that only seems to grow over time. They are no laughing matter.

Notes

1. It is a tradition for cartoonists in Latin America to create pseudonyms for themselves, even though their identity is publicly known.
2. Ilan Stavans, "My Debt to Rius," in Frederick Luis Aldama and Christopher González, eds., *Graphic Borders: Latino Comic Books—Past, Present, and Future* (Austin: University of Texas Press, 2016), 169–77.
3. These words are from the lyrics of a popular 2001 song, "La Memoria" (Memory), by León Gieco. The first line of the verse in which these words appear are "Todo está clavado en la memoria" ("Everything is nailed to memory.") Thus the mural is both a tribute to the memory of the murdered victims and a condemnation of the failures of justice.

The Image of Anne Frank

From Universal Hero to Comic Figure

Liat Steir-Livny

ANNELIES MARIE FRANK (more commonly known as Anne Frank) is one of the most well-known iconic figures of the millions of Holocaust victims. Although canonic collective agents continue to deal with her as a myth, a new subversive path of remembrance has developed in the last two decades that breaks the sanctity of the image by using humor, satire, and parody.[1] It is part of a wider process in which Holocaust humor has become more and more apparent in Western culture.[2]

Scholars who analyze examples of Anne Frank humor in English from American, Australian, and global internet popular culture reveal that they mainly try to deconstruct the "sacredness" of Anne Frank as a myth. But as Barbara Kirshenblatt-Gimblett and Jeffrey Shandler state, "Within its global reach, the Anne Frank phenomenon responds to the particulars of place."[3] In this essay I focus on the specific characterizations of Anne Frank humor in Israel. I claim that, although the previously analyzed Anne Frank humor in English aims to deconstruct the myth of Anne Frank, Israeli humor regarding Anne Frank not only deconstructs the sacred myth but also reflects deeper aspects of memorialization that are an integral part of the debate about Holocaust commemoration in Israel. I open with a discussion of the Anne Frank diary and myth. Then I analyze the developments in worldwide Anne Frank humor. In the main part of this essay I analyze Twitter posts, TV satire, internet jokes, and poetry that reflect the way Israeli Anne Frank humor is used to criticize various aspects of Israeli Holocaust commemoration.

The Diary and Its Worldwide Success

Anne Frank wrote her diary as a young adult between June 1942 (when she received it as a present for her thirteenth birthday) and August 1944. In the diary she describes life in hiding in an Amsterdam attic. The Frank family entered the attic in July 1942. A short time later, the van Pels family joined them and, later on, a dentist named Fritz Pfeffer. The attic was discovered by the Gestapo on August 4, 1944.[4] The Frank family was deported to the transit camp Westerbork and from there to Auschwitz. The mother, Edith Frank, perished in Auschwitz. Anne and her sister Margot were transported to Bergen-Belsen, where both of them died. Otto Frank, Anne's father, the only one among those hiding in the attic to survive, received Anne's diary when he returned to Amsterdam after the war; it was given to him by Miep Gies, one of Otto's former employees, who helped the group of Jews in hiding. Initially, Otto Frank objected to the publication of the painful personal diary and considered allowing only a narrow group of friends and relatives to read it. But after further thought, and having made some changes, he finally gave his consent.[5]

The diary was published in 1947 in Dutch. At first, the book did not have much success. However, slowly but surely, its audience of readers expanded, and a second edition was published and sold out. The diary was published in English in the United States in 1952, with an introduction written by Eleanor Roosevelt. In 1955 the stage adaptation of the book quickly became a hit on Broadway. By the mid-1950s, the diary had become a global asset: 1959 saw the premiere of the film *The Diary of Anne Frank* (directed by George Stevens), which was also, like the play on which it was based, widely successful. The Anne Frank House opened in 1960. This is the same house where the family members hid during the war, and it has hundreds of thousands of visitors every year. The diary was translated into more than fifty languages, and 30 million copies of it, in various languages, have been sold worldwide. Anne Frank's name appears on plazas and streets, coins and stamps, awards, conferences, exhibitions, and monuments. Through its universalization, the diary has become a symbol of human suffering in general.[6] In Israel the diary was published in Hebrew in 1953; the play premiered in 1966 and has since then appeared in several different adaptations, and Anne Frank has become an integral part of the educational system and Holocaust commemoration.⁷

Anne Frank Humor in English

Texts that refer to Anne Frank in a humorous way have been gradually appearing in Western culture since the late 1970s, and this has intensified in the 2010s. In Philip Roth's *The Ghost Writer* (1979), Roth's fictional alter ego, Nathan Zuckerman, meets a woman named Amy Bellet at a dinner party in America. It turns out that this is not her real name and that she is actually the old Anne Frank in disguise. According to the novel, she apparently did not perish but hides so that the diary will continue to be a best seller.⁸

In the last decade Frank has become the protagonist of black humor books, comedy skits, videos, and plays.⁹ Some examples: In the book *Hope: A Tragedy*, by Shalom Auslander (2012), the protagonist moves into a new house and hears strange noises coming from the attic. He finds out that the old Anne Frank is living there. As in Roth's novel, Anne did not perish but is hiding, and in Auslander's rendering she is a bitter old woman with a filthy mouth who constantly swears and lives in frustration. She is working hard on her new novel, but what are the chances it will be equal to the success of the diary?

Comic references to the myth appear in American cartoon satire too, such as *South Park*, *Family Guy*, and *Robot Chicken*. On *South Park*, in the episode "Major Boobage" (2008), the town's authorities decide to deport all the cats. Cartman, one of the four child protagonists of the satire, who is portrayed as a rude, vulgar antisemite, decides to hide a cat named Kitty in the attic. While closing the door he tells the cat to "write a diary." In *Family Guy*, in the episode "If I'm Dyin', I'm Lyin'" (2000), Peter, the overweight protagonist, gets into trouble because of his appetite. He states that this is not the first time his appetite has caused trouble and the scene cuts to a "flashback," a black-and-white scene in which the Nazis break into an attic to find a family hiding. In the center of the attic, a young girl is holding a diary. When the camera pans to the left, it suggests the reason the hiders were discovered was because Peter was hiding with them and eating potato chips very loudly. On *Robot Chicken*, in the episode

"A Toy Meets Girl" (2005), the writers create a parody mock promo for a new Hillary Duff film that is an adaptation of the Anne Frank story done as a Hollywood teen drama. The promo features Hillary/Anne fighting the Nazis, winning and reuniting with Peter, and constantly stating how "awesome" she is.[10]

Anne Frank is also a famous internet meme. Her picture is accompanied by various humorous captions in various languages. For example: "Just noted Twitter is promoting me to 'add a location to your tweets.' Not falling for that one";[11] "Play hide and seek? Sure count me in!";[12] "You guys read my diary? WTF?";[13] and more.[14] These examples deconstruct the sacred myth and imply, as Edward Portnoy claims, that having become too well known, this icon may have lost its power. Frank's iconic stature is precisely what makes her such an easy target of deflationary humor, because sacred cows invite desecration.[15]

Anne Frank Humor in Israel

The way Anne Frank is turning from a myth to a comic figure in Israel is part of a wider process in Israel. In addition to the canonic serious memory of the Holocaust, a new subversive path of memory has evolved, particularly since the turn of the twenty-first century; this new path has been created mostly by the younger generations, who ask to remember, but differently. Holocaust humor, satire, and parody are an integral part of this new memory. Many texts satirize Holocaust commemoration in Israel, parody Hitler and Nazism, use humor to protest against the commercialization and instrumentalization of the Holocaust, vent political frustration through Holocaust humor, and mock Israeli culture by using Holocaust references. Despite the growing popularity of these depictions, they are still controversial and sometimes ignite anger and debate.[16]

As in the Anne Frank humor appearing in Western culture, a group of Anne Frank jokes, which are a subgenre of Israeli Holocaust jokes, apparently tries to deconstruct the sanctity of the myth. For instance, "What are the last words in Anne Frank's diary? 'Just a minute, there's someone at the door . . . ,'" or, "What did Anne Frank tell Hitler when he asked her out on a date? 'Wait, I need to check my diary.'"

These types of jokes also appear in other places in the world, but in Israel the way Anne Frank humor has evolved points to much wider aspects of Holocaust commemoration. In analyzing Anne Frank humor, I have discovered that, as opposed to the humor in the Western world, which mainly deconstructs the sacredness of Anne Frank as a myth, Israeli Anne Frank humor, alongside the deconstruction of the myth, reflects ongoing debates about several themes in Israeli Holocaust commemoration. It is used to ridicule the acting-out of the Holocaust in everyday life, fights religious explanations of the Holocaust, satirizes Holocaust "dark tourism," addresses the ethnic aspects of Holocaust commemoration, and ridicules the right-wing politicization of the Holocaust.

Ridiculing the Acting-Out of the Trauma

Research and public debate indicate that Holocaust awareness in Israel is unique in its intensity, creating a "victimization discourse"[17] or a "religion of the trauma."[18] Holocaust memory is an integral part of the Israeli education system. Jewish Israelis learn about the Holocaust from kindergarten until the end of high school. Since the 1980s, the subject of the Holocaust is included in the matriculation exams, and many high school pupils travel with their class to the former concentration camps in Poland. The subject is also discussed in various ways during the mandatory military service in the Israel Defense Forces. Researchers claim that the Israeli media, educational and cultural fields, and public discourse frame the Holocaust as a current, ongoing local trauma rather than an event that ended decades ago in another place.[19]

Moreover, in the Israeli collective memory, the trauma of the Holocaust is not focused solely on events that occurred in the past. The sensitive relationships between Israel and the Arab nations, the decades-long Jewish-Arab conflict, the threat of annihilation, the continuing terrorist attacks, missile attacks, intifadas, and military operations—all these have created an atmosphere of constant vigilance and ongoing anxiety. The ongoing problematic security situation in Israel, which is accompanied by politicization of the Holocaust by collective memory agents from both sides of the political map, has caused the trauma of the Holocaust to be integrated into present-day Israeli reality and to be replicated within it.[20]

Humoristic references to Anne Frank in social media reveal how deeply the Holocaust is an integral part of the identity of members of the younger generation, who often use Anne Frank references to talk humorously about their everyday life. Through the use of black humor and self-deprecating humor, they rebel against the way Israeli society lives the trauma in the present by deconstructing the fear factor, turning Anne Frank and other Holocaust icons into a common reference, an integral part of the Israeli commonplace.

Checking for humoristic Anne Frank references on Twitter from May 2015 to December 2016, I found ample examples from various areas of everyday life. There are many references in each category, and I present only some examples of the ways that Anne Frank humoristic associations are an integral part of the way Israelis perceive and represent their everyday lives.

Life on the periphery

"If Anne Frank would have hidden in her mother-in-law's house in the Krayot [an area on the periphery of Haifa], her diary would have been much more boring."[21]

Desperate moms

"My son invited ten friends for a BBQ and tried to hide me. I'm Anne Frank just without Peter."[22]

"If I'd write a diary about my mental state two weeks before summer vacation ends, it would be sadder than the Anne Frank diary."[23]

Second floors and attics

"Strange noises from the second floor. I'm home alone. Only the dogs are with me. I have no idea what's going on there and I'm afraid to go up and find out. Maybe it is Anne Frank."[24]

Sex and relationships

"You are less the 'red shoe diary' [an erotic TV show] and more Anne Frank's diary."[25]

Family relations

"I'm at a family gathering. The levels of anxiety I experience resemble the moment Anne Frank was captured."[26]

Everyday trivialities

"I saw a mouse in the dryer. Now I know how the generals who caught Anne Frank felt."[27]

"It became a routine: I look for stamps all over the house. Can't find them. It drives me crazy. I have letters to send and stamps that act like Anne Frank."[28]

Décor

"I think Anne Frank is hiding here," said Moshik Galamin, a designer for a lifestyle renovation show, when he visited the prime minister's house.[29]

Self-criticism

"Anne Frank was 13 when she wrote an entire book. I'm 26 years old and today I've already spilled two cups of coffee on myself."[30]

Hiding

"My wife invited a friend over. I hide in the bedroom like Anne Frank."[31]

"I heard the boss was looking for me, so I went to the toilet. A minute later he appears and shouts 'Are you here?' I've never understood you as well as I do now, Anne Frank."[32]

Bad days

"Let's summarize this morning. It started at 6:30 a.m. I had to drive to Rishon LeZion and now I'm in Tel-Aviv. All in all I would have traded places with Anne Frank right now."[33]

Crummy apartments

"I've wanted to visit Anne Frank's apartment for so long, I didn't know it was so near," said by a disappointed would-be renter after viewing a crummy apartment in Tel Aviv, where the city's rent problems lead landlords to demand high sums of money for substandard apartments.[34]

False hopes for a better future

"Suffering from the side effects of a pill I began taking. Fantasizing how I will pamper myself when it will pass. Feeling like Anne Frank who fantasized about the bath she'll take when the war is over."[35]

Loud knocks on the door

"The most frightening knock on the door on a scale from 1 to 3. 1: The pizza delivery which came to our house tonight. 2: The Nazis in Anne Frank's house."[36]

Dealing with legal authorities

"There is a police car that is following me because they saw I am driving and holding the cellphone in my hand. Feel like Anne Frank."[37]

Sports

"Avramek versus Anna Frank. Auschwitz versus Bergen-Belsen."[38]

Twitter

"Dear diary, today we are in the sixth day in the seventh month. I'm starting the tweet in such a formal way in order to sound like Anne Frank."[39]

Writing abilities

"Reading the diaries I've written from when I was 10 years old till I was 13. Boy, what expressions, what figures of speech. Anne Frank, just without the Holocaust part."[40]

Self-references about looks

"I won't be caught not ready! And when I say 'won't be caught' I think about Anne Frank and when I say 'not ready' I think about her eyebrows."[41]

"I'm pretty sure that 'Anne Frank' was not my response when I was asked what kind of hairdo I want," said by a disappointed woman leaving a salon after a bad haircut.[42]

Social media researchers claim that internet memes and humorous tweets and posts are more than just simple jokes. They go beyond general silliness and are to be taken seriously. They shape and reflect general social mind-sets and can be used as a prism for understanding certain aspects of contemporary culture.[43] There is much research on the complex and diverse effects of digital social media, participatory media, and mass popular platforms in which the circulation of content is increasingly driven by audiences who become the "producers" and not just the "consumers."[44] Research engages in the transfer from a top-down distribution model to a horizontal circulation model, in which the circulation of content is increasingly driven by audiences. Social media offer a new avenue of civic participation, in which citizens are able to express political opinions and participate in important debates. This argument connects with other studies on new media that look at how online networks might inspire conventional political participation and how user-generated content may function as a mobilizer for citizens who are not usually able or willing to convey their opinions in traditional mass media.[45] Humoristic references to Anne Frank in social media are thus part of a technological change that transfers the power to the individuals, the "small citizens" who are directly involved in the circulation of content. It is part of a grassroots political and social movement, a (conscious and unconscious) bottom-up revolution. The way the myth is inserted into everyday lives deconstructs the frightening effect that Holocaust references are supposed to have and therefore tones down the anxiety that canonical agents create.

However, paradoxically, these references, which subvert the collective memory agents' attempts to preserve the acting-out of the trauma in everyday life and aim to deconstruct the fear factor by ridiculing one of its major myths, also strengthen the dominance of the trauma in the present by inserting it even more into everyday life and popular culture. These references demonstrate that for many Israelis the first associations to describe their lives are Holocaust connected. Thus Israeli Anne Frank humor functions, on the one hand, as an attempt to fight the acting-out of the trauma, but, on the other hand, strengthens certain elements of acting-out.

Fighting Religion Through Anne Frank Satire

The question of the presence of God in the Holocaust poses difficult questions. These questions have been answered in Orthodox and ultra-Orthodox Jewish writings through a number of responses, including divine punishment for the sins of Zionism and assimilation.[46] Some writers emphasize the importance of religious holidays and ceremonies in the ghettos and concentration camps and the way this helped Jews to transcend their unbearable everyday lives. Some religious Holocaust survivors, in their writings, have also mentioned "divine miracles" that saved them from death.

One Anne Frank skit engages with religious "answers" for what happened in the Holocaust in order to oppose them. The skit, which was a part of the show *A Place for Worries* (in Hebrew, *Makom ledeaga*, Matar Productions, 2008–2010), opens in a mystical atmosphere: a black-and-white scene of a European city with a bell tower. A young woman's voiceover is heard: "My dear diary, hello." When the camera enters the room and pans across it, the voiceover continues, "I know I haven't written for a long time but I've had very good reasons. We are facing days of fear and danger. And I don't always have the time to collect my thoughts." As the camera pans across her bed, she continues, "Mother again cooked us peas for supper. We didn't have anything to talk about and Uncle van Dam started again to talk about politics. I hate it when he does that." The camera focuses on the protagonist who writes in a diary, an actress whose hairdo suggests that she is Anne Frank. "My dear diary, if you only knew how crowded it is here in the attic," she continues as the camera focuses on her hand writing. "Sometimes it seems that all is lost," she writes as the camera returns to the sad hopeless look on her face and she begins to cry.

Suddenly a bright light appears from the window, the frame turns from black and white to color, and the sound of a voice is heard: "Anne?" The camera returns to Frank, still pictured in black and white, and then in a parallel editing frame, the scene switches from the black-and-white Frank to the color frame, and the voice continues loudly to ask, "Anne Frank?" "Who is it?" asks the frightened Anne. "You know exactly who it is," answers the voice from the frame in color. "God?" "Yes my sweet child. It is me." A blurred image appears through the bright light. Anne seems joyful and relieved. "God. I'm so glad you came," she says through her tears. "I almost started to think that you don't exist." God laughs loudly but then notices her face. Speaking dramatically, he turns to her: "What is it? Are you crying, Anne?" As he steps out of the bright light, the viewers can see that he is a man with long, bushy white hair and a beard. He is filmed through filters and looks as though he has a halo. Anne wipes away her tears. "I'm sorry I'm crying like this. It is just that we are having such a hard time here. It is suffocating." "I know my child," says God, who leaves his color frame and sits on the bed beside Anne, thus entering her black-and-white world. "This is exactly why I wanted to tell you something. I wanted to tell you that . . ." He stops, puzzled. His initially powerful image disappears as the camera focuses on his chubby embarrassed face. "Ah . . . I wanted to say that . . ." It seems as though he is looking for something encouraging to say as he looks around uncomfortably. "Well?" says tearful Frank, who is awaiting his words. He hesitates: "Ah . . . everything will be all right." "What will be all right?" asks Frank. "Everything will be fine," answers God, who now seems a bit more confident, starting to believe his own lie. "I know things are hard and a bit unpleasant now. I understand that it is a bit crowded here and that generally the situation is not . . . ah . . . good, but it is important for me that you'll know that everything will be fine." "Are you sure?" asks Frank. "Yes," replies God. "I'm not just saying that" (his facial expression reveals the opposite). "Everything will work out just fine. Things have a tendency to work themselves out. Well, Anne, I need to go now. I have some . . . never mind . . . anyway don't worry. It will be fine." He stands up and walks toward the bright light from which he appeared. "God?" Anne calls him. "Yes?" he turns to her. "Thank you." Anne seems relieved. "You are welcome," says God and disappears into the bright light. The camera turns from her relieved face to the clock tower.

One of the most basic human needs is having control over one's environment. Control means knowing what is happening in your existential environment at any given moment: the better the control, the better the odds of survival. The saying "knowledge is power" is a result of this primary human need. Humor inherently tends to connect to those significant qualities of human nature. Not knowing is a flaw, and flaws make good platforms for humor. Not knowing is a situation in which one or more details are not revealed to the person or persons involved in the situation or to the viewers. There are two options: The first is that the person performing the action is not aware of a certain detail or event, and the second is that neither is the viewer. It will become known to them at the end of the process.[47]

In the skit the "hidden detail" is the end of Anne Frank, which is known to the audience and to God but not to Frank. She is unaware of the future. This gap creates the black sarcastic humor. Frank was not Orthodox or ultra-Orthodox, and she and her family did not wait passively while putting their trust in God but worked actively to try to save themselves by hiding. Therefore the critique here is not of Frank. This Anne Frank skit reflects a wider secular and even atheist critique of the religious world, belief in God in general, and the explanations of religious people regarding God's role during the Holocaust.

Satirizing Holocaust Dark Tourism

Educational trips to the former concentration camps in Poland have become popular in Israel since the 1980s. Another well-known dark tourism site is the Anne Frank House in Amsterdam, which, in a Holocaust-drenched society, has become almost a mandatory visit for every Jewish Israeli who travels to Amsterdam. As mentioned, one group of Anne Frank jokes simply tries to break the sanctity of the myth. Some of the jokes refer to the Anne Frank House. For example, satirists Shai Goldstein and Dror Rafael telephoned on air during their radio program (2004) to the Anne Frank House in Amsterdam to ask whether she used to smoke marijuana. Comedian Adi Ashkenazi said on the talk show *Yair Lapid* (2004) that she had just returned from Amsterdam; she went to the Anne Frank House but there was no one there. On Twitter, surfers ridicule the "mandatory" visit while in Amsterdam. For example, "I'm in Amsterdam high on drugs after I was with a prostitute in the red light district. My mother calls to ask what I'm doing: going to the Anne Frank house, mom."[48]

On other occasions, Anne Frank humor is integrated into the critique of dark tourism to the former concentration camps.[49] It reflects two major notions that appear in the serious Israeli critique of the trips: commercialization and ethnic conflicts.

Criticizing the Commercialization of the Holocaust
One of the criticisms of dark tourism is the perception that it commercializes traumatic memory and turns it into a commodity.[50] The 2015 poetry book *A Visitor's Guide to Birkenau* (in Hebrew, *Madrich lamevaker bebirkenau*)[51] criticizes the commercialization of the Holocaust in the Auschwitz-Birkenau memorial and museum and the way the historical event is reduced to a series of commodities. The book was written by Shmuel Refael, the son of Holocaust survivors. His parents were deported from Salonika, Greece, to Auschwitz and survived. Refael is a Ladino researcher and has written books about the Holocaust in Greece. His poetry book is the outcome of his journeys to Poland with his students and colleagues.

In Refael's book the graveness, pathos, and national tone that are integral markers of the canonical remembrance and of many poetry books regarding the Holocaust are replaced with cynicism and black humor, providing a different outlook on the traumatic issues. Refael suggests that the Auschwitz museum became a tourist attraction like any other, where the tourists are completely detached from the meaning of the site and are preoccupied with trivialities. For instance, in the poem "Industrialized Memory" ("Zikaron metoas"), he describes things going through the mind of a 15-year-old overweight German high school student who was sent as an outstanding student to Auschwitz "to visit relatives from the near past." Throughout her visit, she constantly deliberates on what she ought to buy: "A Twix bar, for three and a half zloty? / Orange Mirinda / in a can? Or / in a bottle? / Perhaps a Diet Coke." Moreover, the "souvenirs" sold at the museum are devoid of any emotional meaning to her. They are no more than commodities, and her process of choosing resembles the manner in which one decides what blouse to buy in a boutique: "The thoughts would not rest, would not rest / Anne Frank in Swedish, Turkish or Japanese? A poster of leg amputees / or a Jewish dwarf seated on a wicker chair?" The poems illuminate the superficiality of the remembrance. Anne Frank has become a commodity, a souvenir, an item with no historical depth.

Reexamining the Ethnic Conflict in Israel: Mizrahim and Dark Tourism
From the late 1940s to the 1960s, hundreds of thousands of Jews from North Africa and Asia immigrated to Israel in several waves of immigration. Their encounter with the Jewish Israelis already in Israel was problematic and complex. For many years their culture was marginalized and patronized. The persecutions of the Jews in North Africa during WWII was marginalized as well, and Mizrahim were often perceived as alienated from Holocaust commemoration. Because Holocaust awareness is perceived as an integral part of "Israeliness," it marked their marginalization in the Israeli collective identity.[52]

In the last decade, Mizrahi satirists have comically explored notions that appear in serious debates on the subject: the feeling that Mizrahim are not included in the memory and do not relate to the trauma. The humoristic portrayal of Mizrahim being dragged into the domain of Holocaust dark tourism while displaying a lack of knowledge about historical occurrences appeared in the skit show *The Chosen People* (in Hebrew, *Am segula*; Keshet Broadcasting, 2011), in which members of the comedy trio Ma Kashur—three Mizrahi comedians—write and play the lead roles. A central series of skits on the show dealt with two Mizrahi high school students, both named Yossi (who are depicted with an exaggerated, fixed set of negative stereotypical characteristics: ignorant, inarticulate, and vulgar), who join a high school delegation journey to the former concentration camps in Poland. Yossi and Yossi substitute engagement with the horrors of this tragic space with a series of emotionless clichés ("How sad," "Inconceivable," "It's the saddest thing ever," they mumble to each other inarticulately at the beginning of each skit). They have no real interest in the historical events, and they spend their time squabbling and searching for video and online games to pass the time.

In the skit "Yossi and Yossi Meet" (in Hebrew, "Yossi veYossi nifgashim")[53] the two Yossis roam a concentration camp museum, again using their clichés ("How sad it is," "Unbearable"), and then ask themselves what they would have done if they had been in the Holocaust. "If I was back then [the linguistic mistakes are in the original skit], I would have hidden in such a place that no one would have found me," says Yossi. "You are such a hero," mocks Yossi. "Of course they would have found you. Back then there were many snitches. How do you think they caught Anne Frank?" "Of course they caught her," answers Yossi knowingly. "The girl published a diary. You don't want to get caught, don't publish," adding, "What next? Photo on the cover of *Pnai Plus*?" (*Pnai Plus* is an Israeli tabloid dealing with celebrities. Being depicted on the front page is a symbol of success in Israeli popular culture.)

In this Yossi and Yossi skit, Anne Frank humor is used in several ways. It is a part of the critique of dark tourism. Each skit opens with a pseudo-newspaper clip in which the Ministry of Education praises the "fine youth" who travel to Poland. The skits show detached youth. Most of the students just do as they are told: When they are asked to be sad and listen, they do so; when they are asked to check the names of their dead relatives in the museum's computers, they do that. Yossi and Yossi are the only ones who disobey the teacher, and their conversations expose the educational trips as hollow and meaningless. But in addition to the general critique about Holocaust tourism from Israel, the Anne Frank humor has a specific ethnic slant. On the surface, the two Yossis seem to strengthen the stereotype of the ignorant Mizrahim who are detached from the trauma. But on the other hand, the skits can be interpreted as a form of resistance: The fact that Mizrahi comedians repeatedly engage in the issue suggests that they are actually profoundly interested in it rather than detached from it. In addition to and along with claims according to which exaggeration of the vulgarization of stereotypes shatters them,[54] the Mizrahi characters in the skits are a collection of overstated negative stereotypes, and therefore these skits break the stereotypes of the ignorant Mizrahim rather than confirm them. They speak against common concepts in society regarding Mizrahim and their emotional alleged detachment from the Holocaust. In order to rebel against these concepts, they make them absurd and shatter them.

Fighting Right-Wing Politicization of the Holocaust

Since the 1990s, Israeli Holocaust satire has been a part of the left-wing struggle against the politicization of the Holocaust by the right wing. Through satire the creators criticize the right wing and its attempts to relive the Holocaust in the present in order to create constant fear and anxiety that will never enable a dialogue between Jewish Israelis and Palestinians.[55]

Left-wing satirists criticize different figures from the right wing, but the most vilified politician is Prime Minister Benjamin Netanyahu. This emphasis is the result of Netanyahu's constant use of the Holocaust when he discusses the conflicts between Jewish Israelis and Palestinians, Jewish Israelis and Arabs, or Jewish Israelis and Muslims. Left-wing Israelis often speak out against these sorts of analogies from Netanyahu and ridicule his attempts to conjure up atavistic fears. During the preparation for one of his public speeches at the United Nations, one critic tweeted, "I remind you of the 'Bibi drinking game': one reference to Iran = one shot, a reference to the Holocaust = two shots, a reference to Anne Frank = three shots."[56] Another example is the virtual humoristic reaction to his speech on October 20, 2015, to the World Zionist Congress in Jerusalem. Netanyahu stated that Hitler did not want to murder the Jews but only to expel them and that it was the Arab mufti Haj Amin El-Husseini who advised him to murder the Jews. At a tense time in Israel (October–November 2015) that some refer to as the third intifada, Netanyahu's subtext was clear: Every Arab, from the past to the present, is a Nazi. This comparison again turns Jewish Israelis into eternal victims, trapped in a repetitive Holocaust by the Nazis and the Palestinians combined.

Some on the Israeli right hurried to use this equation to prove their claim that Palestinian terror is not related to the Jewish settlements in the West Bank but existed long before the 1967 war.

From the other side of the political map, left-wingers responded in two ways: one serious and one humorous. The narrative of the serious responses emphasized Netanyahu's historical mistake: that the mufti, who indeed was a Nazi sympathizer, was not the one who initiated the Final Solution. The Israeli left also claimed that Netanyahu's speech was another example of the attempts of the right wing in Israel to increase hatred and racism and to dissolve any opportunity for a dialogue. The second way of criticizing and dismantling Netanyahu's statement was through satire and parody. On the internet left-wing surfers released and shared in Israeli social media many humoristic memes[57] mocking this statement.

"The Mufti made me do it" meme was the prominent one. The surfers used various pictures of popular culture icons to claim that the mufti was responsible for everything bad that happened in popular culture. For example, under a picture of Gargamel, the villain in *The Smurfs* cartoons, the caption says that he actually liked the little blue creatures, but one day he met the mufti, who convinced him otherwise. Under a picture of Jerry Seinfeld, the caption says that all Israelis wanted to go to the Seinfeld stand-up show in Israel, but the mufti bought all the tickets. Under a picture of Netanyahu giving his speech, the caption says, "Ito Aviram is the one who wrote the Anne Frank diary." (Ito Aviram is an Israeli writer who, in the 1980s, wrote a successful series titled "Yael and I" for the prominent Israeli teen magazine *Maariv for the Youth* [*Maariv lanoar*]. In the various columns, Aviram wrote first-person diary-like impressions of a female high school student.) In this example Anne Frank humor is another layer that ridicules Netanyahu's statement and shows how far-fetched it is.

Conclusions

By analyzing Anne Frank humor in the Western world, Edward Portnoy shows that these texts do not respond to the tragedy or to the Holocaust itself but rather to the popularization of Anne Frank through the publication of her diary, performance of her life story on stage and screen, and the opening of the Anne Frank House. In his opinion these texts reflect the fatigue of the new generations with that icon.[58] Here, I have shown that in the Israeli sphere, the need to break the myth is only one aspect of Anne Frank humor. The humoristic, satiric, and parodic references to Anne Frank in Hebrew reflect much wider topics than dismantling the icon itself, topics that are an integral part of the debates about Holocaust commemoration in Israel: the acting-out of the trauma, the role of God in the Holocaust, dark tourism, ethnicity and remembrance, and the commercialization and politicization of the Holocaust. These texts are part of a wider change in Holocaust commemoration in Israel, in which the role of humor has grown significantly.

The differences in Anne Frank humor between Israel and the Western world are an example of the special role of the Holocaust in Israeli contemporary life and highlight Israel as a unique sphere of Holocaust awareness. Also, Anne Frank humor, alongside many other examples of Holocaust humor that thrive in Israeli culture, especially since the turn of the millennium,[59] reflects humor's important role as a defense mechanism against the acting-out of the trauma, a tool to vent frustration and fight various aspects of Holocaust commemoration, and an attempt to tone down the constant anxiety that the canonical memory agents create by deconstructing the fear factor. Thus they are much more than an attempt to break the myth or a symbol of fatigue from the icon of Anne Frank; they are a part of a sociocultural revolution that aims to change Holocaust awareness in Israel.

Notes

1. Only a few articles have touched on the subject. These articles do not deal with Anne Frank as a comic figure in Israel. See, for example, Edward Portnoy, "Anne Frank on Crank: Comic Anxieties," in Barbara Kirshenblatt-Gimblett and Jeffrey Shandler, eds., *Anne Frank: Unbound Media, Imagination, Memory* (Bloomington: Indiana University Press, 2012), 309–23; Jeffrey Demsky, "Searching for Humor in Dehumanization: American Sitcoms, the Internet, and the Globalization of Holocaust Parodies," in Rotimi Taiwo, Akinola Odebunmi, and Akin Adetunji, eds., *Analyzing Language and Humor in Online Communication* (Hershey, PA: IGI Global, 2016), 1–19; and David Slucki, "Making Out in Anne Frank's Attic: Humor and the Holocaust in Australia," in Eli Lederhendler and Gabriel N. Finder, eds., *A Club of Their Own: Jewish Humorists in the Contemporary World* (New York: Oxford University Press, 2016), 204–29.
2. Liat Steir-Livny, *Is It OK to Laugh About It? Holocaust Humour, Satire, and Parody in Israeli Culture* (London: Vallentine Mitchell, 2017), 22–34; Gavriel Rozenfeld, *Hi Hitler: How the Nazi Past Is Being Normalized in Contemporary Culture* (Cambridge, UK: Cambridge University Press, 2015); Eyal Zandberg, "Critical Laughter: Humor, Popular Culture, and Israeli Holocaust Commemoration," *Media, Culture, and Society* 28, no. 4 (2006): 561–79; Eyal Zandberg, "'Ketchup Is the Auschwitz of Tomatoes': Humor and the Collective Memory

of Traumatic Events," *Communication, Culture, and Critique* 8, no. 1 (2015): 108–23.

3. Barbara Kirshenblatt-Gimblett and Jeffrey Shandler, "Introduction: Anne Frank, the Phenomenon," in Barbara Kirshenblatt-Gimblett and Jeffrey Shandler, eds., *Anne Frank: Unbound Media, Imagination, Memory* (Bloomington: Indiana University Press, 2012), 13.

4. The mystery of who betrayed the Franks' hiding place has not been completely solved. Until recently it was said that the Gestapo found out about the hiding place because someone betrayed the Franks and exposed their location. (Researchers suggest several theories on the identity of that person.) Recently, a new research study, published by the Anne Frank House in Amsterdam, claims that it was not an act of betrayal and exposure; rather, the attic was discovered during a police raid aimed at finding criminals who were hiding in the building. See Miep Gies, "The Betrayal," *Miepgies*, n.d., http://www.miepgies.nl/en/The%20betrayal/ [accessed 10 August 2018]; Umberto Bacchi, "Anne Frank: Book Identifies Betrayer as Helper's Sister and Gestapo Informer Nelly Voskuijl," *International Business Times*, 9 April 2015, http://www.ibtimes.co.uk/anne-frank-book-identifies-betrayer-helpers-sister-gestapo-informer-nelly-voskuijl-1495662 [accessed 9 April 2015]; Janene Van Jaarsveldt, "Sister of Anne Frank Helper Likely Betrayed Frank Family: Book," *NL Times*, 7 April 2015, http://nltimes.nl/2015/04/07/sister-of-anne-frank-helper-likely-betrayed-frank-family-book/ [accessed 7 April 2015]; and Ofer Aderet, "Research on Anne Frank: This Is How One of the Most Famous Holocaust Stories Changes," *Haaretz*, 17 December 2016 (in Hebrew) http://www.haaretz.co.il/news/education/.premium-1.3162557 [accessed 17 December 2016].

5. Many research studies have been written on the life story of Anne Frank. See, for example, Miep Gies, *Anne Frank Remembered: The Story of the Woman Who Helped to Hide the Frank Family* (New York: Simon & Schuster, 1987); Melissa Müller, *Anne Frank: The Biography* (New York: Metropolitan Books, Henry Holt, 1998); and Carol Ann Lee, *A Friend Called Anne: One Girl's Story of War, Peace, and a Unique Friendship with Anne Frank* (New York: Viking, 2005).

6. The worldwide publication of the diary has also turned it into a milestone in the writings of Holocaust deniers, who have tried over the years to claim that it is unauthentic and even that Anne Frank is an invented image. For more information on the success of the diary and Anne Frank as an iconic figure, see, for example, Dina Porat, "Forty Years of Struggle: Anne Frank's

Diary and Holocaust Deniers, 1958–1998," http://www.yadvashem.org/odot_pdf/Microsoft%20Word%20-%205103.pdf [accessed 2 December 2016] (in Hebrew); Alvin H. Rosenfeld, "Popularization and Memory: The Case of Anne Frank," in Peter Hayes, ed., *Lessons and Legacies: The Meaning of the Holocaust in a Changing World* (Evanston, IL: Northwestern University Press, 1991), 243–78; John Berryman, "The Development of Anne Frank," in Hyman Aaron Enzer and Sandra Solotaroff-Enzer, eds., *Anne Frank: Reflections on Her Life and Legacy* (Urbana: University of Illinois Press, 2000), 76–80; Judith Tydor Baumel, *Double Jeopardy: Gender and the Holocaust* (London: Vallentine Mitchell, 1998), 143–45, 253–58; Christopher Bigsby, *Remembering and Imagining the Holocaust: The Chain of Memory* (New York: Cambridge University Press, 2006); Lawrence Graver, "One Voice Speaks for Six Million: The Uses and Abuses of Anne Frank's Diary," *Yale Holocaust Encyclopedia*, http://www.myjewishlearning.com/article/one-voice-speaks-for-six-million/ [accessed 17 April 2012]; Oren Baruch Stier, "Anne Frank as a Visual Icon," in Oren Baruch Stier, *Holocaust Icons: Symbolizing the Shoah in History and Memory* (New Brunswick, NJ: Rutgers University Press, 2015), 102–18, 119–52; and Tim Cole, *Selling the Holocaust: From Auschwitz to Schindler—How History is Bought, Packaged, and Sold* (New York: Routledge, 1999), 1–22, 23–46.

7. Porat, "Forty Years of Struggle"; Sharon Geva, "A Young Girl's Voice in the Holocaust: The Image of Anne Frank in the Israeli Public Discourse," *Israel* 12 (2007): 81–105.
8. Patrick O'Donnell, "The Disappearing Text: Philip Roth's 'The Ghost Writer,'" *Contemporary Literature* 24, no. 3 (1983): 365–78.
9. Portnoy, "Anne Frank on Crank."
10. See Demsky, "Searching for Humor."
11. http://www.memecenter.com/fun/426598/anne-frank [accessed 5 August 2015].
12. https://knowyourmeme.com/photos/104261-anne-frank [accessed 23 April 2019].
13. https://www.memecenter.com/fun/46896/anne-frank [accessed 23 April 2019].
14. https://ifunny.co/tags/annefrank/1455692745 [accessed 23 April 2019]; https://knowyourmeme.com/memes/anne-frank [accessed 23 April 2019]; https://ifunny.co/tags/annefrank/1455692745 [accessed 23 April 2019]. On Anne Frank humor in Australia, see Slucki, "Making Out in Anne Frank's Attic."
15. Portnoy, "Anne Frank on Crank," 311, 322.
16. Steir-Livny, *Is It OK to Laugh About It?*, 97–132.

17. Alon Gan, *From Sovereignty to Victimhood: An Analysis of the Victimization Discourse in Israel* (Jerusalem: Israel Democracy Institute, 2014), 28–35 (in Hebrew).
18. Avraham Burg, *To Defeat Hitler* (Tel Aviv: Yediot Aharonot, 2007) (in Hebrew).
19. Oren Meyers, Motti Neiger, and Eyal Zandberg, *Communicating Awe: Media Memory and Holocaust Commemoration* (New York: Palgrave Macmillan Memory Studies, 2014).
20. Daniel Bar-Tal, *Living with the Conflict* (Jerusalem: Carmel, 2007) (in Hebrew).
21. Segev Daga, Twitter post, 24 November 2016.
22. Gafi Amir, Twitter post, 23 April 2015.
23. Yehudith, Twitter post, 19 August 2016.
24. Phoebe Ben, Twitter post, 10 August 2016.
25. Goel Pinto, Twitter post, 26 June 2016.
26. Michmecheffendi, Twitter post, 28 May 2016.
27. OK 26, Twitter post, 16 December 2016.
28. Shluli, Twitter post, 22 May 2016.
29. Twitter post, 15 February 2015.
30. One Tweet Wonder, Twitter post, 5 February 2015.
31. Assaf Appelboim, Twitter post, 27 October 2016.
32. Savirush, Twitter post, 19 September 2016 (in Hebrew).
33. Mefazer, Twitter post, 26 August 2016.
34. Avivit Mysnikov, Twitter post, 14 April 2016.
35. Noam Parthom, Twitter post, 28 December 2015.
36. Roei, Twitter post, 22 December 2015.
37. Mor, Twitter post, 6 September 2015.
38. Uricovagerev, Twitter post, 16 June 2016. Avamek Koplowitz perished in the Łódź ghetto when he was 14. He left a notebook with songs. These songs were translated from Polish into Hebrew and set to music, and an album with his songs was produced and released in 2005 by Uri Meiselman and other Israeli musicians.
39. Orel, Twitter post, 6 July 2016.
40. Ronit yamin, Twitter post, 13 December 2016.
41. Rozashwartz, Twitter post, 31 March 2016.
42. Ruthi Grossman, Twitter post, 10 September 2016.
43. Colin Lankshear and Michele Knobel, "Sampling 'the New' in New Literacies," in Michele Knobel and Colin Lankshear, eds., *A New Literacies Sampler* (New

York: Peter Lang, 2007), 1–24; Limor Shifman, *Memes in Digital Culture* (Cambridge, MA: MIT Press, 2013), 119–50.

44. See, for example, Lankshear and Knobel, "Sampling 'the New' in New Literacies"; Jean Burgess and Joshua Green, *YouTube: Online Video and Participatory Culture* (Cambridge, UK: Polity Press, 2009), 58–74; and Henry Jenkins, Sam Ford, and Joshua Green, *Spreadable Media: Creating Meaning and Value in a Networked Culture* (New York: New York University Press, 2013), 153–94.

45. See, for example, Howard Rheingold, "Using Participatory Media and Public Voice to Encourage Public Participation," in Bennet Lance, ed., *Civic Life Online: Learning How Digital Media Can Engage Youth* (Cambridge, MA: MIT Press, 2008), 97–118; and Shifman, *Memes*, 119–50.

46. For example, see a summary of these answers in Porat, "Forty Years of Struggle."

47. Porat, "Forty Years of Struggle."

48. Shlomi Komemy, Twitter post, 17 November 2016.

49. See, for example, Jacky Feldman, *Above the Death Pits, Beneath the Flag: Youth Voyages to Poland and the Performance of Israeli National Identity* (New York: Berghahn Press, 2008); Cole, *Selling the Holocaust*, 1–22, 97–120; and Dan Soen and Nitza Davidovitch, "Educational Trips to Poland: Pros and Cons," in Nitza Davidovitch and Dan Soen, eds., *Holocaust Remembrance: Issues and Challenges* (Jerusalem: Ariel, 2011) (in Hebrew), http://toldotofakim.cet.ac.il/ShowItem.aspx?ItemID=7a596d66-085f-47d7-82f1-b7c8a6fa73b2&lang=HEB [accessed 30 May 2016].

50. Feldman, *Above the Death Pits*; Hanna Yablonka, *Off the Beaten Track: The Mizrahim and the Holocaust* (Tel Aviv: Miskal-Yedioth Aharonot Books, 2008) (in Hebrew); Soen and Davidovitch, "Educational Trips"; James E. Young, *The Texture of Memory: Holocaust Memorials and Meaning* (New Haven, CT: Yale University Press, 1993), 49–80, 119–54.

51. Shmuel Refael, *A Visitor's Guide to Birkenau* (Tel Aviv: Sifreir Itoney, 2015) (in Hebrew).

52. Yablonka, *Off the Beaten Track*.

53. https://www.mako.co.il/tv-choosen-poeple/articles/Article-b91be0ad50d2031006.htm [accessed 23 April 2019].

54. Limor Shifman, *Televised Humor and Social Cleavages in Israel, 1968–2000* (Jerusalem: Magnes Press, 2008), 143–50 (in Hebrew).

55. Steir-Livny, *Is It OK*, 114–32.

56. Yotam Berger, Twitter post, 22 September 2016.

57. I use Limor Shifman's definition of *meme*: "(a) a group of digital items sharing common characteristics of content, form, and/or stance, which (b) were created with awareness of each other, and (c) were circulated, imitated, and/or transformed via the Internet by many users" (Shifman, *Memes*, 41). The "Hitler Rants" meme is defined by her as part of a group called "egalitarian memes"—memes that are based on a certain formula or genre. Surfers relate to a certain formula and modify the text.
58. Portnoy, "Anne Frank on Crank," 322.
59. Steir-Livny, *Is It OK to Laugh About It?*.

"I'm Allowed, I'm a Jew"

Oliver Polak and Jewish Humor in Contemporary Germany After the Holocaust

Gabriel N. Finder

FROM HEINRICH HEINE IN the first half of the nineteenth century through Kurt Tucholsky in the 1920s and before the rise of the Nazis to power, Jewish humor was a fixture in Germany before the Holocaust. In the first thirty years of the twentieth century, many a Jewish comedian made a name for himself in German cabaret and revue, not to mention the new medium of film. The Nazis, of course, devastated Jewish culture in Germany, and humor was not spared. Jewish comedians either left the country or were killed in concentration camps; the same was true of their Jewish patrons. The few Jewish comedians who survived and returned to Germany after World War II no longer had natural and enthusiastic Jewish audiences for their Jewish-inflected brand of humor.[1] In any event, there wasn't much to laugh about. It isn't surprising, then, that in the eyes of many (though not all) contemporary observers, the Holocaust dealt a fatal blow to the tradition of Jewish humor in Germany. Thus in her bestselling book *Der jüdische Witz* (The Jewish Joke), published in Germany in 1960, Jewish sociologist Salca Landman tolled the death knell for Jewish humor in that country: "Wherever one looks, the conditions that produced the Jewish joke are nowhere to be found. One part of the Jewish people managed to survive the Nazi terror, but not the [Jewish] joke. It belongs to the Jewish past, just as German fairy tales belong to the German past."[2]

A well-known anecdote from the life of Mark Twain comes to mind. In 1897 a London cousin of his by the name of James Ross Clemens was seriously ill and almost died. Confusing Twain, whose real name was Samuel Clemens, with his cousin, newspapers reported Twain's demise. As Twain wrote to an acquaintance, "The report of my illness grew out of his illness, the report of my death was an exaggeration." Reports on the death of Jewish humor in Germany are an exaggeration.

Dani Levy, Shahak Shapira, and Oliver Polak are cases in point. Dani Levy's 2004 film *Alles auf Zucker!* (Go for Zucker!) is a comic exploration of Jewish identity after the fall of the Berlin Wall; the main character is a Jewish pool shark from the former East Berlin who is grudgingly reunited with his estranged brother, an Orthodox Jew from West Germany, for the funeral of their mother. In *Mein Führer*, released by Levy in 2007, a Jewish acting coach is recruited from a concentration camp in late 1944 to help an emotionally stunted Hitler prepare a New Year's Day speech, the goal of which is to rally the German people on the eve of Germany's imminent defeat. The Holocaust did not figure in *Alles auf Zucker!* but, of course, it was central to the plot in *Mein Führer*. Although Levy's intention was to satirize Hitler and his Nazi minions, the critics in Germany did not find it funny. (Nor did their counterparts in the United States.)[3]

Shahak Shapira, who was born in Israel and immigrated to Germany with his mother when he was 14, specializes in parody. Repulsed by contemporary commemorative culture in Germany, for his website "Yolocaust," which he created in 2017, he combed social media sites such as Facebook and Instagram for inappropriate selfies taken by people during their visit to the Memorial to the Murdered Jews of Europe in the heart of Berlin. Out of numerous examples, he chose twelve. He then juxtaposed the originals with his own composite image, in which he erased the background of the memorial and replaced it with scenes from concentration camps, leaving the unwitting selfie-takers surrounded by emaciated inmates and corpses and, in effect, shaming them. (He removed the site within a few days of creating it after it had been seen by all twelve selfie-takers, who expressed regret and promised to remove their selfies from their personal social media profiles, not to mention 2.5 million other visitors.)[4]

Then there is Oliver Polak, arguably the most popular among these three prominent Jewish humorists and others in contemporary Germany. If Polak's career in particular is any indication, Jewish humor in Germany after the Holocaust is still alive and kicking. Indeed, it is frequently inflected by the Holocaust. Nevertheless, truth be told, it often appears to be on life support. In other words, Salca Landman was *mostly* wrong.

Of all things, Ephraim Kishon, an Israeli humorist who was a Holocaust survivor from Hungary, represented the salvation of Jewish humor in Germany in the first decades after the Holocaust, taking (West) Germany by storm between the 1960s and 1980s and remaining enormously popular there until his death in 2005. Kishon was so successful because Germans of his generation found themselves able to relate to his humorous sketches of family life and bureaucratic incompetence and venality in Israel without being made to feel guilty for Nazi Germany's persecution and murder of European Jews during the Holocaust. Indeed, with rare exceptions, Kishon studiously avoided the Holocaust in his relatively tame and anecdotal brand of humor.[5]

If any Jewish comedian inherited Kishon's mantle after his death, it is Oliver Polak. But Kishon's and Polak's approaches to humor are like night and day. Kishon's fans must be mortified by Polak. The son of a Holocaust survivor, Polak was born in the German port of Papenburg in 1976. In his edgy and unrestrained brand of stand-up comedy, which has been on display since he appeared on stage for the first time in 2006 in an act titled *Ich darf das, ich bin Jude* (I'm Allowed, I'm a Jew) and published the first of his two bestselling books under the same title in 2008, Polak provocatively and shamelessly reminds Germans of the Holocaust. (His other book is *Der jüdische Patient* [The Jewish Patient], published in 2014.) But Polak does not recoil from deploying antisemitic stereotypes of Jews for his own comic purposes either. Kishon's humor was intentionally inoffensive; both Jews and non-Jews, indeed Germans who lived through and remembered the Nazi period, liked it without compunction. In contrast, Polak is offensive and makes both German non-Jews and German Jews squirm, in part because of his biting satire on the representation of the Holocaust in contemporary Germany. People in his audiences have even been known to leave in the middle of his performances because they aren't sure whether or not they should laugh.[6] Yet Polak has an enthusiastic following in Germany, especially among left-leaning Germans of his generation, and many Jews, even those from the Jewish establishment in Germany, are fans of his.[7] (By 2015, however, he had begun to change direction in pursuit of an alternative comic persona.)

Polak's first appearance on the stage of the Quatsch Comedy Club, a trendy hot spot in Berlin, in 2009 is exemplary of the early stand-up routines thanks to which he made a name for himself. (On YouTube this performance is titled "Gelber Stern zum Anstecken" [A Yellow Star to Stick On].) After an initial round of bantering with the decidedly hip and—if looks are any indication—exclusively non-Jewish audience, Polak declares, "I'm a Jew. However, you only have to laugh if you find it [my act] to your liking. A lot of people are surprised, 'Hmm, they're allowed to perform [on stage] again?' But I think, how long has this history been already, seventy years? Let's make a deal tonight: I'll forget this stupid story about the Holocaust—and you forgive us for Michel Friedman."[8]

Polak pulls no punches—that is clear from his in-your-face declaration of his Jewish identity. Moreover, contrary to conventional wisdom, Jews, he asserts, are back with a vengeance; well out of sight of the non-Jewish population for decades since 1945, they have emerged from the shadows into the limelight (again), whether Germans like it or not. But Polak does not want Germans' (fictitious) sympathy. He wants their ear. For this he is willing to concede the Jews' ace in the hole—the Holocaust—in exchange, this time round, for Michel Friedman. Friedman is a prominent and visible German Jew, a former politician from the conservative Christian Democratic Union (CDU) and talk show host who was vice president of the Central Council of Jews in Germany and president of the European Jewish Congress from 2001 to 2003. In 2003 he was accused of providing drugs to prostitutes in exchange for sex. He was fined for possession of cocaine, but he avoided trial; he resigned from the CDU and the Central Council.[9] As if there was a moral equivalency between Friedman's personal misdeeds and the Nazi genocide of the Jews! Of course, there isn't, and Polak knows this all too well. Polak, for his part, is delivering a stinging satire on the pervasive attitude, entrenched in German society, that blames all Jews in Germany for the conduct of a few bad apples in the Jewish community.

Polak then takes the low road, telling a couple of sexually explicit jokes that exploit antisemitic stereotypes of the supposed Jewish obsessions with sex and money. Here is one:

> What do people know about Jews? Jews are circumcised. Why as a matter of fact?
> Out of hygienic reasons? No, though that's what people still say. Jewish men are circumcised because a Jewish

woman would never touch whatever isn't reduced by twenty percent.¹⁰

The non-Jewish audience squirms—just a bit—and then chuckles. These jokes resemble those told by comedians from the old Borscht Belt school of Jewish comedy. Their function for Polak is to establish a rapport, even intimacy, with his primarily non-Jewish audience, those German non-Jews of his generation who have never heard a Jewish comedian, or, for that matter, any Jew in public, use the stereotypical language of antisemitism, perhaps the language used behind closed doors among their friends and family. It further allows them to eavesdrop on the Jews' inside language. Coming out of Polak's mouth, the message is that it is acceptable to laugh at jokes that poke fun of Jews—as long as a Jew tells them. It's either his terms, or no terms. He can dictate the terms because he's a Jew.

Then Polak switches gears and takes the high road. He riffs on Steven Spielberg's 1993 blockbuster *Schindler's List*. Polak is 14 years old when his high school teachers plan to take the class to see *Schindler's List*, but he doesn't want to see it, as he says, "out of personal reasons, I mean, you wouldn't want to watch *Terminator 2* if your ancestors had been murdered by a cybernetic organism from the future." He goes to the teachers' lounge and asks whether he has to watch *Schindler's List*. After all, the Turkish girls in the class don't have to go to the swimming pool to learn how to swim because they would be required to wear swimsuits (which, it is implied, would force them to violate the Muslim code of female modesty). His protest is, however, in vain.

> My teacher said I had to watch the film, and I thought, it's all the same to me, if it's from the oeuvre of Steven Spielberg—ET, the white egg, Jurassic Park—it can't be so bad, and I really learned something from this film. I didn't know beforehand that Gandhi was Oskar Schindler's secretary.¹¹ At the end of the film, it was really stressful when my history teacher, Mr. Braun—that was his real name—pulled me over to the side and spoke a lot of nonsense with me. He asked me whether I, as a Jew, consider it okay to be eating popcorn at a film like *Schindler's List*, and I pointed to the

screen and said, look over there, Mr. Braun, is that your father holding the assault rifle?[12]

Schindler's List is a sacred cow. Eating popcorn—a Jewish adolescent eating popcorn, no less—during a screening of *Schindler's List* amounts, in effect, to a transgression of proper conduct before "a globally celebrated symbol of the Holocaust," as David Slucki writes. Slucki invokes a famous episode of *Seinfeld* in which Jerry kisses his girlfriend during *Schindler's List*, only to be castigated by Elaine for his "act of defiance against the norms and solemnity of Holocaust remembrance."[13] Eating popcorn while watching *Schindler's List* may not be as egregious as necking during the film, but eating popcorn is disrespectful nonetheless. Moreover, Polak's teacher's name is intended to bring to mind the brown shirts of the Nazi SA (Sturmabteilung) thugs. In other words, who is Herr Braun, the likely heir of the legacy of Nazism, to upbraid a Jewish youth whose father is a Holocaust survivor for juvenile behavior during a screening of *Schindler's List*? Isn't there a world of difference, Polak insinuates, between eating popcorn and shooting innocent Jews?

Polak concludes his performance on a similar note.

> Two weeks ago I received mail from eBay because I had ten positive ratings. So I earned a small present. I don't know, is someone else [here] with eBay? What eBay sends for ten positive rankings is a star, exactly, a star to stick [on your clothing], that's right, a star to stick [on your clothing]. By the way, does anybody know what the color of the star is? Yellow! For ten positive rankings eBay sends me a yellow star to stick [on my clothing]. You have to say one thing, it's as though nothing has changed in Germany. Seventy years ago one negative rating from the neighbor was enough for the yellow star.
>
> So there you have it, from Germany's only Jewish comedian. It's a difficult fate, a hard lot. You know what's happened to the other comedians, don't you? They earn a fistful of money in Hollywood. But I don't want to complain. The Quatsch Comedy Club is also very cool.[14]

In fact, eBay sends yellow stars to its most valued patrons not just in Germany but across the globe. It is normal. Yet Polak's act makes a cogent point, to borrow from historian Michael Brenner, that "even seven decades after the Holocaust, the history of Jews in Germany seems anything but normal."[15] But Polak does not let his fellow Jews off the hook, either. When he refers to "comedians," he means Jewish comedians who, unlike him, have jumped ship in pursuit of wealth—an allusion to the stereotype of the avaricious Jew—while he remains in Germany in spite of his "hard lot." (It is unclear, however, who these other comedians are.) One is then led to ask what his reason for staying in gray and somber Berlin is when he could be enjoying life in sunny California. By the end of the routine Polak has the audience guffawing and eating out of his hand. It is unclear, though, at whose expense.

One might reasonably argue that by suggesting, even facetiously, that Jews have complained enough already about the Holocaust and that there is a moral equivalence between what Germans did during the Holocaust and the deplorable actions of this or that prominent German Jew, Polak is giving young Germans of his generation license to ignore the subtlety of his humor and, in turn, to laugh at the Holocaust and make excuses for contemporary antisemitism. In support of their position, skeptics might well draw attention to the reaction of the audience; what sounds like embarrassed laughter at the start of his show sounds less encumbered, less

Comedian Oliver Polak performing the song "Lasst uns alle Juden sein."

cringing, and more approving by the end. In her popular recent book, *No Joke: Making Jewish Humor*, Ruth Wisse expresses her suspicion that "an excess of laughter might exacerbate the tensions it is meant to alleviate."[16] Seen from this perspective, one might make the case that Polak's humor has the potential to amplify and facilitate anti-Jewish stereotypes in Germany and minimize or trivialize the Holocaust in Germans' eyes. This obviously is not his intention. The question remains, however, What is his intention?

By his own account, Polak models himself largely on Sarah Silverman and Jerry Seinfeld. Like them, he is subversive, transgressive, irreverent, and politically incorrect. He challenges taboos, and his autobiographical skits, which are central to his repertoire, are ironically observational, in the manner that *Seinfeld* made famous. I also see elements of Lenny Bruce in his act. Like Bruce, Polak, performing largely before a non-Jewish audience, does not mince words about being Jewish (think of Bruce's famous bit about Jewish and goyish) and calls a spade a spade when it comes to antisemitism. Unlike Bruce, Polak uses regular setups and punch lines, but what they both have in common is that they place a premium on a personal approach and connecting with their audiences. But the comedian Polak resembles even more so than Silverman, Seinfeld, or Bruce is Richard Pryor. A black stand-up comedian who developed an intimate rapport with his audiences, Pryor mostly took the low road. After the 1970s his comedy was unimaginable without liberal use of the N-word, the F-word, and other choice expletives. But even when he went low, his best routines, epitomized by spoofs of the limitless variety of people to be found in the black community, mined a dark vein of comedy in the stark reality of American racial injustice and the fundamental differences between black life and white life in America.[17]

The difference between Pryor and Polak is that, in his heyday, Pryor played largely, although far from exclusively, to a black audience, whereas Polak's audience consists mostly of non-Jewish liberal Germans of his generation. As Scott Paul puts it in his captivating biography of Pryor, "Richard's use of the *N*-word kissed his entire audience with lightning. Instantly, it established a rapport with those blacks who had never heard a comedian address them in the language of their closest friends and family, and who, in the age of Black Power, were eager to leave *Negro* behind in pursuit of blackness. Less obviously, it connected Richard to those white audience members who wanted to eavesdrop on the black community's inside language, letting them join his black fans in a grand gesture of refusal."[18] In Polak's case it is non-Jews with whom he develops a rapport, leaving his fellow Jews to eavesdrop on their conversation and to wonder who is the actual butt of the joke, who is the insider and who the outsider. As Paul observes of Pryor's white fans, "The problem was not that white audiences became uptight (as Richard saw it), but that they loosened up, flattered themselves for their open-mindedness and tolerance, over the course of the show."[19] The same could be said of Polak's non-Jewish audience.

How are we, then, to understand Polak's act? In the first place, this is not what many would consider typical Jewish humor—"laughter through tears" or self-deprecating humor. And even though the focus of Polak's act is the awkward and pretentious, self-righteous, and self-serving manner in which anything to do with Jews is dealt with in German society in the aftermath of the Holocaust, Polak does not use what for Jeremy Dauber is a distinguishing feature of Jewish comedy: humor as a weapon, in the form of displaced aggression and rebellion, as a defensive retaliatory measure undertaken in reaction to a hostile, antisemitic environment.[20] Indeed, if Polak's fans are representative of a certain demographic subculture in his generation, his audience might even be called philosemitic. In what used to be the ruins of Berlin and, indeed all of Germany—the physical and spiritual homeland of tens of thousands of Jews from the end of the eighteenth century to the rise of Nazism—Polak's humor is arguably Jewish and an incongruous response to the most somber event in Jewish history, but not simply because it is produced by a Jew and has something to do with Jews or even because it evokes laughter in the wake of catastrophe. If Polak's humor is Jewish in some way, it is because it might be said to possess elements of what literary scholar Sidra Dekoven Ezrahi calls a "diasporic aesthetic." Ezrahi examines "the reinstatement of the comic as building block of a post-Shoah universe," and her diasporic aesthetic is animated by an "arrogation of 'the right to speak.'" This arrogation is defined by a comic point of view that is removed from Auschwitz and that is self-consciously utopian or messianic: "The promised happy end is always deferred—and in the deferral is the invitation for imaginative reinterpretations and retellings."[21] But what, then, is the utopian message in Polak's humor, and is it real?

Of course, Polak wants to make people laugh—and he does make people laugh. But there is an intellectual dimension to Polak's comedy. My understanding of Polak's act is informed by a passage in his book *Ich darf das, ich bin Jude*, a comic memoir, in which he discusses his father.

> In Papenburg there were 20 Jewish families before the war, who were completely deported with Emsland thoroughness. Only one person returned and stayed: my father, the living memorial [*Mahnmal*]. At some point the city had a tablet for the victims of the Nazi regime erected in the square where the former synagogue was. . . . One can incredibly easily fail to notice it—[but one can] not [fail to notice] my father, who with his glaring yellow suspenders takes a walk by the canal twice each day. The wandering guilty conscience of Papenburg. And then I came, too: "Memorial—the next generation." Whether I wanted it or not.[22]

In other words, by virtue of being Jewish, Polak is a reluctant symbol whose objective is to remind Germans of their guilt.

But even though being a living memorial is largely the stuff of Polak's comic routine, he has appeared increasingly discomfited by this role because it has impeded him from attaining what he really wants, despite what he has said in the past: the normalization of relations between Jews and non-Jews in Germany.[23] Indeed, in the final analysis, although there are many elements of Richard Pryor's act in Polak's comedy, Polak's act is not primarily an exercise in pricking the collective conscience of his generation; rather, it is his idiosyncratic attempt, through comedy, to reconfigure normalcy between Jews and non-Jews. In the words of cultural historian Caspar Battegay in his analysis of Polak's act, "Jews also are normal Germans . . . and, incidentally, Germans also are normal Jews."[24] This is—or was—key to Polak's act.

In interviews Polak often likens himself—and, by extension, other Jews in Germany—to a panda, an exotic animal kept in a cage in a zoo for viewing from a distance.[25] He does not want to be a panda in Germany. "We Jews in Germany are also just Germans," he writes in *Ich darf das, ich bin Jude*.[26] Thus, what Polak tries to do on stage and in his books—from the distinctive position of a German Jewish comedian born thirty years after the Holocaust—is break the spell of the status quo in contemporary Germany, not to browbeat his non-Jewish contemporaries, most of whom have never met a Jew, but to confront the elephant in the room, to prompt the members of his generation to transcend clichés and clichéd thinking when they meet Jews and when the topic of the Holocaust arises, which it almost invariably does in encounters between Jewish Germans and non-Jewish Germans. In this vein, the title of Polak's popular show and of his first bestseller, *Ich darf das, ich bin Jude,* is telling. According to Polak, it is just "a gag. What matters to me in the first place is comedy."[27] There is an element of truth in this assertion. I would add, however, that, even more important, the title is not meant to confer the mantle of victimhood on German Jews—Polak would reject being labeled a victim—and, with it, a sense of entitlement wielded to nurse and redress their just grievances, in other words, to stick it to Germans. Marching under a banner of victimhood, Jews would only further alienate themselves from non-Jews. What this title does entail, I believe, is that Polak, by virtue of being a Jew born in postwar Germany whose father is a survivor, arrogates to himself the right to speak from a liminal position—it comes, after all, with the territory—about the abnormal state of relations between Jews and non-Jews in contemporary Germany, which he is eager to rectify.

But why does he want to normalize relations between Jewish and non-Jewish Germans? In my opinion, it is because he wants to fit in, indeed to be loved, but he suffers from the isolation or even the existential loneliness that has been the lot of the Jew in Germany both before and after the Holocaust.[28] "I am a Jew" (*Ich bin Jude*)—so Polak begins the show *Ich darf das, ich bin Jude.* As historian Michael Brenner observes, as far as the generation of late-twentieth- and early-twenty-first-century German Jewish writers who often examine Jewish subjects is concerned, "it is still considered somewhat exotic to be a Jewish writer in Germany. The result has been a self-conscious display for a non-Jewish audience."[29] Brenner rightly includes Polak in this group. But there seems to more to his provocative public declaration—or confession—that he is a Jew. Polak may or may not be cognizant of this allusion, but these words, uttered in defiance, are reminiscent of Nathan the Wise in Gotthold Ephraim Lessing's famous late-eighteenth-century play by the same name, *Natan der Weise.* When the eponymous protagonist, who is modeled on Moses Mendelssohn, the dean of the Jewish Enlightenment in Western Europe, humbly introduces himself before Saladin, the Ottoman sultan in Jerusalem, he declares, "I am a Jew" (*Ich bin ein Jud*).[30] Nathan, it should be recalled, is the only Jew on stage, and in the last scene he is left outside the circle of Saladin's reunited relatives, including Nathan's adopted daughter, Recha. It is unclear how Nathan feels, because he gives expression to his emotions only once in the play, when he laments the death of his beloved wife and seven sons in a pogrom. According to literary scholar Benjamin Bennett, Lessing's Nathan is emblematic of the historic mission of Jews to remain ironically detached from the rest of the world, to remain outside the circle of those related by a different blood.[31] Perhaps Nathan is even meant to constitute a critique of the importance still attached to consanguinity in Enlightenment Germany. But regardless of Nathan's apparent indifference to Jews' outsider status in Germany, many Jews in the generation after the iconic Moses Mendelssohn, from the last two decades of the eighteenth century through the first two decades of the nineteenth century, suffered from a deep sense of loneliness. Representative of this generation was Rahel Varnhagen, who regarded her Jewish origins with deep ambivalence and then took advantage of her Jewishness to gain access to German society before she converted to Christianity.[32] Doesn't Polak more or less do the same thing—exploit his Jewish identity because he wants to enter the circle that was closed to Nathan? It goes without saying, however, that conversion is not an option for Polak.

"I want to confess straight away that I am a Jew" ("Von vorn herein will ich bekennen, dass ich Jude bin").[33] One finds this confession in a notorious and rather bizarre article, "Höre Israel!" (Hear, O Israel!), written in 1897 by another Jew anxious to be accepted into German society, Walther Rathenau, the famed industrialist, intellectual, and statesman. Unlike Lessing's Nathan, Rathenau liberally indulges in stock antisemitic behavioral and physical stereotypes. According to Amos Elon, "'Hear, O Israel!' [was] a desperate plea to his coreligionists to accelerate assimilation by consciously imitating Prussian manners. They needed also to work on their physical appearance developing longer limbs and straighter noses."[34] As Rathenau's biographer Shulamit Volkov writes, "Nothing less than a complete metamorphosis" was demanded of Jews in Germany by Rathenau.³⁵ According to Volkov (and other historians), however, Rathenau was not a self-hating Jew.

> Self-hatred, an accusation often hurled at Rathenau on account of "Hear, O Israel!" surely does not exhaust the matter. Rathenau was attacking those Jews whom he considered fundamentally different from himself in every meaningful aspect. He did give vent here to his urgent need to "pass" and to his frustration at remaining an outsider despite all efforts. He blamed the Jews rather than the Germans for what he considered his misfortune, but interestingly, his insistence on remaining Jewish seemed unshaken.³⁶

Indeed, Rathenau fancied himself "a Jewish prophet," so argues Clemens Picht.³⁷ In this vein, one of Rathenau's friends observed that he wanted "to become the messiah of the Jews."³⁸ "In Rathenau's opinion," writes Amos Elon, "Jews would survive as Jews, paradoxically, through assimilation."³⁹ As Picht observes, the demand for the improvement of the Jewish body was not Rathenau's alone. The famous early Zionist leader Max Nordau famously sought to create a "muscular Jewry." Even Theodor Herzl sympathized with Rathenau.⁴⁰ To be sure, Nordau beseeched Jews to build their muscles, but Rathenau took Socialist Darwinist notions to their extreme, demanding of Jews also "to work a couple of generations on the renewal of your outer appearance."⁴¹ Indeed, Rathenau himself was derided by his one of his antagonists for his "Jewish-looking face."⁴² Polak, for his part and for what it's worth, "looks Jewish" with his dark curly hair and beard. He cannot be physically transformed to appear less Jewish and more like other Germans—and, by extension, to be more like other Germans—no matter how hard he tries.

The only other alternative left to Polak was (and is), therefore, to transform non-Jews into Jews. Out of his existential loneliness he tries to create a world in which we are all Jews. As Battegay observes, this is the message of Polak's performance of his song "Let's All Be Jews" ("Lasst uns alle Juden sein").⁴³ There are two versions of this bit: one that Polak performed live during his show *Jud süß-sauer* (Jew Sweet and Sour), starting in 2010, at various venues (including the Quatsch Comedy Club in Berlin); and the other in a music video.⁴⁴ The music video, for its part, spoofs the 1984 film *Ghostbusters*. Polak is seen awakening and getting out of bed with what looks like a hangover, or perhaps he's in a blue funk, and staring out a window as raindrops fall on the windowpane. To the accompaniment of a piano playing in the background, he sings plaintively.

> Occasionally I'm sad and I ask myself where should I go.
> I look out my window and my life has no meaning.
> Why is it complicated? Why can't it be simple?
> Why can't all people simply be Jews?

Then, Polak and the pianist are transported to a pedestrian commercial street in Berlin, and the song is transformed into a rock ballad. Garbed in hazmat suits, he and his ragtag squad, one member of which is black, use high-energy weapons, in the manner of the Ghostbusters, to shoot onlookers—a policeman, a prostitute, a Jehovah's Witness who is distributing the denomination's periodical, *The Watchtower*, mothers pushing baby carriages, schoolgirls, even Japanese tourists—with an intense beam of particles, transforming them into stereotypically identifiable Jews, specifically, Hasidim wearing black hats and coats and sporting earlocks (*payes*), even the women among them. After being zapped, many of them seem to be rocking back and forth in the manner of Hasidim absorbed in prayer, but instead of holding a prayer book, they are holding Polak's book *Ich darf das, ich bin Jude*! Of course, the only Jew in the video is Polak, who, when he is seen singing, gyrates on the street to the music and is dressed like a rock star, defying the stereotypical image of the Jew. All the while he sings, repeating the refrain, "Come, let's all be Jews. / And you and you and you, / You belong, too" ("Kommt, Lasst uns alle Juden sein. / Und Du und du und Du, / Auch Du gehörst dazu"). At the end of the video, Polak, his mission accomplished, encounters a busker, who eyes him with a pensive expression, sighs, and then walks past him out of the frame of the video. As Battegay explains, the street musician is actually Dirk von Lowtzow, the frontman of the band Tocotronic, who, in a variation of the group's popular song "Ich möchte Teil einer Jugendbewegung sein" (I'd Like to Be Part of a Youth Movement), sings instead "Ich möchte Teil einer Judenbewegung sein" ("I'd like to be part of a movement of Jews").⁴⁵ On stage

Polak sings the song backed by an orchestra. His wistful voice rises to a crescendo while he struts across the stage. By the end of the song, he invites the (mostly, if not entirely, non-Jewish) audience to join him, and it does so, with resounding ardor on the refrain, "Come, let's all be Jews. / And you and you and you, / You belong, too."

On the one hand, this is a brilliant reversal of Enlightenment-era and Enlightenment-inspired logic, according to which Jews would be accepted in German (and Western European) society if and when they finally (totally) assimilated by adopting German habits. On the other hand, it is an equally brilliant reversal of anti-Enlightenment, Social Darwinist, and Zionist logic, according to which Jews were urged to refashion their very bodies to look like German ones. For Polak, it is not the Jews who have to change either their habits or their bodies but the non-Jews. In Polak's comic—and messianic—vision, Germany (and the rest of the world) after the Holocaust would be a better place not only if all people were Jews but also, in an unconscious riff on Rathenau's notion, if everyone looked Jewish and, by implication, acted more like Jews! And not just any Jews but Hasidic Jews at that, the epitome Nazi stereotype of the "degenerate" Eastern European Jews, who were poised—"the Jews are coming"—to take over Germany and the world—the Nazis' worst phantasmagoric nightmare. In effect, Polak has created a utopian (or dystopian, depending on one's point of view) post-Holocaust fantasy of Jewry's final victory over Germandom. Now *that's* funny!

"Lasst uns alle Juden sein." Of course, Polak did not expect Germans to become Jews. He was encouraging them, however, to feel Jewish, that is, to feel what it means to feel marginalized in society, the hallmark of feeling Jewish in Germany after the Holocaust.[46] But even if such a transformation was possible to imagine around 2010, when Polak started performing this bit, it no longer seems so with the approach of the end of the new millennium's second decade, when Germany, other European countries, and the United States have retreated to a form of tribalism. In Germany in particular, where Polak plies his craft, times have changed, and what people find funny has changed with time. When Jürgen Habermas, the venerable German intellectual, intrepidly challenged his countrymen in the

1980s to acknowledge and overcome their apologetic approach to the Nazi destruction of the Jews—that is, their making of excuses for the crimes committed by the German army and SS along the Eastern Front where, it was frequently asserted, the war forced the Germans' hands—and take full responsibility for the genocide,[47] he was practically giving license to a comedian like Polak to hurl accusations in the form of jokes in Germans' faces, just as Richard Pryor did to whites in America. And when attitudes like Habermas's still dominated Germany, Polak's humor was funny. But what was funny in Polak's comedy was doomed to near-irrelevance almost from the beginning. His audiences were mostly made up of members of his generation who live fully and unashamedly in the present, yet still accept a certain level of responsibility to confront the Holocaust. But Polak's liberal audiences, whose denizens discharged their obligations to remember and mourn the Holocaust and, by extension, welcomed Jews back into German society from behind the walls where they had sequestered themselves after 1945 by attending his show, have been outflanked by Germans who nurse a deep-seated resentment of Jews and who are determined to relegate the Holocaust to the past and, in the process, mothball any further invocations of German guilt for it—a seed planted by such prominent examples as author Martin Walser. In his acceptance speech on the occasion of having received the 1998 Peace Prize of the German Book Trade, Walser remonstrated "against the perpetual presentation of our shame. Instead of being grateful for the incessant presentation of our shame, I am beginning to look away." Auschwitz, he continued in the same vein, "is not suited to become a routine threat, a means of intimidation or a moral cudgel usable on all occasions."[48] Even a few German Jews, such as Michael Wolffsohn, have gotten into the act.[49]

If you can't beat 'em, join 'em! This seems to have been Polak's guiding principle in the last couple of years, since 2015, when he joined the TV talk show *Das Lachen der Anderen* (The Laughter of Others). In 2016 he started moderating the controversial late night show *Applaus und Raus* (Applause and Out), in which he tosses guests from the program if they bore him. Polak is now part of the problem. He has been known to ridicule the handicapped, and he even expresses racist views, even though in an earlier time he castigated comedians whose humor had racist undertones or even overtones.[50] These shows may be popular, but developments in Germany (and in much of Europe) have overtaken him. After the far-right party Alternative for Germany (Alternative für Deutschland) won its largest share of seats in the German Bundestag in the fall election of 2017, Polak publicly considered even leaving Germany.[51]

The shtick that was at the heart of Polak's act made sense at the end of the first decade of the twenty-first century, when the world was more hopeful, when the end of history was still on the horizon and all people would ultimately—in a sense—be Jews. But the messianic promise of coexistence, let alone brotherhood, seems far-fetched in the contemporary world. In all likelihood, members of Polak's original audience do not feel as good about the laughter he provokes as they did when he first took the world of German comedy by storm, because they cannot help but harbor the doubt that there will be a happy ending. To borrow from the title of Sidra DeKoven Ezrahi's article, "After such knowledge, what laughter?"

It seems that the joke is now on Oliver Polak.

Notes

1. See Michael Brenner, "Als der Humor noch in Deutschland zu Hause war," in Gisela Dachs, ed., *Jüdischer Almanach des Leo Baeck Instituts: Humor* (Frankfurt am Main: Jüdischer Verlag im Suhrkamp, 2004), 11–24. There are also several essays on Jewish humor in Germany before the Holocaust in the marvelous exhibition catalog of the Jewish Museum in Vienna: Marcus Patka and Alfred Stalzer, eds., *Alle Meschugge? Jüdischer Witz und Humor* (Vienna: Amalthea, 2013).

2. Quoted in Gabriel N. Finder, "An Irony of History: Ephraim Kishon's German Triumph," in Eli Lederhendler and Gabriel N. Finder, eds., *A Club of Their Own: Jewish Humorists and the Contemporary World* (New York: Oxford University Press, 2016), 142. A similar sentiment apropos of Jewish humor in America whose source was Eastern European Jewry was expressed by Irving Kristol, who wrote in *Commentary* in 1951 that "Jewish humor died when the Nazis killed off the Jews of Eastern Europe" (quoted in Jeremy Dauber, *Jewish Comedy: A Serious History* [New York: Norton, 2017], 32–33).

3. See Mark Landler, "A Hitler Comedy Goes Over with a Thud in Germany," *New York Times*, 11 January 2007, www.nytimes.com/2007/01/11/world/europe/11hitler.html [accessed 25 May 2018].

4. For Shapira's explanation of his project, see www.Yolocaust.de [accessed 25 May 2018].
5. See Finder, "Irony of History," 147–50.
6. See Marcus G. Patka, "'Jud Süßsauer': Oliver Polak im Interview," in Marcus G. Patka and Alfred Stalzer, eds., *Alle Meschugge? Jüdischer Witz und Humor* (Vienna: Amalthea, 2013), 184.
7. Patka, "Jud Süßsauer," 184.
8. "Gelber Stern zum Anstecken," www.youtube.com/watch?v=5y3jaz7F-uo, 0:58–1:28 [accessed 25 May 2018]. This translation and all others from German are mine.
9. See Michael Brenner, "A New German Jewry?" in Michael Brenner, ed., *A History of Jews in Germany Since 1945: Politics, Culture, and Society*, trans. Kenneth Kronenberg (Bloomington: Indiana University Press, 2018), 428.
10. "Gelber Stern zum Anstecken," 1:30–1:55.
11. Ben Kingsley, the English actor who played Isaac Stern, Schindler's Jewish confidant, in *Schindler's List*, won a number of awards, including the Academy Award for best actor for his starring role as Mohandas Gandhi in the 1982 film *Gandhi*.
12. "Gelber Stern zum Anstecken," 3:48–4:40.
13. David Slucki, "Making Out in Anne Frank's Attic: Humor and the Holocaust in Australia," in Eli Lederhendler and Gabriel N. Finder, *A Club of their Own: Jewish Humorists and the Contemporary World* (New York: Oxford University Press, 2016), 209. In 1994, Oakland high school students made news and raised concerns when they laughed during a screening of *Schindler's List*. See "Laughter at Film Brings Spielberg Visit," *New York Times*, 13 April 1994, p. B11, www.nytimes.com [accessed 25 May 2018]; and Sander Gilman, "Is Life Beautiful? Can the Shoah Be Funny? Some Thoughts on Recent and Older Films," *Critical Inquiry* 26, no. 2 (2000): 281. This incident was also the subject of the radio program *This American Life*; see B. A. Parker, "The Miseducation of Castlemont High," *This American Life*, 27 April 2018, www.thisamericanlife.org/644/random-acts-of-history/act-one-5 [accessed 15 July 2018]. I am indebted to David Slucki for this reference.
14. "Gelber Stern zum Anstecken," 5:12–6:33.
15. Brenner, "A New German Jewry?" 430.
16. Ruth Wisse, *No Joke: Making Jewish Humor* (Princeton, NJ: Princeton University Press, 2013), 25.
17. I am indebted to Richard Libowitz for suggesting that I explore the similarities of Polak's and Pryor's acts.

18. Scott Paul, *Becoming Richard Pryor* (New York: Harper Collins, 2014), 217.
19. Paul, *Becoming Richard Pryor*, 236.
20. See Dauber, *Jewish Comedy*, ch. 1.
21. Sidra DeKoven Ezrahi, "After Such Knowledge, What Laughter?" *Yale Journal of Criticism* 14, no. 1 (2001): 287, 291, 297, 301–2.
22. Oliver Polak, *Ich darf das, ich bin Jude* (Cologne: Kiepenheuer & Witsch, 2008), 31. The words "the next generation" are actually written in English rather than in German. Emsland is a region on the Ems River in western Lower Saxony and northern North Rhine-Westphalia.
23. In an interview published in 2013, Polak claimed that it was no concern of his in his act "to improve Jewish-German relations . . . and to give some kind of absolution" (Patka, "Jud Süßsauer," 185).
24. Caspar Battegay, *Judentum und Popkultur: Ein Essay* (Bielefeld: Transcript, 2012), 130.
25. See Battegay, *Judentum und Popkultur*, 132; see also Patka, "Jud Süßsauer," 183.
26. Polak, *Ich darf das, ich bin Jude*, 177.
27. Patka, "Jud Süßsauer," 185.
28. The longing to be accepted in German society that Polak expresses in his comedy seems to be a topos in German Jewish humor. Dauber notes that German Jewish comedy at the end of the eighteenth and the beginning of the nineteenth century reflected the desire of Jews for acceptance in German society, but the butt of the joke was the Eastern European Jewish immigrants in their midst, who embodied negative Jewish stereotypes. As Dauber observes, German Jews and other European Jews "put their best feet forward by explaining that all those stereotypes they [non-Jews] had about Jews weren't *wrong*, precisely, just geographically inaccurate. They should be aiming their brickbats at these other, far less acculturated and (in their minds) acculturable Eastern European types. . . . That desire by the German Jews to fit in, and the comedy of self-hatred (or self-criticism, if you prefer) that it fueled, was conditioned on hope that if and when this social, cultural, and linguistic transformation *did* take place, the barriers would fall between Jews and their non-Jewish neighbors" (Dauber, *Jewish Comedy*, 21, 22; emphasis in original). What distinguishes Polak from his comic ancestors is that his comic arrows are usually aimed at non-Jews, although Jews are not entirely spared his barbs.
29. Brenner, "A New German Jewry?" 428.
30. Gotthold Ephraim Lessing, *Natan der Weise*, in Gotthold Ephraim Lessing, *Sämtliche Schriften*, ed. Karl Lechmann and Franz Mucker (Stuttgart: Göscher'sche Verlagshandlung, 1887), 3: 88 (Act III, Scene V, Line 326).

31. Benjamin Bennett, *Modern Drama and German Classicism: Renaissance from Lessing to Brecht* (Ithaca, NY: Cornell University Press, 1979), ch. 3.
32. The classic study of Rahel Varnhagen is Hannah Arendt, *Rahel Varnhagen: The Life of a Jewess*, ed. Liliane Weissberg; trans. Richard Winston and Clare Winston (Baltimore: Johns Hopkins University Press, 1997). See also Amos Elon, *The Pity of It All: A Portrait of the German Jewish Epic, 1743–1933* (New York: Picador, 2002), 77–81.
33. Walther Rathenau, "Höre Israel!" in Walther Rathenau, *Impressionen* (Leipzig: S. Hirzel, 1902), 1. The essay was originally published in *Die Zukunft* 5 (1897): 454–62. Rathenau made a similar confession when he went to see Berhard von Bülow, the chancellor from 1900 to 1909, who was considering Rathenau for a ministerial post. When he entered the room, Rathenau made a ceremonious bow, put his hand on his heart, and exclaimed, "Your Highness, ... before I am deigned worthy of an audience, I wish to make an announcement and a confession. Your Highness, I am a Jew!" (Elon, *Pity of It All*, 236). The chancellor, who knew who Rathenau was, apparently found Rathenau's behavior both amusing and wearying.
34. See Elon, *Pity of It All*, 232.
35. Shulamit Volkov, *Walther Rathenau: Weimar's Fallen Statesman* (New Haven, CT: Yale University Press, 2012), 45.
36. Volkov, *Walther Rathenau*, 47.
37. Clemens Picht, "'Er will der Messias der Juden werden': Walther Rathenau zwischen Antisemitismus und jüdischer Prophetie," in Hans Wilderotter, ed., *Die Extreme berühren sich: Walther Rathenau 1867–1922—Eine Austellung des Deutschen Historischen Museums in Zusammenarbeit mit dem Leo Baeck Institut, New York* ([Berlin]: Argon and Deutsches Historsches Museum, n.d.), 118, 124.
38. Picht, "Er will der Messias der Juden werden," 124.
39. Elon, *Pity of It All*, 233.
40. Picht, "Er will der Messias der Juden werden," 121.
41. Rathenau, "Höre Israel," 12.
42. Quoted in Elon, *Pity of It All*, 232.
43. See Battegay, *Judentum und Popkultur*, 130–33. In May 1968 Parisian students demonstrated to pressure the French government to permit Daniel Cohn-Bendit, a leading figure in the demonstrations of May 1968 whose parents were German Jews, to enter France from Germany after it had banned him. The students chanted, "We are all German Jews." In Cohn-Bendit's own words,

"In moral terms, that was 1968's greatest event. Africans, Arabs—all the world called themselves 'undesirable' German Jews. That's when multiculturalism was born." See Claus Leggewie and Daniel Cohn-Bendit, "1968: Power to the Imagination," *New York Review of Books*, 10 May 2018, p. 6. This sentiment is compatible with Polak's own, but there is no indication that Polak had the French protestors' slogan in mind when he conceived "Lasst uns alle Juden sein."

44. For Polak's performance of "Lasst uns alle Juden sein" on stage, see, for example, "Oliver Polak—'Lasst uns alle Juden sein,' Live at Admiralspalast / Berlin Revue," https://www.youtube.com/?v=MHDKr1br30o [accessed 25 May 2018]; for the music video, see "Oliver Polak & Carsten Erobique Meyer, 'Lasst uns alle Juden sein,'" Jan Becker videos, https://vimeo.com [accessed 25 May 2018]. The name of the show in which Polak performed, "Lasst uns alle Juden sein," is itself, perhaps consciously, a play on the notorious 1940 anti-Jewish film *Jud Süss* (Jew Süss), produced at the behest of Nazi propaganda minister Joseph Goebbels. The eponymous villain of the film, set in the 1770s, befriends the Duke of Württemberg and becomes his financial adviser. Süss opens the gates of Stuttgart to a horde of Jews, uses deception to extort the duke's subjects, and seduces unsuspecting beautiful German maidens. When the duke suddenly dies of a stroke, his subjects take revenge. They arrest Süss, put him on trial, sentence him to death, and hang him in a cage. After the trial the Jews are expelled from the dukedom. On *Jud Süss*, see Eric Rentschler, *The Ministry of Illusion: Nazi Cinema and Its Aftermath* (Cambridge, MA: Harvard University Press, 1996), ch. 6. Polak's act and the song "Lasst uns alle Juden sein" in effect annul Süss's sentence, the expulsion decree, and ultimately Goebbel's nefarious intent with a vengeance. Not only have the Jews returned to Germany, but also now all Germans are, at least symbolically, Jews!

45. Battegay, *Judentum und Popkultur*, 133.

46. In her recently published book, Devorah Baum argues that in a rapidly changing global society, large segments of society feel marginalized, dislocated, and imperiled—the trademarks of feeling Jewish. Baum suggests that the commonality of these feelings could serve to bring Jews and non-Jews closer together. Devorah Baum, *Feeling Jewish: A Book for Just About Anyone* (New Haven, CT: Yale University Press, 2017). In other words, many non-Jews are already Jews; they just don't know it.

47. See Jürgen Habermas, "Eine Art Schadenabwicklung: Die apologetischen Tendenzen in der deutschen Zeitgeschichtsschreibung," in Jürgen Habermas,

"Historikerstreit": Die Dokumentation der Kontroversen um die Einzigartigkeit der nationalsozialistischen Judenvernichtung (Munich: Piper, 1987), 62–76.
48. Martin Walser, "Erfahrungen beim Verfassen einer Sonntagsrede," in Martin Walser, *Unser Auschwitz: Auseinandersetzung mit der deutschen Schuld*, ed. Andreas Meier (Reinbek bei Hamburg: Rowohlt Taschen, 2015), 236, 238.
49. See Michael Wolffsohn, *Ewige Schuld? 40 Jahre deutsch-jüdisch-israelische Beziehungen* (Munich: Piper, 1988).
50. Patka, "Jud Süßsauer," 183.
51. "Comedian Oliver Polak: 'Zum ersten Mal denke ich an Auswandern,'" https://www.stern.de/kultur/humor/comedian-oliver-polak---zum-ersten-mal-denke-ich-ans-auswandern---7657932.html [accessed 25 May 2018].

"The Holocaust Was the Worst"

Remembering the Holocaust Through Third-Generation Jokes

Jordana Silverstein

> I am grateful to the friends and family members who let me listen to their conversations and learn from their jokes and their general approach to Holocaust humor. I could not have written this chapter without being able to spend ethnographic time among them all. Thanks also to David Slucki for the invitation, to all the editors for their comments, which vastly improved the chapter, to the copyeditor for all her hard work, and to Ben Silverstein for many invaluable conversations about Holocaust humor over the years. I am grateful to the Humanities Research Centre at the Australian National University for a Visiting Fellowship, which provided me with the time and space to edit this chapter. This chapter was written with support from the Australian Research Council through the Laureate Research Fellowship Project "Child Refugees and Australian Internationalism from 1920 to the Present" (FL140100049).

THERE ARE ALWAYS MOMENTS when certain jokes are made, seemingly out of the blue but in a flash revealing that, for some, memories of the Holocaust lie just beneath the surface. For instance, sitting at a family Rosh Hashanah dinner in 2017, where among the conversations about jobs, arguments over the state of Australian politics, and discussions about new pregnancies, we started sharing stories about movies and TV shows we had recently seen. One cousin rhetorically asked us, "You know what's a hilarious movie?" "*Schindler's List*?" another cousin satirically rapid-fire responded, using wit to bring the Holocaust into our conversation, seemingly where it should not belong. These memories, familial and collective, are, to use Marianne

Hirsch's terminology, postmemories. As she explains, they are belated, a symptom of inherited memory and trauma.[1]

In another postmemorial moment, a friend's toddler walked over to the oven and opened it, trying to climb in. One parent's family is non-Jewish German, the other Jewish Polish. "It's his conflicted heritage," one parent joked to the other, as they laughed together. This would turn out to be a story they would recount to Jewish friends and family in the future, always drawing out laughter in the retelling. This is another instance of the Holocaust bubbling over the surface, coming up with an absurdist edge. It is in the seemingly out-of-placeness, which reminds us of the way the Holocaust is a constantly held memory for these descendants of survivors and relatives of descendants of survivors, that the humor can be found. In the retelling others still are bound together in a community of laughter. This is a laughter created by an absurdist humor that is both self-deprecating and a reaffirmation of survival.

Holocaust humor varies across time, space, and people. Different generations of descendants perform their jokes in diverse manners, creating a wide variety of grammars and languages through which a joke's meaning is made. These jokes, though, always carry a serious edge. They are a way of engaging with the enduring traumas and horrors of the Holocaust, with the continuing aftermath, and of speaking to the present moment. In this chapter I focus on two interlinked examples of Holocaust humor produced by members of the third generation, that is, the grandchildren of Jewish Holocaust survivors, in Melbourne, Australia: ephemeral jokes and short films. In doing so, I examine these formations as examples of memory and explore the ways that jokes serve to keep a memory of the Holocaust within the vernacular of descendants of Holocaust survivors. Through autoethnography and ethnographic research, I explore the nuanced and engaged memory tropes that Holocaust humor instantiates in order to understand the performative historical work that such jokes do.[2] I take these approaches to try to capture the diversity and specificity of Holocaust humor among Melbourne-based Jewish grandchildren of Holocaust survivors, some of whom understand themselves to be members of what has been called the third generation, in the early decades of the twenty-first century.[3] In this chapter I argue that these normally absurdist jokes function as postmemorial moments of memory, instantiating deeply felt inherited memories of family histories of loss, trauma, violence, destruction, and survival. These memories, as I will show, do not articulate precise events or moments but rather touch on the feelings that these memories induce. They are testimony to the depth of feeling, of the continuation of trauma and memory, rather than to "what happened."[4] The jokes, which bring the tellers and listeners into a space of humor, produce an emotional and memorial shared space.

These moments of humor come out of what Jonathan Boyarin, in a different context, calls "a palpable desire for communion with the dead." But they are also a yearning for communion with the present and with the legacies that the ghosts, hauntings, and traumas of the Holocaust bring into the real life of the present.[5] The grandchildren of survivors seek not only communion with their ancestors who variously survived or were murdered during the Holocaust but also a connection with the continuing destruction that that genocide wrought on family lives and the modes through which it infiltrates the everyday lives of those who are the descendants. Many of these modes are ephemeral, and thus it becomes necessary to adopt this ephemeral approach to investigate the symptoms and effects.[6] In this chapter I therefore seek to stitch together an ephemeral archive of jokes, bon mots, one-liners, and throwaway enunciations to explore the jokes that members of the third generation in Melbourne tell.[7] These are jokes that are not "about" the Holocaust per se but rather ones that invoke the Holocaust and its long aftermath. That is, these jokes are not stories set during the Holocaust; rather, they mention the Holocaust (or an aspect of it) in passing. These jokes are, as I will make clear, part of a social process of creating a community of humor-makers. I begin this chapter by describing the contours of this group, which we can understand as being part of the third generation in Melbourne, before moving on to explore some of these instances of memory in more detail, exploring the ways in which they act as a form of collective and social memory, producing and articulating an experience of being a member of the third generation. As explored in the classic essay by Mary K. Rothbart and Diana Pien, these jokes often play with "incongruity," bringing the Holocaust into an incongruous moment where it might not be expected to reside.[8] They also self-consciously sit on the margins of good taste, demonstrating the ways that these joke tellers themselves sit between humor and tragedy. These jokes, as it will become clear, are by definition not humorous to everyone.

How Can We Understand the Third Generation?

We must begin, then, by asking what precisely is meant by the term *third generation*. I choose to avoid using capital letters when using the term in this chapter to point to the ways that the third generation is not one thing, not one clearly definable group. There are currently approximately 113,000 Jews living in Australia, with just over half being Australian-born. Of those, large numbers are the descendants of Holocaust survivors, but there is unfortunately no clear data available to determine precisely how many.[9] As many others have noted, though, the Holocaust retains a large hegemonic presence in Australian Jewish life, serving an important social role in formulating a group identity built through collective traumatic memory.[10] However, although many grandchildren of Holocaust survivors are present in Australia, not all identify as being part of a collective generation. Others might take on this self-definition but maintain their own understanding of what it means. As articulated in the introduction to *In the Shadows of Memory: The Holocaust and the Third Generation*, a book I co-edited with David Slucki and Esther Jilovsky,

> We start from the idea . . . that there is no one way in which this sense [of being a member of the third generation] is manifested in our memories, histories, identities and emotions; that there is no one way of being a survivor, or being a member of the third generation. It is clear, though, that the grandchildren of Holocaust survivors have a particular relationship to the Holocaust.[11]

But even given this openness and flexibility, critiques of the idea of a third generation are vital. Karolina Krasuska offers one when she reminds us of the ways that writing about biological or familial generations can become "another tool instrumental in making normative gender relations and reproductive heterosexuality both obvious and inevitable."[12] The normalization of heterosexual gender and sexual relations is indeed a key way in which Holocaust postmemories have become instantiated in the Melbourne Jewish community.[13] In this chapter I propose that Holocaust humor can be a binding and productive force for some members of the third generation:

What if, alongside a relationship to a particular survivor or a place within a family being constitutive of one's membership—or not—in the third generation, one felt oneself to be a member through one's relationship to Holocaust humor? As David Slucki has sketched elsewhere, broadly, members of the third generation in Melbourne appear to feel differently about Holocaust jokes from those of other age groups or relationships to survivors.[14] I should note, however, that although this is generally true, it is not a strict rule: Slucki provides examples of people who might be considered members of the third generation but oppose Holocaust memorializations that venture into the comedic. Of course, there are also people outside the third generation who might see comedic value in these jokes and members of the third generation who might joke in a different way from the one I am outlining in this chapter. Like many other aspects of humor, what one enjoys and deploys is also often a matter of personal taste.

What Are These Jokes?

Following Jonathan Boyarin's autoethnographic lead, I predominantly rely on the snippets of conversation, the moments betwixt and between, the formative utterances, that scatter themselves throughout my interactions with my family, friends, and community.[15] It is these ephemeral moments of speech that constitute most of the third generation's approach to humor in Melbourne in the present moment. Indeed, this is gradually becoming evident to many throughout the Jewish community. In December 2017 I participated in a panel of four third-generation writers and scholars for an adult education short course about Holocaust literature being taught by Sue Hampel, a local Holocaust educator. After each of us spoke, in turn outlining our personal histories, our relationships to Holocaust memory, and the ways in which the Holocaust is expressed in our work, we took questions from the audience. One audience member picked up on a current that had threaded throughout our words and asked about the jokes that we had each thrown in. These jokes included jovial mentions of the therapy that some of us had undergone to deal with our inherited trauma, the large place that the Holocaust occupied in our lives and thinking, and the lack of knowledge we had about our families. These were knowingly absurdist and incongruous jokes that peppered our speech. She asked whether this was something that we felt the third generation regularly did, and all of us agreed that, indeed, it is.

Holocaust jokes are woven throughout the interactions that my brother and I have. As the grandchildren of two Holocaust survivors—our maternal grandparents, both from southwestern Poland, spent the war years in ghettos and camps—we have known about the Holocaust all our lives. There was never a moment of learning, although in recent years we have undertaken more research to find information about the addresses, dates, and relatives whose details we did not previously know.[16] We have researched the camps they were in and examined their applications for naturalization in Australia.[17] This search for knowledge has been deeply moving, raising questions about what each of us knew about the family structure, those ancestors who were murdered, and the stories about the family we had been told as we were growing up. As others have charted, these stories that families pass on to the third generation within the Melbourne Jewish community are often attenuated and uncertain, and carry heightened emotions.[18] But instead of regularly recalling the stories that have emerged, my brother and I are more likely to articulate a postmemory of the Holocaust through its invocation in joke form, throwing around, for instance, examples of how something is "worse than" the Holocaust. (Sometimes we get more specific and riff in the vein offered by Monty Python's "Four Yorkshiremen" sketch.)[19] There is, we could say, an absurdist twist in these jokes, which gets to the heart of the pain.

When David Slucki, Esther Jilovsky, and I were putting together the call for papers for the book that would eventually become *In the Shadows of Memory*, one idea that David and I half-jokingly discussed was that we would ask all contributors to supply a Holocaust joke. Even though this did not end up being a request we made, this anecdote is indicative of the ways that Holocaust humor is prevalent among the third generation in Melbourne. Conversations between members of the third generation are peppered with jokes about being afraid of heights, fearing sudden death or dismemberment, seeing therapists, dealing with our families and their intimate involvement in our lives, or analyzing our eating habits (inevitably disordered in some way). Any train travel provides the possibility of joke making, particularly train travel in Europe. Warnings to avoid trains going east are de rigueur. At a workshop for members of the third generation, held in early 2017 at the Jewish Museum in Sydney, one participant asked, "Who doesn't love to talk about their shit?" to laughs of recognition. Another spoke of the "everyday guilt" we carry, again to comic effect. One friend, who lived at the time in New York with her American partner and who was regularly visited by friends from Melbourne, would find her partner commenting on the ways that the Holocaust would come up in every conversation that her Melbourne friends had. This became a source of humor for my friend in her conversations with other Melbourne Jews who were in on the joke.

After several friends and I watched a film screened as part of the Northside Jewish Film Club—a Jewish film club that a friend and I ran out of the cinema at the back of a bar in North Fitzroy, in Melbourne's inner city—we talked about Holocaust jokes, and one person asked whether I had ever played the dinner-party game where each letter of the alphabet is allocated to a different Holocaust item: A is for Auschwitz, B is for Bergen-Belsen, through to Z, which is for Zyklon B. This is, it turns out, a common game among her friends. Earlier in the conversation, when we were talking about where in Melbourne we all live, someone commented that they live "in the ghetto" (by which they meant Caulfield, a suburb across town from where we sat, around which the majority of Melbourne's Jews live), and another said that they live in the "original ghetto," implying Carlton, where large numbers of Eastern European Jews first settled upon arriving in Melbourne, post-Holocaust.[20] At the mention of a ghetto another person jokingly asked, "Warsaw?" provoking laughter among the others at the table.

We can understand that this Holocaust humor shared among third-generation Melbourne Jews is an example of the leaking-out of traumatic memory. It is testament to an excess of feeling that needs to go somewhere and so is pushed out in the form of words and laughter. It demonstrates a leakiness of bodies and histories, the ways in which this past that sits within us in the form of postmemory is in so many ways *too much*.[21] It is a living connection to the past, the present, and even the future. It is also a way of creating a shared space of memory.[22] As Sara Ahmed has sketched, rather than being natural, emotions are social, cultural, historical, and political productions that stick people together.[23] Through the sharing of emotions, through their affective work, people are brought together. Emotions do sticky work. The laughter, or knowing smiles, that members of the third generation have learned—and taught each other—to enunciate, is a production of that sticky work. Moreover, there is a shared knowledge or understanding that these jokes sit at the margins of good taste, but this is rarely a source of concern. Indeed, this is perhaps part of the point: knowledge that these jokes can be told only by certain people or in a certain way. These jokes create communities; these communities create these jokes. These jokes, and these communities, rest on a bedrock of a great trauma and are produced by, and are productive of, collective (post)memory.[24] As Cathy Caruth has, by way of Freud and Lacan, made clear, "The transmission of the psychoanalytic theory of trauma . . . cannot be reduced . . . to a simple mastery of facts and cannot be located in a simple knowledge or cognition, a knowledge that can see and situate precisely where the trauma lies."[25] The "performance" is central and allows for recognition of "the ethical imperative of an awakening that has yet to occur."[26] The jokes, we can thus understand, are deadly serious representations of belated familial pain and grieving, along with the recognition and celebration of survival. They bond together in a community those who joke in the same way, with the same reliance on absurdism, the same belated pain. They mark a loss, an absence, a reckoning with mass death.

That is, the jokes serve a social process, as symptoms of memory and builders of a community of rememberers. Joan Scott's description of experience as a type of sociality can be helpful here in understanding the ways that Holocaust humor, or the production and dissemination of jokes about the Holocaust, particularly ephemeral jokes, function to produce a third generation. What does it mean to carry the histories and experiences, the memories, of the third generation? We can follow the lead of Joan Scott and consider the jokes that members of the third generation make as being productive of the third generation, while also understanding that these experiences of joking are produced as a result of the collective and individual histories that bring this third generation into existence. "It is not," Scott writes, "individuals who have experience, but subjects who are constituted through experience."[27] The "experience" of the ephemeral joke, following Scott, can be understood as being "a discursive event" that aids in the "emergence of a new identity": the experience of the joke does not preexist the identity.[28] One does not naturally have the experience of telling the joke, or listening to, or laughing with, the joke. Rather, as Scott explains, to approach the experience of the joke in this way, as productive discourse, "is to refuse a separation between 'experience' and language and to insist instead on the productive quality of discourse . . . Subjects do have agency. They are not unified, autonomous individuals exercising free will, but rather subjects whose agency is created through situations and statuses conferred on them."[29]

Scott continues, asserting that "subjects [here, members of the third generation] are constituted discursively and experience is a linguistic event (it doesn't happen outside established meanings), but neither is it confined to a fixed order of meaning. Since discourse is by definition shared, experience is collective as well as individual."[30] Scott poignantly explains that "experience is a subject's history."[31] That history is collective and individual: it shapes both the group and the person. And the histories that the joke-telling subjects can be understood to carry are therefore histories of the Holocaust, which are put into memorial form in these jokes. These jokes both narrate and further a set of histories; these histories are individual, familial, generational, and collective.

Moreover, as Scott explains, we should understand categories (of identity or practice) as historical. Thus humor functions as an ephemeral memory, not as a way to retell specifics of what happened during the Holocaust or in its long aftermath but rather to mark the place of the Holocaust in everyday third-generation memories and histories.[32] This humor, in this telling, helps to construct the category of the third generation. That is, this category is not natural or inevitable, nor does it exist outside discourse or practice. The Holocaust jokes that I am exploring in this chapter are produced by and through the third generation, and that generation is produced by and through these jokes. This is not to suggest that every member of the third generation necessarily tells such jokes, but I have observed that this humor plays a formative role for many. These jokes, and the emotions they produce, stick people together in a circuit of teller and laugher. The jokes do affective work; they are productive social significations.

I have described these jokes as social products and as a form of memory. They are both, because memory is a social, collective process. These jokes can be most usefully understood as postmemories, a formation of memory described by Marianne Hirsch. Speaking about the relationship between those who came after the Holocaust and those who endured it, Hirsch asks, "How can we best carry their stories forward, without appropriating them, without unduly calling attention to ourselves, and without, in turn, having our own stories displaced by them? How are we implicated in the aftermath of crimes we did not ourselves witness?"[33] It is this long aftermath, and our implication in it—however understood or defined, however tenuous or vital—that makes these stories ours also, in part. The jokes that I am exploring here are testimony to the ways that the long aftermath of the Holocaust ensures that its long story is one that is not only of those who were there but also a story of those who have come after. At times these are stories of what happened, but they are also, especially in this chapter, stories of a series of emotional effects and experiences of loss. As Eva Hoffman has written in contemplating "the long afterlife of loss," rather than precise memories, what was "often received with great directness were the emotional sequelae of our elders' experiences, the acid-etched traces of what they endured."[34] Although Hoffman, like Hirsch, is writing of the Second Generation (the children of Holocaust survivors), she recognizes the ways that this can transfer to the third generation. "Loss leaves a long trail in its wake," she writes. "When the losses are as enormous as those that followed from the Holocaust—when what was lost was not only individuals but a world—the disappearances and the absences may haunt us unto the third generation."[35]

In her work on postmemory Hirsch focuses largely on the Second Generation, and the force of this form of memory means that it is handed down to further generations as well.

> Postmemory's connection to the past is thus actually mediated not by recall but by imaginative investment, projection, and creation. To grow up with overwhelming inherited memories, to be dominated by narratives that preceded one's birth or one's consciousness, is to risk having one's own life stories displaced, even evacuated, by our ancestors. It is to be shaped, however indirectly, by traumatic fragments of events that still defy narrative reconstruction and exceed comprehension. These events happened in the past, but their effects continue into the present. This is, I believe, the structure of postmemory and the process of its generation.[36]

The jokes that I am exploring in this chapter are testimony to the "traumatic fragments" and ways in which descendant generations seek not to make narrative meaning and coherence out of the past but rather to incorporate and enact the memories as fragmentary. These ephemeral jokes testify to the ways in which the Holocaust, and its continued traumatic affects, "exceed comprehension" and stand as constant memories. The ephemeral nature of the jokes, as I have shown, is a result of the constancy and force of the Holocaust memories that are held, carried, and articulated. Furthermore, these are jokes in which memory and identity themselves are the subject of the joke. The humor arises in part from the self-referential nature of the jokes: They are not jokes that laugh at the Holocaust but jokes that mock those of us who are doing the constant remembering. In doing so, these jokes also perform the work of continuing the remembering while acknowledging the rememberers. Even as they potentially skirt the margins of good taste, they articulate a vital set of memories and the presence of a collective. The pleasures, and the pains, of the constant carrying of some sort of inherited trauma sits on the surface of the comedy.[37]

If we consider who, or what, is being identified in these jokes, we can understand that it is perhaps the joke itself, as a marker of memory. There is an identification with the trauma and the memory of the Holocaust and an identification with the joke teller as another person who experiences these dripping symptoms of intergenerational trauma. The jokes work to bind people together in a community of humor hearers and tellers.[38] The laughter, when there is laughter, is always meant to carry a tinge of the horror. It is not (necessarily) the laughter of guffaws or belly laughs, but the laughter of knowingness, of incredulity, of memory of trauma. The question then becomes, what are we remembering when we tell these jokes? I believe that the work these jokes do is to create an ephemeral memory of the Holocaust and to produce a social community of rememberers. The intention, and the result, is not a memory full of precision of what happened. It is not a focus straight on the horrors, but a grazing of the horrors, a remembering of a set of feelings, and a location within the inherited (post)memories. These jokes are a way of keeping within daily memory the long aftermath of the Holocaust and its impact on the histories and memories we carry, without encountering the disaster that is the Holocaust fully. Because, indeed, who would want to encounter it fully! And we know well that we can never know what it was like to be *there*.³⁹ These comic moments, then, are testament to the imprecision of the memories that are handed down to those who came after the survivors, and to the affect these memories carry and institute. Ephemeral jokes serve as a marker of a bigger, barely known, history. They touch on the trauma that is being carried intergenerationally and ease the feelings of this trauma and its dominant place in Melbourne Jewish life. These are absurdist and incongruous jokes that deliberately push the boundaries of good taste. There is a self-conscious edginess to these jokes. They walk a tightrope.

This Absurdist Humor on the Screen: *"Minority Report"*

Before I conclude, let me turn to one longer example of this type of humor. Two Melbourne Jewish members of the third generation, Carla Silbert and Justin Olstein, have created the web series *Echo Chamber*.⁴⁰ In one short (3-minute) episode called "Minority Report," a scene plays out between a couple, Aviva and Jack.⁴¹ Jack is sitting at the kitchen table, writing a grant application for his short film about "a seven-year-old boy winning a billy cart race," while Aviva makes a cup of tea. Jack, a straight white man, bounces ideas around, looking for a way to produce a minority status within his application, as he believes this will enhance his chances of receiving the grant. He raises the possibility of mentioning his sister coming out to him and his subsequent embracing of the LGBTIQ community (the initials of which he struggles to remember), casting a Sudanese man as the race marshal because "there aren't really enough roles for black actors," and the fact that his "cinematographer is a Torres Strait Islander." When Aviva reacts in disbelief to his proposals, Jack, exasperated, argues, "Well what am I supposed to do? I've got no minority cards of my own to play, but my work is very inclusive, so shoot me." He continues, "Aviva, you're a Jewish woman whose grandparents survived the Holocaust. You've no idea what it's like not to be marginalized." "Are you saying that I got the Moshinsky Foundation Grant because I'm Jewish, or because I'm a woman? Just not because I'm a good writer?" asks Aviva. "Aviva, you're a great writer who also happens to be part of a historically persecuted minority *and* disadvantaged by the patriarchy, and you know what? It's OK to use it." "I know it's OK," Aviva retorts, "and I won that grant on creative merit." "Exactly!" says Jack. "And so will you," concludes Aviva, as she walks away, pausing just before exiting the kitchen to turn around and say, "But, maybe briefly mention your partner's Holocaust background in your application, just to be sure." And Jack continues to write, clearly inspired and motivated.

This is a joke that deliberately plays at the margins of acceptability, working to place one's third-generation status as something that can be exploited but whose exploitation is owned by those in the third generation.[42] It is inherently a joke about survival—one could not be making a joke about being the granddaughter of Holocaust survivors and how to exploit that status if there were no granddaughters of survivors—thus participating in what Louis Kaplan has identified as the "transgressive commemorative practice [that] values the power of laughter as liberating and as a means of survival in the face of death."[43] Although Kaplan is referring to jokes and laughter produced at the time of the Holocaust, and as part of the Holocaust, we can understand that this web series episode continues this tradition, albeit in postmemorial fashion.

It is an ephemeral joke that binds together the writers and directors of the episode, together with their audience, in a shared third-generation identity. Whereas within the filmic world Aviva is not making a joke, the line plays as a joke for the audience, thus instantiating this comedic moment for those in the know. Importantly, the experience of those watching the joke unfold—and the laughter payoff at the end—will be vastly different for those who are members of the third generation and those who are not: Those in the audience who are third generation are brought into a sphere of humor different from those who are not. This is an instance of comedy that uses experience—familial, generational, peer-based—to produce comic effect. As Boyarin writes, "Identity (personal and collective)" should be understood "as always contingent, always in need of maintenance, reinvention, repair," but also as being constituted through an "emphasis on its boundaries, its points of contact and repulsion vis-à-vis the other."[44] This video and this joke can be understood to produce both the identity and its boundaries. How we laugh is a product of the histories we carry. Although this is true of almost every joke, the boundaries and identities that are being drawn here are particular to the histories being carried: They are a product of that experience of being a member of the third generation, both thoroughly within the community of descendants of survivors and living with and among peers who are not. It is the straddling of those worlds, the living in the edges, boundaries, and points of contact, that produces that experience. This brief filmic scene reminds viewers of the ways that the generational trauma can be carried, exploited, integrated, and given meaning.

Australian comedian Hannah Gadsby has recently described self-deprecating comedy as releasing a pressure valve, allowing the pain of a difficult situation to become bearable.[45] A well-timed joke, she makes clear, can help to deal with the excessive feelings raised by a traumatic memory. As Melbourne-based filmmaker Freda Freiberg has noted, "Comedy celebrates [our] capacity to endure the most excruciating trials and tribulations, humiliations and oppressions, and because of its irreverent attitude towards figures of authority, it has been especially popular with the powerless."[46] The types of jokes explored in this chapter are often absurdist, or silly, existing in the realm of what is commonly called gallows humor. They rarely appeal to everyone: It is our personal histories—a combination of how we were raised, who we interact with, what stories we rely on—rather than any psychological, neurological, or pathological process that determine how we respond to these jokes and whether we make them. Like the jokes themselves, their existence and what they create is ephemeral and social. This is the contingency of the "experience" of the joke.

Conclusion

In 2009 I gave a guest lecture in a third-year Holocaust and genocide studies course, for which I was one of the tutors, at a university in Melbourne with an ethnically diverse student body, many of whom were the first in their families to attend university. Throughout the semester, the main lecturer and I had many private conversations about jokes and genocide and about how essential a sense of humor is to understanding the worlds of genocides. About halfway through my lecture—my first ever guest lecture—I started to worry that the students were no longer paying attention. It was a Thursday afternoon at the end of the semester, and I was anxious. So, seemingly apropos of nothing, I told the students two jokes. One I have since forgotten. The other was: "What's the difference between Sarajevo during the siege and Auschwitz? In Auschwitz at least there was gas." The jokes, maybe unsurprisingly, fell flat. From memory, I blushed, watched the students look at me curiously, and returned hurriedly to my lecture.

A few things distinguish this (potentially) comic moment from the others I have described in this chapter. The jokes that I have been concentrating on here are one-liners, thrown in from the side, designed, however unconsciously, to elicit a smirk and to bond the speaker and the listener in remembrance of a common Holocaust heritage. The joke I told to the class, besides being structurally different in form, had an audience that could not be brought into the affective circle. As a moment of third-generation memory, then, it failed. It perhaps had the potential to work on a different level—through it I could mark myself as a member of the third generation, as someone who could claim access to this subject matter as grounds for humor—but it was unable to bring others into the circuit. Third-generation Holocaust humor, then, can function as a marker of difference, as a memorial act that declares the speaker as someone different from their audience.

People carry stories within them.[47] The jokes that I have sketched in this chapter carry both history and memory; they are an embodied and enunciated enactment of postmemory. They remember that the trauma and aftereffects of the Holocaust continue, that the aftermath of genocide is long, and that our collective and individual psyches are touched by the deep loss in innumerable ways and with innumerable symptoms and effects.

Notes

1. I explore Marianne Hirsch's ideas of postmemory in more detail later in this essay.
2. On the performative, see Judith Butler, *Gender Trouble: Feminism and the Subversion of Identity* (New York: Routledge, 2006), xv (and throughout).
3. Although I use the term *third generation* as a shorthand, in this chapter I am referring to Jewish people living, or who once lived, in Melbourne, Australia.
4. See Shoshana Felman and Dori Laub, *Testimony: Crises of Witnessing in Literature, Psychoanalysis, and History* (New York: Routledge, 1992).
5. Jonathan Boyarin, *Jewishness and the Human Dimension* (New York: Fordham University Press, 2008), 5.
6. As Marianne Hirsch writes, "The bodily, psychic, and affective impact of trauma and its aftermath, the ways in which one trauma can recall, or reactivate, the

effects of another, exceed the bounds of traditional historical archives and methodologies." This is why we need to use a particular methodology and archive, using autoethnography and an ephemeral archive. Marianne Hirsch, *The Generation of Postmemory: Writing and Visual Culture After the Holocaust* (New York: Columbia University Press, 2012), 2.

7. In bringing together and using the methodology of an ephemeral archive, I was influenced by recent turns in Australian feminist and queer scholarship. See, for instance, Alison Bartlett and Margaret Henderson, eds., *Things That Liberate: An Australian Feminist Wunderkammer* (Newcastle upon Tyne, UK: Cambridge Scholars, 2013); Gemma Killen, "Archiving the Other or Reading Online Photography as Queer Ephemera," *Australian Feminist Studies* 32, nos. 91–92 (2017): 58–74; and Petra Mosmann, "Encountering Feminist Things: Generations, Interpretations, and Encountering Adelaide's 'Scrap Heap,'" *Journal of Australian Studies* 40, no. 2 (2016): 172–89. For a consideration of an ephemeral archive in the aftermath of trauma, see, for instance, Kay Turner and James Merrill, "September 11: The Burden of the Ephemeral," *Western Folklore* 68, no. 2/3 (2009): 155–208.

8. Mary K. Rothbart and Diana Pien, "Elephants and Marshmallows: A Theoretical Synthesis of Incongruity-Resolution and Arousal Theories of Humour," in Antony J. Chapman and Hugh C. Foot, eds., *It's a Funny Thing, Humour* (Oxford, UK: Pergamon, 1997), 37–40.

9. See David Graham and Andrew Markus, *Gen17 Australian Jewish Community Survey: Preliminary Findings* (Melbourne: Australian Centre for Jewish Civilisation, 2018), 9.

10. See, for example, Graham and Markus, *Gen17*, 12–14. See also the various Holocaust-centered chapters in Michael Fagenblat, Melanie Landau, and Nathan Wolski, eds., *New Under the Sun: Jewish Australians on Religion, Politics, and Culture* (Melbourne: Black, 2006).

11. Esther Jilovsky, Jordana Silverstein, and David Slucki, "The Third Generation," in Esther Jilovsky, Jordana Silverstein, and David Slucki, eds., *In the Shadows of Memory: The Holocaust and the Third Generation* (London: Vallentine Mitchell, 2016), 1.

12. Karolina Krasuska, "Narratives of Generationality in 21st-Century North American Jewish Literature: Krauss, Bezmozgis, Kalman," *Eastern European Jewish Affairs* 46, no. 3 (2016): 288.

13. See Jordana Silverstein, "'If Our Grandchildren Are Jewish': Heteronormativity, Holocaust Postmemory, and the Reproduction of Melbourne Jewish Families," *History Australia* 10, no. 1 (2013): 167–86.

14. David Slucki, "Making Out in Anne Frank's Attic," in Eli Lederhendler and Gabriel N. Finder, eds., *A Club of Their Own: Jewish Humorists and the Contemporary World* (New York: Oxford University Press, 2016), 204–29.
15. See, in particular, Jonathan Boyarin, *Thinking in Jewish* (Chicago: University of Chicago Press, 1996), 8–33. See also Boyarin, *Jewishness*, 25–44.
16. I always think of the contrast between those of us who *always knew something* (what we knew is unclear, but we knew)—which is perhaps in some ways constitutive of a certain type of member of the third generation—and those who had a moment of learning. Susan Sontag's description of finding photos from Bergen-Belsen and Dachau in a bookshop in Santa Monica is perhaps the archetype of this other coming to knowledge. Susan Sontag, *On Photography*, 19–20, cited in Hirsch, *Generation of Postmemory*, 103.
17. See "Stawski, Sofia," National Archives of Australia, MT874/1, V1956/44232; and "Stawski, Wladislaw [Wolf]," National Archives of Australia, MT874/1, V1956/44231.
18. See, for instance, the following essays in Esther Jilovsky, Jordana Silverstein, and David Slucki, eds., *In the Shadows of Memory: The Holocaust and the Third Generation* (London: Vallentine Mitchell, 2016): David Slucki, "The Third Generation and the Responsibility to Remember," 295–307; Dalit Kaplan, "'But What About Our Persian Rugs?' Inventing a Family History," 77–86; Esther Jilovsky, "Grandpa's Letters: Encountering Tangible Memories of the Holocaust," 135–48; and Ben Silverstein and Jordana Silverstein, "A Politics of the Third Generation: Two Siblings Converse," 231–44. See also Bram Presser, *The Book of Dirt* (Melbourne: Text, 2017).
19. Monty Python, "Four Yorkshiremen," http://www.montypython.net/scripts/4york.php [accessed 1 January 2018].
20. Julie Meadows, ed., *Fun Himlen Blayene Tsu Bloye Teg (From Leaden Skies to Blue Days): 45 Stories of Growing Up in Jewish Carlton, 1945–1975* (Melbourne: Australian Centre for Jewish Civilisation, Monash University, 2014).
21. See Sigmund Freud, *Jokes and Their Relation to the Unconscious*, trans. and ed. James Strachey (New York: Norton, 1989).
22. Boyarin, *Jewishness*, 37.
23. Sara Ahmed, "Affective Economies," *Social Text* 22, no. 2 (2004): 117–39.
24. For useful discussions of trauma, see Cathy Caruth, *Unclaimed Experience: Trauma, Narrative, and History* (Baltimore: Johns Hopkins University Press, 1996); and Felman and Laub, *Testimony*.
25. Caruth, *Unclaimed Experience*, 111.

26. Caruth, *Unclaimed Experience*, 112.
27. Joan Scott, "The Evidence of Experience," *Critical Inquiry* 17, no. 4 (1991): 779.
28. Scott, "Evidence of Experience," 792.
29. Scott, "Evidence of Experience," 793.
30. Scott, "Evidence of Experience," 793.
31. Scott, "Evidence of Experience," 793.
32. Scott, "Evidence of Experience," 778.
33. Hirsch, *Generation of Postmemory*, 2.
34. Eva Hoffman, "The Long Afterlife of Loss," in Susannah Radstone and Bill Schwarz, eds., *Memory: Histories, Theories, Debate* (New York: Fordham University Press, 2010), 407.
35. Hoffman, "Long Afterlife of Loss," 406.
36. Hirsch, *Generation of Postmemory*, 5.
37. For a discussion of the inherited traumas among Jews in Melbourne, see Vivien Silbert, "Three Degrees of Separation: Processes and Outcomes in Intergenerational Transmission of Trauma in Second and Third Generation Holocaust Survivors," PhD diss., Swinburne University of Technology, 2010.
38. For a discussion of the way that humor can create a space to bring people together, see, for instance, Sigmund Freud, *Wit and Its Relation to the Unconscious*, trans. A. A. Brill (London: Kegan Paul, Trench, Trubner, 1916).
39. There is a large body of scholarship exploring the ways in which we cannot know the Holocaust. See, for instance, the discussions in Saul Friedlander, ed., *Probing the Limits of Representation: Nazism and the "Final Solution"* (Cambridge, MA: Harvard University Press, 1992).
40. Carla Silbert and Justin Olstein, *Echo Chamber: A Web Series*, https://www.facebook.com/pg/echochamberwebseries/videos/?ref=page_internal [accessed 10 January 2018]. For additional meditations by Justin Olstein on third-generation Holocaust memory and its presentation as intergenerational trauma, see his short film *The Visitor* (2018).
41. Carla Silbert and Justin Olstein, "Minority Report," *Echo Chamber: A Web Series*, 11 November 2016, https://www.facebook.com/echochamberwebseries/videos/vl.1470659253025361/1173622976039617/?type=1 [accessed 10 January 2018].
42. Louis Kaplan, "'It Will Get a Terrific Laugh': On the Problematic Pleasures and Politics of Holocaust Humour," in Henry Jenkins, Tara McPherson and Jane Shattuc, eds., *Hop on Pop: The Politics and Pleasures of Popular Culture* (Durham, NC: Duke University Press, 2002), 343.

43. Kaplan, "It Will Get a Terrific Laugh," 354.
44. Boyarin, *Jewishness*, 39.
45. Hannah Gadsby, *Nanette*, Netflix, 2018, https://www.netflix.com/au/title/80233611 [accessed 6 August 2018].
46. Freda Freiberg, "*Life is Beautiful* (1998): An Appreciation," *Screening the Past*, 7 June 1999, http://www.screeningthepast.com/2014/12/life-is-beautiful/ [accessed 6 August 2018].
47. Boyarin, *Jewishness*, 35.

"Yad Vashem, You So Fine!"

The Place of the Shoah in Contemporary Israeli and American Comedy

Avinoam Patt

IN THE AFTERMATH OF the Holocaust, survivors in postwar Europe deployed humor as a way to process the recent traumas of the war, to cope with the enormity of the destruction, and to endure the seemingly absurd nature of continued Jewish life after the Holocaust. Humor helped survivors to maintain a sense of psychological advantage and served as an outlet for subversive and cynical observations on the postwar world.[1] After the war, humor directed at non-Jewish audiences often focused on using humor as a weapon, to minimize and belittle Nazis (most famously in the work of Mel Brooks). In recent decades, however, as the place of the Holocaust has grown in contemporary Jewish culture and identity, references to the Holocaust in Jewish humor have grown more frequent, although the function and deployment of such Holocaust humor is substantively different in form and agenda. Rather than deploying humor as a psychological coping mechanism or weapon against Nazis, Holocaust humor has taken on a decidedly more political tone, often used as a means to critique the place of the Holocaust in contemporary Jewish society, politics, and culture.

In this chapter I compare the deployment of Holocaust humor in recent Israeli and American Jewish sketch comedy to assess what humor can teach us about the place of the Holocaust in contemporary Jewish life.[2] I focus on several examples from Israel and the United States, including *Eretz Nehederet* (Wonderful Country), *HaHamishia HaKamerit* (The Camera Quintet), and *HaYehudim Ba'im* (The Jews Are Coming) in Israel and the work of Larry David, Sarah Silverman, Amy Schumer, and Nathan Fielder in America. Unlike Holocaust humor used as a weapon to attack Nazis and Nazism or humor used to alleviate suffering, these more contemporary uses of humor often use the Holocaust as a backdrop for jokes precisely to reinforce or emphasize the absurdity of the joke. Most frequently, these jokes use the motif of the Shoah to satirize the current political climate, memorial practices, Holocaust education, and more but also to reflect the prominent place of "remembering the Holocaust" in contemporary American and Israeli Jewish identity. In many ways, Holocaust (sketch) humor has played a similar function in both Israel and the United States: to make fun of the tendencies in both countries to sacralize and, by the same token, to trivialize the Holocaust. Most recently, however, Holocaust-inflected humor in Israel has been deployed to draw attention to abuses of power in Israeli politics and society; on the other hand, in the United States, Holocaust-inflected humor has increasingly drawn attention to the current and mounting powerlessness of American Jews, reflecting a cautionary tale of a different sort.

The Place of the Shoah in Israeli Sketch Comedy

Although comparatively few scholars have examined the place of the Holocaust in contemporary American Jewish humor, Liat Steir-Livny's recent study, *Is It OK to Laugh About It? Holocaust Humour, Satire, and Parody in Israeli Culture*, argues that in Israel, "a unique post-traumatic society where the trauma of the Holocaust lives as an integral part of the present, Holocaust humour in Hebrew functions as an important defence mechanism that challenges and deconstructs the fear factors."[3] Steir-Livny contends that satirical skits about the Holocaust in Israel do not minimize or trivialize the Shoah but instead simultaneously reinforce the centrality of the Shoah in Israeli society and allow for commentary on the political instrumentalization of the Shoah in Israel. Steir-Livny's research also crucially points out that in Israel, where widespread Holocaust education has helped a younger generation of Israelis assimilate the Shoah as a central event in the formation of the state, a great familiarity with Holocaust history allows for a more nuanced engagement with aspects of the Jewish past through humor (compared with the United States, where the humor deals with certain symbols of memory or Holocaust icons, but in a more superficial way).

> In Israel, where there is a massive use of Holocaust rhetoric by politicians, journalists and educators . . . the Holocaust has been assimilated as a central event, and young Jewish-Israelis perceive the Holocaust as the historical event that has had the greatest impact on them and their future, even more than the founding of the State. Other research has shown that the knowledge the second- and third-generation Holocaust survivors have about the Holocaust in Israel, and the way the Holocaust has shaped their identity is similar to those Israelis of the same age who are not biological offspring of Holocaust survivors. This phenomenon is very different from other places in the world.[4]

Since Menachem Begin's rise to power in 1977, exploitation of the Shoah for political purposes has become commonplace in Israeli life. Under Prime Minister Benjamin Netanyahu's government, the Holocaust is invoked frequently, especially to underscore the threat posed by a potentially nuclear-armed Iran. For example, in his 2012 Yom HaShoah speech at Yad Vashem, Netanyahu invoked memory of the Holocaust as a defense against Iran.

> I will continue to tell the truth to the world—but first and foremost, to my nation. The truth is that a nuclear-armed Iran is an existential threat to the State of Israel and also a grave threat to the rest of the world. The memory of the Holocaust is not just a ceremonial matter. The memory of the Holocaust is a practical commandment to learn the lessons of the past in order to guarantee the foundations of the future. We will never bury our heads in the sand. The People of Israel lives and the Eternity of Israel shall not lie.[5]

In Israel, nearly seventy years after the creation of the state, we might ask why the place of the Shoah has assumed more centrality in the national identity of the state as time has passed and distance from the event has grown. Why and how have we come to the place and time where the president of Israel (Rivlin) can state, "All of us, each and every one of us, have a number tattooed on their arm"?⁶ Why and how has the Shoah become a central component of Israel's educational curriculum, with trips to Poland a necessary rite of passage for students and Yad Vashem a required visit for all foreign political leaders? Israelis generally do not question the place of the Shoah in contemporary Israeli politics and society, although the centrality of the event in Israeli life, more than seventy-five years after the outbreak of World War II, demands investigation. Does Holocaust humor in Israel indicate that all Israelis are now survivors of the Holocaust, that is, with "a number tattooed on their arm"? And if this is true, what do mentions of the Shoah in American comedy reveal about the place of the Holocaust in American society? How might a comparative analysis of Holocaust humor in Israel and America reveal differences in the ways in which the Holocaust informs the identities of Jews in Israel and America?

HaHamishia HaKamerit

Over the last twenty years, as Liat Steir-Livny argues, sketch comedy in Israel has often focused on satirizing the politicization and trivialization of the Shoah while simultaneously highlighting how the saturation of the Shoah in the public sphere minimizes the meaning of the Shoah and shapes the worldview of Israelis. In the 1990s the sketch comedy show *HaHamishia HaKamerit* (The Camera Quintet) included sketches on all aspects of Israeli society, with occasional references to the Holocaust. Several of these addressed the nature of Israel's relationship with Germany, such as the skit "Feldermaus at the Olympics," which included the bumbling Israeli diplomat Feldermaus interceding at a track and field event in Stuttgart in 1995. The sketch makes fun of Jewish athletic ability (or the lack thereof) while appealing to German guilt to allow a Jewish runner to gain some advantage in the race.⁷ After asking the German track and field judge for a competitive advantage for the little Israeli runner "with legs like popsicle sticks" but receiving no assistance, Feldermaus plays the "Holocaust card."

> Haven't you seen *Schindler*? Haven't the Jewish people suffered enough? . . .

His mother is in the stadium, after everything she has been through [implies she is a survivor] she has come back to see him compete.

Once the judge agrees to give the Israeli athlete a small head start to lessen the "historical suffering," the two Israeli diplomats promise to honor the heroism of the judge: "We will take your details and get you a place on the Righteous Persons Boulevard." The skit does not make light of the Holocaust itself, although it does lampoon the Israeli tendency to make use of memory of the Holocaust, particularly in its relationship with Germany, to secure every competitive advantage. Likewise, the joke about the "Righteous Persons Boulevard" also highlights the degree to which a Holocaust memorial and museum like Yad Vashem can be politicized.[8]

In another skit called "Ghetto," which jokes about trivialization through street-naming practices in Tel Aviv, two friends talk about how to drive to a party in Tel Aviv.[9]

> Are you coming with a car?
> Here's what you have to do: drive on Warsaw Ghetto, make a U-turn on Concentration Camp Boulevard, and park in Dachau Square.
> Is it close?
> What? Dachau? It's here, just around the corner.

In making light of Israeli street-naming practices, the sketch also highlights how such practices might trivialize historical places and events and emphasizes the centrality of concentration camps and ghettos in the Israeli collective psyche.

Another *HaHamishia HaKamerit* short sketch called "Schindler," which is modeled after Claude Lanzmann and *Shoah*, shows two men walking in a field in the distance, speaking French and a pigeon hybrid of Polish and Yiddish. A survivor (played by Rami Heuberger, who also acted in the film *Schindler's List* as Josef Bau) describes being lined up in formation on a cold night. Suddenly a big black car pulls up: "Afterward they told us it was Schindler." He describes a lot of shouting.

What happened on that night?

[speaking as if in Polish] I remember it as if it was yesterday.

It was a very cold night, they told everyone to stand in lines.

The ladies, too?

Men, women, all. All around guards, screams of the guards.

And then, what happened then?

Then, he arrived. We saw from far away a black car . . . and HE got out. A very handsome man. Very elegant. Very impressive.

Was that Oskar Schindler?

[Long pause] Afterwards, they told us it was Schindler.

But that night? That night we didn't know. Didn't know anything.

Afterwards?

Afterwards? Lots of shouting. What is this? Like this.

Was it Schindler?

What Schindler? Spielberg. Screaming at us. This was no good. That was no good. Screaming at us to run faster. Do it again. And they returned us to the train cars and told us to start over. It was horrible. Really horrible.

And afterwards? [in French]

Afterwards? They paid us and we went home.

What?

We went home. It was really, really late. But they paid us very, very little.

Spielberg?

He received the Oscar.

The punch line is in fact a commentary on forms of representation and the ease with which the lines can be blurred between genres—documentary, feature film—and who the actual hero of this historical episode actually is—Schindler or Spielberg—with an ironic pun at the end: He won the Oscar![10] Like the scene in *Seinfeld* where Jerry gets in trouble for "making out during *Schindler's List*," the comedians remind us that the representation of the Holocaust is not sacred, but that in sanctifying cinematic representations of the Shoah, we distance ourselves from the actual meaning of the event.

Eretz Nehederet

Even though such satirical representations of the Shoah may have been more biting in the 1990s, since 2000, audiences in Israel and America have grown more comfortable with seeing representations of the Holocaust on film and on television—and just as representations of the Holocaust have been more common, so have jokes and satire that use motifs of the Shoah in popular culture. More recent examples continue this trend, as in the late 2010 sketch "Hope Kindergarten" from *Eretz Nehederet* (A Wonderful Country). That sketch imagines a right-wing kindergarten run by the ultra-nationalist *Im Tirtzu* organization, which educates (or indoctrinates) Israeli children with such games as "Who Are They to Preach Us Morals?" reminding the children that European nations such as Italy "helped the Nazis" and that the French had the "Vichy Regime" while Turkey massacred the Armenians and the Kurds and Norway "killed all the salmon." "What do we tell the world? Don't preach morals to us! There won't be another Auschwitz!" In this case both the politicization and the manipulation of the memory of the Holocaust for educational purposes are critiqued, as is the debate over whether or not to start Holocaust education for Israeli youth beginning in kindergarten.[11]

A 2012 *Eretz Nehederet* sketch makes fun of American Jewish youth on Birthright trips, stereotyping lazy, spoiled American Jews on their tour of Israel while making light of the cynical fundraising aimed at American Jews in a scene reminiscent of Sallah Shabbati planting trees for wealthy American Jewish donors.[12] Riding on the bus, the mostly American Jewish youths reflect on their visit to Masada, which was so emotional, so powerful, and just "awesome!" The tour guide, Ze'ev, asks them to tell their parents that Israel is not what they thought; it is a progressive and developed place (not just camels in the desert). Then he asks for men to sit in the front, women in the back. With "Heveinu Shalom Aleichem" playing in the background, the *madrich* (guide) Ze'ev informs the group:

> Here is the schedule for the rest of the day. At 12:00 we will arrive at the Haganah Museum [the tour groups screams and claps in joy; Josh shouts, "Fucking awesome!"], from there we will continue to Hasmonean village to see the olive press [more cheers and applause], and at the end, only if there is time, only if we have time and all goes according to plan ["please, please, please," says Melissa, the New York Jewish princess], I intend to take you to . . . Yad Vashem Museum [kids are beside themselves, "Fucking awesome," screams Josh, while Melissa and her friend sing "Yad Vashem, you so fine, you so fine you blow my mind!"].

Ze'ev continues with his explanation: "Yad Vashem is a museum dedicated to the Holocaust [as he plays a recording of the theme from *Schindler's List*]. We will give you some time to yourselves to be sad and at the same time to SMS your parents to continue donating to the state of Israel so there won't be a second Holocaust, because the sequel is never as good as the original." ("No problem," says one of the girls. "My parents have lots of money; *abba sheli* has tons of *kesef rav* [my dad has tons of money].") Ze'ev passes around a blue JNF *pushke* (charity tin) equipped with a credit card swiper to collect donations.

The skit pokes fun at the degree to which the Holocaust has become a tourist attraction ("Yad Vashem, you so fine") and at the fact that, by some estimates, at least 95% of Birthright trips make Yad Vashem a required stop on the standard 10-day itinerary. The commentary extends, however, to the willingness to make use of the Shoah as a philanthropic tool—please continue to support Israel "so there won't be a second Holocaust, because the sequel is never as good as the original." Playing the theme from *Schindler's List*, which absurdly accentuates the artificial sadness of such a limited visit within the framework of a tightly scheduled itinerary, the tour guide, Ze'ev, like Prime Minister Netanyahu, is willing to invoke the prospect of a second Holocaust to justify defense of Israel (where there are now 6 million Jews).

Another *Eretz Nehederet* sketch from the tenth season in 2013 examines another aspect of contemporary society: the universal fascination with reality television, in this case asking how far unsuspecting Israelis would go to be contestants on a reality TV show called "The Camp: Only One Wins."[13] The sketch uses a mockumentary style that both criticizes the willingness of ordinary Israelis to sell their moral principles for a chance to appear on a reality television show and exposes (in a Sacha Baron Cohen–esque way) the failures of Holocaust education, as typical Israelis, who are presumably familiar with the historical details of the Holocaust, are all too willing to imprison and persecute their fellow Jews for a chance to win 6 million shekels. The producer of the show, the self-styled "Mr. Reality," explains that the game is "a German format that was a big success all over Europe" in which contestants will be divided into "two groups, Germans and Jews" and that "the prize is 6 million." He interviews prospective contestants.

> "Are you willing to be a kapo?" he asks one woman.
> "Sure," she responds.
> "Would you send your friends to die in your place?"
> "Of course!" [and she cracks a whip]
> "Amazing," he responds.

Whereas most of the prospective contestants express a preference for living on the German side of the camp, which resembles a "boutique hotel," rather than living with the Jewish contestants, who will live in barracks, behind barbed wire, with armed guards and German shepherds, one contestant responds, "I'm willing to live with the Jews until death, until death." The mockumentary format is designed to trick participants into an ethically questionable exchange of information in order to satirize,[14] but the use of such an extreme format on an Israeli sketch comedy show for allegedly humorous purposes does highlight the degree to which Israeli society has been saturated with Holocaust icons and references, making the premise of a reality show based on a concentration camp plausible. But what is the butt of the joke here? The absurd nature of reality television? The greed of average Israelis willing to sell out their ethical principles, sense of morality, and memory of the Holocaust for 6 million shekels? Or the overall failure of Holocaust education? All of the above, it would seem.

HaYehudim Ba'im

A more recent entry into the Israeli sketch comedy scene is *HaYehudim Ba'im* (The Jews Are Coming), a satirical TV show that completed its first broadcast season in January 2015 and recorded two more seasons in 2016 and 2017–2018. The show has been broadcast on Israel's historic Channel 1—for many years the only TV channel in the country—and it is devoted not to spoofs of contemporary Israeli politics but to sketches that target the entire history of the Jewish people since biblical times. Unlike *Eretz Nehederet*, which like the *Daily Show* tends to focus on politics and current events, *HaYehudim Ba'im* analyzes central moments in Jewish history and culture through a comedic lens.[15] The show features one of the foremost veterans of Israeli sketch comedy, Moni Moshonov (star of *Zehu Zeh*), along with newer stars Yossi Marshek and Yaniv Biton, among others. In addition to skits on Masada, the Dreyfus affair, the kibbutz movement, the Hebrew poetess Rachel, and the Bible, the show offers satirical looks at World War II history and the Holocaust.

One episode includes a skeptical Hannah Senesh worrying about her fate before she is deployed as a parachutist; or in the same episode, "Art Academy in Vienna," Adolf Schickelgruber's artwork is rejected and a committee member ridicules him, explaining his work must have some emotion, some anger in it. A young Hitler is encouraged by Jewish committee members to change his name "to something more catchy," stop painting fanciful portraits of cats, and channel his inner rage into something productive. In the sketch "Final Solution 2.0," situated in 1956, the last surviving Nazis in Europe are meeting in a bunker to discuss the ultimate Final Solution. This time the final plan is to scatter Nazi sympathizers among all the media enterprises in Europe and guarantee that Israel does not receive one point in the Eurovision Song Contest. The plan is greeted with enthusiasm by all in the bunker, and one of the Nazis announces in German-accented Hebrew, "Zeh yaharog otam [That will kill them]!" The sketch concludes with the Nazis gathered around the table singing the West German entry to the 1979 Eurovision song contest, "Dschinghis Khan" (Genghis Khan).[16] A seemingly farcical addition to the end of the sketch, this song is by itself meaningful on multiple levels: The 1979 Eurovision contest in Jerusalem marked the first time Israel hosted the contest as well as the first time Eurovision was held outside the European continent. The performance by the West German group was groundbreaking, as they performed in German, in Israel, for the first time. The irony is that although the sketch parodies the Israeli tendency to perceive every slight against Israel as antisemitic, Israel in fact won Eurovision in back-to-back years in 1978 and 1979 for the songs "A-Ba-Ni-Bi" and "Hallelujah." (Israel would triumph again in 1998, with Dana International's "Diva" and in 2018 with Netta Barzilai's "Toy.")

In line with examining famous moments in Jewish and Israeli history, another *HaYehudim Ba'im* sketch imagines the execution of Adolf Eichmann in Ramle prison in 1962, but the bumbling and inept guards are incapable of executing Eichmann, incapable of stooping to the depths of evil represented by Eichmann himself. In the end, Eichmann places the noose around his own neck, concluding that "if you want something done right, you have to do it yourself." Whereas the actual trial was meant by Israel's leaders to exhibit Jewish power, the sketch seems to highlight Jewish weakness, which, according to Zionist ideology, Jews in Israel had shed. By the same token, this sketch and others are also a subtle reflection of Israeli Jews' exercise of power and the ethical responsibility that comes along with it. Are Jews capable of "acting like Nazis"? Is the State of Israel even capable of stooping to the same level as the Nazis? (Moni Moshonov, who plays Eichmann in the sketch and one of the Nazi officers in "Final Solution, 2.0," is

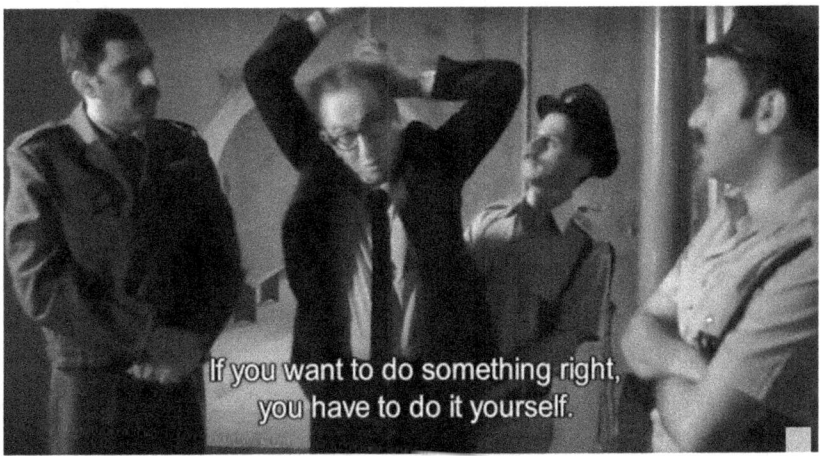

"The Execution of Adolf Eichmann," *HaYehudim Ba'im*.

Shoah in Contemporary Israeli and American Comedy • 271

one of Israel's most recognizable comedic actors.) The "Mr. Reality" sketch on *Eretz Nehederet* asks the same questions. And although these questions are posed in a satirical manner, the answers are nonetheless uncomfortable, to say the least.

Holocaust Humor in American Sketch Comedy

This brief chapter reveals the degree to which satirization of the politics of Holocaust memory and education in Israel has become a staple of Israeli sketch comedy. Although it is also possible to trace a parallel rise in the frequency of references to the Holocaust in American sketch comedy, it is worth noting that Israeli shows such as *HaHamishia HaKamerit*, *Eretz Nehederet*, and *HaYehudim Ba'im*, broadcast on Israeli television (and online), can count on a largely educated Jewish audience. The producers and creators are making insider jokes in a country immersed in Holocaust education and collective memory, as opposed to Holocaust humor for an American audience, which, out of necessity, must be translated for a broader audience who is less likely to understand references to the Holocaust. Nonetheless, it is possible that increased Holocaust education in the United States (particularly since the opening of the United States Holocaust Memorial Museum in 1993 and the passage of legislation requiring Holocaust education in certain states since then) has increased general awareness of the Holocaust among an American audience, though it has not necessarily instilled a deeper knowledge of the historical specifics associated with the genocide of European Jewry.

At the same time, in the background of this examination is a question raised by data from the 2013 Pew Portrait of Jewish Americans that asked American Jews to take into consideration the place of "remembering the Holocaust" in contemporary American Jewish identity; 73% of respondents to the Pew survey identified remembering the Holocaust as an essential part of what being Jewish means to them.[17] Even though this finding needs to be analyzed in much greater detail, the fact that remembering the Holocaust ranked highest among nine possible responses for an "essential component of Jewish identity" indicates the significance of the Holocaust for Jewish Americans in the twenty-first century. The same survey found that 42%

of American Jews felt that "having a good sense of humor" was "an essential part of what being Jewish means to them."

Finally, there are more platforms than ever for the deployment of comedy, and it seems that the standards for what is considered acceptable or even funny continue to evolve. In the 1950s, when Sid Caesar and Imogene Coca along with writers Mel Brooks, Neil Simon, Carl Reiner, and others pioneered the sketch comedy series *Your Show of Shows* on NBC, sketches such as "The German General," which made masterful use of Caesar's double-talk, made fun of Germans (and presumably Nazis) while avoiding the subject of the Holocaust. As David Slucki's chapter in this volume demonstrates, treatments of the Holocaust have evolved over the past several decades of sitcoms, just as the media environment has expanded from broadcast networks to cable television to a plethora of offerings on streaming services. And even so, as Larry David's appearance on the sketch comedy staple *Saturday Night Live* in November 2017 demonstrated, the viewing public still seems to hold broadcast television to a higher standard.

Larry David

In his November 2017 appearance on *Saturday Night Live*, Larry David made a joke about sex in concentration camps that many observers found to be in poor taste because he situated the joke in a concentration camp and insinuated that Jews may have had sexual urges there (in the context of Harvey Weinstein's sexual abuse charges and the fact that Jewish women and [and men] were subjected to widespread sexual violence during the Holocaust).[18] "I know I consistently strive to be a good Jewish representative," said David during his monologue, after expressing his discomfort with the fact that so many of those accused of sexual harassment, particular in the entertainment sphere, are Jewish. His joke reflected his own thoughts on the matter: As a Jewish man, would he have been focused on sex, even during the Holocaust?

> I've always been obsessed with women, and I've often wondered—if I'd grown up in Poland when Hitler came to power and was sentenced to a concentration camp—would I still be checking out women in the camp? I think I would.

> "Hey Shlomo! Shlomo! Look at that one over there by barracks 8. Oh my God, is she gorgeous! I've had my eye on here for weeks. I'd like to go over and say something to her." The problem is, there are no good lines in a concentration camp. . . . "How's it going? They treating you okay? You know, if we ever get out of here I'd love to take you out for some latkes. You like latkes? What? What'd I say? Is it me, or is it the whole thing? It's 'cause I'm bald, isn't it?"[19]

Many observers considered the joke not to be the finest moment in Larry David's career (Jonathan Greenblatt, CEO of the Anti-Defamation League, tweeted the next morning that David "managed to be offensive, insensitive & unfunny all at same time. Quite a feat"), but the fact that he told the joke as part of his opening monologue on *Saturday Night Live* before an audience of millions presents an interesting starting point to examine the place of Holocaust humor in American society. What is the focus of such humor? Can we draw a distinction between jokes that satirize the sacralization and politicization of memorial culture and jokes that are situated in the Holocaust, perhaps making light of Jewish suffering or Nazi persecution? David can segue from reflections on the nature of his own Jewish identity (consistently striving to be a good Jewish representative) to the Holocaust without missing a beat. For an American audience, this would not be surprising, because their most likely association with Jewishness is the Holocaust. (It is not coincidental that the "Jewish" museum on the National Mall in Washington, D.C., is the Holocaust Museum.)

The deployment of Holocaust humor in the American context functions in a similar way to Israeli Holocaust humor, satirizing the place of memorial culture in contemporary Jewish identity while also pointing out the slippage that takes place in the use of certain terms that have expanded beyond Holocaust usage (camps, survivor, ovens, etc.). How much do the conventions of Holocaust memory become the targets of satire? In contrast to Larry David's joke, "safer" targets of Holocaust humor in the American context, less likely to provoke outrage, focus on Schindler, Anne Frank, references to "camps," the "survivor," Hitler memes, and so on. In general, the punch lines, as in Israel, satirize the place of the Holocaust in contemporary Jewish culture and political identity. At the same time, frequent use of the Holocaust by Jewish comedians in America may also reflect the central place of the Holocaust in contemporary American Jewish identity, often in lieu of religion, tradition, or other ethnic markers of Jewish identity.

Curb Your Enthusiasm

Larry David returns frequently to the Holocaust in his material. For example in the "Trick or Treat" episode (or Wagner episode) of *Curb Your Enthusiasm* (season 2, episode 3), Larry points out the hypocrisy of a Jewish identity predicated on hatred of Wagner's music. The episode begins with Larry's neighbor attacking him for being a "self-loathing Jew" because he enjoys the music of Wagner as he whistles "Siegfried Idyll" for his wife, Cheryl. "I do hate myself," Larry responds, "but it has nothing to do with being Jewish." As the neighbor becomes more irate, asking Larry, "Where is your heritage?" and reminding Larry that the music of Wagner played as "millions of Jews were being taken to the concentration camps," Larry responds by whistling the opening bars of "Springtime for Hitler." At the end of the same episode, Larry becomes a victim of a hate crime; but in this case not antisemitism but anti-baldism (being labeled a "bald asshole" by his anti-Wagner neighbor's daughter). David questions the nature of a Jewish identity based on boycotting German culture, a negative Jewish identity based in a memory of the Holocaust that raises children to commit hate crimes (if spray-painting "bald asshole" on a neighbor's door can be labeled a hate crime).

Earlier in his career, as a creator of and writer for *Seinfeld*, Larry David, along with Jerry Seinfeld, asked whether it was possible for dentist Tim Whatley (played by Bryan Cranston) to convert to Judaism for the jokes; was it possible to adopt a history of suffering? Can he convert to Judaism just for the jokes, along with the implicit underlying belief that much of Jewish humor is a response to thousands of years of Jewish suffering (which he just adopted)? And can a Jew who has not suffered adopt a shared history of suffering? Again, David and Seinfeld question what defines prejudice and discrimination, as Jerry's suspicion of the dentist's motives lead him to be labeled a "rabid anti-dentite."[20] In both cases, Larry asks about degrees of persecution and an identity based on collective suffering: What is the difference between anti-baldism, anti-dentism, and antisemitism?

In the "Survivor" episode of *Curb Your Enthusiasm*, David not only satirizes the cultural slippage that takes place through the widespread use of the term *survivor* and the relative levels of suffering (when the Holocaust survivor Solly is introduced to Colby, the contestant from the reality TV show *Survivor*), but also introduces another current usage of the Holocaust in contemporary American comedy: using the Shoah as a stand-in for 9/11 and asking questions about who gets to claim the mantle of suffering. (In the same episode the rabbi's brother-in-law died on 9/11, even though he was killed in a cycling accident uptown, not in the towers. Is he a victim of 9/11?) When Larry and Cheryl renew their vows, Larry offends the rabbi by using the phrase "let's roll" and the episode concludes with an earthquake and Colby from *Survivor* telling Larry, "We survived!"

My Crazy Ex-Girlfriend

To cite another recent example that plays on the notion of survival and suffering, in the CW show *My Crazy Ex-Girlfriend*, Patti Lupone and Tovah Feldshuh temper the joy of a Jewish wedding by exhorting Rachel to "Remember that we suffered."

> We sing in a minor key to remember that we suffered! I don't want to bring up the Holocaust, I know, I know, the Holocaust, but the Holocaust is a really big deal . . . remember that we suffered!
>
> [The DJ announces]: My Grandmother's a survivor, remember that she suffered! The Sweet and the Bitter, Streisand and Hitler—Remember that we suffered! Spielberg and Hitler—Remember that we suffered![21]

Jewish identity is thus reduced to a few key buzzwords: a hora, a singing Tova Feldshuh, the Holocaust, survival, and a vague notion of collective suffering. The humorous commentary is not far from the truth, as Jewish wedding ceremonies include the breaking of a glass that recalls the destruction of the Temple in Jerusalem. Again, what's the punch line? "The Holocaust, I know, I know, the Holocaust, but the Holocaust is a really big deal."

Inside Amy Schumer

Although each of these examples reflects references to the Holocaust that seem to question a Jewish identity based in the Holocaust or that implicitly criticize identities based in vague notions of collective suffering and survival, Amy Schumer's "Museum of Boyfriend Wardrobe Atrocities," a sketch from the 2015 season of *Inside Amy Schumer* (season 3, episode 7), represents a much more direct satire of contemporary Holocaust memorial practices (even more spot-on than Sarah Silverman's "Wowschwitz" episode of *The Sarah Silverman Show*; see David Slucki's chapter in this volume for a more detailed discussion of this episode). In this short but powerful spoof of Holocaust museums, Amy Schumer narrates an audio tour with sad classical music in the background that follows a group of female visitors (with one exception) to a museum that highlights wardrobe atrocities perpetrated by fashion-challenged boyfriends.[22]

Alana O'Brien plays a visitor to the museum listening to the audio tour. Standing before a tacky male outfit, she hears the narrator explain, "This is what Josh wore to meet her parents; tragically, the relationship perished soon after." In another display, visitors see Mark and his bowling shirt, learning that "he insisted on wearing calf high tube socks; she hid them in her attic, but sadly they were discovered and forced back into rotation." In another part of the exhibit, viewers learn they "are in the accessory wing. One survivor recorded the following words: first he wore a braided belt and . . . I said nothing. Then came that hat . . . and I said nothing. Then he wore that fucking hemp necklace and I was like . . . PEACE!!" One female visitor nods in recognition and understanding. In the next room: "You are entering the Hall of Sighs. You will hear recordings of real girlfriends the moment they bore witness to their boyfriend's mistakes." The wall is a hall of photos of boyfriend wardrobe atrocities that evokes the tower of faces at the United States Holocaust Memorial Museum in Washington, D.C. (In the background we hear recordings of girlfriends complaining about men wearing ugly shorts, Birkenstocks, etc.) The only man on the tour (an angry white guy with a red beard who represents a boyfriend wardrobe-atrocity denier) says, "I don't think this many guys wore this stuff. These numbers are exaggerated." In the final scene of the short clip, visitors stand before a giant pile of Crocs that evokes the piles of shoes at Holocaust museums and concentration camps. "There are 5,200 pairs of Crocs in front of you. Each one represents a relationship that was real and tangible until poor judgment tore it apart." At the end of the tour a little girl in a red coat modeled after the girl in the red coat from *Schindler's List* asks, "Did this really happen?" As the screens fades to black and white, only the girl's coat remains in color and the adult with her answers, "It did, Gabby, it did."[23]

The museum tour includes references to relationships that have "tragically perished," articles of clothing "hidden in the attic," a reference to the famous Martin Niemoller quotation, deniers of wardrobe atrocities, piles of Crocs, and a not so subtle final reference to *Schindler's List*. Even the exhibit descriptions (barely visible in the sketch) carry the hyperbolic wardrobe atrocities to their most extreme, such as this one below a bowling shirt: "It is now considered Charlie Sheen's most heinous crime to have been the inspiration for this outfit."

As Rachel Shukert writes in *Tablet*, the sketch is a "pitch-perfect send up of the kind of solemn, often self-imposed field trip we've all taken

The 5,200 pairs of Crocs shown in the sketch "Museum of Boyfriend Wardrobe Atrocities," *Inside Amy Schumer*.

to various Holocaust museums the world over, from the United States Holocaust Memorial in Washington D.C., where . . . you are given the identity of one of the perished, like one of those troubling games one used to play at one of your more Jewish-inflected summer camps; to Yad Vashem, in whose tomb-like, black marble walls the numbers of the dead are ominously listed by country."[24] At the same time, the sketch satirizes how mundane and commonplace Holocaust commemorative practices have become—and the kind of slippage that can take place when the terms *evil* or *atrocity* are used casually. Likewise, as we become overly saturated by all kinds of violence and catastrophe, the term *atrocity* loses its power.

Nathan for You

Another recent parody of Holocaust memorial culture in contemporary American sketch comedy comes from the 2015 "Summit Ice" sketch on the Comedy Central show *Nathan for You*.[25] Nathan Fielder is a Canadian Jewish comedian whose show on Comedy Central describes him as "a business advisor who implements strategies that no traditional consultant would dare attempt." In "Summit Ice" Fielder concocts an absurd business strategy that is a critique of the ridiculous extremes of Holocaust memorialization and education; at the same time, he uses the new line of outerwear clothing he has developed for the show as a means of funding Holocaust education, raising hundreds of thousands of dollars for the Vancouver Holocaust Museum. In the sketch Nathan, disappointed to learn that his favorite brand of winter outerwear, Taiga, also supports Holocaust deniers, decides to create his own brand of outerwear, called Summit Ice, to confront deniers, with a model who announces in advertisements, "Deny Nothing." As Fielder has explained in interviews:

> When I was younger, and until recently, I used to wear a jacket brand called Taiga, which is from a shop just down the street. I discovered recently that they published a tribute to a Holocaust denier in their winter catalogue, but I was wearing their jacket on my TV show. I felt like that was bad because I was giving them publicity. I didn't know what

jacket company to trust, so I thought it was easiest to start my own company.²⁶

In the mockumentary-style sketch, Nathan consults a real Los Angeles rabbi (who is, in fact, the butt of the joke), who helps Nathan design a retail display for his outerwear clothing line that will confront Holocaust denial. The display mixes mannequins in concentration camp uniforms wearing Summit Ice outerwear, educational posters on the history of the Holocaust, a replica of the Auschwitz "Arbeit macht frei" entrance gate, photos of the clothing model wearing Summit Ice and reminding shoppers to "deny nothing," and, of course, Summit Ice apparel for sale. In the end, it is the hippie, laid-back storeowner who has to be the voice of reason: Retail and the Holocaust don't mix. Fielder takes "Museum of Boyfriend Wardrobe Atrocities" and ups the ante. What are the limits of extreme memorialization? And why can't he wear the jacket of his favorite apparel company because Taiga supports Holocaust deniers? Are we supposed to boycott Nazis? Is financial resistance real resistance?²⁷

What are the limits of Holocaust memorialization? For American Jews who advocated boycotting the Nazi movement in the 1930s, why can't contemporary Holocaust memorialization take the form of boycotting a clothing line that supports Holocaust deniers? Fielder probes the limits of the commercialization of Holocaust memory while using his critique to fund Holocaust education. In the new post-Trump reality, Fielder's 2015

Holocaust retail display in the sketch "Summit Ice," *Nathan for You*.

satire seems prescient, highlighting the limits of education and boycotts to confront antisemitism and Holocaust denial. Do American Jews actually have the tools with which to confront such threats, or does such Holocaust-inflected humor draw attention to the current and mounting powerlessness of American Jews?

Conclusion

What is the difference between Holocaust humor in America and that in Israel? Does humor in America reflect an anxiety over forgetting, over the ways in which "remembering the Holocaust" has become a stand-in for Jewish identity, whereas humor in Israel—where the Shoah is too central to Israeli national identity to be forgotten—instead becomes a political tool to criticize that very centrality in the culture? Israelis fear instrumentalization by their leaders; in a country where Jews exercise sovereignty, the target is the state and political culture is turned inward, as Jews are no longer the outsiders. On the contrary, Jews in Israel must deal with exercising power and the fear that they now abuse power as a majority that "subjugates" a minority; at the same time, the Shoah is used to justify political choices and the exercise of power. In America, Jews also have power, especially to shape culture. However, in the American context the function of the Holocaust is to remind American Jews of who they are, of their otherness, and in the age of Trump and the reminders of persistent forms of antisemitism, Holocaust humor functions as a form of satire invoked to again critique the powerful and to reinforce the minority status of the Jews, lest they become too white or too privileged. At the same time, the historical specificity of the Shoah in the American context is reduced to a number of "Holocaust icons." American sketch comedy about the Holocaust does not make fun of specific historical events but of symbols and terms the audience will be able to identify: survivor, the Anne Frank "game," Spielberg, Schindler, and a vague sense of collective suffering.[28] As distance from the event grows, the Shoah continues to assume a central role in both Israeli and American Jewish identity. Humor about the Holocaust not only mirrors the concerns of each society but also reflects the degree to which a vague sense of collective memory of the Holocaust has replaced any historical specificity of the event itself.

Notes

1. Avinoam Patt, "'Laughter Through Tears': Jewish Humor in the Aftermath of the Holocaust," in Eli Lederhendler and Gabriel N. Finder, eds., *A Club of Their Own: Jewish Humorists and the Contemporary World* (New York: Oxford University Press, 2016), 113–31.
2. The genre of sketch comedy, unlike situation comedy (or sitcoms), allows for short explorations of a concept or a situation; longer than a skit generally built around one joke, the sketch allows for the development of an idea over several minutes but can be strung together with several other sketches to form a show. The genre has its origins in vaudeville and is an ideal format to allow talented comedic actors to play off one another.
3. Liat Steir-Livny, *Is It OK to Laugh About It? Holocaust Humour, Satire, and Parody in Israeli Culture* (London: Vallentine Mitchell, 2017), book jacket blurb.
4. Steir-Livny, *Is It OK*, 40.
5. Benjamin Netanyahu, Yom HaShoah speech, 2012; see text in various sources, for example, http://www.israelnationalnews.com/News/News.aspx/154895 [accessed 1 August 2017].
6. President Reuven Rivlin, Yom HaShoah Memorial Day Ceremony, 15 April 2015, http://www.president.gov.il/English/ThePresident/Speeches/Pages/news_150415_01.aspx [accessed 1 August 2017].
7. "Feldermaus at the Olympics," *HaHamishia HaKamerit*, 3 July 2013, https://www.youtube.com/watch?v=1FPRYXbIxDc [accessed 1 August 2017].
8. In the sketch "Feldermaus at the White House," the two bumbling diplomats attempt to surprise Bill Clinton at the White House with a request to play saxophone at a small party at the Israeli embassy. Rebuffed by a secretary who insists the president is a "very busy man," Feldermaus loses his patience, insisting he will wait no more: "We will not be taken like lambs to the slaughter!" https://www.youtube.com/watch?v=lLIWCW4ewb8 [accessed 1 August 2017]. It should also be noted that the name of the diplomat "Feldermaus" is itself an ironic inversion. In Hebrew the name of the opera by Strauss, *Die Fledermaus*, can also be mistakenly read as Feldermaus. In so doing, the "bat" from Strauss's humorous farce is transformed into a common "field mouse."
9. https://www.youtube.com/watch?v=nRTI_yI7-Oc&feature=youtu.be [accessed 1 August 2017].
10. https://www.youtube.com/watch?v=liYGNXMtIhw [accessed 1 August 2017]. Steir-Livny points out that, in this case in a postmodern sense, "the satirists remove themselves and their audiences even more from the historical event.

This skit turns the Holocaust from an historical event to a representation of the representation, a situation in which the creators do not refer to actual historical events from the Holocaust, but rather respond to other texts representing the Holocaust as acts of homage to them." Steir-Livny, *Is It OK*, 103–4.

11. In 2014 Israel's Ministry of Education released a Holocaust education curriculum for kindergartners, in conjunction with Yom HaShoah. See http://www.tabletmag.com/scroll/170448/israel-to-teach-about-holocaust-in-kindergarten [accessed 30 November 2017]. See also http://cms.education.gov.il/EducationCMS/UNITS/Moe/Shoa/ganeyeldim [accessed 30 November 2017].
12. *Eretz Nehederet*, https://vimeo.com/35660324 [accessed 1 August 2017].
13. "Mr. Reality," *Eretz Nehederet*, http://www.mako.co.il/tv-erez-nehederet/season10-articles/Article-e1ea8be897bbe31006.htm [accessed 1 August 2017].
14. See, for example, M. Campbell, "The Mocking Mockumentary and the Ethics of Irony," *Taboo: The Journal of Culture and Education* 11, no. 1 (2017): art. 8, https://digitalcommons.lsu.edu/taboo/vol11/iss1/8 [accessed 1 August 2017].
15. See Wendy Zierler, "'The Jews Are Coming' Offers Hebrew Satire of Jewish History," 28 March 2016, http://jewishstudies.washington.edu/hebrew-humanities/the-jews-are-coming/ [accessed 14 January 2018].
16. "Final Solution 2.0," *The Jews Are Coming*, 20 May 2016, https://www.youtube.com/watch?v=Pp3Qi07nJK4 [accessed 14 January 2018]. "Dschinghis Khan" became the basis for several popular covers of the song, including the Hasidic hit song "Yidn, Yidn Kumt a Heym," by Mordecai Ben-David.
17. See Pew Research Center, "A Portrait of Jewish Americans," 1 October 2013, http://www.pewforum.org/files/2013/10/jewish-american-full-report-for-web.pdf [accessed 7 July 2015].
18. https://www.youtube.com/watch?v=G0eeNijdv3I [accessed 11 January 2018], starts at 5:30.
19. Jenny Singer, "Why Larry David's Holocaust Jokes Didn't Go Far Enough, and Four Comedians Whose Did," *The Forward*, 6 November 2017, https://forward.com/schmooze/387012/why-larry-davids-holocaust-jokes-didnt-go-far-enough-and-four-comedians-who/ [accessed 11 January 2018].
20. "The Yada," *Seinfeld*, 1997, http://www.imdb.com/title/tt0697814/ [accessed 11 January 2018].
21. https://www.youtube.com/watch?v=iLNa-ocdryY [accessed 11 January 2018].
22. "Fight Like a Girl," *Inside Amy Schumer*, 2 June 2015 (season 3, episode 7); see https://www.hulu.com/watch/800365#i0,p4,s3,d0 [accessed 30 November

2017]; or for video of just the sketch, see https://vimeo.com/141682826 [accessed 30 November 2017].

23. In the *South Park* episode "Death Camp of Tolerance" (season 6, episode 14, 2002), the boys are taken to "tolerance camp" as punishment for their insensitivity to their teacher, Mr. Garrison, who hopes to be fired by the school district for being a homosexual. The scenes in the tolerance camp are shot in black and white (a direct reference to *Schindler's List*), and the boys are also taken on a field trip to the Museum of Tolerance, where they also learn many other harmful stereotypes and forms of hate speech. http://southpark.cc.com/clips/104220/museum-of-tolerance [accessed 11 January 2018].

24. Rachel Shukert, "Amy Schumer Satirizes the Rite of Visiting Holocaust Memorials and Nails It," *Tablet Magazine*, June 2015, https://www.tabletmag.com/scroll/191741/amy-schumer-satirizes-the-rite-of-visiting-holocaust-memorials-and-nails-it [accessed 30 November 2017]. See also https://www.pastemagazine.com/articles/2015/07/the-10-best-sketches-from-inside-amy-schumers-thir.html?a=1 [accessed 30 November 2017]. For a literary take on summer camp games that evoke the Holocaust, see Ellen Umansky's short story "How to Make It in the Promised Land," which was made into a film of the same name in 2013.

25. http://www.cc.com/episodes/05z29h/nathan-for-you-horseback-riding-man-zone-season-3-ep-302 [accessed 28 January 2018].

26. See, for example, "I Went to Nathan Fielder's 'Holocaust Awareness Outdoor Apparel Sale,'" *Vice*, 27 March 2017, https://www.vice.com/en_us/article/mgdp7y/i-went-to-nathan-fielders-holocaust-awareness-outdoor-apparel-sale [accessed 28 January 2018].

27. http://www.cc.com/episodes/05z29h/nathan-for-you-horseback-riding-man-zone-season-3-ep-302 [accessed 28 January 2018].

28. The term "Holocaust icons" comes from Oren Baruch Stier, *Holocaust Icons: Symbolizing the Shoah in History and Memory* (New Brunswick, NJ: Rutgers University Press, 2015). Nathan Englander plays with the idea of the "Anne Frank game" in his short story "What We Talk About When We Talk About Anne Frank," https://www.newyorker.com/magazine/2011/12/12/what-we-talk-about-when-we-talk-about-anne-frank [accessed 28 April 2019]; in this story the characters examine the meaning of living a Jewish life predicated on remembering the Holocaust while also grappling with the question of whether they would have sheltered one another during the war.

"Did You Ever See Our Show?"

Holocaust Comedy in American Sitcoms

David Slucki

"My grandma's a survivor," proclaims the DJ at a Scarsdale bar mitzvah in a season 2 episode of Rachel Bloom's musical sitcom *Crazy Ex-Girlfriend*. The bar mitzvah of a cousin of Rebecca Bunch, played by Bloom, descends into farce in Bunch's mind as she tries to convince her non-Jewish boyfriend that Jews do not know how to have fun. While he is enjoying the festivities, in Rebecca's imagination she can only be reminded of the Jews' bitter past. The episode culminates in a hora titled "Remember That We Suffered," in which Broadway stars Tovah Feldshuh (playing Rebecca's overbearing mother) and Patti Lupone (as Rebecca's rabbi) remind Rebecca that, although it is a joyous occasion, Jews cannot simply celebrate without the shadow of persecution constantly haunting them. As she is lifted onto a chair, Rebecca's mother and rabbi sing to her, "The sweet and the bitter / remember that we suffered / Streisand and Hitler / remember that we suffered!"[1]

The song is a gibe at an American Jewish society that even in the happiest moments insists on invoking the sanctity of the Holocaust and draws a certain kind of cachet from its connection to the suffering of European Jews. It is high farce: a festive Jewish dance with joyful participants insisting on remembering the worst times in Jewish history; a juxtaposition of the best of American Jewish culture (Streisand, Spielberg) with the worst villain in Jewish memory (Hitler); a DJ who initiates a call and response to bring the whole community into the conspiracy ("When I say 'we,' you say 'suffered'")—all performed by two of Broadway's biggest stars, who insist that "the Holocaust was a really big deal."[2]

In this chapter I highlight the rise of Holocaust-related humor in sitcoms since the 1990s, a period in which such humor became commonplace, even pedestrian. Whereas once Holocaust jokes might have been considered transgressing social and cultural mores, today they are ubiquitous. This is, I argue, a reaction against the increasing sacralization of the Holocaust. This shift has taken place largely since the early 1990s and has been typified by television comedies that criticize a culture of Holocaust memory as grotesque. Whereas the Holocaust as subject of satire had been proscribed until recently, today comedians regularly invoke the Holocaust in their programs as they seek ways to further push the boundaries of humor. The comics who write and star in these shows are the inheritors of a long legacy of Jewish comics who have transgressed conventional mores and refused to accept a staid and shallow version of Jewishness that hinges on collective victimhood. These comics lampoon what historian Peter Novick dubbed a "culture of victimization," in which all American Jews were able to benefit from the moral privilege that their identification as vicarious victims gave them.[3] Focusing on what have come to be inscribed as holy symbols or icons of the Holocaust—survivors, memorials, Anne Frank, *Schindler's List*—comedians level a serious critique at the American Jewish community and American society more broadly for fetishizing Holocaust victims and survivors and performing rituals stripped of meaning and understanding.[4] One challenge inherent in this approach is that by desacralizing the Holocaust, we run the risk of trivializing it, making it appear mundane, just another instance of state-sponsored violence. Yet these comedians seem to suggest that it is precisely the process of sacralization—at a time when Holocaust education is ubiquitous yet knowledge of the Holocaust seems superficial—that has resulted in the minimization of Jews' suffering.

More effectively perhaps than any other medium, sitcoms have held up a mirror to their audiences, demanding that they think about their own role in participating in and perpetuating certain ways of thinking about the Holocaust. They have challenged their audiences to consider the danger of a memorial culture that disembodies the victims from the events and turns the Holocaust into a spectacle, bereft of real meaning and reduced to entertainment, another show to be consumed, a role to be performed. These shows have much to tell historians about how popular memory of the Holocaust has changed and will continue to transform in the years to come.

Holocaust Taboos

The Israeli philosopher Adi Ophir identified the taboos surrounding the Holocaust in a 1987 article in the magazine *Tikkun*. His "Anti-Theological Treatise" argues against sanctifying the Holocaust, which he claims has become commonplace in Israel and the United States.[5] He identifies four "commandments" that rule the new "religious consciousness built around the Holocaust": "Thou shalt have no other holocaust before the Holocaust of the Jews of Europe; Thou shalt not make unto thee any graven image or any likeness; Thou shalt not take the name of the Holocaust in vain; Remember." Ophir warns against the danger of enforcing these commandments, through which historians and community leaders seek to "establish the boundaries of Jewish legitimacy; they establish the Holocaust as a transcendent event which precedes and qualifies any attempt to fashion a modern Jewish identity."[6]

The commandments also reinforce the impossibility of representing and understanding the Holocaust and warn against drawing parallels or comparisons to the Holocaust. The greatest danger in all this, according to Ophir, is the way that such rules have the reverse effect of what they intend to do: Instead of preserving the memory of victims and learning important lessons, sanctification only "blurs the humanness of the Holocaust" and encourages us to be preoccupied with the past without understanding its implications for the future.[7] It insists on the Holocaust as specifically a Jewish tragedy, when, as Ophir forcefully claims, it is much more than that. These commandments are enforced and reinforced by Jewish historians, politicians, and educators worldwide and dare not be violated.[8]

That critique was reinforced around the same time by literary scholar Terrence Des Pres. Writing on the intersection of humor, literature, and the Holocaust, Des Pres highlighted three unwritten conventions governing the representation of the Holocaust, not so different from what Ophir had identified: that the Holocaust needed to be represented as "unique" and "above or below or apart from history," that such representations must be as "accurate and faithful as possible to the facts and conditions of the event," and that the Holocaust should be seen only as a "solemn or even a sacred event."[9]

These critiques came nearly a decade after the Holocaust had become much more prominent in the public sphere. The TV miniseries *Holocaust*, which aired in 1978, brought representations of the Jews' suffering into people's homes.[10] President Jimmy Carter established a president's commission on the Holocaust in 1979, headed by Elie Wiesel, by then America's preeminent survivor figure. And plans were well underway to erect a memorial to the Jewish victims on the National Mall.[11] Ophir, Des Pres, and others were responding to this atmosphere in which the Holocaust and its victims and survivors were increasingly venerated, inscribed with sacred qualities. As these scholars identified, the Holocaust was the ultimate taboo. It soon followed that Ophir's sardonic and satirical critique gained wider traction, as comedians directly lampooned the very symbols associated with this culture of veneration.

Taboos and Television

Television is the medium where this critique spread most widely. Until the mid-1990s, jokes that referred to the Holocaust or lampooned Nazis had been mainly the domain of film and literature.[12] The taboo against Holocaust laughter remained intact on television until as late as the 1990s. Once Holocaust- and Nazi-related jokes reached television screens, however, they spread quickly and widely.[13] Within a decade, it was perfectly common for sitcom, sketch show, and late night talk show writers to include jokes about Nazis or any of the emblems of the Holocaust that audiences would recognize. These television programs dealt more squarely with the nature of Holocaust remembrance and its impact on Jews and American society more broadly. In this medium, comics targeted the sacred cows of Holocaust remembrance: Anne Frank, Auschwitz, survivors, *Schindler's List*, the United States Holocaust Memorial Museum. It was on television, more so than in film, literature, or stand-up, that Holocaust humor found its most sustained expression, to the point where Holocaust jokes might now be considered passé. Television has changed the landscape and the possibility of Holocaust comedy, just as it has shaped Holocaust memory.[14] It has played a major role in the way that the world, in particular Americans, have come to understand the Holocaust; the broadcast of the Eichmann trial, for example, brought Holocaust stories to the forefront of American popular consciousness. Television brought the Holocaust to wider audiences and told a wider range of stories, ensuring that it was not simply the domain of filmmakers on the margins but part of the American mainstream.

Television is an intimate medium. People watch it in their homes, with their families, or alone. Televisions are a fixture in homes worldwide, often a focal point. People watch television each night, and televisions are instrumental in the way people understand the world around them, whether through news and current affairs programming or in other ways that their societies are mirrored back to them. When people watch television, they do so in the knowledge that many others are watching and reacting to exactly what they are viewing. In this way, watching television creates communities. As television historian Horace Newcomb observed, "Movie and radio had done positive work, but there was something about sitting in the living room, knowing that something almost dangerous was taking place on the screen, that others sensed it too, and that they were reacting very differently."[15]

Sitcoms, particularly network sitcoms, straddle a fine line between mass entertainment seeking to appeal to the broadest possible audience and transgressive comedy. To build a wide audience, geographically and culturally, television comedies often seek to be as inoffensive as possible, following the "LOP" (least objectionable program) logic. Especially on network television, it is the advertisers and commercial sponsors that have historically policed content. "Let's face it," conceded TV writer Allan Neuwirth, "if you're a salesman and your goal is to sell as many cans of dog food or tubes of toothpaste as you possibly can, the last thing you want to do is offend any potential customers."[16] Yet this approach also creates opportunities for sitcoms to rub up against the boundaries and taboos around controversial subjects and to broaden what audiences will accept.[17] Moreover, the mere fact of transgression on television can be compelling for audiences. The rules and conventions are what allow transgressive humor to flourish. Media scholar Michael Teuth argues that "the societal taboos and the misbehavior that satire wishes to end must remain, so that one can experience the delight of the entry into forbidden realms, a childish joy in simply breaking all the adult taboos."[18] Or, as Neuwirth puts it, "Humor derives much of its power from *pushing against* limits. If there were no limits, would there be comedy?"[19] This raises even bigger questions about the limits of representing the Holocaust at all. The sitcoms under investigation here raise moral questions about how we treat the past in art, particularly traumatic events such as the Holocaust.[20]

Seinfeld to The Sarah Silverman Program: Transgressing the Taboo

The first series to push against the Holocaust taboo was the critically acclaimed *Seinfeld*, created by stand-up comics Jerry Seinfeld and Larry David. Vincent Brook, whose work on Jews and sitcoms is unrivaled, notes that *Seinfeld* was "not only the most popular comedy series of the 1990s (according to the Nielsen ratings) but also the 'decade-defining' one (according to the popular and trade press)."[21] *Seinfeld* is, as cultural studies scholar Jon Stratton has noted, a commentary on "the experience of civility," a comedy about the day-to-day interactions between people and the rules and conventions that inform them.[22] With Holocaust memorials and representations a ubiquitous part of American culture by the mid-1990s, it was natural that they would become part of what *Seinfeld* sought to lampoon, another part of the ordinary daily life of urban Americans with which the show was preoccupied.

Numerous jokes about Nazis appeared in the series, most famously one in which a cranky local soup purveyor is dubbed the "Soup Nazi."[23] Another episode has Jerry and George unwittingly occupy the limousine of a leading neo-Nazi speaker and play the role of the Nazi leader. That same episode features a monologue in which Seinfeld wonders about why Hitler's version of the Nazi salute was so much more casual than that of the rank-and-file.[24] In yet another episode, Elaine's boss, Mr. Pitt, unwittingly smears ink on his upper lip, which makes him look like Hitler, and gives an expressive speech in which he declares, "We will annex Poland in the spring at any cost" (referring to his pending merger with the bottled water company, Poland Spring).[25] Each of these episodes suggests that two and half decades after *The Producers*, jokes about Nazis were coming into the mainstream.

Most significant, though, is the two-part episode titled "The Raincoats," co-written by Larry David, which came in the series' fifth season in 1994. By then, *Seinfeld* was at the height of its popularity, with the creators confident that they could push any boundaries and break any taboos. "At that point," Seinfeld recalled, "there was nothing we couldn't pull off."[26] The episode's main story line has Jerry seeking privacy with his Jewish girlfriend, Rachel, while his parents are visiting from Florida. Seeking a quiet place, he takes her to the recently released blockbuster *Schindler's List*.[27] There, they are caught making out throughout the movie by Jerry's archnemesis and neighbor, Newman, who promptly informs Jerry's parents of their son's indiscretion. "He was moving in on her like the storm troopers into Poland," complains Newman. "A more offensive spectacle I cannot recall." Jerry's parents, Morty and Helen, who had urged him to go see the film, are mortified: "You were making out during *Schindler's List*?" Later, when Elaine's "close-talking" partner Aaron regrets that he was not hospitable enough to Jerry's parents on their visit, he melodramatically chastises himself in a manner that parodies the emotional final scene of *Schindler's List*, in which Oskar Schindler (Liam Neeson) regrets that he did not save more Jews ("This watch . . . this watch could have paid for their whole trip. This ring . . . this ring is one more dinner I could have taken them out to").

Critics mostly applauded the episode's audacity. One reviewer in the *Los Angeles Daily News* said that *Seinfeld* is "the only show around that could get away with a *Schindler's List* joke. Perhaps the only show with the sort of adventurous spirit to even try a Holocaust movie har-har."[28] Phil Kloer of the *Atlanta Journal-Constitution* acknowledged that "the [show's] flirtation with Holocaust humor never veers into bad taste,"[29] and Alan Pergament of the *Buffalo News* wrote that "the show gets some of its biggest laughs from its sacrilegious treatment of the movie 'Schindler's List,'" but he conceded that it was one of the season's best episodes.[30]

Not all viewers were so enthusiastic. In a letter to the *Columbus Dispatch*, one viewer wrote how offended she was that *Seinfeld* would "debase Steven Spielberg's epic film about the Holocaust, possibly the most tragic period in the history of the Jewish people, with such scum." The letter writer's blurring of the lines between the actual events of the Holocaust and their representation in a Hollywood movie is perhaps the exact situation that the episode criticizes. It is not the Holocaust that *Seinfeld* satirizes, but the supposed sanctity of a movie *about* the Holocaust. This reflects one of Peter Novick's major critiques of Holocaust memorial culture: that audiences have conflated representations of the Holocaust with the event itself. This will ultimately be one of the major focuses of the comedians' critique. They recognize that audiences have blurred the boundaries between reality and fiction and see the comic potential in the confusion. Norman Kleeblatt, curator of the Jewish Museum of New York's Mirroring Evil exhibition, wrote in this vein that "visual culture at large confuses the represented and the real."[31] Returning to the now familiar charge that one cannot understand what it means to be Jewish without demonstrating the appropriate reverence for the gravity of the Holocaust, the letter writer continued her tirade against *Seinfeld*: "Has Jerry Seinfeld (who is Jewish) no feelings about his Jewish heritage? How can he equate what he defines as comedy to the worst tragedy mankind could perpetrate upon itself. . . . Is his mind sick?"[32]

Years later, reflecting on the series as it finished its final season, television critic Tom Shales complained about Seinfeld's apparent disdain for his own Jewishness generally and the *Schindler's List* episode specifically. He thought it crude that the show would parody Spielberg's "appropriately traumatizing film about the Holocaust." Even though Jerry "making out" with his girlfriend was "one of the more tasteless 'jokes' in the series," Judge Reinhold's parody of Schindler's closing monologue really raised Shales's ire: "The satiric point of this completely eluded me," he protested. "Perhaps it was just the *Seinfeld* writers bragging again about how tasteless they could be and still get away with it."[33] The Seinfeld writers were clearly poking fun at the phenomenon of the film, and the episode contained an underlying critique of the taboo against Holocaust laughter. They were also commenting on the ways in which people conflated the hyperrealistic *Schindler's List* with the events of the Holocaust themselves. Clearly, the episode struck a nerve with certain segments of American Jewry, who sought to reinforce an approach to Holocaust representation that was reverent and serious. By then, though, the taboo had been broken, and the theme would be taken up much more regularly by many other sitcoms.[34]

After *Seinfeld*, satirizing *Schindler's List* and other symbols of the Holocaust became regular fare in sitcoms, such as the animated series *South Park*, *American Dad*, and *Family Guy*, and in other popular sitcoms, including *Sex and the City*, *It's Always Sunny in Philadelphia*, *Broad City*, *Difficult People*, *The Office*, and most recently *The Marvelous Mrs. Maisel*. By far the most sustained engagement with Holocaust memorialization in the post-Seinfeld era is throughout the nine seasons of *Curb Your Enthusiasm*, the HBO comedy by Seinfeld's co-creator Larry David. Like *Seinfeld* before it,

Curb Your Enthusiasm is, in part, a comedy of manners, in which David and his circle of friends and acquaintances comment on the absurdities and trivialities of daily life (at least, of the daily life of a white liberal millionaire in Hollywood). Playing a fictionalized version of himself, David pulls no punches, not scared to make any group look bad.[35] Given that the show was produced on HBO, a network premised on breaking taboos and pushing boundaries, David was given far greater freedom to explore and experiment. Unconstrained by the demands of advertisers and network censors, he was freer to take some of the ideas and approaches that underpinned *Seinfeld* much further in testing the boundaries of comedy.[36]

The Holocaust, and how Americans engage with it, is a theme that comes up regularly from the first episode, when Larry lands in hot water for referring to his wife as Hitler in front of his friend's parents, offended because they had lost a gay Jewish cousin during the Holocaust.[37] In other episodes Larry refuses to fire a chef with Tourette's syndrome in his restaurant, mistaking the lottery numbers the chef scribbled on his arm for an Auschwitz tattoo.[38] In season 8 David unwittingly teaches a 7-year-old about Hitler and Nazi antisemitism. This backfires when the boy embroiders a pillow slip with a swastika, using the sewing machine Larry had given him as a gift.[39]

By far the most famous Holocaust story line appears in the season 4 episode, "The Survivor" (2004). Larry and his wife, Cheryl, invite their rabbi to dinner at their house; the rabbi wants to bring his friend, a survivor. Larry decides to invite his father's friend Solly, who is himself a Holocaust survivor. What transpires is an uproarious misunderstanding. The survivor that the rabbi brings turns out to be not a Holocaust survivor, but Colby Donaldson, a contestant from the high-rating television series *Survivor*. The two "survivors" engage in a competition about who is really a survivor and who suffered the most. For example, in response to Solly angrily recounting that they had no food in the concentration camps, Donaldson counters by complaining that in his forty-two days "trying to survive," he could not work out and "didn't even have a gym." "You know," he continued, "I wore my sneakers out and the next thing you know I've got a pair of flip-flops." The exchange climaxes as an exasperated Donaldson asks Solly if he had even seen the television series. Solly responds—incensed—demanding, "Did you ever see our show? It was called the Holocaust!"[40]

Solly's retort is a meta-critique of America's Holocaust memorial culture. Not only is the debate between a Holocaust survivor and a contestant from the television series *Survivor* absurd, but the Holocaust itself has also become nothing more than a "show," consumed by millions. What David seems to be suggesting through this exchange is that remembering the Holocaust has become itself a kind of performance, a reality show comparable to *Survivor*, to which audiences are transfixed but remain remote. The Holocaust has become simply a form of entertainment, the stories of survival no worse than other made-for-TV enactments of suffering and survival. Further, when Solly complains that Donaldson "never suffered a minute in your life compared to what I went through," the episode mocks the tendency toward competitive suffering, the convention pointed out critically by Des Pres that the Holocaust is "a unique event" or "a special case and kingdom of its own, above or below or apart from history."[41] Donaldson is a stand-in for the viewing public, who would idolize a figure like Donaldson and give him the designation "survivor," with all the cachet that confers on him. David is mocking our tendency once again to put all other kinds of suffering in the same ballpark as the Holocaust. Even the rabbi, a figure of religious and moral authority, is not immune to this minimization of the Holocaust and to the pull of celebrity worship.

The irony here is that, in this episode, the survivor is also the butt of the joke. Traditionally, survivors are treated with reverence. They are noble, strong, sympathetic—they have overcome terrible odds to rebuild their lives and are the symbols of Jewish continuity despite their ordeals during the Holocaust. In David's version, though, the survivor is an unhinged, defensive, competitive, quivering *nudnik*. These traits—borne from a kind of toughness or stubbornness that may have been what helped him to survive—are seen as comic, whereas Donaldson, whose "suffering" cannot be compared, is ironically the one with social cachet. With his volatile temper and willingness to exaggerate, Solly is a long way from the heroic survivor archetype. Here, David takes a cue from comic artist and author Art Spiegelman, whose magisterial memoir *Maus* veers from the typical representations of survivors as heroic and infallible. As Jewish Museum of New York curator Norman Kleeblatt notes, Spiegelman's decision to "portray his own father as unsympathetic, cold, misogynist, and—even more paradoxically—racist" broke an unwritten convention that survivors were beyond reproach. "As victims," Kleeblatt notes, "survivors are usually shown as morally unblemished."[42] Similarly, Anne Rothe points out that American popular culture, particularly through the talk show genre that emerged in the 1980s, underwent a radical transformation in the understanding of victims and survivors after the Eichmann trial. According to Rothe, visible figures such as Elie Wiesel sought to turn Holocaust survival "into an exceptional achievement," something to be lauded. This, she argues, was an unethical development, because with this shift, the victim "functioned as the survivor's weak Other who died for lack of survival skills."[43] As Rothe shows in her discussion of this episode, David's survivor is "antithetical to trauma culture's romanticized survivor figure, paradigmatically embodied by Elie Wiesel."[44]

Curb Your Enthusiasm routinely mocked the tendency to sacralize the Holocaust in American Jewish life. David's character regularly made faux pas and never himself understood the boundaries that had been constructed over decades. David paved the way for even more transgressive humor with the Holocaust at its core. The apex—the television program that pushed the boundary further perhaps than any other—came in the final episode of Sarah Silverman's cable sitcom in 2010, *The Sarah Silverman Program*. Holocaust jokes had long been part of Silverman's stand-up act, which pushes the boundaries of gender, sex, religion, and identity.[45] The TV series, though, gave Silverman greater creative freedom and a bigger audience to play out this critique. In the final episode of the series, Silverman's title character, a fictionalized version of herself, puts together a Holocaust memorial—not that she particularly cares about remembering the Holocaust. The memorial is instead conceived as a way to one-up her earnest sister Laura's planned unveiling of a memorial plaque.[46] The memorial is high farce: a dunk tank, "sexy Hitler," an alpaca, and "a real person who was at Auschwitz," who we later discover was a Nazi guard. The carnivalesque commemoration has at its center a memorial fountain that draws on a particular Jewish stereotype: a giant, "crying nose." Sarah's interest in the Holocaust stems only from her instincts to compete with her sibling, who herself is only performing a role she is expected to play.

"Wowschwitz" was the final episode of a series that had been canceled as a result of plummeting ratings. Perhaps because of this, Silverman took Holocaust humor further than her predecessors had. The "Wowschwitz" episode takes the *Seinfeld* and *Curb Your Enthusiasm* critiques to their logical endpoint, incorporating an attack on the tendency to both sacralize the Holocaust (per *Seinfeld*) and trivialize it (per *Curb Your Enthusiasm*). It is a comment on the all-pervasive nature of Holocaust memory, on its fragility, and its tendency to be characterized by empty symbols and gestures. It is not just the archetype of Sarah that is the target, with her scarcely believable and buffoonish lack of knowledge of the Holocaust, a comment, perhaps, on American Jewry writ large. Silverman is also attacking the Laura archetype, a sanctimonious stand-in for an American Jewish community that fetishizes and sacralizes the Holocaust. In showing Laura's obsession with the Holocaust, Silverman shows that often such reverence lacks substance and meaning. In the end, although the audience might be uncomfortable with or horrified by Sarah's "Holocaust memorial smackdown," they may be equally as ambivalent about Laura and her husband's morbid fascination, characterized not necessarily by understanding or empathy but by an expectation to perform Holocaust memory. Silverman shows us that, with both these tendencies prevalent in American life—sacralization and trivialization—American Jewry is unable to properly engage in dignified commemoration of the Holocaust.

The episode signaled that the ground had shifted when it came to discussing the Holocaust in twenty-first-century America. The unwritten rules governing representation and public discussions of the Holocaust were under fire by the turn of the new century, and television comedies were at the forefront of this shift. Silverman was only the most recent in a line of television comedians to bring these challenges to the small screen, reacting against taboos that they felt had come to overshadow Holocaust memorial culture in the United States and had rendered memorialization of the Holocaust either sanctimonious and hollow or shallow and insincere, despite all good intentions.

Transparent: Whose Holocaust?

More recently, the Amazon series *Transparent* has been subtler in treating how the Holocaust has come to be remembered, but it takes the critique of Seinfeld, David, and Silverman even further, claiming that we are too narrow in what we remember. The series itself is pathbreaking for numerous reasons. To date, it is the most widely viewed and distributed representation of the challenges transgender people in the United States face, treating the issue with sensitivity and care. Moreover, it employs more transgender people on and off screen than any other film or TV set, providing a pathway into the film industry and ensuring that transgender voices help drive the story's narrative. It also part of a new wave of television that is produced by streaming studios, eschewing the more traditional formats of broadcasting on network and cable television stations.

Television production and consumption has been revolutionized since the days of *Seinfeld* and the laugh-track-laden 22-minute sitcom. The possibilities on Netflix and Amazon are different from those on NBC or even HBO. The streaming format has given television writers greater freedom in terms of format and narrative than shows bound to the conventions of traditional programming, particularly compared with network television with its more rigorous regulation and concern for advertisers.[47] This is partly the outcome of sheer volume, with large streaming services such as Netflix, Hulu, and Amazon spending large amounts of money on new programming. The result is a massive increase in content, as more shows are being produced than ever. Dan Harmon, creator and writer of the canceled Yahoo Screen series *Community*, told *New York* magazine, "If I'm hiring writers, I'll meet with ten, and seven of them have a show on Amazon that I've never heard of."[48] Between 2015 and 2016 alone, online scripted television boomed, with the number of series more than doubling from forty-six to ninety-three.[49] This in turn creates greater scope for writers and producers to target more specific niche audiences and for studios to take greater risks in terms of content and the topics they are willing to cover. Without consideration of advertisers and networks, the opportunities to push boundaries have multiplied exponentially with the rise of streaming.

At first glance, the Amazon hit *Transparent* does not fit neatly into the sitcom world, because it eschews many of the conventions of the traditional sitcom. It is a series underpinned by dramatic elements, deeply flawed characters, and the enormous sadness and angst surrounding the central family, the Pfeffermans. Aesthetically and technically, it departs from sitcom norms with its season-long story arcs and the ways the episodes are filmed. Yet, as media scholar Maria San Filippo has argued, *Transparent* highlights recent developments in which streaming television series have transformed the traditional sitcom's capacity for telling dramatic stories. She claims that *Transparent* is a hybridized sitcom that challenges the conservatism of the genre. It is the show's "newfangled narrative mode, which balances conventional sitcom pleasures with a heightened verisimilitude that revalidates the sitcom as industrially and ideologically relevant."[50] The show also seems to suggest the borders of what constitutes comedy. A show can have serious, dramatic, and even sad story lines but still elicit laughter, as we recognize and empathize with the characters and their all-too-human struggles.

Transparent tells the story of a transgender woman, Maura Pfefferman, revealing her true gender identity to her family. The show focuses on her struggle as a 70-year-old finally trying to live as her true self but also on the different ways her family comes to terms with the new revelation. The comedy lies partly in the absurdity of the situation—a parent (Moppa, a neologism coined by Maura's youngest daughter, Ali) transitioning—and the program examines the possibility of continued existence in the aftermath. Each character responds differently to the new set of circumstances: Shelley, Maura's ex-wife, is not surprised by the revelation; Maura's daughters, Sarah and Ali, try to be supportive, but with so much of their own baggage in the background fail to do so; Josh, Maura's son, struggles to come to terms with the new family dynamic. Each of the main characters reexamines their own sexuality in the wake of their Moppa's announcement, often creating deeper wounds for themselves, each of them preconditioned by earlier traumas and relationships.

Transparent is a show that wears its Jewish heart on its sleeve. The Pfeffermans are an unruly, tight-knit, complicated Los Angeles Jewish family, descended from German Jewish refugees. The show does not shy away from the family's Jewishness, depicting it in all its beauty and messiness. Jewish themes underpin some of the major story arcs, and one of the central spaces in which much of the action takes place is the family's synagogue.[51] And although it is not a traditional sitcom, *Transparent* does draw heavily on Jewish comedic tropes. Shelley is an overbearing Jewish mother who peppers her speech with Yiddishisms;[52] Maura is a frustrated professor;[53] there is a generational and cultural gap between the parents and children, a trope in Jewish sitcoms dating back to *The Goldbergs* in the 1950s. The children respond to their parents' neuroses with sarcasm and often inappropriate jokes. The show also highlights contrasts between Jews and Gentiles. For example, in the first episode of season 2, at a family wedding, the chaotic and expressive Jewish family is juxtaposed with the stuck-up and stuffy WASPy Gentile family of Sarah's partner.[54]

As the show delves deeper into Jewish themes, it inevitably explores the Pfeffermans' connection to the Holocaust. We learn of this connection early, when Josh impulsively proposes to his young girlfriend with his grandmother's "Holocaust ring," which we later learn was the only family relic connecting the children to their family members who were killed by the Nazis. The only thing they really know about it is that they had a family member who was in Treblinka, something that the family brags about. This version of "competitive suffering" foreshadows what will come later, as we learn more about Maura's aunt who was killed by the Nazis. But this impulse for Jewish families to claim social status on the basis of their relatives' suffering elicits laughter from the audience, if only for its absurdity.[55]

Ultimately, we learn that Maura's mother, Rose, escaped Germany just after the Nazis took power, joining her father, a refugee, in Los Angeles. The twist, though, is that Rose's sister, Tante (aunt) Gittel, was a trans woman living in Magnus Hirschfeld's Institute for Sexual Research.[56] It is after the Institute was ransacked and its founder and inhabitants taken prisoner that Rose's mother finally convinces her to leave. In episode 9 viewers witness the heartbreaking scene where the Institute is destroyed and its books and archives burned by bands of SA thugs.

The story arc of Rose and her sister Gittel challenges the viewers' assumptions that those persecuted by the Nazis were targeted simply because they were Jewish. Most likely, the Pfefferman family myth highlighted the family's Jewishness as the key reason Gittel was ultimately murdered and Rose was forced to flee. But as the story unfolds, it becomes clearer that their Jewishness was but one reason they suffered. For Gittel, it was perhaps even a minor factor in why she was killed. The show offers ambiguity, reinforcing the positions of Ophir and Des Pres, who protest the sacralization of the Holocaust because it leads to narrow, shallow, and reductive conceptions of the Holocaust. *Transparent* demands that the viewer reconceptualize the Holocaust, to see nuance and complexity in the stories, to see the stories that have been hidden for more than seven decades. Even the Pfeffermans are on this path of discovery, not knowing much about how or why they came to America or what happened to the mysterious Tante Gittel, with only a vague idea that they had a family member who had been killed at Treblinka.

Season 2 is where this story line unfolds, as Ali searches for a connection to that past. The season is punctuated by flashbacks to 1933, when Gittel is finding her community inside Hirschfeld's Institute but with the Nazis' ominous rise to power in the background. Throughout the season the youngest Pfefferman daughter, Ali, explores her sexual and ethnic identity as she enters grad school. At the same time, Ali takes a renewed interest in her family history and in the Nazi persecution of gay and lesbian people in Germany, two interests that, for her, are deeply intertwined. As Ali tries to make these connections, she proposes a thesis title to her adviser: "It's like phallus is to crucifix, as vagina is to Holocaust," clumsily trying to show connections between misogyny and antisemitism.[57]

It is through this exploration that audiences see the connections between the persecution of Jews and the LGBTQ community more clearly, as Ali seeks to understand the story she has truly inherited, what the source of her family's trauma is. In episode 4 Ali muses on the genetic transmission of trauma—epigenetics—inviting audiences to consider whose trauma she claims to be inheriting: that of her grandmother, who fled Nazi Germany as a Jew, or that of her great-aunt, (presumably) killed because she was a transgender Jewish woman. Epigenetics posits that descendants of those who have experienced trauma have had their DNA altered by that experience, demonstrating their own signs of trauma.[58]

Ali's dabbling in epigenetics is complicated, and her third-generation story is not a typical one, because she struggles to come to terms not only with her Jewishness as a result of the inherited trauma but also with her sexuality. Ali's efforts throughout the season to reach out to her grandmother suggest that there is a concrete, albeit fading, link, between Gittel's suffering and her own struggles to make sense of her own sexuality and gender. For Ali, her grandmother is the key to unlocking some of the secrets and to offering some answers, some pathways to come to terms with her own sexual and ethnic identity. As she readjusts to life with her transitioning parent, Ali reassesses how her family history has shaped who she has become. And, as is established early in the season, she approaches the issue with sarcasm and a wicked sense of humor.

Yet it is not clear that it is Tante Gittel with whom Ali identifies. In the story's climax, in episode 9, Ali takes Maura to a women's music festival, where she is shunned as a trans woman. The link between Gittel's persecution in 1933 and Maura's exclusion in the present day are made clear. Yet Ali's link is not Gittel, but her grandmother; both Ali and Rose are witnesses to injustice against their loved ones. Ali sees the ghosts of Rose and Tante Gittel as the storm troopers come to shut down Hirschfeld's Institute and arrest its inhabitants. As past and present intersect, flashbacks overlapping with present-day action, Ali and Rose hold hands as they watch the books burning in the bonfire. As the grandmother and granddaughter connect over the family and the lives lost, we see that it is not Gittel whom Ali is identifying with, but Rose, who has struggled to make sense of Gittel's transition, just as Ali has been trying to make sense of Maura's. It is a third-generation story but with a twist, one that renders the viewer unsure about how exactly the traumas intersect and which injustice—antisemitism or transphobia—is at the story's center.[59] Season 2 ends with Rose and her mother escaping and finding Rose's father in Los Angeles, and we are left to assume that Gittel was murdered by the Nazis. The big question that lingers is whether the Holocaust narrative that haunts the Pfeffermans stems from the family's Jewishness or from its hidden history of gender queerness. Does Ali identify with the Holocaust narrative because of her ethnic identity or her sexual identity?

There are good reasons for the intersections here between Jewish and queer identities. First, Jews were prominent among twentieth-century advocates for LGBTQ rights. As Josh Lambert argues in his review of season 2 of *Transparent*, "Jews were crucial, ardent supporters of sexual science and minority rights throughout the 20th century, for many reasons; often because, being Jewish, they understood that persecution or prejudicial treatment of any minority is actually a threat against all of us."[60] Second, a story that tells of that intersection is easier to tell than a story of a non-Jewish queer victim. Dorthe Seifert argues that this is because Jewish queer survivors already have an existing language and framework that they can tap into; non-Jewish queer survivors, however, lack an adequate language to describe their experiences. This has both positive and negative aspects, according to Seifert: "On the one hand, Jews have been able to draw on an existing literary tradition when wanting to speak about other Nazi persecutions. On the other hand, this tradition has also determined the ways in which other Nazi crimes have been viewed."[61] In this way, telling the story of a Jewish trans woman and her suffering can fit into a recognizable framework. Finally, the intersection presented between Jewish suffering and queer suffering stems from the Nazis' own conception of the link between Jewishness and homosexuality, which they saw as inherently linked. Historians have more recently been recognizing that examining these links in greater depth give us a fuller understanding of Nazi ideology. In other words, by looking at the ways in which Nazism understood gender and sexuality, we can better make sense of Nazi antisemitism.[62]

Season 3 of *Transparent* mostly leaves the Tante Gittel story line behind, but a significant moment takes place in episode 8, which centers around flashbacks to Maura's childhood among Jewish refugees in 1950s Boyle Heights, the Jewish neighborhood of Los Angeles. Here we see 12-year-old Mort/Maura exploring her gender identity, only to have her grandfather, the family patriarch and a refugee from Nazi Germany, stamp out any possibility that she will be able to live the life that she sees for herself. As Maura secretly inhabits her true self, hidden away in the family's nuclear bunker, she is caught by her grandfather during an unexpected air raid siren test. He loses his temper: "Gershon burned to death in the oven," he shouts, "because your mother and grandmother let him run around in a skirt."[63] The bunker, a safe space from the realities of the Cold War, from the family's secret trauma, a place where post-Holocaust anxieties have been mapped onto fear about an impending nuclear war, has been rendered unsafe. Maura will carry her own secret for another six decades.

This is the first time we see the material impact of the Holocaust on the Pfeffermans, a departure from the season 2 focus on the transmission of trauma, where we see the less tangible ways that Holocaust trauma comes to be inherited. In other words, it is not simply the memory hovering in the background that shapes the Pfeffermans' view of the world, often in confusing and opaque ways. Instead, in 1940s Los Angeles the wounds of life under Nazism are still fresh and the memory of the Holocaust in the Pfefferman family makes it impossible for a young Mort/Maura to express who she really is. It is a reversal of the more familiar situation in which Jewish families emphasize their commitment to their Jewishness, which assumes greater importance because of their suffering. In this narrative, being

Jewish becomes urgent, even holy, as survivors and their families seek to deny Hitler a posthumous victory. This reassertion of Judaism, captured in the survivors' postwar invocation *Mir zaynen do!* (We are here!), is a common trope in representations of survivors. Of course, the Holocaust led many survivors to question or hide their Jewishness, but for many survivors and refugees, outward expressions of their ethnic and religious identity were quickly seen as acts of defiance and a clear message of perseverance and courage. When it comes to sexuality and gender, though, the suffering endured by Gittel leads to the impossibility that the Pfeffermans will accept young Mort's gender exploration. The earnest grandfather, having witnessed (from afar) his own child's persecution, will not allow his family to stray from the cis-gendered heteronormativity of the postwar United States. The anxiety that they will be taken away, like Gittel in 1933, hovers in the background and explodes in the climactic bunker scene, where Maura's secret, and the family secrets, will remain buried for a generation.

This shift comes against the backdrop of growing scholarly interest in how gender and the experience of the Holocaust intersect. In particular, the last decades have seen growing interest in the persecution of gay men and lesbians by the Nazis.[64] The innovative approach to sitcoms that *Transparent* takes, blending pathos with laughter, asks new questions about the Holocaust, eschewing narrow interpretations of it as simply a Jewish tragedy, one left in the past. It shows the Holocaust to be more multilayered and ever present in Jewish families generations later. The Holocaust and the way it is remembered are not principally the subject of our laughter here (although there a few jokes). What is important here is that the sitcom becomes a vehicle to tell Holocaust stories, in this case, unexpected ones. The series reflects a greater willingness to incorporate a range of different stories, not only of Jewish victims and survivors but also of other groups who experienced the worst of the Nazis' excesses, in particular, those whose stories are largely invisible in efforts to commemorate the Holocaust. *Transparent* goes a step further than previous series in its reconsideration of Holocaust remembrance; it is not critiquing Holocaust commemoration per se but using a comic medium, reconceiving what the Holocaust was.

Conclusion

By now, it has become ever clearer that the Holocaust and its revered symbols are no longer off-limits. Comedians regularly use them to critique societal conventions and to test the limits of comedy, to the point where Holocaust humor is so commonplace on television that it is no longer edgy. As Lenny Bruce, Sarah Silverman, Mel Brooks, and so many others have shown, comedy can be harnessed as a means to speak truth to power and to upend outdated and oppressive social mores. If Ophir and Des Pres are correct that cultural taboos limit how the Holocaust can be represented, sitcoms have played a key role in challenging those taboos through their transgressive approach to a serious matter. These sitcoms raise serious questions not only about how we talk about and represent the Holocaust but also about how and by whom such conversations are regulated.

Comedy is part of the vast tapestry of Holocaust remembrance. It allows audiences to engage with victims and survivors in different ways, to show their abhorrence of perpetrators. Holocaust humor may all be in bad taste, yet that is not the pertinent issue. Rather, we must consider whether the incongruity between form and content can be made productive for producers and consumers of humor. The question we must ask is not whether the Holocaust can be the subject of comedy, satire, parody, or black humor, but how and within what ethical framework it can be incorporated into the broader context of representing and remembering the Holocaust.

Still, many questions remain. There are further questions around the issue of gender and sexuality in Holocaust representation: How do these experiences of the Holocaust get emphasized or erased by the memorial culture? How does the positioning of the comic shape our reading? Are the rules different based on our gender or sexual identity? There are questions of generation: Do different generations have different sensibilities and senses of humor? How will this shape the future of Holocaust-related humor? The issue of the medium is crucial: Will changing media landscapes shape what we view as permissible or how we define and redefine good and bad taste? The issue of power and privilege are important: As Jews discover greater security and prosperity, does the function and meaning of their humor change? Finally, the issue of antisemitism cannot be ignored: How will the rise of the alt-right and the prevalence of antisemitism in American public discourse influence ideas about comedy and the Holocaust?

Notes

1. "Will Scarsdale Like Josh's Shayna Punim?" (season 2, episode 10), *Crazy Ex-Girlfriend*, 13 January 2017. The song can be viewed at https://www.youtube.com/watch?v=iLNa-ocdryY [accessed 22 June 2018].
2. The song is a rewritten version of Bloom's "Think About All the Dead Jews," written for a parody Chanukah album in 2013. See Katie Atkinson, "'Crazy Ex-Girlfriend' Star Rachel Bloom Breaks Down Four Standout Songs from New Season 2 Soundtrack," *Billboard*, 3 March 2017, https://www.billboard.com/articles/news/7710180/crazy-ex-girlfriend-rachel-bloom-season-2-soundtrack-interview [accessed 21 May 2018].
3. Peter Novick, *The Holocaust and Collective Memory: The American Experience* (London: Bloomsbury, 2001), 8–11.
4. On how figures such as Anne Frank or sites such as Auschwitz are imbued with their iconic status, see Oren Baruch Stier, *Holocaust Icons: Symbolizing the Shoah in History and Memory* (New Brunswick, NJ: Rutgers University Press, 2015).
5. Adi Ophir, "On Sanctifying the Holocaust: An Anti-Theological Treatise," *Tikkun* 2, no. 1 (1987): 61–67.
6. Ophir, "Sanctifying the Holocaust," 62–63.
7. Ophir, "Sanctifying the Holocaust," 63.
8. That year, *Tikkun* also carried a debate on the topic between literary critic Philip Lopate and historians Deborah Lipstadt and Yehuda Bauer. See Phillip Lopate, "Resistance to the Holocaust," in Phillip Lopate, *Getting Personal: Selected Essays* (New York: Basic Books, 2005), 263–79.
9. Terrence Des Pres, "Holocaust Laughter?" in Berel Lang, ed., *Writing and the Holocaust* (New York: Holmes & Meier, 1986), 217.
10. After *Holocaust* aired, Elie Wiesel anticipated the critique that such representations are incapable of capturing the essence of the Holocaust and simply reduce the Jews' suffering to mass entertainment. He argues not only that the medium is incapable of representing the truth of the Holocaust but also that to do so is dangerous, because it puts viewers at a remove rather than bringing them closer

to the event. See Elie Wiesel, "Trivializing the Holocaust: Semi-Fact and Semi-Fiction," *New York Times*, 16 April 1978, pp. 1, 29.

11. These are just a few of the many developments that made the Holocaust a national concern through the 1980s. For an excellent discussion on this, see Deborah Lipstadt, *The Holocaust: An American Understanding* (New Brunswick, NJ: Rutgers University Press, 2016).

12. On comedy and Holocaust films, see Lawrence Baron, *Projecting the Holocaust into the Present* (Lanham, MD: Rowman & Littlefield, 2010), 135–70; Aaron Kerner, *Film and the Holocaust: New Perspectives on Drama, Documentaries, and Experimental Films* (New York: Continuum, 2011), 79–100; and Annette Insdorf, *Indelible Shadows* (Cambridge, UK: Cambridge University Press, 2009), 59–74. On literature, see Des Pres, "Holocaust Laughter."

13. There are earlier examples of television humor that pokes fun at Nazis. A couple of examples are *Hogan's Heroes* and the German general sketch on Sid Caesar's *Your Show of Shows*. These were, however, exceptions, and even Nazi-related jokes were not widespread until the 1990s.

14. The definitive work on the representation of the Holocaust on American television is Jeffrey Shandler, *While America Watches: Televising the Holocaust* (New York: Oxford University Press, 1999). On other contexts, see Wulf Kansteiner, *In Pursuit of German Memory: History, Television, and Politics After Auschwitz* (Athens: Ohio University Press, 2006); Emiliano Perra, *Conflicts of Memory: The Reception of Holocaust Films and TV Programmes in Italy, 1945 to the Present* (Oxford, UK: Peter Lang, 2010); James Jordan, "Assimilated, Integrated, Other: An Introduction to Jews and British Television, 1946–1955," *Jewish Culture and History* 12, nos. 1–2 (2010): 251–66; and Eyal Zandberg, "Critical Laughter: Humor, Popular Culture, and Israeli Holocaust Commemoration," *Media, Culture, and Society* 28, no. 4 (2006): 561–79.

15. Horace Newcomb, "Studying Television: Same Questions, Different Contexts," *Cinema Journal* 45, no. 1 (2005): 110–11.

16. Allan Neuwirth, *They'll Never Put That on the Air: An Oral History of Taboo-Breaking TV Comedy* (New York: Allworth, 2006), vii.

17. Chiara Bucaria and Luca Barra, "Taboo Comedy on Television: Issues and Themes," in Chiara Bucaria and Luca Barra, eds., *Taboo Comedy: Television and Controversial Humor* (London: Palgrave Macmillan, 2016), 9.

18. Michael V. Teuth, "Breaking and Entering: Transgressive Comedy on Television," in Mary M. Dalton and Laura R. Linder, eds., *The Sitcom Reader: America Re-Viewed, Still Skewed*, 2nd ed. (Albany: SUNY Press, 2016), 253.

19. Neuwirth, *They'll Never Put That on the Air*, x; emphasis in original.
20. The seminal work on this topic is Saul Friedlander, ed., *Probing the Limits of Representation: Nazism and the "Final Solution"* (Cambridge, MA: Harvard University Press, 1992). Interestingly, this book was published in 1992, around the same time that comedians were beginning to approach the intersection between humor and Holocaust representation more seriously. This might help explain the rise of the "Holocaust comedy" genre in this period.
21. Vincent Brook, *Something Ain't Kosher Here: The Rise of the "Jewish" Sitcom* (New Brunswick, NJ: Rutgers University Press, 2003), 3.
22. Jon Stratton, *Coming Out Jewish: Constructing Ambivalent Identities* (London: Routledge, 2000), 255–56.
23. "The Soup Nazi," *Seinfeld* (season 7, episode 6), 2 November 1995.
24. "The Limo," *Seinfeld* (season 3, episode 19), 26 February 1992.
25. "The Gymnast," *Seinfeld* (season 6, episode 6), 3 November 1994. For Mr. Pitt's speech, see https://www.youtube.com/watch?v=nN8V6SYm164 [accessed 17 July 2018].
26. "Inside Look," *Seinfeld*, DVD Extras, season 5, episodes 18–19, https://www.youtube.com/watch?v=J28M7ambckA [accessed 16 May 2018].
27. It is worth noting that Jerry's girlfriend was Jewish in this episode. Typically, his girlfriends tended not to be Jewish, but in this episode, in which Jewish communal and familial obsessions with the Holocaust are at the fore, it hammers home the point of Jerry's ultimate offense, the desecration of *Schindler's List*.
28. Mike Duffy, "New Seinfeld Worth Wait," *Los Angeles Daily News*, 28 April 1994, p. L6.
29. Phil Kloer, "TV Review: Seinfeld," *Atlanta Journal-Constitution*, 28 April 1994, p. C10.
30. Alan Pergament, "'Seinfeld' Soars on Sacrilege; 'Tonya and Nancy' Stumbles," *Buffalo News*, 28 April 1994, p. B4.
31. See Norman Kleeblatt, "The Nazi Occupation of the White Cube: Transgressive Images/Moral Ambiguity/Contemporary Art," in Norman Kleeblatt, ed., *Mirroring Evil: Nazi Imagery/Recent Art* (exhibition catalogue) (New York: The Jewish Museum; and New Brunswick, NJ: Rutgers University Press, 2001), 15.
32. Julia Keller, "Folks Decry How, When TV Ads Air Seinfeld Smooching During 'List' Seen as Deeply Offensive 'Humor," *Columbus Dispatch*, 19 June 1994, p. 4G.
33. Tom Shales, "So Long, *Seinfeld*: Let Me Show You to the Door," *Washington Post*, 16 April 1998, p. B1.

34. There was a limit that the show would not cross: *Seinfeld* would not make fun of Holocaust survivors. The farthest the show was willing to go in this regard was in an episode written by Spike Feresten, in which George competes with an elderly survivor of the *Andrea Doria* shipwreck to secure a plum apartment; the survivor was granted priority because of his past suffering. The story line was based on Feresten's finding out that Holocaust survivors were granted priority access to his local tennis courts. The basic story made it to the show, but clearly making fun of survivors was still a taboo that the program was not yet ready to tackle. See Jennifer Keishin Armstrong, *Seinfeldia: How a Show About Nothing Changed Everything* (New York: Simon & Schuster, 2016), 184.
35. On *Curb Your Enthusiasm*'s Jewish overtones, see Benjamin Wright, "'Why Would You Do That, Larry?': Identity Formation and Humor in *Curb Your Enthusiasm*," *Journal of Popular Culture* 44, no. 3 (2011): 660–77; and David Gillota, "Negotiating Jewishness: *Curb Your Enthusiasm* and the Schlemiel Tradition," *Journal of Popular Film and Television* 38, no. 4 (2010): 152–61.
36. Larry David discusses the origins of *Curb Your Enthusiasm* in James Andrew Miller, "Curb Your Enthusiasm: Larry David Interview," *Origins Originals*, podcast, 27 September 2017, https://art19.com/shows/origins-originals-with-james-andrew-miller/episodes/2a50cdc3-f56f-4f09-8cac-04b8ba9a4a12 [accessed 17 July 2018].
37. "The Pants Tent," *Curb Your Enthusiasm* (season 1, episode 1), 15 October 2000.
38. "The Grand Opening," *Curb Your Enthusiasm* (season 3, episode 10), 17 November 2002.
39. "Larry vs. Michael J. Fox," *Curb Your Enthusiasm* (season 8, episode 10), 11 September 2011.
40. "The Survivor," *Curb Your Enthusiasm* (season 4, episode 9), 7 March 2004. This line also is reminiscent of Elie Wiesel's critique of the miniseries *Holocaust*, in which he closes by saying, "The Holocaust *must* be remembered. But not as a show" (Wiesel, "Trivializing the Holocaust," 29).
41. Des Pres, "Holocaust Laughter," 217.
42. Kleeblatt, "Nazi Occupation of the White Cube." For a reading of *Maus* that further discusses these transgressions, see Michael Rothberg, *Traumatic Realism: The Demands of Holocaust Representation* (Minneapolis: University of Minnesota Press, 2000), 202–19.
43. This is in contrast to Primo Levi's discussion of the ways in which notions of victim and survivor developed and were deployed in the decades after the war,

in which survivors felt shame at having survived. "We, the survivors," he wrote, "are not the true witnesses." Survivors were the exception to the rule, since they survived at best because of luck, privilege, or dishonesty. See Primo Levi, *The Drowned and the Saved* (New York: Simon & Schuster, 2017), 70.

44. Anne Rothe, *Popular Trauma Culture: Selling the Pain of Others in the Mass Media* (New Brunswick, NJ: Rutgers University Press, 2011), 38–41.
45. Sarah Silverman, *Sarah Silverman: Jesus is Magic*, DVD, Visual Entertainment, 2006.
46. "Wowschwitz," *The Sarah Silverman Program* (season 3, episode 10), 16 April 2010, http://www.cc.com/video-clips/1q4p7e/the-sarah-silverman-program-dueling-memorials [accessed 20 June 2018].
47. On the theory of media displacement and audiences' willingness to replace old forms of media with new forms, see Alec Tefertiller, "Media Substitution in Cable Cord-Cutting: The Adoption of Web-Streaming Television," *Journal of Broadcasting and Electronic Media* 62, no. 3 (2018): 390–407. On viewers' experience of streaming services, see Michael Samuel, "Time Wasting and the Contemporary Television-Viewing Experience," *University of Toronto Quarterly* 86, no. 4 (2017): 78–89.
48. David Marchese, "Swimming Upstream," *New York*, 29 May–11 June 2017, p. 112.
49. Michael L. Wayne, "Netflix, Amazon, and Branded Television Content in Subscription Video On-Demand Portals," *Media, Culture, and Society* 40, no. 5 (2017): 726.
50. Maria San Filippo, "*Transparent* Family Values: Unmasking Sitcom Myths of Gender, Sex(uality), and Money," in Mary M. Dalton and Laura R. Linder, eds., *The Sitcom Reader: America Re-Viewed, Still Skewed*, 2nd ed. (Albany: SUNY Press, 2016), 307–8.
51. On the Jewishness of *Transparent*, see Joshua Louis Moss, "'The Woman Thing and the Jew Thing': Transsexuality, Transcomedy, and the Legacy of Subversive Jewishness in *Transparent*," in Michal Renov and Vincent Brook, eds., *From Shtetl to Stardom: Jews and Hollywood* (West Lafayette, IN: Purdue University Press, 2016), 73–98.
52. On the Jewish mother stereotype, see Joyce Antler, *You Never Call! You Never Write! A History of the Jewish Mother* (New York: Oxford University Press, 2008).
53. This is a stereotype that comes up in the works of Philip Roth, Woody Allen, and the Coen brothers.

54. This image is well-worn, best exemplified in the works of Lenny Bruce and Woody Allen.
55. "The Letting Go," *Transparent* (season 1, episode 2), 26 September 2014.
56. Hirschfeld founded the Institute for Sexual Research in Berlin in 1919, and it was liquidated by the Nazis in May 1933. The scholarship on Hirschfeld in English is still scant, but he is increasingly recognized as a pioneer in research into sexuality and gender. See Ralf Dose, *Magnus Hirschfeld: The Origins of the Gay Liberation Movement* (New York: Monthly Review Press, 2014); Elana Mancini, *Magnus Hirschfeld and the Quest for Sexual Freedom: A History of the First International Sexual Freedom Movement* (New York: Palgrave Macmillan, 2010); Simon LeVay, *Queer Science: The Use and Abuse of Research into Homosexuality* (Cambridge, MA: MIT Press, 1996), 11–40; Robert Beachy, *Gay Berlin: Birthplace of a Modern Identity* (New York: Knopf, 2015), 160–88; Vern L. Bullough, "Magnus Hirschfeld, an Often Overlooked Pioneer," *Sexuality and Culture* 7, no. 1 (2003): 62–72; Heike Bauer, "'Race,' Normativity, and the History of Sexuality: Magnus Hirschfeld's Racism and the Early-Twentieth-Century Sexology," *Psychology and Sexuality* 1, no. 3 (2010): 239–49; and Toni Brennan and Peter Hegarty, "Who Was Magnus Hirschfeld and Why Do We Need to Know?" *History and Philosophy of Psychology* 9, no. 1 (2007): 12–28.
57. "Bulnerable," *Transparent* (season 2, episode 6), 11 December 2015.
58. Rachel Yehuda, Nikolaos P. Daskalakis, Linda M. Bierer, Heather N. Bader, Torsten Klengel, Florian Holsboer, and Elisabeth B. Binder, "Holocaust Exposure Induced Intergenerational Effects on FKBP5 Methylation," *Biological Psychiatry* 80 (2016): 372–80; Natan P. F. Kellermann, "Epigenetic Transmission of Holocaust Trauma: Can Nightmares Be Inherited?" *Israel Journal of Psychiatry and Related Sciences* 50, no. 1 (2013): 33–39.
59. One other way it is a third-generation story is in Ali's use of humor and Holocaust jokes. On the third generation and Holocaust jokes, see the chapter by Jordana Silverstein in this volume.
60. Josh Lambert, "Pfefferman Family Matters," *Tablet Magazine*, 7 December 2015, https://www.tabletmag.com/scroll/195620/pfefferman-family-matters [accessed 19 July 2018].
61. Dorthe Seifert, "Between Silence and License: The Representation of the National Socialist Persecution of Homosexuality in Anglo-American Fiction and Film," *History and Memory* 15, no. 2 (2003): 94–129.
62. See, for example, William J. Spurlin, *Lost Intimacies: Rethinking Homosexuality Under National Socialism* (New York: Peter Lang, 2009).

63. "If I Were a Bell," *Transparent* (season 3, episode 8), 23 September 2016.
64. There is still a dearth of research on this topic in English, but the pioneering works in this field are Richard Plant, *The Pink Triangle: The Nazi War Against Homosexuals* (New York: Henry Holt, 1986); and Gunter Grau, ed., *Hidden Holocaust? Gay and Lesbian Persecution in Germany, 1933–45* (Chicago: Fitzroy Dearborn, 1995).

The Last Laugh?

Ferne Pearlstein and Robert Edwards

OUR INTEREST IN THE relationship between humor and the Holocaust began seven years before we even met. In 1991, early in her previous career as a documentary photographer, Ferne found herself on assignment in Miami at its then new Holocaust Memorial. After touring the memorial with an old friend, Kent Kirshenbaum, they approached the elderly survivor who had been their guide and asked what she thought of Art Spiegelman's *Maus*, which had just been serialized and was about to win the Pulitzer Prize. The guide was distressed by the graphic novel's very conceit. "There's nothing funny about the Holocaust!" she told them. "You can't tell this story through 'the funny pages'!" Kent and Ferne tried to explain that they did not feel *Maus* was funny, except in the darkest sense, and that it merely used the comic strip form to tell a poignant story. But their guide was not moved and remained appalled by the idea.

That moment stuck with both of them. Later, on the road to his PhD, Kent wrote a paper asking whether there was a legitimate and honorable way to use humor in connection with something as horrific as the Holocaust. When he finished the paper, he handed it to Ferne and said, "Make this into a movie." That was 1993. It would take twenty-three years to actually do so: eighteen to get funding and another five to make the film. The resulting feature documentary, *The Last Laugh*, which we produced along with Jan Warner and Amy Hobby and Anne Hubbell of Tangerine Entertainment, was released theatrically in over 25 cities and broadcast nationally on PBS's Independent Lens on Holocaust Remembrance Day, after screening at over 100 film festivals including Tribeca, London, Rome, and Jerusalem.

The Long Haul

The Last Laugh wrestles with the question of whether or not humor has a socially redeeming role in approaching an atrocity on this epic scale and, if so, under what conditions. Going into making the film, we knew how controversial the topic would be. We expected hate mail and protests. But what we did not expect was how much the passage of time—one of the major themes of the film—would affect the reaction over the course of those twenty-three years and how much the reaction would continue to evolve even since the documentary's premiere in 2016.

Naturally, it was challenging to raise financing and get interview subjects to agree to be in the film. Many of the people we approached professed to love the topic, but no one wanted to be the "first one in," whether it was on camera or as a funder. Some talent agents and managers bluntly refused even to present the project to their clients. "Not no, but hell no!" one told us and then turned around and told us a Holocaust joke off the record. The legendary Hollywood manager Bernie Brillstein, now sadly deceased, whose firm represented Robert at the time, championed the project but was candid about its prospects, telling us we did not have a chance in hell of getting it made.

Another hurdle was the appearance of *Life Is Beautiful*, which was released not long after we met in 1998 and began working on this project in earnest. That film, by the Italian actor and comedian Roberto Benigni, ignited great controversy for blending comic moments into the story of a father trying to distract his son with humor when they are sent to a Nazi concentration camp. That film was so polarizing and so dramatically changed the nature of this conversation that we knew we could not make our documentary in its wake, at least not immediately, because it loomed too large. We knew we had to wait a few years until Benigni's film settled into its appropriate place in the discussion, which it ultimately did.

We also encountered the phenomenon of our culture simultaneously becoming both more and less accommodating of free speech. Obviously, many more topics are now fair game than they once were. But at the same time, we have become far more skittish about certain words and ideas that were once commonplace. In part, that is a healthy development; for example, certain slurs are no longer readily excused and condoned. But in the process, there has been collateral damage to freedom of expression, in that we can no longer even refer to those words or ideas, even in a constructive context.

The best example from our own work had to do with Norman Lear's groundbreaking TV series *All in the Family*. When the show premiered in 1971, it shocked audiences with its blunt use of racial, sexual, and other slurs, principally from the mouth of the lead character, Archie Bunker. The show's creators used that device to expose and destroy prejudice. But when we interviewed the film director Rob Reiner, who as a young actor had been one of the key cast members on the show, and asked him to list some of those slurs, he declined—laughing—on the grounds that he would be pilloried if he did so, even as a teaching point.

It is hard to argue that he was wrong. Thus we are presented with the curious irony that today, when our society is undeniably more enlightened on such issues, one cannot even say words that one of the most socially conscious and progressive television shows in U.S. history routinely used to combat that very bigotry. Even at the time, of course, *All in the Family* was controversial; some critics thought that a certain segment of the audience missed the satire inherent in Archie Bunker's bigotry and instead took it at face value, applauding it even. As the critique put it, some people weren't laughing *at* Archie; they were laughing *with* him.

There were other challenges, even after we finally obtained our initial development money in 2011. We found it hard to work old jokes into the film, even highly relevant ones, especially those from the wartime era itself, because they simply did not resonate with a modern audience seventy years later, particularly young people. We also knew from the start that we wanted to broaden out from the Holocaust to other subjects that might be taboo for humor, but we found that to be a sensitive balancing act. Putting any other atrocity next to the Shoah simultaneously invited criticism that we were equating the two ("You think 9/11 was as bad as Auschwitz?") or, conversely, that we were placing the Holocaust in a special category of human history all its own (which some observers do and some pointedly do not, a contentious debate in its own right). Yet we found that the film did not quite work unless we could point to other tragedies for the sake of context. For instance, the younger audience could only appreciate the fearlessness of Mel Brooks making Holocaust jokes in the Catskills just five years after the war when they themselves physically felt the discomfort of hearing a 9/11 joke nearly twenty years after that tragedy.

In other words, we discovered that, as taboo as the Holocaust is presumed to be, there has actually been a fair amount of comedy about it over the decades, creating a desensitizing effect. We had to refer to fresher, more recent tragedies—even lesser ones—for the audience to get even a small sense of how transgressive Holocaust humor was in, say, 1946.

The Risks Involved

It is easy to understand the uproar over humor that touches on the Holocaust; it is much harder to understand the ways in which a comedic approach might be not only acceptable but even healthy and constructive under the right circumstances. The potential for such humor to turn hostile is ever present, particularly as resurgent antisemitism worldwide reminds us that, as Faulkner said, the past not only isn't dead, it's not even past. The image of neo-Nazis marching in Charlottesville, Virginia, in August 2017 without censure or even complaint from the highest governmental authorities attests to how easily that specter can again arise in a time and place that until recently we never imagined possible.

Needless to say, going into *The Last Laugh*, we understood that any use of comedy in connection with the Holocaust would be highly charged and would risk diminishing the suffering of millions. But if we make the Holocaust off-limits, are we not on the slippery slope to the same suppression of free speech that characterized the totalitarianism that led to that atrocity? What, then, are the implications for other controversial subjects—slavery, 9/11, racism, AIDS—in a society that prizes freedom of expression?

More to the point, it is not even a matter of *if* we wish to allow humor about the Holocaust. The fact is, as the Shoah itself becomes ever more part of the distant past, such humor is inevitably becoming less and less charged and more and more common. What are the implications of that development, and how should we deal with it?

The Last Laugh examines the issue through three intertwined threads: the remarkable cinema verité story of 94-year-old Auschwitz survivor Renee Firestone; a Greek chorus consisting of interviews with comedians, writers, and thinkers led by Mel Brooks and including Sarah Silverman,

Mel Brooks, in his office in Culver City, California, for the documentary *The Last Laugh*. Photo by Ferne Pearlstein.

Carl Reiner, Rob Reiner, Susie Essman, Alan Zweibel, Harry Shearer, Gilbert Gottfried, Judy Gold, Jeffrey Ross, Larry Charles, Etgar Keret, Deb Filler, David Cross, Shalom Auslander, Jake Ehrenreich, Lisa Lampanelli, David Steinberg, Robert Clary, Roz Weinman, Hanala Sagal, and Abraham Foxman; and, lastly, clips from movies, TV, stand-up comedy, and other archival material ranging from *The Producers* and *Hogan's Heroes* to rare propaganda footage of cabarets inside the concentration camps themselves.

Time

When it comes to gallows humor, the famous, almost hackneyed formulation is "Tragedy plus time equals comedy." It is a maxim attributed to many sources, from Lenny Bruce to Steve Allen, and memorably repeated by Alan Alda's fatuous TV producer character in Woody Allen's *Crimes and Misdemeanors*.[1]

No work of comedy more perfectly exemplifies that effect than Mel Brooks's first feature film, *The Producers*, and its trajectory from scandal in 1967 to Broadway smash thirty-four years later. The film turns on the idea that the disreputable theater producers played by Zero Mostel and Gene Wilder are *trying* to make a flop and so choose the most offensive idea imaginable: a musical comedy about the Third Reich. In *The Last Laugh* the great satirist Harry Shearer neatly captures the irony.

> The whole essence of the joke of *The Producers* was, how could you possibly think that a musical about Hitler was acceptable? That was the whole MacGuffin of the picture. But by the time it gets to Broadway, a movie about a spectacular Broadway failure because it was in such bad taste becomes a Broadway hit because it's not in bad taste anymore! The passage of time alone has made it almost sweet. People sing along with "Springtime for Hitler"—there's no revulsion. If it had been "Springtime for Saddam Hussein" when it appeared on Broadway, it would have had the original kick.

"Of course time makes a difference," actress and comedian Susie Essman says in her interview for the documentary. "Nobody cares if you make Inquisition jokes." Her claim seems indisputable, but as our film cuts to Mel Brooks singing and dancing as Torquemada in a Busby Berkeley–style auto-da-fé from his 1981 comedy *History of the World, Part 1*, we begin to wonder. In our screenings at more than a hundred film festivals and elsewhere we have indeed had one or two audience members stand up and insist that people today do not realize the horrors of the Inquisition and that it remains unconscionable to joke about it, half a millennium of distance notwithstanding.

Although the passage of time undeniably reduces sensitivities as we grow further and further from the trauma of a given incident, it does not alter the concrete facts of the horror. That dynamic of desensitization is accelerated when the last living victim or witness is no longer with us, a moment that is rapidly approaching with the Holocaust. Robert frequently posits that someday the Shoah will be as remote as the Inquisition is to us now and will possibly be treated with the same nonchalance. It is our hopeful contention, however, that the existence of film footage and other visceral documentary evidence not available in 1492 might alter that. Future generations will have to be the judge. Certainly something valuable will be lost, but is it possible that something new can be gained?

Who better to answer these questions than an actual survivor?

Renee

The heart of *The Last Laugh* is Renee Firestone, now 94, who survived Auschwitz but lost most of her family, including her parents and her younger sister Klara, who was experimented on by Dr. Josef Mengele's staff. Early in the documentary, Renee tells a story about being examined by Mengele himself, a story that has the feel and structure of a joke and manages to be both bone-chilling and genuinely funny—hard as that is to believe, until you hear Renee tell it.

> One day, the doctor arrives, and who is it, it's Dr. Mengele. And we have to get undressed; he's going to check us, and we were wondering, why are they checking us? That was itself funny. But I come in front of him, and he puts his hand on my shoulder and he says to me in German, "Genug Speck noch"—"There is still enough fat." And then he says to me, "If you survive this war, you better have your tonsils removed. You have big tonsils." So, I was thinking, "Is he insane? Tomorrow I may die. I'm worried about my tonsils?" But when I survived and came back, and I thought about what he said, it was *funny*!

In that same scene, Renee's daughter Klara—who is named for her murdered aunt whom she never knew—expounds on the phenomenon of her mother's jet black humor. "Most people don't expect survivors to have much humor after the Holocaust, but that's really not the case at all," she says. "The survivors actually have some of the worst gallows humor ever. And I guess that they're the only ones allowed to do that!"

After the war Renee immigrated to Los Angeles, where she had a remarkable career as a pioneering fashion designer, among other adventures, before turning to anti-genocide activism full-time. Renee's mindset toward the topic focuses less on what is offensive than on the value of humor in maintaining humanity.

Renee traveled with Ferne extensively over the past eighteen months, promoting the documentary. Recently, a reporter in Montana asked her what she thought when Ferne first approached her about being in the film.

Theatrical poster for the feature documentary *The Last Laugh*, directed by Ferne Pearlstein; poster designed by Yen Tan.

At first I was surprised when she told me it was about humor. But then I thought about it and I figured it's wonderful. Ferne is the first person that really showed that we were still human beings while we were in the camps. Because if you're human, you laugh at something if it's funny. Even in the camps, if something was funny, you would have laughed at it. You don't decide that you're going to laugh at something; laughter and smiling are things that come to you automatically. I can remember being in the camp and seeing a guard trip over her gun. We laughed at that. People think of Holocaust survivors as not human. How can you live through such a thing? Well, this inner sense of humor and of wanting to see the good in life, not just the bad, that is what kept me alive. . . . I thought people will think I'm crazy to be in this film, but this is one of the most wonderful Holocaust films I know.

Who Can Make These Jokes?

It is hardly surprising that Jewish inmates of the concentration camps would seize on humor as one of the few tools they had to cope with their ordeal. Deb Filler, the New Zealand–born comedian, writer, and performer who figures in an important scene in *The Last Laugh*, quotes her late father, who survived four camps, including Auschwitz and Buchenwald: "If you were funny before the camps, you were funny in the camps." In that regard, Holocaust humor is a subset of the important place humor has always held among Jews as perennial objects of attack by the outside world. Tribally, humor functions as a means of both bonding and self-defense and carries with it all kinds of unspoken protocols.

But this dynamic turns precisely on membership in the oppressed group. By that standard, only Jews can ever use humor in connection with the Holocaust (and even that is not a blank check). The legendary comedy writer Alan Zweibel, whose career stretches back to the earliest days of *Saturday Night Live*, puts it this way in the film: "I think the initial reaction when a non-Jew makes a Holocaust joke is that they're making fun of the Holocaust, and who are you to make fun of that? You weren't there, you weren't affected. We were, and we're allowed to joke about it, okay?" Zweibel's comment, partly made in jest, implies another level of comedic inclusion and exclusion: the idea that all Jews, even those who weren't "there" in the Shoah itself, have inherited this right.

Yet there are also non-Jewish comedians who do Holocaust jokes with varying degrees of acceptance. Ricky Gervais somehow seems to get away with a scabrous routine about Hitler meeting Nietzsche and crediting him with the idea of the genocide of the Jewish race, to Nietzsche's horror. By contrast, the American insult comic Lisa Lampanelli made a joke at a Comedy Central Roast of David Hasselhoff, addressing his remarkable popularity as a pop singer in Germany, that raised hackles: "If they'd played your music at Auschwitz, the Jews would have sprinted for those ovens." Even Renee, who responds to many of the Holocaust jokes in our film by saying, "I'm not offended. I just don't find it funny," was offended by that.

Once we allow for any humor about the Holocaust—even if only by its victims, or their descendants, or more broadly by Jewish people at large—we have opened the door to acceptance of all kinds of humor about the Holocaust, and by a wider range of commentators. That in turn runs the real risk of fueling antisemitism, racism, and hate, a risk that is very much on the minds of many Americans at this moment. What happens when that insular, positively oriented humor is taken as license for all, when it is co-opted by outsiders—or worse, by the oppressors themselves—and is turned into a weapon of abuse and further victimization? On the other hand, should we proscribe all humor related to the Holocaust (or any sensitive subject) simply because some people will misunderstand or abuse it? Does that not subject us all to the limitations of the lowest common denominator?

"You can't control how your joke will be inferred," says comedian Sarah Silverman in the film. "I had a friend named Tom Giannis who called it 'mouth-full-of-blood' laughs, where the audience is laughing at the wrong thing. And that's hard, but it's just no longer yours." This dynamic, again, is the same one that animated fears of audience members laughing with Archie Bunker and his bigotry rather than at him.

The issue then becomes, What are the acceptable parameters for such transgressive humor? In a society like the United States, where freedom of speech is sacrosanct and protected (for the moment), and presuming that the humor does not cross into hate speech as defined as actual incitement to violence, this is not a question of government censorship but of social norms. What kind of humor as a form of free expression do we consider reasonable and acceptable, even if "tasteless"?

Context Is King

In a monologue on *Saturday Night Live* in late 2017, Larry David joked about picking up women in a concentration camp, igniting a national firestorm over the use of humor that invokes the Holocaust. It is a controversy that cuts right to the heart of this debate: context. In the monologue David does one side of a fictional conversation in which he hits on a female inmate, only to have her respond with shock and horror.

> How's it going? They treating you okay? You know, if we ever get out of here, I'd love to take you out for some latkes. You like latkes? [He mimes her offended reaction.] What? What did I say? Is it me, or is it the whole thing? It's because I'm bald, isn't it?

When scrutinized, the bit is really about his own crassness—or the crassness of the character he regularly plays—than about the Shoah itself. Indeed, the whole joke turns on the idea that the fictional woman is offended by the fact that he's hitting on her in a concentration camp of all places. So David is obviously aware of the transgressive nature of the bit. But, understandably, in the minds of many that does not mitigate what for them is offensive by its very definition.

It is fair to wonder whether the bit would have generated such outrage if it had been in an episode of *Curb Your Enthusiasm*. David's audience expects this sort of humor from him, and he has successfully gotten away with what most would consider far more off-limits material in the context of his own show. But it plays differently to the more general audience—and much bigger one—of *Saturday Night Live*. How you feel about David's bit has everything to do with your familiarity with his comic persona and body of work, his Jewishness and your own (or not), your comfort level with gallows humor, and the presumption of good intent in his routine (or not).

In fact, the beauty of Larry David's humor (and the success of *Seinfeld* and *Curb Your Enthusiasm*) is the way he calls attention to the awkwardness of the taboo. A prime example is the memorable line in *Seinfeld* about homosexuality: "Not that there's anything wrong with it." In the 1990s we laughed at that because even the characters knew that what they were saying was taboo and felt obliged to qualify it.

Another thing that makes David's *Saturday Night Live* joke difficult to digest is that it was told in the context of a flood of recent revelations of rape and sexual assault that makes that area taboo for humor at the moment and perhaps going forward in perpetuity. (David led into the bit with an equally fraught observation about his discomfort that so many of the male perpetrators being named in the post–Harvey Weinstein and "Me Too" era are Jewish.)

Another of the interview subjects in *The Last Laugh* is the eloquent Larry Charles, who wrote for *Seinfeld* and has directed many episodes of *Curb Your Enthusiasm* (as well as Bill Maher's documentary *Religulous* and three of Sacha Baron Cohen's movies—*Borat*, *Bruno*, and *The Dictator*—among other films). In our documentary, Charles says that a joke is only taboo is if we have not sufficiently dealt with the subject being joked about, and we are very much in the middle of dealing with the topic of sexual harassment right now.

In other words, context is everything. In her interview for *The Last Laugh*, the TV producer, writer, and former sociology professor Roz Weinman—who headed NBC's Standards and Practices Division for many years, including during *Seinfeld*'s run—describes how show runners often complained to her about material that she had nixed for their shows but allowed on others. "I had to explain that I assessed material on a case-by-case and show-by-show basis, rather than employing some one-size-fits-all standard. The audience for *SNL* or *Seinfeld* was different than the audience for another given show, and vice versa, and I had to weigh the expectations of each specific audience." Weinman, as it happens, is herself the child of Holocaust survivors.

These days, probably no American comedian takes on the Holocaust with as much boldness and frequency as Sarah Silverman. In one bit from her stand-up act, she says that her grandmother was a survivor of the Holocaust, then corrects herself—"I'm sorry, alleged Holocaust"—as she carries on with the main part of the joke. It is a rapier slash not only at Holocaust denial but also at deconstructionism and relativism. Even for those who find it offensive, Silverman's Holocaust-related comedy arguably serves a noble purpose as social criticism and not just as an attempt to get a cheap laugh by means of shock value.

Over a decade ago, we saw Silverman do a lot of this material live in her one-woman show *Jesus Is Magic*. The audience loved it and laughed uproariously. But it was one thing to watch that act in a tiny black box theater on Bleecker Street with a self-selecting group of her fans; it was quite another to stand next to Renee Firestone while she watched the same routine on YouTube. But it was extremely important to us that we remind the audience of *The Last Laugh* what they were laughing at. It was easy to laugh in that space in Greenwich Village with no one watching us; it is an entirely different matter listening to Silverman's jokes through the eyes of an Auschwitz survivor. Admittedly, Sarah doesn't attract a lot of 90-year-olds in her audiences. But we deliberately filmed Renee watching Silverman that way, heightening the awkwardness and the discomfort to make that point about context. We did not want to let the audience off the hook or ever let them forget—for more than a couple of minutes at least—what they were laughing at.

Does It Have to Be Funny?

Larry David's bit on *Saturday Night Live* is similar to an intensely dark joke that the comedian Judy Gold tells in *The Last Laugh*, in which she admits to privately wondering, "If I was standing on line, naked, for the gas chambers, would I hold my stomach in?" Yet no one in any of our screenings has ever objected to Gold's joke, even though it is similarly structured and takes place in the same setting as David's. We have always wondered if it is in part because Gold's joke is really about the highly relatable topic of body image, in a way that David's joke about picking up women is not. Indeed, David's joke feels especially uncomfortable when predatory male behavior is on everyone's minds. Gold's joke was also not told on national television on *Saturday Night Live* in front of an audience of millions.

In many ways, Gold's line is a perfect embodiment of the very nature of a "joke" in Woody Allen's formulation: the surprising juxtaposition of incongruent things, typically the profound and the petty. At that point it is fair to ask, Are these jokes even about the Holocaust at all, except tangentially—itself a technique that presents worries of its own? Comedian Jeffrey Ross goes to the heart of that question.

> To me, you don't have a Holocaust joke. You have a joke about dating, you have a joke about politics. . . . For me, the joke's always about something else, and then the punch line is the shocker. That's when you mention Hitler, or the Holocaust. "Auschwitz" is a funny punch line—not a funny topic, but a funny punch line. You don't want to walk out on stage and go, "How's your Friday night going everybody? Let's talk about Auschwitz!" That's not gonna fly. No one's getting laid after that show.

The fact that Gold's joke is so funny to many forgives all, a point that also figures heavily in these debates. "If you're going to cross the line, you'd better be funny," Susie Essman says. Harry Shearer adds, "A great joke really does trump all rules. But it's got to be a great joke, and the higher the stakes, the higher the standard for how good the joke has to be."

But therein lies the rub. It is by no means clear that being funny is a credential that should immunize and authorize transgressive humor. That said, there is no doubt that if people laugh, they are far more ready to accept a given bit, almost involuntarily, by sheer virtue of its success. But even if that were the crucial metric, "funny" is inherently subjective. Nazis undoubtedly find jokes about gas chambers funny. So it is no easier to define "funny" than it is to define "offensive."

Weaponizing Ridicule

Another issue for Holocaust humor is who is the butt of the joke, and that can lead to some complex gymnastics. Ferne began almost all the interviews for the film by asking, as a sort of icebreaker, "Do you have a Holocaust joke?" Many of the interview subjects would think for a moment and then reply, "I don't have a Holocaust joke, but I do have a Nazi joke." We quickly realized that comedians—and many audiences—make a distinction between the two, if only subconsciously. One is humor at the expense of the perpetrators, which is a long-standing tradition in satire and comedy in general, at which almost no one bats an eye. The other is humor at the expense of the victims, and that is where most people draw the line. It is the difference between "punching up" and "punching down," as comedians put it.

But even that is not a bright line. Even jokes that are indisputably at the expense of the Nazis can set off outrage just by invoking the imagery of the death camps, as when Joan Rivers said of a dress worn by German supermodel Heidi Klum, "The last time a German looked this hot was when they were pushing Jews into the ovens." Even Mel Brooks winced at that one. He admitted, however, that he thought it was funny, noting, "Even the rhythm is good." The Anti-Defamation League and others did a lot more than wince, roundly condemning Rivers and the joke.

It is true that when you parse it, it is really a joke at the expense of the Germans. But we have found that just evoking the machinery of the Holocaust—the camps, the gas chambers, the ovens—is a third rail for many people. It is also true that the furor over the joke may stem from its ephemeral subject—kibitzing about fashion—as opposed to one that, however dark, aims to make more substantive social commentary. Although it relies on the same dichotomy of the petty and the profound as Judy Gold's joke, its balance is more extreme and accordingly generated much more indignation.

For her part, Rivers fiercely defended that joke and all her Holocaust humor by arguing that it was her way of keeping the memory of the Shoah from disappearing from the public mind. One of her most persistent critics, longtime Anti-Defamation League president Abraham Foxman, strongly disagreed, arguing that jokes like that only trivialized the horror.

The ultimate example of humor at the expense of the victims is the subgenre of Anne Frank jokes.[2] For seventy years Anne Frank has stood as the ultimate personification of the victims of the Shoah. Accordingly, jokes about her murder in Bergen-Belsen are among the most taboo in the already fraught genre of Holocaust humor. But for that very reason in the last decade there has been an outright burst of such jokes, from *Family Guy* to *South Park*, from Shalom Auslander's satirical novel *Hope: A Tragedy* to a savage stand-up routine from Ricky Gervais ("She had time to write a novel for Chrissakes! And no sequel—lazy!"). Whereas some may see this phenomenon as a mere attempt to be as transgressive as possible for transgression's sake, more generously it might be seen as a harbinger of how society is adjusting its relationship to the Holocaust.

Not surprisingly, the proudly transgressive comedian Gilbert Gottfried rejects and ridicules the distinction between perpetrator-based and victim-based humor altogether, arguing that Nazi jokes are by definition Holocaust jokes. "Like you can separate the two," he scoffs, "because the Nazis had nothing to do with the Holocaust." (Not surprisingly, Gottfried also disregards the "tragedy plus time" rule, saying, "I always thought, 'Why wait?'")

A Change in Context

One aspect of *The Last Laugh* that stands out much more now than when the film first premiered is the long-standing debate over the power of humor, specifically satire, as a force for political change, made freshly relevant by the political situation in the United States at the time of its release in the fall of 2016. As it happened, Ferne had to travel with the film to several U.S. film festivals within days of the election, offering our first taste of how differently that aspect of the film—and indeed, the whole film—played after the election of Donald Trump than it had before.

"Humor is the weapon of the weak," offers Israeli satirist Etgar Keret in *The Last Laugh*. His formulation is not a criticism but rather an assertion that comedy is one of the few arrows the oppressed have in their quiver. But how effective is it? Historically, tyrants are resistant to comedic attacks; ridicule did not stop a single tank from rolling into Poland. Hitler, of course, was famously dismissed by many as a joke when he first came to power. Speaking to a group of schoolchildren in Los Angeles, Renee recalls going to her father in 1933 with her fears about the new German chancellor and his antisemitic tirades. "My father told me, 'Don't listen to that comedian. Don't you see he looks like Charlie Chaplin? He'll be out of power in no time.' Well, my father was wrong." This line in particular makes U.S. audiences audibly gasp in a way they never did before. Previously, its main function in the film was as a simple verbal connection to Chaplin. After Trump, it carried far more weight.

Because most U.S. film festival audiences tend to be politically progressive, we were accustomed to liberal crowds for the most part; we were not encountering a lot of Trump supporters. But the Jewish film festivals in the United States are a different story; it just so happened that the American Jewish film festival circuit starts more or less in the second week of November. Suddenly we were seeing a different reaction. Festival directors would privately warn us what percentage of their audiences was pro-Trump and anti-Trump. They would often introduce the film by saying things like, "We are living in divided times and *The Last Laugh* offers us a way to have a civil discussion." In two of the major Jewish festivals where we screened, people left in significant numbers before the Q&A—the Trump factions, we were told by the festival directors. The film did not alienate those viewers; they just did not want to have the "divided times" discussion surrounding it.

Another danger with satire is that we are merely comforting ourselves with jokes that only like-minded people appreciate while the true horror rolls merrily along unimpeded. In his interview for *The Last Laugh*, Larry Charles discusses this exact phenomenon in terms of Slavoj Žižek's maxim that "resistance is surrender." Žižek's argument is that a certain amount of dissent, comedic and otherwise, is built into the system to prevent real resistance from coalescing. That mechanism also allows the authorities to deflect charges of censorship or suppression of free speech, making it doubly useful to the powers that be.[3] Likewise, in his book *Dead Funny: Humor in Hitler's Germany*, author Rudolph Herzog surprisingly declared that the Nazis were actually tolerant of a certain amount of low-level political humor, a measure of how unthreatened they were by it. The Nazis were happy to have a terrorized populace harmlessly vent its anger with a few jokes rather than channeling that anger into political action that could truly threaten the regime.[4]

But the present moment seems to offer a different landscape. In fact, it is quite possible that never before in U.S. history has satire been a more potent weapon than right now. Donald Trump is the ripest possible target for satire precisely because he is such a voracious consumer of pop culture (especially TV), so attuned to what comedians and others are saying about him, and so thin-skinned and easily enraged. Because of his particular set of foibles, Trump presents a rare opportunity for satire to have an outsized effect.

But he presents some hazards as well.

To Žižek's point, there remains the possibility that something like Alec Baldwin's imitation on SNL is normalizing his buffoonery for the general public rather than serving as a call to arms, regardless of whether it angers Trump personally. Even that anger carries some risks. By some accounts, Trump's quixotic presidential quest began as his own attempt at vengeance for the 2011 White House Correspondents' Association dinner, where he sat fuming as he was roundly roasted by President Obama and host Seth Meyers. The right-wing political operative and Trump confidant Roger Stone has mused that this was the moment the eventual forty-fifth president of the United States thought, "Maybe I'll just run. Maybe I'll show them all."

Now, of course, the joke is on us.

Reactions

As we stated, when we started production on *The Last Laugh* we expected an angry response from many viewers. But for the most part we did not experience that. It's hard to say why. We would like to think it is in part because the respectfulness with which the film approaches the topic is self-evident, even when we are treading on dangerous ground. We like to say that we made a film about bad taste, but we feel we made it in good taste. But it is equally possible that the simple passage of time creates an ever-changing landscape in which the reaction to these jokes is constantly evolving. Indeed, a recent upsurge in hate crimes has made these jokes more controversial than ever.

One of the other characters in our film, Elly Gross, is also a survivor of Auschwitz, but she differs radically from Renee in that she carries a deep sorrow within her that is evident every moment of the day, with none of Renee's optimism or resilience. She expresses that in the film. Because she lives in Queens, we invited her to the premiere, in New York City, but Ferne was worried about her reaction and repeatedly reminded her of the film's subject matter. She came anyway and was not offended; in fact, in front of the premiere audience, she requested tickets for the following night's show. We were pleasantly surprised, to say the least.

The reaction to the film has also varied outside the United States. We had two festival screenings in Israel, where we were told by many, including Etgar Keret, that Holocaust humor is something Israelis grow up with—especially given the large number of survivors—in a way that is not true in the United States. Our first screening was for a secular audience that was supportive and not at all bothered by the film's content. The second screening was in a modern Orthodox neighborhood where Ferne was more concerned about the response. But that also went smoother than she expected. Although people were definitely on guard entering the theater, they were reassured once they viewed the film and were able to discuss it with Ferne. Indeed, the Q&A was so crucial that it continued beyond the allotted time in the lobby of the theater.

In Germany, by contrast, where the taboo against joking about the Holocaust is strong and there are actual laws against Nazi-related hate speech, we found that audiences at our European premiere in Munich were quiet. If they laughed at all, it was only when a survivor like Renee or Robert Clary made a joke that somehow gave them permission to follow suit. We had a sense going into the German screenings that that might be the case. In the course of production, one of our co-producers had an intern watch the film and was alarmed by his stoic response. Afterward, she asked what he thought, to which the intern replied, "I loved it!" The producer said, "Really? Because you didn't smile or laugh once." And the intern explained, "I'm Austrian! I'm not allowed to laugh at the Holocaust!" But what was alarming in Munich, especially for Ferne—most likely the only Jewish person in an audience of 350 Germans—was what audiences actually felt comfortable laughing at, which were crass "Jews are cheap" jokes. Somehow they didn't see this as a problem, but it was deeply disturbing to her. Once again, context was crucial—and in this case, worrying.

The Future

So where does that leave us going forward?

In the course of researching *The Last Laugh*, we were introduced by Art Spiegelman to Yann Martel, author of the Man Booker Prize–winning *Life of Pi*. After the triumph of that book, Martel's next novel, the allegory *Beatrice and Virgil*, was met with condemnation for telling the story of the Holocaust through a pair of stuffed animals. Baffled by what he saw as the myopia of his critics, Yann argued to us that it is absurd that there is only one approved artistic approach to the Holocaust—which is to say, sober realism (black-and-white footage scored with cello in a minor key, as Woody Allen dryly observes in another of his films). And why is that, Martel asks. Why is the Holocaust alone among human tragedies limited to just one narrow aesthetic treatment? War is horrific, yet no one objects to the black comedy of *M*A*S*H* or *Catch-22*. Everyone understands that the intent of those novels and their film adaptations is serious and noble, not disrespectful or mocking.

Sarah Silverman argues that comedy is not given the same respect as an art form in storytelling. ("Comedians sit at the children's table," as the famous complaint goes.) But we have seen that dynamic changing even in the course of making our film. In the post–Jon Stewart era, more and more Americans look to comedians for serious social criticism, even as respect for traditional journalism and media has waned, partly because of dishonest, politically motivated attacks on it. Perhaps even as the traditional ways of dealing with the Holocaust begin to disappear with the last survivors, humor and satire will open up new ways of helping us understand the Shoah and prevent other genocides from happening. (Too late, some might argue.)

As noted, these questions are not going away but in fact will become only more pressing as the Holocaust recedes further and further into history. Alan Zweibel again: "Are there things that go over the line? I'm sure that there are. But I don't know if my kids would consider it over the line." Humor can have a role in helping us to come to terms with tragedy, even a tragedy on the scale of the Holocaust; it can serve as a weapon to fight against the powerful, or it can act as a beacon to illuminate even the darkest moments. This is ultimately a truth as plain as the existence of humor in the human condition in the first place. If humor offers us a way to do those things, albeit with strict vigilance for the many attendant dangers, its value is self-evident. It might even be a solution to so-called Holocaust fatigue, which, of course, is dangerous in its own right.

At the conclusion of *The Last Laugh* Mel Brooks tells us, "Comics are the conscience of the people, and they are allowed a wide berth of activity in every direction. Comics have to tell us who we are, where we are, even if it's in bad taste." Or as David Steinberg puts it, "Sometimes it's important to be ahead of society. Just because it's uncomfortable doesn't mean that it's the wrong thing. Sometimes it means it's exactly the right thing."

Notes

1. In a more academic formulation, Sidra DeKoven Ezrahi writes, "The comic reflex comes into being . . . in the intersection of tragic historical knowledge and a reconsecration of the universe. It is in constant dialogue with messianic temptation and apocalyptic despair; released by the messianic promise of resolution, the comic is then animated by the *deferral* of that resolution." Sidra DeKoven Ezrahi, "After Such Knowledge, What Laughter?" *Yale Journal of Criticism* 4, no. 1 (2001): 288; emphasis in original.
2. See the chapter in this volume by Liat Stier-Livny on Israeli humor and Anne Frank.
3. Slavoj Žižek, "Resistance Is Surrender," *London Review of Books* 9, no. 22 (2007): 7.
4. Rudolph Herzog, *Humor in Hitler's Germany*, trans. Jefferson Chase (New York: Jefferson House, 2011).

Contributors

David Slucki is the Loti Smorgon Associate Professor in Contemporary Jewish Life and Culture at the Australian Center for Jewish Civilization at Monash University. He is the author of *Sing This at My Funeral: A Memoir of Fathers and Sons* (Wayne State University Press, 2019) and *The International Jewish Labor Bund after 1945: Toward a Global History* (Rutgers University Press, 2012). He is co-editor of *In the Shadows of Memory: The Holocaust and the Third Generation* (Vallentine Mitchell, 2015). He has published widely on Jewish life after the Holocaust and is currently working on projects focusing on Holocaust survivors in the United States and on the grandchildren of survivors.

Gabriel N. Finder is professor of Germanic languages and literatures and former Ida and Nathan Kolodiz Director of Jewish Studies at the University of Virginia. He is also associate editor of the journal *Holocaust and Genocide Studies*. *Jewish Honor Courts: Revenge, Retribution, and Reconciliation in Europe and Israel after the Holocaust* (Wayne State University Press, published in association with the United States Holocaust Memorial Museum, 2015), which he coedited with Laura Jockusch, was named a 2016 National Jewish Book Award finalist in the Holocaust category by the Jewish Book Council. He is coeditor with Eli Lederhendler of *A Club of Their Own: Jewish Humorists and the Contemporary World* (Studies in Contemporary Jewry 29) (Oxford University Press, 2016) and coauthor with Alexander Prusin of *Justice Behind the Iron Curtain: Nazis on Trial in Communist Poland* (University of Toronto Press, 2018).

Avinoam Patt is the Doris and Simon Konover Chair of Judaic Studies and director of the Center for Judaic Studies and Contemporary Jewish Life at the University of Connecticut. He is the author of *Finding Home and Homeland: Jewish Youth and Zionism in the Aftermath of the Holocaust* (Wayne State University Press, May 2009), coeditor (with Michael Berkowitz) of a collected volume on Jewish Displaced Persons, titled *We are Here: New Approaches to the Study of Jewish Displaced Persons in Postwar Germany* (Wayne State University Press, 2010), and contributor to several projects at the USHMM including *Jewish Responses to Persecution, 1938–1940* (USHMM/Alta Mira Press, September 2011). He is coeditor of an anthology of contemporary American Jewish fiction titled *The New Diaspora: The Changing Landscape of American Jewish Fiction* (Wayne State University Press, 2015) and of a new volume on *The Joint Distribution Committee at 100: A Century of Humanitarianism* (Wayne State University Press, 2019). He is currently writing a new book on the early postwar memory of the Warsaw Ghetto Uprising and together with Laura Hilton is coeditor of a new volume on *Understanding and Teaching the Holocaust* (University of Wisconsin Press, June 2020).

JENNIFER CAPLAN is an assistant professor of religious studies and the program director for undergraduate Jewish studies at Towson University. Her work is primarily on contemporary Judaism and popular culture, and she has published or taught on topics related to Jewish graphic novels, popular portrayals of gendered Jews, and the pedagogy of the Jewish studies classroom. Her book *All Joking Aside: Judaism and Humor from The Borscht Belt to Broad City* is forthcoming from Wayne State University Press.

MARC CAPLAN is a native of Louisiana and a graduate of Yale University. In 2003 he earned his Ph.D. in comparative literature from New York University. Since then he has held professorial appointments at Indiana University, Johns Hopkins University, and Yale. In 2011 he published *How Strange the Change: Language, Temporality, and Narrative Form in Peripheral Modernisms*—a comparison of Yiddish and African literatures—with Stanford University Press. His second book, *Yiddish Writers in Weimar Berlin: A Fugitive Modernism*, is forthcoming from Indiana University

Press. He is currently a visiting professor in the Taube Department of Jewish Studies at the University of Wroclaw, Poland.

ROBERT EDWARDS is a graduate of Stanford University's MA program in documentary film and the writer/director of the feature films *Land of the Blind* (2006), starring Ralph Fiennes and Donald Sutherland, and *When I Live My Life Over Again* (2016), aka *One More Time*, starring Christopher Walken and Amber Heard. Formerly he was an infantry and intelligence officer in the US Army, with service in Germany in the late 1980s and Iraq during the first Gulf war.

FERNE PEARLSTEIN is a prize-winning documentary filmmaker whose work has been screened and broadcast around the world. An acclaimed cinematographer, she won the Sundance Cinematography Prize for *Imelda* and is one of a handful of women featured in Kodak's long-running "On Film" campaign. As a director, her most recent film is the critically acclaimed *The Last Laugh*, which was released theatrically in over 25 cities, broadcast on PBS's Independent Lens, and screened at over 100 film festivals including Tribeca, Jerusalem, and Munich. Ferne is a member of the Academy of Motion Pictures Arts and Sciences and the Brooklyn Jewish Hall of Fame.

JAN SCHWARZ received his Ph.D. at Columbia University in 1997 in the fields of Yiddish and comparative literature. Since 2011, he has been associate professor of Yiddish studies at Lund University, Sweden, the only academic position in the field of Yiddish in Scandinavia. He was senior lecturer at University of Chicago, 2003–2011, and assistant professor at University of Illinois, Urbana–Champaign, 1998–2002. He held academic appointments at Northwestern University, 2003–2005, and University of Pennsylvania, 1994–1995. He is the author of two scholarly monographs about Yiddish culture and literature: *Imagining Lives: Autobiographical Fiction of Yiddish Writers* (2005) and *Survivors and Exiles: Yiddish Culture after the Holocaust* (2015). He has published articles and edited volumes as well as lectured widely about Yiddish, Jewish, American, and Scandinavian literatures, world literature and translation, and Jewish responses to the Holocaust. He is the Danish translator of Abraham Sutzkever's *Grønt akvarium Fortællinger fra Lithauens Jerusalem* (2017) and Scholem-Aleichem's *Mælkemanden*

Tevje (2009) and editor of *Den gyldne kæde. En antologi af jiddisch litteratur* (Rhodos 1994). He is currently working on a project that has been funded by the Swedish Research Council (2014–2016), *The Bilingual Works of Isaac Bashevis Singer: Novels, Translations, World Literature* as well as editing I. B. Singer, *In the World of Chaos: Early Writings, 1925–1936*.

DAVID SHNEER is a writer and teacher and serves as the Louis P. Singer Chair in Jewish History and professor of history and Jewish studies at the University of Colorado. His award-winning works include *Yiddish and the Creation of Soviet Jewish Culture* (Cambridge University Press, 2004), *Through Soviet Jewish Eyes: Photography, War, and the Holocaust* (Rutgers University Press, 2011), and *Grief: The Biography of a Holocaust Photograph* (Oxford University Press, forthcoming 2020).

JORDANA SILVERSTEIN is a historian based at the University of Melbourne. She is the author of *Anxious Histories: Narrating the Holocaust in Jewish Communities at the Beginning of the Twenty-First Century* (Berghahn, 2015) and co-editor of *In the Shadows of Memory: The Holocaust and the Third Generation* (Vallentine Mitchell, 2016). Her research focuses on histories of Jewish Holocaust memory, Australian Jewish sexuality, and Australian child refugee policy.

ANNA SHTERNSHIS holds the position of Al and Malka Green Professor of Yiddish studies and the director of the Anne Tanenbaum Centre for Jewish Studies at the University of Toronto. She received her doctoral degree (D.Phil) in modern languages and literatures from Oxford University in 2001. Shternshis is the author of *Soviet and Kosher: Jewish Popular Culture in the Soviet Union, 1923—1939* (Indiana University Press, 2006) and *When Sonia Met Boris: An Oral History of Jewish Life under Stalin* (Oxford University Press, 2017). Together with artist Psoy Korolenko, Shternshis created a Grammy-nominated *Yiddish Glory* project, the initiative that brought back to life the forgotten Yiddish music written during the Holocaust in the Soviet Union.

LIAT STEIR-LIVNY is an assistant professor in the Department of Cultural Studies, Creation and Production at Sapir College and a tutor and course coordinator for the cultural studies MA program and the Department of

Literature, Language, and the Arts at the Open University of Israel. Her research focuses on the changing commemoration of the Holocaust in Israel from the 1940s until the present. It combines Holocaust studies, memory studies, cultural studies, trauma studies, and film studies. She has authored numerous articles and five books.

ILAN STAVANS is Lewis-Sebring Professor of Humanities, Latin American and Latino Culture at Amherst College, the publisher of Restless Books, the host of the NPR podcast *In Contrast*, and a columnist for the *New York Times en Español*. Among his most recent books are *Quixote: The Novel and the World* (2015), the anthology *Oy Caramba!: An Anthology of Jewish Stories from Latin America* (2016), the photographic meditation *I Love My Selfie* (2017), the graphic novel *Angelitos* (with Santiago Cohen), the one-man play *The Oven* (2018), and the booklong poem *The Wall* (all 2018). The recipient of numerous awards and honors, his work, translated into twenty languages, has been adapted to the stage, TV, radio, and film.

JARROD TANNY is associate professor of history and the Charles and Hannah Block Distinguished Scholar in Jewish History at the University of North Carolina Wilmington. He received his PhD from the University of California at Berkeley. His monograph, *City of Rogues and Schnorrers* (Indiana University Press, 2011), examines how the city of Odessa was mythologized as a Jewish city of sin, celebrated and vilified for its Jewish gangsters, pimps, bawdy musicians, and comedians. He is currently working on a larger study on Jewish humor in post–World War II America and its place within the larger context of the European Jewish past.

STEPHEN J. WHITFIELD is emeritus professor of American studies at Brandeis University, where he taught the intersection of politics and ideas in the twentieth century. He is the author of *The Culture of the Cold War* (1991, 1996), *In Search of American Jewish Culture* (1999) and, most recently, *Learning on the Left: Political Profiles of Brandeis University* (2020) as well as six other books. Whitfield has served as a visiting professor at the Hebrew University of Jerusalem, the Catholic University of Leuven/Louvain-la-Neuve in Belgium, the Sorbonne, and the Ludwig Maximilians University of Munich.

INDEX

Page numbers in *italics* refer to figures.

absurdism, 242–43, 245–46, 248, 252, 254, 262
Absurdistan (Shteyngart), 174
Adenauer, Konrad, 162
Adorno, Theodore, 5
Adventures of Huckleberry Finn, The (Twain), 106
Adyar Club, Amsterdam, Netherlands, 59, 61–62, 65
"Afn Hoykhn Barg" ("On the High Mountain"), 21–23
After (Bukiet), 173
Ahmed, Sara, 247
AIDS, jokes about, 107
Allen, Woody, 119, 134, 140, 144–48, 149, 161, 325
Alles auf Zucker! (*Go for Zucker!*; Levy), 220
All in the Family (CBS), 315
Amsterdam, Netherlands, 59, 60, 61, 64–65, 72
Anne Frank House, Amsterdam, Netherlands, 196, 206–7
Annie Hall (Allen), 144, 145–46
Ansky, S., 61
Ansky Society, 59, 60–61, 62
Anti-Defamation League, 274, 327
anti-fascism: in East Germany, 60, 69–70, 79; interwar, 60; Jewish, 16, 71; Yiddish humor and, 17, 32
Antiochus IV Epiphanes, 19–20
antisemitism, 109, 139, 144, 172; anti-Zionism and, 185; contemporary, 7, 193, 281, 305, 316; historical factors, 183–84; Holocaust consciousness and, 173; Holocaust representation and, 6; interwar, in U.S., 135; language of, 223; in Latin America, 181–85, 187–90; Soviet, 31; stereotypes, countering, 138
anti-Zionism, 185, 193
Arab-Israeli conflict, 182–83, 199, 210–11
Argentina, 156, 182, 189–92
Arvin, L., 73, 75
Asch, Sholem, 89–90
Ashkenazi, Adi, 206–7
assimilation, 89, 93, 160, 231
audience response: as changing during performance, 225–26, 227; contextualized, 325; controversy, 323; discomfort, 2–3, 4, 117, 221, 223; misunderstanding, 322; offense, 291–92; positive, 78–80, 124, 253, 330–31
Auerbach, Rachel, 40
Auschwitz, 50, 60, 66, 319; Anne Frank's family in, 196; God and, 158; as Holocaust icon, 288; jokes about, 254, 326
Auschwitz-Birkenau Memorial and Museum, Oświęcim, Poland, 207
Auslander, Shalom, 159, 160–61, 168–69, 170–71, 174–75, 197
Australia, 244
"Az der Rebbe Elimelekh," 75–76

Barney's Version (Richler), 172–73
Battegay, Caspar, 228, 231
Bavohuis, Amsterdam, Netherlands, 62
Beatrice and Virgil (Martel), 331–32
Ben-Gurion, David, 52
Benigni, Roberto, 5, 314
Benny, Jack, 114, 117
Bergen-Belsen, 60, 66, 196
Bergson, Henri, 106
Berle, Milton, 143
Berlin, Germany, 60, 70

341

Berliner Zeitung, 70
Birthright trips, 267–68
Black, Lewis, 158–59, 167–68
Bloom, Rachel, 285
Bloshteyn, Hirsh, 15–16, 18, 27–28
Bonato, Raúl A. "Catton," 191
Borowski, Tadeusz, 49–50, 181, 193
Boyarin, Jonathan, 243, 253
Brenner, Michael, 225, 229
Brook, Vincent, 290
Brooks, Mel, 4, 122–24, 134, 156, 261, 317, 317–18, 327, 332
Bruce, Lenny, 121–22, 134, 139, 140–44, 146–48, 156, 157; gender and, 145, 149–50; influence of, 226
Buenos Aires, Argentina, 86, 189–91
Bukiet, Melvin Jules, 173
Burns, Christy, 149
Butler, Judith, 142, 148

cabaret, 61, 62, 64–65, 70, 74; political, 79
Caesar, Sid, 273
caricaturas, 181, 182–83, 185, 189–90, 192–93
caricature, 18, 25, 28
cartoons, television, 197–98
Catton. *See* Bonato, Raúl A.
censorship, 17, 26, 110, 323, 329
Chaplin, Charlie, 109–10, 124, 156, 328
Charles, Larry, 324, 329
Chelmno, 113
Chelm stories, 90
children, 157, 160–61, 168; in postwar film, 45, 46–47, 48–49; songs of, 23–25
children's stories, 90, 91
Chosen People, The (*Am segula*; Keshet Broadcasting), 208–9
circumcision, 141
Cocksure (Richler), 119
Cold War, 42, 73, 118
collective conscience, 228
collective guilt, 162–64
comedians, 40–41, 120–22, 134, 139, 144, 156, 158–59, 167–68, 206–9, 221–29, 254, 270–72, 275–77, 279–81, 324–28; in fiction, 164–65; masculinity and, 140–48; non-Jewish, 322
comedy of manners, 90
Communism, 42, 45, 46

Communist Party: Netherlands, 61, 67; Poland, 47
competitive suffering, 294, 299
concentration camps, 43, 60, 75, 112, 113, 168, 319; in cartoons, 191, 192; educational trips to, 199, 206, 207–9; God and, 158; humanity in, 321; humor in, 43, 66, 321; jokes set in, 2, 269, 273, 323, 325–26; non-Jews in, 50
Copenhagen, Denmark, 67
Corliss, Richard, 115
Crazy Ex-Girlfriend (CW), 276, 285
Crimea, 21, 22
critical response: anger, 4; condemnation, 327, 331; contextualization, 2–3; negative, 2, 115, 123, 220, 274, 292; positive, 75, 124, 291
Crocodile magazine, 28
cross-dressing, 63–64, 65, 67, 68, 70
crypto-Jews, 183, 187
Curb Your Enthusiasm (HBO), 3, 161, 275, 276, 292–95, 296, 323

Dachau, 50
dance, 60, 61–64, 285
Dance of Genghis Cohn, The (Gary), 120, 164–65
dark tourism, 206–9
Dauber, Jeremy, 2–3
Davar, 52
David, Larry, 2–3, 4, 161, 273–76, 290, 292–95, 323–24
Davis, Christie, 29
Day and Night (*Tog un nakht*; Ansky), 61, 62
Day the Clown Cried, The (Lewis), 120–21
"Dead Fiddler, The" ("Der toyter klezmer"; Singer), 87–89
Dead Funny: Humor in Hitler's Germany (Herzog), 329
desensitization, 316, 318
DesHechos Históricos, 186, 188
Des Pres, Terrence, 5–6, 155, 287, 294, 304
Diary of Anne Frank, The (book; Frank), 184, 196
Diary of Anne Frank, The (film; Stevens), 196
Diary of Anne Frank, The (play; Goodrich and Hackett), 75, 196

"Diary of the Evil One, The" (*Der togbukh fun yeytser-hore*; Singer), 85
diasporic aesthetic, 227
Diner, Hasia R., 118
displaced persons camps, 67
displacement, 5, 42
Dos poylishe yidntum, 87
Douglas, Mary, 142
Dritte Walpurgisnacht, Die (Kraus), 107
Dr. Strangelove (Kubrick), 119
Duck Soup (McCarey), 136–37
dybbuks, 86, 88–89, 120, 165
Dzigan, Shimen, 40, 41, 46–47, 48–49, 50, 52

East Germany. *See* German Democratic Republic
Echo Chamber (Silbert and Olstein), 252–54
effeminacy, 25–26, 135, 139, 144
Efimov, Boris, 18
Efron, John, 52
Eichmann, Adolf, 144, 156, 184; laughter and, 105; portrayals of, 121, 271; trial of, 118, 166, 288–89, 295
Eisenstein, Bernice, 167, 171–72, 174
El-Husseini, Amin, 210–11
Enemies, A Love Story (film; Mazursky), 86, 98–99
Enemies, A Love Story (*Sonim, a geshikhte fun libe*; Singer), 86–87, 90–99; adaptations of, 86, 91; comedy in, 88
enemies: failures of, 19–20, 22–23; historical, 19–20, 159, 160; revenge humor and, 44–45; satirical images of, 17
entitlement, 171–72
epigenetics, 300
Eretz Nehederet (*A Wonderful Country*), 267–69
Eshkol, Levi, 52
Essman, Susie, 318, 326
Eulenspiegel, Die, 74
Exodus (Uris), 134, 139, 147
Eynikayt (*Unity*), 15–16
Ezrahi, Sidra DeKoven, 6, 8, 227

Fackenheim, Emil, 161
Family Guy (Fox), 197
farce, 86, 88, 90, 99, 116, 285

Federal Republic of Germany (FRG), 71, 110–11, 118, 162
Feinstein, Rachel, 3
Feldshuh, Tovah, 276, 285
feuilletons, 40, 41–42
Fielder, Nathan, 279–81
Filler, Deb, 321
film, 5–8, 40, 74, 119, 144–46, 149–50, 156–58, 220, 288
Finkielkraut, Alain, 171
Firestone, Renee, 316, 319, 321, 325, 328, 330
folk culture, German, 69; reclaiming of, 73–74
folklore, 19; academic study of, 16, 32–33; ideology and, 17, 31; patriotic, 23
folk music: German, 69, 71–72, 73–74; Yiddish, 71–72
Folksshtime, 73, 75
Forverts, 87, 89, 90–91
France, 7, 18, 120
Franco, Francisco, 30
Frank, Anne: as commodity, 208; dark tourism and, 206–7, 209; hidden diary pages, 1–2, 4; humor about, categories of, 200–203, 327–28; humor about, in Israel, 198–211, 212; humor about, in West, 197, 211, 212; as iconic, 195, 196–97, 198, 211, 212, 286, 288, 327; life and death of, 66, 75, 196; myth of, 195, 198–99, 211, 212; political satire and, 210, 211; portrayals of, 3–4, 170, 174–75, 197; religious satire and, 204; sanctification of, 169–70; as tragic hero, 158
Frank, Otto, 196
free speech, 314, 316, 322–23, 329
Freiberg, Freda, 254
Freud, Sigmund, 106, 125
FRG. *See* Federal Republic of Germany
Frick, Wilhelm, 15, 18

Gadsby, Hannah, 254
Gary, Romain, 120, 164–65
GDR. *See* German Democratic Republic
Gebirtig, Mordkhe, 39
Gelekhter durkh trern (*Laughter Through Tears*; Nudelman), 40, 41–46, 47–48

Index • 343

gender, 244, 302; binary, 142–43; construction of, 134; differentiation, 145–46; expectations, 137; Holocaust experience and, 303; in Holocaust representation, 304; Judaism and, 139; performance of, 143, 148; presentation, 143
generations, 7, 46, 166–74, 228, 242, 250–51, 303, 304. *See also* Second Generation; third generation
German Democratic Republic (GDR), 60, 69–75, 76
Germany: acceptance of guilt, 162, 234; anti-Nazi laws, 331; culpability of, 162–63; Holocaust humor as taboo in, 331; Holocaust representation in, 221; relations between Jews and non-Jews, 228–29. *See also* Federal Republic of Germany; German Democratic Republic
Gervais, Ricky, 322, 327
ghettos, 75, 247; humor in, 17, 21, 27, 29, 32, 43–45
Ghost Writer, The (Roth), 120, 197
ghostwriting, 86, 91–93
Gilman, Sander, 141, 157
"Gimpel the Fool" ("Gimpel tam"; Singer), 85, 93
Glatstein, Jacob, 39
Glick, Hirsh, 26
God, 158–61, 204–6
Goebbels, Joseph, 15
Gold, Judy, 325, 326
Goldstein, Chaja, 64–65
Goldstein, Eric, 135
Goldstein, Shai, 206
Göring, Hermann, 18, 44
Gottfried, Gilbert, 3, 328
graphic novels, 5, 167, 294–95, 313
Great Britain, 44
Great Dictator, The (Chaplin), 108, 109–14, 115, 156
Gross, Elly, 330
Gross, Natan, 40, 41, 46
"Gute Nakht, Velt, A" ("Good Night, World"; Glatstein), 39

HaHamishia HaKamerit (*The Camera Quintet*), 264–67
Haman, 15, 18–20
Hasidic culture, 61–62
Hasidic dances, 59, 61

Hasidim, 232, 233
hate speech, 323
HaYehudim Ba'im (*The Jews Are Coming*), 270–72, 271
Hebrew language, 40
Heller, Binem, 40, 46
Herzog, Rudolph, 329
Himmler, Heinrich, 15
hipsters, 139
Hirsch, Marianne, 249–50
Historical Roasts (Netflix), 3–4
historietas (comic books), 185, 186, 187–89
History of the World, Part 1 (Brooks), 318
Hitler, Adolf: death of, satirized, 15, 43; as evil incarnate, 107–8; failures of, satirized, 22, 23–26, 44; fascination with, 107; Haman comparison, 15, 18–20; humor targeting, 108, 156; as iconic villain, 18, 285; imagery of, 25; laughter and, 105, 106; portrayals of, 3–4, 123, 124, 220; Yiddish jokes about, 25, 27
Hoffman, Eva, 250
Hogan's Heroes (CBS), 157
Holmgren, Beth, 64
Holocaust (NBC), 157, 191, 288
Holocaust: approaches to, 5–7, 292, 331–32; as background, 8; centrality of, in Israel, 262–64, 265, 281; commercialization of, 198, 207–8; consecration of, 155, 158; exploitation of, 263; icons of, 197, 281, 286, 288; inheritance of, 167–68, 171, 322; instrumentalization of, 198, 262; as off-limits, 4, 304; politicization of, 199, 210–11, 264, 267, 274; resumption of life after, 42; seen as propaganda, 184, 186; as separate from Nazism, 120, 123, 125, 157, 273, 326–27; trivialization of, 264; as unique, 5, 287, 294, 332; as unrepresentable, 6, 112
Holocaust commemoration, 40, 173, 195, 212, 279; changes in, 211; debates about, 211; exclusions from, 208; in Israel, 198, 199
Holocaust consciousness, 118, 155, 157–58, 161, 169; expansion of, 167–68; museums and, 173; proliferation of, 172; as tool, 174
Holocaust denial, 121, 184, 279–81, 325
Holocaust etiquette, 5

344 • Index

Holocaust fatigue, 332
"Holocaust laughter," 155
Holocaust memorialization, 279, 280–81
Holocaust memory, 9, 155–56, 166; culture of, 286; exploitation of, 172; in Israeli education system, 199; as performance, 294; politics of, 272; popular, 286; shaping of, 288; subversive, 198
Holocaust remembrance, 4–5, 262, 288; comedy as part of, 304; methods of, 6; reconsideration of, 303; shaping of, 6–7, 8; trajectory of, 7
"Holocaust Tips for Kids" (Auslander), 160–61
homosexuality, 143
Hope: A Tragedy (Auslander), 168–71, 174–75, 197
"How Does the Tsar Live?" ("Vi Azoi Lebt der Kayzer?"), 59–60, 62–63, 64, 70, 75–80
Humor, 191–92
humor: antisemitic, 7, 8, 30–31, 185; as attractive, 140; as bonding, 248, 251, 255, 321; boundaries of, 4–5, 8; as challenging Holocaust conventions, 8; compensatory, 25; contemporary relevance of, 3–4, 32–33; as coping strategy, 8; deflationary, 106, 198; as destabilizing, 175; as educational, 4; ethics of, 2–3, 4, 304; functions of, 4, 8; moral neutrality of, 106; as motivational, 17, 18, 31; as normalizing, 7, 330; officially approved, 16–17, 20–21, 23, 26, 32–33; patriotic, 17, 28; permissibility of, 4–5, 7, 223, 229, 255, 321–22, 331; physical, 23, 98; as preserving Holocaust memory, 6, 281, 327; resilience and, 5; as resistance, 43; role in Holocaust experience, 2; role in memory, 2; as survival strategy, 95, 253; as therapeutic, 49, 155; as trivializing, 327; as weapon, 8, 52, 124–25, 328; during World War II, 8, 15–33. *See also* Yiddish humor
Hungary, 18
hypermasculinity, 134, 138

Ich darf das, ich bin Jude (*I'm Allowed, I'm a Jew*; Polak), 221, 228–29

ideology, 49, 50, 186; humor as supporting, 16–17, 21, 31
"If I Were Rothschild" (Aleichem), 78
I'll Never Heil Again (White), 109
Imhoff, Sarah, 148
incongruity, 243, 245–46, 252, 304
Indonesia, 61, 62
Inglorious Basterds (Tarantino), 149, 165
Inquisition, 20, 183, 187–88, 318
Inside Amy Schumer (Comedy Central), 277–79, *278*
internet, 198, 200–203, 211, 220, 296–98
In the Shadows of Memory: The Holocaust and the Third Generation (ed. Jilovsky, Silverstein, and Slucki), 244
Is It OK to Laugh About It? Holocaust Humour, Satire, and Parody in Israeli Culture (Steir-Livny), 262–63
Israel. *See* State of Israel
Israeli-Palestinian conflict, 186, 188, 210–11
I Was a Child of Holocaust Survivors (Eisenstein), 167

Jacobson, Howard, 155, 167
Jakob the Liar (Kassovitz), 5
Jaldati, Lin, 59, *65*, *68*; critical response to, 75–76; Anne Frank and, 75; interwar career, 60–63, 64–66, 70, 79; life of, 60–61, 66–67, 69; postwar career, 67, 70–72, 73, 74–76, 79–80; during World War II, 66–67
Jewish identity, 150, 220; Holocaust and, 262, 272, 274, 275, 277, 281; markers of, 276
Jewish masculinity, 133–34, 148–50; as active, 147; interventions into, 141, 143–44; post-Holocaust, 139–48; pre-Holocaust, 135–38; sexuality and, 146
Jewishness, 63–64, 93, 138, 286; associated with Holocaust, 161–62, 274; commitment to, 302–3; portrayals of, 298; sexuality and, 302
Jews: as actors, 3; as chosen people, 159–60, 161; demographics, Australia, 244; demographics, Latin America, 182; as sexual threat, 135–37, 141, 142, 146; as soldiers, 26–27, 135, 156; viewed as victimizers, 185, 192; viewed as victims, 133, 135, 145, 149, 150, 210; World War II leaders, corruption of, 30, 32

Jew's Body, The (Gilman), 141
jokes, 16–17, 27–31, 44, 95, 144–45, 254–55, 273; ephemeral, 241–43, 245–52, 253; as form of memory, 249; in Anne Frank's diary, 1; as historical documents, 32; revenge, 43–44; as social process, 243, 248, 249; taboo and, 324
Joselit, Jenna Weissman, 137
Joshua Then and Now (Richler), 162–63
jüdische Witz, Der (*The Jewish Joke*; Landman), 219

Kalooki Nights (Jacobson), 167
Kamadjaja, Indra, 62
Kaplan, Louis, 253
Kasrilevker sreyfes (*A Conflagration in Kasrilevke*; Aleichem), 48–49
Kassovitz, Peter, 5
Kaufman, David, 138, 139, 149
Kazakhstan, 15, 17–18, 19, 27
Keough, William, 106
Keret, Etgar, 328
Khurbn (destruction), 39
Kiev, Ukraine, 47
Kiev Cabinet for Jewish Culture, 16, 32
Kimmel, Michael, 135
Kirshenblatt-Gimblett, Barbara, 195
Kishon, Ephraim, 221
Kivel, Paul, 138
Kleeblatt, Norman, 294–95
Klein, Robert, 120
Klötzer, Sylvia, 74
Kowadlo, Boris, 61
Kraus, Karl, 107, 108
Kristallnacht, 66, 69
Krushevan, Pavel, 19–20
Kubrick, Stanley, 119
Kunstwereld, 59, 61–62
Kupershmidt, Sholem, 21

Lampanelli, Lisa, 322
Landman, Salca, 219
Lanzmann, Claude, 111–12, 118
Last Laugh, The (Pearlstein), 313, *317, 320,* 326–28; audience response to, 330–31; context of, 328–30; on funniness, 325–26; production challenges, 314–16
"laughter through tears" tradition, 5, 50, 72, 89, 99
Lavado, Joaquín Salvador "Quino," 189
Lehrer, Tom, 119
Leipzig, Germany, 72–73, 75
Lessing, Gotthold Ephraim, 229–30
"Let's All Be Jews" ("Lasst uns alle Juden sein"; Polak), 231–32
Levitt, Laura, 133
Levy, Dani, 220
Lewis, Jerry, 120–21
LGBTQ persons, 252, 300, 301–2; Nazi persecution of, 303. *See also* transgender persons
Life Is Beautiful (Benigni), 5, 6–7, 8, 314
literary journals, 39, 85
Łódź, Poland, 41, 46
Łódź ghetto, Poland, 30
Lovitz, Jon, 3
Lubitsch, Ernst, 29, 114
Lupone, Patti, 276, 285

Mad Magazine, 157, 158
magazines, 15–16, 28, 74, 156, 157, 158; cartoons in, 191
Mailer, Norman, 139–40, 143, 145
Man, Mendel, 26
Manger, Itzik, 26
Manhattan (Allen), 147
manhood, 139, 141
Martel, Yann, 331–32
Marx, Julius "Groucho," 136–37
Marx Brothers, 136–37
masculinity: Gentile, 138, 145, 149; Jewish women and, 139; lack of, 26; performative, 139, 140–48, 149. *See also* hypermasculinity; Jewish masculinity
Maus (Spiegelman), 5, 294–95, 313
Mazursky, Paul, 86, 98
Mein Führer (Levy), 220
Meir, Golda, 52
Melbourne, Australia, 242, 243, 244–47, 252
memes, 198, 203, 211
memoirs, 163–64, 168, 228
Memorial to the Murdered Jews of Europe, Berlin, Germany, 220
memory: collective, 164, 199, 203–4, 281; ephemeral, 249, 251; markers of, 251; process of, 249; traumatic, 207, 247, 254. *See also* Holocaust memory; postmemory
Menakhem-Mendl (Yiddish comedy character), 47–48

"Menakhem-Mendl the Emigrant" (Nudelman), 47
Mengele, Josef, 184, 319
Meshugah (Singer), 86
Messe (Leipzig fair), 72–73, 75
messianism, 227, 231, 233, 235
Mexico, 181–82, 187–89, 192–93
Mihăileanu, Radu, 5
Mintz, Alan, 166
Miron, Dan, 40
Mizrahim, 208–9
mockumentary, 269, 280
Modern Times (Chaplin), 109
Moina, Amsy, 61
monologues, 85–86, 90, 92, 273–74
Monsieur Verdoux (Chaplin), 114
Moore, Deborah Dash, 135
moral authority, 7
Moshonov, Moni, 270, 271–72
"Mountain of Shoes, A" ("A Barg Shikh"; Shulshteyn), 75–76
muscular Christianity, 137, 147
museums, 173–74, 207, 277–79
musicals, 4, 30, 124
music videos, 232
"My Machine Gun," 26

Natan der Weise (*Nathan the Wise*; Lessing), 229–30
Nathan for You (Comedy Central), 279–81, *280*
National Revue (Netherlands), 60, 65
"Naye Khasene, Di" ("The New Wedding"), 23–27
Nazism: German folk culture tainted by, 73; mocking of, 44–45, 147, 156–57, 198, 261, 326–27; as separate from Holocaust, 120, 123, 125, 157, 273, 326–27
nebbish, 140, 144–45, 146, 149–50
neo-Nazis, 7, 125, 316
Netanyahu, Benjamin, 210–11, 263
Netherlands, 66, 67
Neuwirth, Allan, 289
newspapers, 28, 41; cartoons in, 185–86, 192; serials in, 86, 87, 90, 94
New York, New York, 96
Night (Wiesel), 158
9/11, 276, 315, 316
Ninotchka (Lubitsch), 117
No Joke: Making Jewish Humor (Wisse), 226

Nordau, Max, 231
normalization, 175
novels, 86–87, 120, 159, 162–67, 168–71, 173–74, 197
Novick, Peter, 158, 161, 166, 171, 286, 291
Nudelman, Moyshe, 40, 41–46, 47–48, 49–51
Nuremberg trials, 44, 162

Olstein, Justin, 252
One, Two, Three (Wilder), 119
Ophir, Adi, 287, 288, 304
Ostjuden, 61–62

Página/12, 192
Palestinians, 182, 184, 186, 188, 210
Paris, France, 48, 51
Peres, Shimon, 52
Perlina, Shifra, 15, 18, 20
Pilcer, Sonia, 167, 172
Place for Worries, A (*Makom ledeaga*; Matar Productions), 204–6
play on words, 44, 92, 93, 97
poetry, 207–8
pogroms, 72, 73, 90, 161, 188; in Latin America, 190
Polak, Oliver, 220, 221–25, *225*, 228–30, 231–35; models for, 226–27
Poland, 8, 41, 64, 115–18; Communism in, 42; deportation of Jews from, 16; as Jewish, in Yiddish comedy, 45; postwar life in, 45, 47; travel to, from Israel, 199, 206–7, 264; works suppressed in, 40, 42, 45, 50; Yiddish civilization in, 18
Portnoy, Edward, 198, 211
postmemory, 242–43, 244, 246, 247–48, 249–50
Potsdam, Germany, 74
Prince Bettliegend, 30
Producers, The (film; Brooks), 4, 8, 108, 122–23, 124, 156–57, 290, 317–18
Producers, The (musical; Brooks), 4, 8, 124, 317, 318
Producers, The (musical film; Stroman), 124
propaganda: Holocaust seen as, 184, 186; humor as, 7, 31; jokes about, 29–30
Protocols of the Elders of Zion, 20, 184
Pryor, Richard, 226–27
Punchlines (Keough), 106

Purim, 18–20
"Purim Gifts for Hitler," 19–20

Quatsch Comedy Club, Berlin, Germany, 221–22
Quino. *See* Lavado, Joaquín Salvador

"Raboysay." *See* "How Does the Tsar Live?"
radio, 206
Rafael, Dror, 206
Rathenau, Walther, 230–31
Rebling, Eberhard, 65, 66, 67
Rebling, Jalda, 77–78
Refael, Shmuel, 207–8
Reik, Theodor, 156
Reiner, Carl, 156
Reiner, Rob, 315
Repiso, Miguel "Rep," 190–91
resistance, 17, 26, 52; humor as limiting, 329
revenge, 20, 149, 165; humor as, 43–44
Ribbentrop, Joachim, 15, 18
Richler, Mordecai, 119, 159–60, 162, 165–66, 172
Río García, Eduardo Humberto del "Rius," 187–89
Rire, Le (Bergson), 106
Rius. *See* Río García, Eduardo Humberto del
Rivers, Joan, 327
Robb, David, 74
Robot Chicken (Cartoon Network), 197–98
Roosevelt, Franklin Delano, 3, 44, 110
Rosenberg, Alfred, 15, 18
Rosenberg, Joel, 117
Rosenberg, Klara, 23
Rosenfeld, Alvin, 175
Ross, Jeffrey, 3–4, 326
Rossen, Rebecca, 63–64
Roth, Philip, 120, 161, 197
Rothe, Anne, 295

sacralization, 155, 166, 274, 295, 299; reactions against, 286; as trivializing, 262, 296
Sahl, Mort, 119
Sala, Gustavo, 192
Sarah Silverman Program, The (Comedy Central), 295–96
sarcasm, 22, 45, 50, 206

Satan in goray un andere dertseylungen (Singer), 85, 86
satire, 62–63, 72, 74–75, 262, 274; antisemitic, 185; as memorial, 76; as normalizing, 7; political, 66, 328–30; religious, 204–6; Soviet, 18; as transgressive, 125
Saturday Night Live (*SNL*; NBC), 2–3, 4, 273–74, 323–24, 330
"S'brent" ("It Burns"; Gebirtig), 39, 48, 67
Schindler's List (Spielberg), 5–6, 157, 173, 265–67, 291–92; as iconic, 286, 288; inappropriate behavior during, 223–24, 267, 291; in Latin America, 184; references to, 268, 278
"Schmeed Memoirs, The" (Allen), 119
Schuman, Rebecca, 163–64
Schumer, Amy, 277
Scott, Joan, 248–49
Second Generation, 166–74, 207, 221, 250
Seghers, Anna, 69, 71
Seidman, Naomi, 138
Seifert, Dorthe, 301–2
Seinfeld (NBC), 224, 266–67, 275, 290–93, 296, 324
Seinfeld, Jerry, 224, 226, 275, 290–92
self-deprecation, 26, 254; lack of, in Soviet Yiddish humor, 20, 21
sexual abuse, 2, 273, 324
sexuality, 168, 244, 273–74, 302, 303; in Holocaust representation, 304; as taboo, 324
Shadows on the Hudson (Singer), 86, 90
Shandler, Jeffrey, 158, 195
Shapira, Shahak, 220
Shargorodskii, Veli, 21–22
Shearer, Harry, 318, 326
Shevrin, Aliza, 90
Sheyne-Sheyndl (Yiddish comedy character), 47–48
Shoah (Lanzmann), 111–12, 118
Sholem Aleichem, 5, 47–49, 78, 89, 90, 161
Shteyngart, Gary, 173–74
Shub, Elizabeth, 91
Shulshteyn, Moyshe, 75
Shumacher, Yisroel, 40, 41, 46–47, 48–49, 50, 52
Siege of Leningrad, 30
Sierkowiak, David, 30

Silbert, Carla, 252
Silverman, Sarah, 226, 295–96, 322, 324–25, 332
Singer, Isaac Bashevis: artistic universe of, 93; as bilingual, 86, 99; early career, 85–86; inspirations for, 90, 99; translation and, 94–95, 98
sitcoms, 285–86, 289–94, 304; hybridized, 298
Six-Day War, 118, 147
sketch comedy, 261–62; in Israel, 264–72; in United States, 272–81
slapstick, 98, 156
Slate, 163
Slave, The (Singer), 88–89, 90, 96
Slucki, David, 224, 245
SNL. See *Saturday Night Live*
social media, 200–203, 211, 220
Song of the Peoples (*Das Lied der Völker*), 70–71
songs, 119, 231–33; in concentration camps, 67; ghetto, 43, 67; satiric, 73–75; Soviet Yiddish, 15–16, 19–20, 21–26, 31–32. See also folk music; Yiddish music
South Park (Comedy Central), 197
Soviet humor, 21, 30–31
Soviet Union, 117; fall of, 32; humor in, vs. ghetto humor, 29–30; Jewish fear of, 16; Jews in, 16, 21; popularity of, 28–29; Yiddish civilization in, 18
"Soyne Fun Vakatsyes, Der" ("The Enemy of Vacations"; Nudelman), 50
Spain, 186
Speer, Albert, 106
Spiegelman, Art, 5, 294–95
Spottlieder, 73–74, 76
Stacheltier, Das (*The Porcupine*), 74
Stadner, S. Hanala, 155, 157, 166–67
Stalin, Joseph, 107; Soviet Yiddish praise of, 15, 20, 25; Western support for, 28
Stalingrad, Soviet Union, 18, 28
stand-up comedy, 120, 122, 139, 140–43, 144, 150, 156, 158–59, 221–22, 324–25
State of Israel, 147, 181, 188, 264–72, 274, 330–31; Anne Frank humor in, 195, 198; Latin American view of, 182, 184, 186; postwar life in, 50–52; relocation to, 41, 45; Yiddish humor in, 50–52
Steinberg, David, 332

Steir-Livny, Liat, 262–63
stereotypes, 136–37, 150; antisemitic, 138, 188, 222–23, 331; subversion of, 26, 146–48
story collections, 41–42, 47–48, 49–50
Streicher, Julius, 44
Streisand, Barbra, 285
St. Urbain's Horseman (Richler), 159–60, 162, 165–66
survivors: as absolving guilt, 71; elevation of, 158; humanity of, 321; humor as coping strategy for, 8, 49; as humorists, 221; Jewishness and, 303; moral authority of, 7; in New York, 86; non-Jews as, 50; representations of, 99; treatment of, 294; unconventional representations of, 96–98, 294
Svive, 39

taboo, 4, 125, 142, 155, 287–88, 316, 324, 331; television and, 288–96, 304
talk shows, 295
Tarantino, Quentin, 149, 165
Tashkent, Uzbekistan, 26, 30
Tel Aviv, Israel, 51
television, 156–58, 197–98, 288, 289–96, 315; cable, 2, 293; network, 2–3, 289–92; skit shows, 208–9; streaming, 296–98
Tenenbom, Tuvia, 163
Teuth, Michael, 289
theater, 62, 75, 196. See also cabaret; musicals
third generation, 242, 244–45, 300; humor of, 245–50, 252–55
This Way for the Gas, Ladies and Gentlemen (*Proszę państwa do gazu*; Borowski), 49–50, 181
Three Stooges, 108–9, 156
Time Magazine, 28
Timerman, Jacobo, 191
Tip Top Cabaret, Berlin, Germany, 64–65
To Be or Not to Be (Brooks), 124
To Be or Not to Be (Lubitsch), 29, 108, 114–18, 123–24
Tog-Morgn Zhurnal, Der, 41
Torquemada, Tomas of, 19–20
tragicomedy, 86, 90, 99
Train of Life (Mihăileanu), 5
transgender persons, 297, 298, 299, 300–302

transgression, 141–43, 149, 289, 304, 328; parameters for, 322
Transparent (Amazon), 296–303
trauma, 199, 248, 250–51; acting-out of, 203–4, 211, 212; engaging with, 242; identification with, 251; intergenerational, 251–52; intersectional, 301; transmission of, 300, 302. *See also* memory: traumatic
Treblinka, 43, 112
Truffaut, François, 113, 114
Trump, Donald, 281, 328–30
"Tsip Tsapkl," 75–76
Tsukunft, Di, 39
"Tsvey Yidn Khapn Fish" ("Two Jews Fishing"; Nudelman), 50
Twitter, 200–203, 207
2000 Years with Carl Reiner and Mel Brooks (Reiner and Brooks), 156

Ukraine, 18, 22, 23
Undzere kinder (*Our Children*; Gross), 8, 40, 41, 42, 45–47, 48–49, 50
United States Holocaust Memorial Museum, Washington, D.C., 173, 272, 274, 279, 288
Uris, Leon, 133–34, 139, 147, 149
Uzbekistan, 21

Venezuela, 183
victimhood, 167, 170, 174, 229; collective, 286
victimization, 169–70, 199; culture of, 286; humor used for, 322
Vilna ghetto, Lithuania, 26
Vilna Troupe, 62
violence: anti-Nazi, 147; humor as promoting, 15, 20; masculinity and, 139, 141–42
Visitor's Guide to Birkenau, A (*Madrich lamevaker bebirkenau*; Refael), 207–8
Volk, Het, 65
von Braun, Wernher, 119
Vrije Kunstenaar, De (The Free Artist), 66

Waldheim, Kurt, 119–20
Warsaw ghetto, Poland, 17, 29; humor in, 43
weapons, 24, 26; humor as, 43, 52, 328
web series, 3, 252–54
Weinman, Roz, 324
Weinstein, Harvey, 2, 273, 324

Westerbork, 66, 196
West Germany. *See* Federal Republic of Germany
"white negro," 139–40, 143
Wiesel, Elie, 107, 158, 288, 295
Wilder, Billy, 118–19
Wisse, Ruth, 226
Witz, Der (Freud), 106

Yad Vashem, Jerusalem, Israel, 263, 264, 268, 279
"Yankl der Katsev" ("Yankl the Butcher"; Nudelman), 50–51
"Yeshiva Boy, The," 63
Yiddish culture: destruction of, 60; modern perception of, 20–21, 22
Yiddish humor: anti-fascist, 15–16, 17, 32; censored, in Soviet Union, 17, 29; development of, 39–40; government ideology and, 21, 31; interwar, 60; in Israel, 50; modern reaction to, 20–21; as motivational, 17; official, 32; patriotic, 16, 17, 32–33; postwar, 40–42, 60; publishability of, 16, 21; Soviet, 15–28, 31; as survival strategy, 95; uncensored, in Poland, 17, 29–30; during World War II, 15–28
Yiddish language, 39, 40, 42, 76, 80; in Israel, 52
Yiddish literature, 39–40, 144, 161; interwar, 85–86; postwar, 86–87
Yiddish music, 15–16, 19–20, 21–26, 31–32, 62, 69–71, 74–76; army songs, 26; interwar, 59–60; revenge songs, 43; socialist interpretation of, 72, 73
Yiddish press, 41, 50, 86–87, 90, 94, 96–97
"Yidn Hobn in Geto Oykh Gelakht" ("In the Ghettos Jews Also Laughed"; Nudelman), 43
"Yolocaust" (Shapira), 220
"Yosl Ber" (Manger), 26
You Nazty Spy (White), 109, 156
Your Show of Shows (NBC), 273

Zelig (Allen), 150
Zionism, 45, 46, 47, 147–48, 192, 231
Žižek, Slavoj, 6, 329, 330
"Zog Nit Keynmol" ("Never Say"; Glick), 26, 67
Zweibel, Alan, 321–22, 332

www.ingramcontent.com/pod-product-compliance
Lightning Source LLC
Chambersburg PA
CBHW070259240426
43661CB00057B/2589